TO THE THIRD EMPIRE
Ibsen's Early Drama

THE NORDIC SERIES
Volume 4

Other Titles in the Series

TO THE
THIRD EMPIRE

Ibsen's Early Drama

Brian Johnston

UNIVERSITY OF MINNESOTA PRESS ☐ MINNEAPOLIS

Copyright © 1980 by the University of Minnesota.
All rights reserved.
Published by the University of Minnesota Press,
2037 University Avenue Southeast,
Minneapolis, Minnesota 55455
Printed in the United States of America.

Library of Congress Cataloging in Publication Data

Johnston, Brian, 1932-
   To the third empire.

   (The Nordic series; v. 4)
   Bibliography: p.
   Includes index.
   1. Ibsen, Henrik, 1828-1906 — Criticism and inter-
pretation. I. Title. II. Series: Nordic series;
v. 4.
PT8895.J59   839.8'226   79-28329
ISBN 0-8166-0902-0

The University of Minnesota is an equal opportunity
educator and employer.

THE NORDIC SERIES

In carrying out general plans for this series,
the University of Minnesota Press is advised on various
aspects by the following scholars:

DEDICATION

To Eric Bentley
whose courage, past
and present, is the
only true Ibsenism.

PREFACE

*I believe that the ideals of our time, while
disintegrating, are tending toward what in my play*
Emperor and Galilean *I designated "the third empire."
Therefore, permit me to drink a toast to the future—to
that which is to come.*

Ibsen's speech at a banquet in Stockholm,
September 24, 1887

Wordsworth's subtitle to his poem *The Prelude, "Growth of a Poet's
Mind,"* could be the subtitle to this volume. The poetic odyssey
that took Ibsen from the writing of *Catiline* (1848-49) to the completion of *Emperor and Galilean* (1873), and which constitutes, as
Rolf Fjelde has observed, the first half of Ibsen's career, is one of
the clearest as well as one of the most consequential examples of
aesthetic and imaginative evolution known to us. It would be hard
to find a parallel to this Grimstad poet from a culturally backward
nation. Inheriting a language not only ignored by the rest of the
world but unenriched through significant ideological and cultural
commerce with it, Ibsen emerged as the world-historical dramatist
of *Emperor and Galilean* and as the poet of whom James Joyce
could declare, "It may be questioned whether any man has held so
firm an empire over the thinking world in modern times."[1] James
Joyce himself, of course, was to enjoy a similar fate. But Joyce
had at his disposal the rich legacy of English literature, and his
impact upon the "thinking world" (in distinction to the academic
world) was to be considerably less than Ibsen's.

Had Ibsen been born twenty years earlier or twenty years later,
it is doubtful that he could have achieved his astonishing success.
He is the poet of the great bourgeois civilization of the second half

ix

of the nineteenth century, a period of unparalleled social and technological change and of ideological conflict. To find an equivalent
period one would have to return to the Renaissance or to the vital
period of the Greek city-state with its confident rationalism and
its proud humanism. The scientists, thinkers, engineers, financiers,
artists, statesmen, doctors, architects, priests, and prophets of the
nineteenth-century bourgeoisie make up a brilliant assemblage of
human types equal to any in history. And when this brilliant culture became deeply reflective, self-questioning, "tragic," it gave
rise to a literature (in poetry, the novel, drama, and the critical or
moral essay) that addressed itself to an entire "thinking world" in
a way impossible today. One has only to read the great nineteenth-
century periodicals to appreciate the level of moral and intellectual
discourse, the manner in which the sciences, arts, politics, and
religion of the times intertwined as urgent and conscious dialogue
between the different disciplines. The impact of Darwinism, for
example, was immediate and universal and not an event primarily
of interest to biologists. Ibsen becomes the dramatic poet of this
brilliant and profound thinking world, I believe, with the publication of *Brand* in 1866, and from that year he begins to increase his
"empire" over it.

Without the emergence of the new theater public from the more
settled middle classes of the growing cities of Europe and without
the nationalist movements that eagerly established national
theaters and national theater companies from the Balkans to Ireland, and thereby created an ideologically responsive theater audience throughout Europe in the later part of the nineteenth century,
Ibsen could not have gained so wide a public. Twenty years later,
and the Ibsen of the plays that made his international reputation,
from 1877 on, would have encountered a different, more fragmented bourgeoisie and would have become a "minority" dramatist of a different culture whose later work would have had to
compete with motion pictures. The conditions that permitted Ibsen
to extend his empire over his art and over his public, gradually and
surely extending its form and substance from the uncertain explorations of the early plays to the total mastery of the great
realistic cycle, were not to be repeated. Bernard Shaw, who might
not have become a dramatist without Ibsen's example, did not

exercise his tremendous hold on the public by his drama alone; moreover, his influence was not as great as Ibsen's and his relationship to his culture was not as fruitful for his art, as the works that follow *Heartbreak House* bear witness.

Although it is true that Ibsen was to a great extent the *product* of his culture, he was also, to a degree almost unheard-of for an artist, a *creator* of that culture, not only providing it with a new idea of the place of the theater in society but also creating a new conception of the individual within society. With Falk, Brand, Peer Gynt, and the individuals of the realistic cycle, a novel idea of spiritual heroism, attainable by any individual, displaces the older concept of hierarchical heroism. Where earlier writers of "bourgeois tragedy" had failed to establish this idea, Ibsen succeeded simply by making it aesthetically persuasive. But the aesthetic success was, of course, grounded in deep philosophic convictions. Precisely at the time when the great bourgeois culture had become most self-reflective and most troubled about its identity, its compulsions and forces, its history and its destiny, Ibsen presented it with a theater whose psychic ritual was a resurrection of the old powers and demons, a questioning of identity, history, and destiny for what he was to call "a judgment-day upon the soul." In the present volume one can follow the process whereby Ibsen makes himself the poet of such a theater, an act of self-creation impressive for its will, its intellectual comprehension, and its imaginative daring.

The formidable will is detectable from the beginning. Ibsen may falter or occasionally drop below his own best level, living as he did in a cultural backwater; nevertheless, when reading the sequence of plays from *Catiline* to his first masterpiece, *Love's Comedy* (1862), one gains the impression that within the dozen years between the two works the poet consciously and firmly is extending the range of his dramatic argument. Each successive play in the series is not merely a new idea or subject to be theatrically exploited; it is a deliberate and pondered advance of his form and subject matter.

The self-consciousness of this program of intellectual and imaginative mastery may repel those who prefer that a poet's evolution be more spontaneous and mysterious. Ibsen, as we claimed, is the poet of a highly self-reflective and self-critical culture, and from his first plays and critical writings he accepts the responsibility of mastering and adopting the great heritage of human history and culture, and even of bringing his own nation to claim this heritage. Although their imaginative worlds are much the same, in many ways Ibsen and Richard Wagner are polar opposites. Wagner renders the cultural heritage of Europe utterly subservient to his own subjective drama. He dissolves the world, as it were, within the abyss of his drama of feelings so that the spectator of the great music-dramas feels he or she is confronted by a form of personal psychic allegory whose surface details merely obscure true comprehension. Indeed, modern Wagnerian productions sweep these surface details from the stage altogether. Ibsen's spiritual dialogue with the objective world, which goes at least as deep as Wagner's, is too evenly balanced to permit this disregard of its objectivity, so that we will find that his surface details, his "props," are actually indispensable guides to the depths beneath. Even the "mental dramas," *Love's Comedy, Brand, Peer Gynt,* and *Emperor and Galilean,* are compellingly *visualized,* shown as actual worlds, in addition to being manifestations of spirit. The modern experience of our alienated world, from which Wagner turned away in despair, is an essential part of the reality of Ibsen's mature work.

The imaginative daring of this artistic odyssey was possible because the poet had intellectual integrity. Each of the plays, from *Catiline* on, is a dramatized concept in which characters, dialogue, actions, and the scenes in which they take place are all elements of a detectable argument. As the dramatist matures, this concept is gradually subtilized and enriched, so that what begins as the clash of antithetical forces within the subjectivity of Catiline expands into the world-historical conflicts and perspectives of *Emperor and Galilean.* Within the framework of these increasingly complex concepts, we find one or two (seldom more) heroic or self-aware characters with consciousnesses that are more advanced than the cultural environment of which they are the products, and that represent this culture at its most self-reflective. Such characters become aware of their inward spiritual divisions, and in their struggle to overcome this inward opposition they not only vividly bring to light what is more obscurely or inadequately understood or some-

times even denied by others but actually become the instruments
of essential change. They consciously or unconsciously reveal and
work upon the contradictions within existence that need to be
transcended, and thus their heroism or their activity is not unlike
that of the poet Ibsen, who similarly strives to be a force for change
in reality. By this similarity, Ibsen is able to identify with his characters and their actions, and so give to his dramas passionate life;
yet, because their situations are not his own, he is able to objectify
the dramatic situation into works of finely controlled artistry. The
plays thereby exemplify T. S. Eliot's idea of the "objective correlative" in which the poet simultaneously is passionately implicated
in yet aesthetically detached from his or her artwork. Ibsen's
exemplary heroes usually are tragic victims of this process of dialectic change in much the same way that the heroes and heroines of
Greek tragedy are: they are the pioneers of consciousness, their
unhappy histories becoming a means of "showing forth" the unacknowledged forces and powers.

Such a dramatic process is presented naively and ardently in
The Burial Mound. But where a lesser poet would then merely
have continued with a whole series of such complacently exemplary dramatized concepts, progressing only in the skill and breadth
of presentation, Ibsen, with true imaginative daring, pushes his
dramatic argument to the almost despairing limits of *Brand, Peer
Gynt,* and *Emperor and Galilean.* The poet's intellectual/imaginative
quest is so inextricably bound up with his dramatic development
that he continually breaks with achieved dramatic forms in order
to develop more adequate and more authentic ones.

Engaging seriously with philosophic issues, Ibsen allows his art
to reflect the confusions and complexities of philosophic problems.
He develops the terms of his basically Hegelian concepts until they
evolve into the painful confusions of part 2 of *Emperor and Galilean* in which the poet is temporarily defeated by the great argument he has raised. To have contrived a more congenial dramatic
action and a more assured structure was well within the capacity
of a poet of such consummate dramatic skill. Ibsen's refusal to
employ the devices and skills of his art to hide the confusions of
his argument is what gives us faith in the integrity and authenticity
of his best art. In the realistic cycle, for example, the dramatic

skills are powerfully successful, and we can be assured that the poet of *Emperor and Galilean* is employing them for the deepest and truest purposes.

Ibsen's critical writings suggest that the concept and the form of an Ibsen play imitates what he believes to be the structure both of the individual and of the general mind/spirit. This would mean that the mind of the poet and that of his people unite, during a theatrical presentation, in the recognition of commonly held impulses, aspirations, and heritage. The mind instinctively recognizes its first expressions in the form of myths, which are the general shapes that the natural impulses and intuitions take on and which are most closely attuned to the natural forces within the as yet undeveloped world. Such a condition of mind is responsive to the spiritual import of changes of scene, weather, light and darkness, vegetation, and so on. Human conflict at this level is simple, heroic, egoistic; the heroic will might come into conflict with the love impulse, for example. As this dialectic develops, the structure of the mind and of the world it is responsive to becomes more elaborate, adding to the natural dimensions of action the familial, societal, historical, and ideological. This is a dialectical continuum, for the later stages, i.e., ideological stages, are developments from, and sublimations of, the earlier stages. The pagan-Christian conflict of *Emperor and Galilean*, for example, is as much grounded in the erotic passions of the individuals as it is in the vast historical/ philosophical travail of the culture and vice versa, for the condition of eros is affected by the cultural condition. Thus it always is a mistake to "reduce" an Ibsen play to only one component of its total concept—to the erotic at one level, for instance, as in facile neo-Freudian interpretation, or to the merely ideological, at the other extreme. An Ibsen play is the sum of all its "moments," and because each moment is of such consequence the dramatist, as has often been remarked, refuses to indulge in redundant detail.

As the surrounding world of an Ibsen drama becomes increasingly tamed and problematic (in *The Feast at Solhoug*), the individual mind becomes separated and even alienated from the purely natural and becomes the more unnerving arena of cultural and ethical conflict. External reality now comprises a nation, its history, its identity within a community of other nations, and individuals now define themselves in these more concrete terms. They may find that their elaborate individual impulses, inclinations, and desires come up against a "higher" national identity which they also should serve and which they may become conscious of betraying (as in *Lady Inger*). This higher ideological realm may imperiously override all others, as with Haakon in *The Pretenders*, Ibsen's one portrait of the man of destiny; or it may lure its tragic victim to honorable defeat, as with Julian in *Emperor and Galilean*. In either situation, this ideological realm is as powerful an incitement to action as the inner psychological or the instinctual realm, and, in fact, it cannot be separated from them.

Although the more elaborate later stages of consciousness contain all the earlier stages, they are responsive to broader perspectives of both nature and history, so that the landscape, and the spiritual past, become increasingly vital elements of the dramatized concept, or "argument." Higher consciousnesses like Falk, Brand, Peer, and Julian are responsive to this larger surrounding medium and, because of this, are also responsive to the heights and depths of their own psyches; for the individual spirit's extension into the cosmos is an extension of its own being, just as, in Hegelian philosophy, the individual's comprehension of the cosmos, of the Absolute, is the Absolute's comprehension of itself.[2]

This synthesis of subjective and objective realities, in which the individual's drama is the drama of his world, is fully developed in *Brand, Peer Gynt,* and *Emperor and Galilean*. (Peer Gynt's inability successfully or meaningfully to engage with subjective and objective reality is depicted in a chaotic landscape of desert, storm and shipwreck, and a wasteland.) In the later realistic cycle, from *Pillars of Society* to *When We Dead Awaken*, the same concept is present. The twelve plays in the cycle build up an even more ambitious landscape of heights and depths where changing weather, light, and shade become the delicate theatrical notation of spiritual meanings. The spiritually most advanced consciousness of each play responds to and richly embodies its total pattern of meanings, as in the earlier plays, so that Margit of *The Feast at Solhoug* and Mrs. Alving of *Ghosts* are different stages of the same conception of dramatic character.

What we term the "argument" of Ibsen's dramas is not unlike

the procedure of all great drama. We detect expanding circumferences of meaning and action from the most immediate impulses of
the individual ego to the farthest limits of metaphysical implication—a Peer Gynt's onion of layer upon layer of reality. Ibsen
seems to have understood in advance what Bernard Shaw was to
proclaim: that, because the Wagner music-drama had done all that
could be done with the drama of emotional expression, the future
for modern spoken drama lay in its intellectual, its conceptual,
adequacy. In Ibsen's greatest plays there is great emotional resonance but it is always steadied by a firmly established intellectual
integrity and by a demanding aesthetic of realistic credibility which
does not permit the poet to "get away with" a cloud-castle building
that is not also "firmly established."

Ibsen is the heir to the Romantic movement, but he has learned
that the mere rhetorical affirmation of Romantic values, their
impressive "poetic" presence, as in so much Romantic posturing,
does not test these values sufficiently in terms of actual life-
possibilities. The Romantic metaphor underlying Alfhild's descent
into the self-divided and alienated world of Olaf Liliekrans is the
same as that of Hilde Wangel's descent into the self-divided and
alienated world of masterbuilder Solness; the immense difference
in artistic subtlety and power is greatly due to the fact that, in the
later work, both the Romantic themes and the human realities
they work upon have evolved into more potent and more multilayered aspects of the poet's imagination. At least from *Love's
Comedy* on, Ibsen progressively narrows the gulf between "poetry"
and "life" or, in Goethe's phrase, between poetry and truth (*Dich-
tung und Wahrheit*). The transfigured reality which is the mature
Ibsen's medium is as much truth as it is poetry, involving continuously shifting levels of meaning. (Henry James described the texture of *The Master Builder* as resembling that of shot silk.)

In this volume I begin with the critical writings of Ibsen because
in these writings the terms of his aesthetic program are presented
most lucidly. We all are in debt to J. W. McFarlane for assembling
many of these writings in his *Oxford Ibsen*, vol. I, and, although
I have not always used these translations it has been a great relief
to have them at hand when dealing with Ibsen's often tortuous
Hegelian terminology. Because this book is addressed to non-

Norwegian-speaking readers, I have referred to McFarlane's volumes in the Oxford series. At this point I also would like to acknowledge a debt to Rolf Fjelde, whose translation of Ibsen's article on Paludan-Müller's mythological poems in *The Drama Review* (Winter 1968) alerted English-speaking readers to Ibsen's critical writings and made me aware of their possible significance. The standard Norwegian text to which all translations, including my own, should be referred is the *Samlede Verker [Hundreårsutgaven]*, edited by Francis Bull, Halvdan Koht, and Didrik Arup Seip, in twenty-one volumes (Oslo: Gyldendal, 1928-58). A less complete but more convenient Norwegian text is the *Samlede Verker* edited by Didrik Arup Seip, in three volumes (Oslo: Gyldendal, 1960). Where I have found English translations particularly felicitous, I have used them in order to direct readers to them, as with Rolf Fjelde's translation of *Peer Gynt*, now out of print in its New American Library edition but fortunately reprinted in a revised version (Minneapolis: University of Minnesota Press, 1980).

The idea of reality emerging from these plays is that the changing spiritual form of a culture is reflected in the subjective movements of one or two advanced consciousnesses, so that the conflicts between individuals becomes a paradigm of universal conflicts. Such an idea is Hegelian. For Hegel, Art was one of the highest means by which Spirit reflected upon itself, superseded only by religion and philosophy; and drama was the highest form of this aesthetic self-reflection precisely because it could most adequately depict, through suffering individuals, universal forces in dialectical conflict. Whatever the paths by which Ibsen received his Hegelian aesthetics, they indisputably are *there* in his work, as anyone reading Hegel's lectures on *Aesthetics* (now available in a fine new translation by T. M. Knox [Oxford: Clarendon Press, 1975]) will discover. Ibsen's early critical writings and creative practice seem permeated by Hegelian terminology and procedures from the *Aesthetics*—so much so that I would suggest that any serious interpretation of these early works, and of Ibsen's later dramas, must involve some acquaintance with Hegel's aesthetic writings. This, indeed, is no very dismaying requirement, for not only are these writings profoundly interesting and illuminating in their own right; they also are the most congenial and accessible of the philosopher's works. It is because Hegelian aesthetic theory can help us see what Ibsen is doing that I make occasional use of it. Indeed, I suspect I make too little use of it and that much more of Ibsen's artistic intention would be open to us if we could establish a more thorough-going Hegelian interpretive discipline, or hermeneutics.[3] The present study seeks to move the boundary posts out a little farther but is painfully conscious of the immense *terra incognita* beyond.

There has been a distressing tendency in much modern Ibsen interpretation to restrict the poet's range to the narrowest circumference of meaning—generally the psychological circumference. Both admirers and detractors conspire in this, and the unhappy result has been to transform Ibsen's lifelong act of spiritual and aesthetic liberation into a succession of modest and even deceptive strategies, with the multilayered texture of the realistic plays serving "to fool his audience."[4] To be sure, we all can comprehend such an Ibsen without effort, and, self-gratifyingly, we all can measure up to and even feel a little superior toward him. A poet who is attempting to "fool" us and thus imprison us in deception—employing "literary tactics," we are told, that "spilled over into Ibsen's own private life"[5]—would be contemptible both as an artist and as a human being and it would be better not to waste any more time on him. Such is the verdict of Ronald Gray whose unremitting attack upon Ibsen as artist and man derives much of its sustenance from the work of those who purport to be Ibsen's admirers. It is easy for Gray to show that a dramatist whose goals are as modest as these modern interpreters claim is unconvincing, clumsy, narrow-minded, and shallow.[6] Indeed, Gray's work is hardly the "dissenting view" he proclaims, for the interpreters he opposes share his determination to remove from Ibsen's art all the visionary and universal content that gives it such tremendous significance. It almost is as though Ibsen's opponents, in the early years of the great Ibsen controversy (when he was defended by such men of vision as Henry James, James Joyce, Bernard Shaw, Oscar Wilde, Thomas Hardy, E. M. Forster, Thomas Mann, Rainer Maria Rilke, Hugo von Hoffmansthal, and others), decided to change their tactics to inflict more harm by interpreting Ibsen.

Fortunately, the situation for Ibsen studies is not as desperate as this, and in this book I acknowledge my debt to many who are engaged in restoring to Ibsen the "empire over the thinking world" that he once enjoyed and that he still deserves. If, in my contribution to this effort, I sometimes overreach myself, I still prefer to err in the direction of exposing my faults while indicating the greatness of the poet than in the already well-trodden direction of establishing a safely modest discipline that reveals only a safely modest artist and an impregnable critic.

I wish to thank Rolf Fjelde for his advice on many points of style. To Lindsay Waters, editor at the University of Minnesota Press, and to Victoria Haire, who combed my tangled manuscript into order, my special thanks.

CONTENTS

TO THE THIRD EMPIRE
Ibsen's Early Drama

THE CRITICAL WRITINGS

Anyone coming to Ibsen's critical writings with the expectation of finding an equivalent of Friedrich Schiller's ardently eloquent enunciation of exciting new aesthetic principles and categories, or of Richard Wagner's more ponderous formulation of principles for the redemption of art, society, and humankind in general, will be disappointed. Ibsen produced few critical writings, all of them products of his early, formative years as a poet. They are, for the most part, merely short occasional pieces, reviews, replies to reviews; only one piece is the length of an essay. The critical writings show no consciousness of doing or saying anything new (as do, say, the critical writings of Wordsworth and Coleridge); rather they clarify and assent to preexisting aesthetic principles. These principles derive from German idealist thinking; in particular the aesthetics of Hegel.

The critical pieces are emphatically intellectual, scrupulously objective, and, occasionally, even pedantic. There hardly is a trace of subjective "enthusiasm," apocalyptic manifesto writing, or brilliant originality. Ibsen insists on clear distinctions, on accurate use of terms, on assigning correctly to categories, and on making precise definitions in the manner of one to whom intellectual integrity and objectivity are never to be sacrificed to the empty depth of speculative profundities. The reader who comes to these critical writings hoping to witness a young rebel flinging his gauntlet boldly at the feet of a contemptible society will experience a deflation similar to that of one who goes to hear a noted revolutionary in the hope of indulging in heady elation only to find oneself confronted with a dry lecture given by a slightly odd and very earnest academic. The pieces are peppered with the often difficult-to-digest terminology of Hegelian aesthetics and are structured upon Hegelian concepts of literature and drama. At first this terminology and these concepts do not seem particularly earthshaking; only on deeper reflection does one discover that they are seeds as pregnant with consequential growth as those of Aristotle's dry little treatise on poetics.

Ibsen gives a sarcastic account, in the introduction to the second edition of *The Feast at Solhoug,* of how one became a drama critic in Christiania (Oslo) in the 1850s—the period when he wrote virtually all his criticism. The account derides the meager learning of most critics: they would read Heiberg's essay *On Vaudeville* and read about Oehlenschläger's quarrels with his critics and from this insubstantial intellectual foundation embark upon critical judgments. Ibsen's irony is directed not against Heiberg's Hegelian aesthetics nor against Oehlenschläger and his critics but against the paucity of learning of the Norwegian critics, suggesting that Ibsen considered rigorous and extensive knowledge to be a requisite of critical judgment. When we detect behind the terminology of Ibsen's critical writings a firm and an extensive commitment to Romantic and Hegelian aesthetics and when, furthermore, we proceed to show that Ibsen's early plays are conscious experiments in Hegelian aesthetic theory, we merely confirm Ibsen's own pronouncements on these matters. Whether or not the current Hegel revival will restore Hegelian aesthetics to their former authority, these aesthetic theories are sufficiently deep and sufficiently extensive to provide a young poet in a cultural backwater of Europe a welcome means of spiritual liberation, for Hegel's subject, in his aesthetics as well as in his philosophy of spirit and of history, is the entirety of human expression.

In many ways Hegel was the great schoolmaster of nineteenth-century Europe. He is authoritative about everything under the sun (and beyond) and demonstrates how everything exists to fulfill its purpose within the great system of things, so that the world he finally describes is a schoolmaster's world. He is always a brilliant, perceptive, and profound schoolmaster, who frowns upon arbitrariness (or, worse, "understands" it and puts it in its place!) and sets up a world of knowledge against spontaneity of action. It is no wonder that this produced a somewhat desperate reaction among his pupils: Kierkegaardian existentialism and Nietzschean irony were tactics of the more wayward. Model pupils, like Karl Marx, adapted the system to their own understanding of the world, and Ibsen seems to have been one of the model pupils rather than one of the rebels.

Anyone who seriously studies Hegel experiences a strong ambivalence toward the philosopher. On the one hand, the depth and the breadth of the philosophic analysis, the cosmopolitan and unprejudiced sweep of the philosopher's sympathies and interests, are exhilarating, so that one enjoys the true excitement of the educative process. On the other hand, the seeming rational inevitability of the great march of spirit in the world as it gradually fulfills the grand design, or Absolute, can seem deadly, its goal not unlike that which Clov dreams of in Samuel Beckett's *Endgame:*

I love order. It's my dream. A world where all would be silent and still and each thing in its last place, under the last dust.[1]

In Ibsen's day one could not ignore Hegel nor "refute" him. One lived under his shadow either as rebel or as model pupil. If one acknowledged this fact, one could discover what one could "do with" it, e.g., as a dramatist, for one's own personal development. If the early Romantics, in Matthew Arnold's phrase, "did not know enough," post-Hegelians, one might say, knew too much for their own comfort. The burden and pressure of knowledge lies upon Ibsen's work, and he takes it too seriously to play with it. The consequence is that his early work is curiously clumsy and tentative, and one feels the discrepancy between the complex intention and the crude performance; but gradually this leads to a depth and scope of intention and a mastery of dramatic means unrivaled in the nineteenth century—or, indeed, in world drama since Shakespeare. Ibsen is the great dramatist of his age because he dramatizes its burdened consciousness, the accumulations of spiritual history and conflict that are "there" to those who will only "see".

The notion of so self-conscious a dramatic artist simultaneously acquiring the aesthetic philosophy of his art and its better and better realization in practice, conceding almost from the beginning that the essential rules and principles of his art already have been theoretically established, conflicts with the idea of Ibsen as the revolutionary path breaker for modern drama. There is an almost "Augustan" aspect to the way Ibsen perceives and acknowledges a certain order, with its own established high standards, to which he wishes to align his individual practice and to which he wishes to raise the consciousness of his audience. It is typical of the complexity of Ibsen as an artist that this attitude toward the world should be deeply conservative in many ways and radical, in others.

For the modern reader, the particular difficulty of Ibsen's critical writings is that they assent to a certain order of intellectual achievement and invoke this order often, employing its terms and everywhere reflecting its spirit, without spelling out for the reader's benefit what this order is. The interpreter must detect the sources of Ibsen's critical terms, gloss his texts, and point out the implications of his arguments. For example, in one of his first, and slightest, pieces,[2] written in March 1851, Ibsen already employs a strongly Hegelian aesthetic terminology a little comically at odds with the subject of the review: a student vaudeville. In vaudeville, the youthful Ibsen observes, the "epic" element is dominant, in that the situation influences the characters and not vice versa. This is not an uncanny anticipation of Brechtian theory but derives from the source of Brechtian theory: Hegel's distinction between the epic, "objective" mode, the lyric "subjective" mode, and the dramatic mode, which synthesizes the two. The epic spirit, Hegel observed, was one in which the individual heroes embody great national purposes rather than exist as independent, "self-concentrated" characters, as in drama, whose "inner will" determines actions.[3]

In conclusion, Ibsen notes that student comedy, which revolves around themes rather than characters with serious volitions, is different from comedy proper where "the lyric element is dominant."[4] In Hegelian theory, lyric poetry is the expression of subjectivity, in which the poet gives us not the imaginative rendition of *external* reality, as in epic, but "an inner vision and feel of it."[5] The lyric poet internalizes the world and gives it the coloring of subjective consciousness, at the same time disclosing the poet's heart and its feelings. This is a stage leading to the development of dramatic poetry, which will produce characters who express their inward states. So far, Ibsen's Hegelian references are slight enough and could have been picked up secondhand; but later we will observe them growing into a Hegelian discipline while also being put to practical use in such dramatic experiments in Hegelian structure as *The Feast at Solhoug, Olaf Liliekrans* and *The Vikings at Helgeland.*

In another article,[6] Ibsen takes up the cause of Norwegian nationalist drama, a theme which was to engage him deeply in the years to follow. He attacks French (meaning Scribean) drama for its ethical tawdriness, its aesthetic ineptitude, and its baneful influence upon the development of a truly nationalist tradition of drama in Norway. This concern with nationalism was a major element of the *Zeitgeist,* for in nation after nation, from the Balkans to Ireland, the political movements for liberation from foreign rule drew upon the intellectuals' vivid need for ethnic identity within a unique national tradition. A tragicomic aspect of this movement was that the common people, or peasantry, from whom the great national tradition was supposed to derive, frequently were indifferent to or hostile toward such re-creations of the native tradition, which often involved the academic resurrection of strange gods and outlandish cults, so that the supposed popular national and folk traditions increasingly became an exotic creation of eccentric intellectuals. (Ibsen takes up this theme in *St. John's Night.*) In its most extreme form we have W. B. Yeats's plays, in which Celtic legends, insofar as they have been academically restored, are blended with modern adaptations of Japanese Noh-theater, to be performed in drawing rooms before highly select and sophisticated audiences; what began as a self-proclaimed art of the whole people evolved inevitably into an exotic art of the few.

The history of cultural nationalism is long and complicated.

As with so much else in the modern world, it seems to have originated in Germany; at least one can see the movement coming to life there. There are intimations of cultural nationalism even in Lessing, otherwise an Enlightenment universalist in his thinking; his *Hamburg Dramaturgy*, in its plea for a modern German drama free from pernicious Gallic influences, at least sets the argument in motion. Herder gave to the concept of cultural liberation deeper themes of ethnic uniqueness, the *Nationalgeist,* or *Geist des Volkes,* from which much that was to become so disturbing in subsequent German history can be seen to have originated, even though he himself was not responsible for the sinister use of his ideas.[7] At the same time men like the brothers Grimm, with their immense learning, were recovering for the modern mind the folktales of the people with their mythological streams feeding from the dim past into the life of the present. The movement found its greatest and most alarming artist in Richard Wagner, in whom we find at once so much that is admirable and so much that is frightening in cultural nationalism. Folktales, folk songs and music, ethnic history, and national mythologies, invaded the literature and music of nation after nation in a Europe that earlier, in the age of the Enlightenment, had sought to suppress cultural and national uniqueness in favor of a rationalist universalism. Although we, today, so often associate cultural nationalism with so much that is reactionary, we should remember that it was seen as a force of liberation in the nineteenth century; the advocacy of nationalist institutions was a direct attack upon oppression by foreign rule.

Cultural nationalism is the major dividing line between the Enlightenment and the age of Romanticism. In Enlightenment Germany, for example, Lessing and Schiller or Mozart and Beethoven, so different in many respects, are united in the universalist emphasis of their art. Lessing might wish to see German drama and German culture free itself from Gallic influence, but not in terms of a specifically German culture; in fact, he points to Aristotle and Shakespeare (in a reformulation of that ever-recurring Augustan duality of *Art*—Aristotle—and *Nature*—Shakespeare) as the best models for Germans to follow because both are universal writers, whereas the French, for all their rules, remain peculiarly

Gallic. Mozart's *The Magic Flute*, Lessing's *Nathan the Wise*, Goethe's *Iphigenia in Tauris* seek to address the same universal human audience as does Beethoven's Ninth Symphony, which suitably sets to music Schiller's universalist *Ode to Joy*. If one puts beside these works Wagner's *The Ring of the Nibelungs* or Mussoursky's version of *Boris Godunov*, or the many nationalist operas and dramas of the European countries emerging from foreign rule, one detects that the latter are addressed to a particular people in all its depth of response and not to a theoretical universal humanity.

Through his art, Ibsen desired to stir deeply the spirit of the Norwegian people as well as to lift its dramatic art to the highest level of achievement; and for this purpose the spirit of the people must be felt to be deeply and authentically present in the artwork. In his article on nationalist drama Ibsen defines the nature of his ideal audience as much as he defines his ideal dramatic form and method. Richard Wagner, at about the same time, insisted that modern dramatic artists return, for their subject matter, to folk-myth, "that native, nameless poem of the folk,"[8] to give their people the deepest expression of its timeless spirit: that essential spiritual identity freed from the arbitrary and accidental events in "alienated" historical time and from the promptings of merely abstract reason.

Ibsen, similarly, needed to create the audience to which he could addresss his art. The highest and deepest art would call upon the highest and deepest elements in the spirit of that audience, which would conceive of itself as a nation and a people whose collective spirit was greater than its accidental historical individuality. This collective spirit could extend itself spatially into the world of nature and temporally into its total past. Unlike Wagner, however, Ibsen never was to establish a shortcut to mythic grandeur by bypassing the historically created and rationally understool realities that intervened between modern man and his prehistorical, mythic, and natural origins.

"The truly national author," Ibsen observed in a review of a nationalist play,[9] "is one who knows how to impart to his work those undertones which ring out to us from mountain and valley, from meadow and shore, and above all from our own inner souls."

Beneath the youthful rhetoric is the Romantic belief that the "spirit of the Universe" is interfused with the mind of man just as the mind of man is extended into the universe as *Geist*, or Spirit. In the revised version of *The Burial Mound* Blanka's speeches are rewritten to express this consciousness of an interfusion of the spirit of the universe with that of the human mind; but *The Burial Mound* also is a play in which highly momentous historical and rational processes are shown to be at work.

Cultural nationalism, Ibsen believed, should extend itself from the individual spirit to the collective racial spirit, through the world of a commonly inherited nature as well as back through time to the very origins of consciousness where even the most distant myths can be seen as contributing to the huge evolution of the human spirit. This idea informs the argument of the review *"Professor Welhaven on Paludan-Müller's Mythological Poems."*[10] This unpromising title actually introduces one of Ibsen's most important statements of his aesthetic principles, although it must be conceded at the outset that the Hegelian terminology is employed with more than justified difficulty: it is far harder going than Hegel's own writings on the subject!

Welhaven, a poet and critic whom Ibsen admired, had deplored the use of old mythological figures in modern verse, and Ibsen finds the issue important enough to come to the defense of the mythologizing poets. It has not been proved, Ibsen argues, that myth is unsuited for use in modern times as poetic material for an "intellectual poem." In myth, Ibsen argues, the original content of the folk consciousness (i.e., the first perceptions and formulations of the race) manifests itself as a synthesis of "speculation and history" (i.e., the tendency to imaginative speculation works upon historical events and converts them into myth). One might call this the "objective" phase of spirit that precedes the "subjective", lyric phase. Myth, therefore, originates at about the same time as epic and can "rightly claim to act as clothing for speculative tendencies in that it simultaneously functions as a justifiable category in the genre of epic, since one element in its content is historical." Lyric poetry, on the other hand, is the "expression of subjectivism," and so cannot manifest itself as myth "in so far as the latter is ideally conceived." That is, lyric poetry, which attempts to express subjective reality and feelings with the greatest authenticity, cannot *ideally* originate as mythic (i.e., objective) expression. "But since the emergence of every myth lies outside that point in time when the immediacy of the folk consciousness was still absolute" (i.e., since myth is the creation of a phase of spirit coming after that in which the people's consciousness was wholly *immediate,* that is, limited to purely non-self-reflective modes such as perception and memory[11]), " . . . so in every myth the beholder (the original or primitive observer) will appear self-consciously aware of that which he observes" (i.e., because myth is the product of such objective and advanced tendencies as speculation and history, the observer, confronting this more complex human expression, is aware of himself being aware of the object (myth), for it is not an object of "immediate" perception) and " . . . subjectivity will come into its own, and lyricism will thereby appear as a necessary element of myth" (i.e., from this *self*-conscious awareness the observer of myth enters into subjectivity of which the lyric is the fitting expression, and this subjective or lyric apprehension of the objective myth is the necessary later development of the myth in the consciousness of the race.)[12]

This means that a modern self-consciousness, such as Henrik Ibsen's can make use of mythic expression, but in a higher subjective mode rather than in the objective mode in which the myth originated. This will have consequences for Ibsen's playwriting; we will find characters in a "subjective" and lyric drama, such as *The Feast at Solhoug,* frequently resorting to, quoting, and reflecting upon objective mythic and balladic material. A far more consequential development of this theme runs through all the plays from *Love's Comedy* to *When We Dead Awaken,* where the gulf detected between the original and spontaneous life of mythic characters and the manner in which they are travestied in the present modulates through the most diverse examples. Emperor Julian, who tries to return to the pagan myths and their sources and cults, which belonged to an earlier, more spontaneous, less reflective, and less divided age, but who is the most reflective and divided of all, is the greatest example. We will discover the same themes in the plays of the realistic cycle, where the lost vitality and instinctual health of a nonreflective past, which had what Hilde

Wangel will call "a robust conscience," is poignantly played off against a crushingly subjective and self-reflective present. The cycle ends with the clearest example of this contrast between the "naive" and the "sentimental" consciousness in the Ulfheim-Rubek, Maia-Irene pairs.

In this unprepossessing little article on Paludan-Müller's poems, therefore, we can see the seed from which the entire dramatic world of Ibsen will grow. This theme of synthesizing the modern, alienated, reflective, and sentimentalisch mind with the primitive, immediate, naive consciousness has its origins in pre-Romantic thought—in the Rousseauist contrast between a decadent complex modern civilization and simpler, more primitive, and more nobly honest societies (the theme of Ibsen's earliest plays). For Friedrich Schiller, our alienation from nature had to be overcome to attain to present freedom, but Schiller did not advocate a return to the primitive condition. His famous contrast of the naive and the sentimental consciousnesses, that is, of the spontaneous and the self-reflective, ends in favor of the self-reflective and alienated, but Schiller envisages a synthesis of the two. The greatest and most massive development of the theme of integrating all earlier phases of consciousnesses into the life of the present was in Hegel's *Phenomenology of Spirit,* which maintained that only by acknowledging the necessary deaths of all prior phases of spirit could one incorporate them into the ever-living Spirit. If one denied their necessary death and sought to resurrect these past phases as vital elements of the present—as an artist might try to create exactly in the spirit of classical Greece, for example—the result would be only a confirmation of their demise. *The Vikings at Helgeland* is Ibsen's attempt to write within the spirit of the pagan-warrior culture just as it is undergoing the transition to Christianity, and the result, although impressive in its perverse way, only confirms the mistaken nature of the endeavor. In *Emperor and Galilean* Julian fails to see that the spirit of classical Greece, to which he wishes to return, is alive, and only can be alive, as it has been transmuted into the vital currents of the present.

The rest of the article on Paludan-Müller's poems develops this idea. Ibsen comments that the period of original mythological poetry is over but that myth, because it "bears infinity within itself," will undergo continuous evolution. The myth should not, and indeed cannot, be changed, yet it can be ever newly examined and pondered "on the level of speculation," which constitutes "a necessary stage of its continuing development."[13] To denounce the use of myth in modern literature, Ibsen writes—and we should take note—is to denounce the whole age and its cultural trends. In the present age, he observes, one does not sail like Columbus across the sea to discover new land, but one investigates the nature of that which already is known. Considering that Ibsen lived during a time of almost unparalleled scientific discovery and technological innovation, this comment seems surprising. But a constant theme of his pronouncements upon his time was that it represented a closure, the end of a spiritual phase from which something new but unknown would be born. For Hegel, the great ages of exploration, expeditions, national migrations, and the like are the age of the Epic:

Drama is the product of a completely developed and organized national life. For in essence it presupposes as past both the primitive poetic days of the epic proper and the independent subjectivism of lyrical outpourings, because, comprising both of these, it is satisfied in neither of these spheres taken separately. For this poetic combination, the free self-consciousness of human aims, complications, and fates must have been already completely aroused and developed in a way possible only in epochs of the halfway or later development of a national life.[14]

To claim that the present age, therefore, no longer was one of significant discovery was to claim that it was an age ready for a major dramatic art. (Perhaps Bertolt Brecht's desire to write drama for an age of consequential *change* led him to formulate the somewhat paradoxical concept of an "epic theater.")

That Ibsen uses such difficult philosophical terminology in a short critical article indicates to what extent he belongs to the tradition of German idealist thought. A perennial problem for the Romantic imagination was that of liberating the modern spirit from the erroneous and often oppressive burden of the past while helping the modern spirit acquire its true and complete heritage, from the very origins of consciousness to the most advanced developments of the present.

In this endeavor, Romantic writers from many different disciplines—imaginative literature, aesthetics, philology, history, philosophy—were united. M. H. Abrams, in his impressive study of Romantic thought entitled *Natural Supernaturalism*, gives a good account of the ubiquity of this tradition, observing:

At no other time and place have literature and technical philosophy been so closely interinvolved as in Germany in the period beginning with Kant. The major German poets and novelists (as well as Coleridge, and later Carlyle, in England) avidly assimilated the writings of the philosophers; many of them wrote philosophical essays; and all incorporated current philosophical concepts and procedure into the subject matter and structure of their principal works of imagination. And on their part philosophers remained closely in touch with literature; Schelling and Hegel themselves wrote poetry and both these thinkers gave literature and arts a prominent—Schelling in his central period, the cardinal—place in their metaphysical systems. It is not by chance nor by the influence of a mysterious non-causal *Zeitgeist,* but through participation in the same historical and intellectual *milieu,* through recourse to similar precedents in the religious and cultural tradition, and by frequent interaction, that the works of philosophy and literature of this age manifest conspicuous parallels in ideas, in design, and even in figurative detail.[15]

It was this tradition which Scandinavia, with its inevitable time lag, absorbed, a tradition in which there was no rigid demarcation between imaginative and conceptual writing and in which aesthetic structures reflected conceptual structures. However, although the intellectual tradition of Scandinavia reflected the tendencies of German culture, its *theatrical* tradition, like that of most European countries, was dominated by the French school of playmakers and their imitators who followed the example of the prolific Eugene Scribe. In a review of a performance, in Christiania, of Karl Gutzkow's *Zopf und Schwert,*[16] Ibsen contrasts the French with the German contribution to modern drama while recording his dismay at the cultural level of the Norwegian theater audience—the audience to whom Ibsen would have to address his art. For many years the Norwegian theatrical repertory was almost exclusively French and Danish, and the Norwegian public's taste had been corrupted by a lavish diet of "Scribe & Co.'s sugar candy drama." Gutzkow's play was a drama of the modern German school—a first from that school for the Norwegian audiences—and Ibsen finds the contrast between the two schools, the French and the German, highly instructive. French drama cannot claim to be *literature* since it needs to be performed to come to life, whereas German drama exists primarily as literature and only secondarily as theater.

Ibsen makes a distinction, here, that also must strike any reader of nineteenth-century drama: that the technical development of the nineteenth-century theater, from early Scribe to Victor Hugo, emphasized theatrical effectiveness at the cost of literary merit. It was an art of the maximum *theatrical* excitement with the minimum of *conceptual* risk, and such an essentially mindless theater, with opera, becomes the popular and fashionable theater of the day. The *literary* drama, extending the conceptual as well as the expressive range of drama, now pursues a separate course, as, in France itself, the career of de Musset illustrates. English Romantic poets from Blake to Tennyson attempted or completed unactable closet drama while Byron, the most gifted in specifically dramatic talent, forbade his plays to be acted, insisting he was writing for a "mental theater"—a form to which Ibsen was to devote a great part of his career (from *Love's Comedy* to *Emperor and Galilean*). The great names of the literary drama—Heinrich von Kleist, Georg Buechner, Alfred de Musset, Franz Grillparzer (admired by Byron), Friedrich Hebbel—are not the great names of the *theater* in the nineteenth century. The supreme exception, Richard Wagner, is too *great* an exception, in all areas of art—and life—to qualify this rule.

The achievements of nineteenth-century literary drama, which seeks to establish Byron's "mental theater," separate from the theatrical development, so that the two traditions that Ibsen distinguishes, German "literary" and French "theatrical," exemplify a drastic separation in public taste, a separation that would have to be overcome by an author who wished to address an entire "people" or nation and not just an intelligentsia. Ibsen's own dramatic practice, in his early years, showed a very awkward alliance of highly abstract and idealist dramatic concepts and a clumsily handled French (Scribean) technique—although he was never as bound to the latter as has often been supposed.

German dramatists, Ibsen writes, offend against the essential *unity* of art, drawing characters in extenso and thereby transgressing the limits of drama. With this emphasis upon character, German drama attempts to achieve reality, but, "in the realm of art, reality, pure and simple, has no place; illusion, on the contrary, has".[17] French drama, on the other hand, suffers from overformalism; it has no reality *within it,* and the characters appear as mere abstractions, as either angels or devils, created purely for formal contrast. (If to some readers it seems too great a paradox that the unintellectual, commercial plays of Paris should be more "abstract" than the more intellectual works of Germany, they might refer to a brilliant little essay by Hegel called "Who thinks abstractly?" in which he demonstrates that the unreflective language of common discourse is guilty of abstractness in the sweeping simplicities of its terms. The simple moral stereotypes of French drama similarly are "abstract.") German dramatists, Ibsen continues, portray "the most trivial, ordinary people such as we see and hear every day. But the ordinary person's character is by no means trivial from an artistic point of view; as represented by art, it is just as interesting as any other."[18]

The antinomies of this argument—reality versus art, formless triviality of detail versus unrealistic formalism—recognize strengths and weaknesses in both traditions. The argument shows that Ibsen is conscious of, and seeking to reconcile, the claims of both reality in art and aesthetic form. "Reality," in his own art, will come to embrace the world we inhabit, with its history, its ideologies and conflicts, its intimations of metaphysical dimensions of experience, as well as its immediate, everyday content. Form will be more than a mere shell enclosing this reality; it will become the best means for revealing it. So dramatic form must be responsive to all dimensions of reality, just as the poet's understanding must be responsive to the requirements of the aesthetic intelligence.

The article ends with an attack upon the Norwegian public for the abysmal level of its taste, for it was not the merits of Gutzkow's play that found favor, but the most trivial piece of stage buffonery, featuring a well-known actor who appeared in his underpants. One begins to see Ibsen's great artistic problem. He wishes to be a major dramatist in a country where the cultural traditions are imported in debased form and where the audience, for whom the poet must write, cannot attain even the level of these debased forms.

Cultural nationalism therefore was all the more to be welcomed as a partial broadening of both the audience's range of interests and the poet's permitted subject matter, for cultural nationalism at least extended that subject matter in terms of the nation and its history, its scenography and its inherited identity. The cast of characters then could extend beyond the present or, if of the present, could be responsive to echoes and ghosts from the past—the theme of *St. John's Night.* In a "Prologue" written by Ibsen in 1851 in celebration of Ole Bull's visit to Christiania to raise funds for his Norwegian theater in Bergen, the themes of the earlier articles are gathered under a program of cultural nationalism.[19]

Viking times, the Prologue states, were wild and rough, yet Viking actions were a living poem made of sword and shield. This "warrior poetry," however, was too powerful for the common people, and so the skald or minstrel appeared, to transpose the harsh poetry of battle into the modes of music and words that could entertain the warrior kings. (Ibsen, here, seems to follow Hegel's account of the emergence of epic poetry, at a necessarily later stage, out of the actually lived heroic life.[20]) But then an awesome winter fell over the north, the noble skald fell silent, "dedicated to death like one bewitched who has forgotten the word with which he can find release from his enchantment."[21] The spirit of the Norwegian people slept a long winter's sleep, and its Viking past was like a faded memory. Other phases and other customs came to Norway, but these were unresponsive to the submerged "harp of longing"[22] within the Norwegian spirit.

Art alone could interpret the longing of the people and, through art's power, bring back the glorious images of the past, sound again the forgotten music, and so awaken the people's spirit. That spirit once again was responsive to valley and mountain, forest and meadow. Art now will sing, not just about the past but about this reawakened life of the present, when it possesses its new temple— the Bergen theater.

These themes are sounded with an unskeptical Wagnerian ardor suitable to the fund-raising occasion; there is no hint here of the grim exploration of the darker areas of the spirit's past that Ibsen's art actually will undertake. Instead we find what are to be the constant Ibsen themes of the reawakening of the human spirit through the recovery of the past and through dialectical struggle (a mental sublimation of the old warrior combativeness), which we will encounter from *Catiline* to *When We Dead Awaken.*

The most extensive excursion into critical writing made by Ibsen was a paper, *"The Heroic Ballad and Its Significance for Literature,"*[23] read to a literary society in Bergen in 1857. As it is the most considered account of literary history that has survived from his critical writings (a paper on Shakespeare, written for the same society, has not survived), it will repay careful study, despite the often dubious nature of his argument. The theme throughout the paper is the relation of literature to "the consciousness of the people."[24] The heroic ballad was the one enduring art of "the ordinary people,"[25] and through the ballad, which was not composed by any one individual, the people found a satisfying expression of its own inner life. Richard Wagner proposed the identical argument when he called upon artists to draw only upon "that native, nameless poem of the folk."

Paraphrasing Hegel's description of the epic poet and the folk singer, "who must retire in face of his *object* and lose himself in it... [so that only] the product, not the poet, appears...,"[26] Ibsen observes that a basic element of the heroic ballad, and of the epic, is "objectivity," for

literary subjectivity has no significance for the people; they do not care about the poet, only about his work insofar as they recognise in this a particular aspect of their own personality... If the new is to appeal to the people it must also in a certain sense be old; it must not be invented but rediscovered; it must not appear as something strange and incongruous, and in which our national strength mainly resides; it must not be presented like some foreign utensil whose use is unfamiliar and which is inappropriate for the familiar routine; it must be reproduced like some old family piece which we had forgotten but which we remember as soon as we set eyes upon it, because all kinds of memories are linked with it—memories which, so to speak, lay within us fermenting quietly and uncertainly until the poet came along and put them into words.[27]

The implications of this passage for our understanding of Ibsen's method and intentions are enormous. He repeats the same argument much later in his career when commenting on the public's reception of *Ghosts:* "A writer dare not alienate himself so far from his people that there is no longer any understanding between them and him. But *Ghosts* had to come..."[28] Art must explore, must extend the limits of human consciousness, because, as Ibsen wrote in an album presented to Leopold von Sacher-Masoch, "in these times every piece of writing should attempt to move the frontier markers."[29] But this did not and could not mean that poets should cultivate eccentric isolation from their people, retreating into intellectual dandyism or esoteric aestheticism. True to Romantic thought, Ibsen's self-explorations always are simultaneously explorations of that which he has in common with his people, for, as he once remarked, we all share the guilt of the people to which we belong. Although poets must at all times remain within the conceptual range of their people, this is less of a limiting proscription than it seems for this conceptual range includes areas that the public possesses only unconsciously and that will need to be reawakened by poets, areas "forgotten but [remembered] as soon as we set eyes upon [them]." Poets, therefore, are not forced to be unoriginal and conventional; on the contrary, as Ibsen's own career will exemplify, the task of reawakening the people to the full possession of its spiritual wealth (the task, also, of a work like Hegel's *Phenomenology of Spirit)* will require the greatest originality and inventiveness.

Such a belief, that all artists have a responsibility to the whole spirit of their public and their nation — that they must share the people's conceptual range, help it better to grasp it — has given rise to such widely different and original art forms as those of Richard Wagner, Henrik Ibsen, and Bertolt Brecht. Wagner sought, through the agency of myth, to resurrect from the depths of the consciousness of the German people its deepest feelings and intuitions, and to express these with the utmost power in an art form that although revolutionary, still was the embodiment of the timeless. The determined individualist, Ibsen, and the equally determined collectivist, Brecht, refuse to separate their artistic explorations from the communal needs that such explorations are serving, and it is no accident that both draw upon a rich storehouse of folk proverb and folk legend. Such plays as Brecht's *The Caucasian*

Chalk Circle and *The Good Person of Setzuan* are as filled with folktale elements and a common stock of proverbs (the anonymous and collective wisdom of the people) as are *Peer Gynt* and *Brand,* yet for all this reliance upon the common legacy of the people and its conceptual range at its most articulate, no more startlingly innovative works could be imagined than these plays.

Ibsen's cultural nationalism is part of the poet's deep desire to be the expression of the people's consciousness, and this is neither intellectual timidity on Ibsen's part nor the desire to be popular (for few writers took less pains to court popularity). Rather, it represents his resolve not to remove himself from the general consciousness while fulfilling his unique identity and destiny as an artist. In Hegelian aesthetics, dramatic art is not only the highest form of poetry; it is also the highest form and culmination of the entire realm of art. Great drama requires that the dramatist write not for the sake of the self but for humanity in general, that the artist therefore deal with themes that are of universal importance, at the same time giving them concrete individuality and contemporaneity.[30] If Ibsen followed Hegel in this, as he follows him in so much else, he would conceive of his entire career as a dramatist in such universalist terms, would make his art express more and more adequately the totality of human consciousness. In one fascinating passage Hegel considers the possibility of a poet who might take as subject matter the entire history of the human spirit, in epic form, but then he dismisses the idea as being either too cumbersome or too nebulous to be effective epic art.[31] To any reader of Hegel, however, the idea would remain as a tantalizing invitation. The Hungarian dramatist Imre Madàch was lured to attempt this in his *The Tragedy of Man,* and I have argued elsewhere that Ibsen embarked upon just such a project in his realistic cycle, giving compellingly concrete form to the nebulous spiritual drama.

Ibsen now develops the most dubious part of his argument, with a contrast between the poetry of "Germanic" peoples and that of "southerners." Southern peoples, Ibsen declares with what seems to be astonishing inaccuracy, never possessed a folk poetry corresponding to the heroic ballads of the north, for southerners "did not make poetry themselves; they had their poets and minstrels.

The southerner had artists to glorify him and his past; the north-
erner glorified himself."[32] Even in Ibsen's day, the fact that
behind Homer and Hesiod stretched a long tradition of oral and
ballad poetry generally was conceded—to the point, in fact, that
Hegel decried the academic fashion of denying the existence of
Homer.[33] The unfortunate contrast between the arts of the north
and the south, which is to lead Ibsen, in this essay, through thickets
of bad reasoning, seems to be based on a misunderstanding of a
passage in Hegel's *Aesthetics:*

This inclination towards a lyrical treatment is essentially grounded in the fact
that the entire life of these [i.e., medieval German, Latin, and Slavonic]
nations has been developed on the basis of the principle of the personality
which is forced to produce out of its own resources as its own what is substantive and objective, and to give a shape to that, and this process of plumb-
ing its own depths it pursues more and more consciously. This principle is
effective in the most perfect and unclouded way in the case of the Germanic
races, while the Slavonic ones, on the other hand, have first to struggle out of
an oriental immersion in the universal substance of things. In the middle
between these are the Latin peoples who found available to them in the con-
quered provinces of the Roman Empire not only the remains of Roman learning and civilization generally, but a completely developed social and political
situation, and in order to be assimilated to it they had to abandon part of
their original nature.[34]

Even if Ibsen, like Hegel, is discussing only the post-Christian,
medieval times, his argument strikes me as wholly untenable. The
artistically fertile south is depicted as divided between a majority
of passive consumers of art and a minority of artistic producers (as
if incredibly beautiful and intricate craftsmanship did not exist at
all levels of "southern" culture), and, again following Hegel, Ibsen
uses this division to explain why *dramatic* art belongs to the south
more than to the north. Northerners, on the other hand, Ibsen
goes on, do not want to see their ideas and concepts rendered by
another; each wishes to be given only the outlines of the design
and to put on the finishing touches, as in the variations with each
individual retelling of the folk ballad. By such reasoning Ibsen actually is able to make the artistically poorer north seem richer
than the south.

The ballad tradition, Ibsen continues, is necessarily an oral tradition, which enjoys continuous spontaneous modification by the people. "In print the ballad looks old and gray, indeed old-fashioned, if you will; on the lips of the people age does not concern it."[35] Yet it is right that these ballads should now be written down while there is still time, for "the people's season of poetic productivity can now be regarded as more or less over."[36] If it *is* over, the "north" would be similar in situation to the "south" and so would be ready for the development of *dramatic* art, whose hour in the north, presumably, has been historically and dialectically prepared. (Ibsen's own interests as an aspiring dramatist are obviously closely involved in this argument!) "With the rise of civilization, the present age no longer is the strong and vigorous period that produces the rich events and distinguished personalities among the people that are the subject of the heroic ballad"[37] — as Hegel also argued when contrasting the conditions suitable to the emergence of epic and of dramatic art.[38] Folk poetry, however, does not therefore die; it holds within itself "the potential of some new and higher existence"—i.e., its "sublimation" into dramatic art. As civilization progresses, naive spontaneity must be lost, but later generations will turn to the ballad poetry as to a gold mine; when "refined, restored to its original purity and elevated by art, it [ballad poetry] will once again take root in the people."[39]

The continuity between this and the article on Paludan-Müller's mythological poems, of six years earlier, is evident. Both contain the same idea of psychological, historical, cultural, and aesthetic evolution, as a single totality, where the past is complexly built, layer upon layer, into the structure of the present. Such an idea is Hegelian, whether at first- or at second-hand; before Hegel, except in the untypical case of Vico, such an evolutionary concept of history did not exist. Its continuation, especially after the Darwinian theory of evolution, in the writing of such influential thinkers as Marx, Freud, and their followers, allows us to forget how distinctly "Germanic" Ibsen's thinking in these articles actually is and how the strengths and weaknesses of this tradition are "built into" his ruminations on cultural history.

Ballad, he continues, is more suitable for dramatic treatment than is saga because the latter "is a great cold epic, closed and complete within itself, essentially objective and remote from lyricism"[40] (in Hegelian theory, lyric poetry, coming after epic, is closer to dramatic poetry). "If then, the poet is to create a dramatic work from the epic material, he must necessarily introduce a foreign element into this given material: he must introduce a lyrical element; because, as is well known, drama is a higher synthesis of lyric and epic."[41] Two years earlier Ibsen had worked the epic material of the Volsunga saga into the "lyric drama" *The Feast At Solhoug.* In such plays as *Lady Inger of Ostraat, The Feast at Solhoug, Olaf Liliekrans,* and *The Vikings at Helgeland* Ibsen deliberately creates Hegelian dramatic structures in which ideas of cultural history, psychological orientation (i.e., "objective" or "subjective"), and poetic form (epic, lyric, dramatic) taken directly from Hegel's aesthetic philosophy are rigidly adhered to. Although this accounts for much of the inadequacy of these plays, we can see this deliberate philosophical-aesthetic structuring on Ibsen's part as the apprenticeship that will produce the great mastery of the series of plays from *Love's Comedy* to *When We Dead Awaken*, in which the Hegelian structuring and the philosophical content, deepening with Ibsen's own deeper understanding of and reflection upon life, become a far more subtle, flexible, and searching artistic principle.

The introduction of lyric elements into the saga material, Ibsen goes on, violates the saga's form, and it is only through some national *form* that national *themes* can emerge. The poetry and themes of the saga, though written down in the Christian period, essentially are pagan; for this reason, the saga material is more suited to ancient Greek than to Christian poetic style. (The reason for this apparently is that both cultures, the Viking and the classical Greek, were pagan, although one hardly can imagine two more disparate cultures than the Vikings of the sagas and the Athenians of the age of Pericles.) The heroic ballad, on the other hand, is essentially Christian, for though there are heathen elements in it, "these elements are present on a quite different and higher level than in the mythic stories, and it is by reason of this that the poetic offshoot of Christianity, romanticism, manifests its influence on the ballad."[42] (Like Hegel, Ibsen means by "romanticism" the culture of the Middle Ages and after, in contrast with the "classic" period of Greece and Rome.)

The reader will note the dynamism of Ibsen's concept of cultural change: its Hegelian and dialectical series of transitions from earlier to later, lower to higher phases, all the time preserving (sublimating) what is most essential in the discarded phase. This is the method of Hegel's *Phenomenology of Spirit;* in his *Aesthetics,* we see the same process operating in the sphere of the human imagination. From *The Burial Mound* on, Ibsen creates dramas in which this spiritual working-through from lower to higher phases of cultural consciousness is the major action of the play. To give the reader an idea of the nature of Ibsen's concept of historical/cultural evolution, of the complexity of the spiritual substance that the poet must dramatize, I have selected the following passage from his article on the heroic ballad:

The Aesir worshippers who did not know the power of faith where reason fails, constructed a world for themselves in which no rational laws were valid. In this world, therefore, everything—but consequently also nothing—was supernatural; and this was their solution, for in this way they were able to reconcile faith with reason. The romantic philosophy, on the other hand, takes a different path, venerating Shakespeare's phrase that "there are more things in heaven and earth than are dreamt of in your philosophy." This allows rational things a right and a validity; but alongside it, above it, and through it goes the mystery, the inexplicable, the Christian if you like, for Christianity is of course itself a mystery. It preaches faith in those things "beyond all understanding." It is in this that the mythic tales differ fundamentally from the heroic ballad; the former is to the latter as the fable is to the fairy tale. The fable does not know the miraculous, the fairy tale is rooted in it.

   This world, at once natural and supernatural, is the one which the heroic ballad exposes to us. In many of the ballads it is the heroes and the events of the Aesir doctrine which form the actual content, but always in a more modern guise, always under a more or less explicable Christian form. Tor and his battle with the Tursers, Sigurd Fafnirsbane and his exploits, the sagas of Tyrfing etc., are all recognisable enough in their medieval dress and names; from being gods and saga heroes, the characters have descended to being warriors and mortal knights; but one surely is in error if one seeks the reason for this transformation either in the religious feelings of the people or in any political or ecclesiastical pressure on the part of those in power. The myths presumably continued to live among the people long after the introduction of Christianity; and it is doubtful whether the understanding of Christianity was clear and pure enough to kill faith in the ancestral gods. The many apparent points of contact between the old and new doctrines rather make it probable that both persisted for a long time alongside each other, and that the Christian doctrines in the first instance probably served more as a civilizing power than actually as a religion. Either the priests, the advocates of the new doctrine, had not grasped the situation with sufficient clarity, or else they were unable to tear themselves free from the traditions they had inherited; but instead of proclaiming the merely imaginary nature of the existence of the Aesir, instead of declaring their annihilation along with the faith that abandoned them, they presented them as evil, hostile powers, dangerous to the new teaching and to its true believers. No wonder, therefore, that the old spirits were long-lived, for they had a good footing. St. Olaf might well summon them in stone to a day of judgement—they nevertheless continued to live in the consciousness and faith of the people and there they have continued to live until our own day.[43]

What this passage describes is a collective consciousness, a national consciousness, evolving in time (later, Ibsen will broaden his subject to include human consciousness in its entirety) through historical, ideological, cultural forms. New spiritual phases are dialectically generated, together with their forms, which then attempt to suppress but finally assimilate prior phases which are altered within the consciousness they in turn are altering. This was to remain Ibsen's subject matter to the end of his career, although he evolved greatly modified dramatic means of revealing it.

The poetry of the heroic ballad is not subjective, for the poet does not sing of his individual experience: "he simply wakes to conscious life that which lay dreaming and fermenting within the people itself. His poetic talent consists essentially in his clear vision of what the people wish to see expressed, and in a certain ability to give that expression a form in which the people can most easily recognise what is said as belonging to them."[44]

Ballad poetry represents the continuing life of the old, prehistoric, mythic form of consciousness of pagan times undergoing transformation "along with the shifting manifestation of the spirit of the age in successive periods."[45] It is a truer expression of the people's consciousness than the court-centered scaldic poetry, and in the heroic ballad can be detected "an intimate connection between the ballad and the mythic themes," which make it probable that the entire pagan doctrine, far back in time, was given expression and given currency among the people in age-old songs which formed the skeleton for our heroic ballads."[46]

Ibsen's argument mainly is concerned with proving that the ballads are a genuine native expression of the folk consciousness and not an alien importation nor a creation of the individuality and subjectivity of particular poets. As much as Richard Wagner, Ibsen needs to believe in such an existing, objective, evolving, and universal people's consciousness which is both the subject matter, what the artist is shaping as a play, and the audience's "mind" which, in responding to the play, is responding to its own awakened and clarified deeper reality. Consciousness, therefore, (what Ibsen and Hegel both call "spirit") becomes the reality the artist must discover, the material to be shaped, the subject it is shaped into, and the means by which the drama exists in the audience's mind. The artist, therefore, must be humbly, profoundly responsive to the spirit of the people; and to attempt to modify that consciousness or to exorcise its demons is to take on the gravest responsibility. To be a poet, Ibsen once wrote, is to war with devils that infest the mind and heart and to conduct a ceaseless judgment day upon one's soul. Such an artist is something of a mantic, and Ibsen *does* seem to believe in the objective reality of the spiritual forms he is summoning to appear in the great séance of his art:

Let us not object that the world of the heroic ballad is merely a fictional world that has nothing to do with reality. The poetry of the people is equally its philosophy: it is the form in which it expresses its sense of the spirit's existence in concrete fashion.[47]

In *Emperor and Galilean* Julian will make the same point when he replies to the Christian Basilios's argument that the Greek poems and myths were mere "fiction,": "Are not the poetic imagination and the will subject to the same creative laws?"[48]

The series of critical writings, from the first brief reviews to the extended essay on the heroic ballad, show the steady evolution of a single, consistent, Hegelian idea of the poet's literary heritage and his or her function within that heritage—an argument not dissimilar to that in T. S. Eliot's *Tradition and the Individual Talent*. The poet should not strive to evolve new and startling forms, should not be an eccentric talent or genius standing apart from his or her fellowmen. The poet is to be the adequate articulator, through art, of the people's consciousness, both of its acknowledged and of its hidden and unconscious areas. The poet shares with the people a rich spiritual heritage, built up through dialectically evolved conflicts through the ages to a multilayered and organic structure of spiritual phases, once appearing separately in time but now coexisting as a given reality for the poet to explore in all its diversity. The artist should be aware of the appropriate means of expression for his or her art and the type of form best suited to the spiritual phase of culture that is being expressed. This concept of the artist and of the artist's subject is Hegelian, and it is adapted by Ibsen to his own cultural and artistic situation. Ibsen's subsequent dramatic practice will be the gradual development and enrichment of this Hegelian concept of art in terms of both his dramatic structures and his greater comprehension and mastery of his subject matter.

THE SUBJECTIVITY OF
CATILINE/THE OBJECTIVITY
OF *THE BURIAL MOUND*

At the outset of his career Ibsen creates, with *Catiline* and *The Burial Mound*, a pair of almost antithetical works. Proceeding by contraries is to become a recurring method of his, as is revealed by such pairs as *Brand/Peer Gynt*, *The League of Youth/Emperor and Galilean*, and by the dialectic sequence of the realistic cycle. *Catiline*, dark and enigmatic in message and intention, is a drama of extreme subjectivity; *The Burial Mound*, as if by deliberate contrast, is almost painfully lucid and explicit and is emphatically *objective* in its treatment of its material. In addition to inaugurating such a subjective-objective dualism, these two plays, in spite of all their obvious defects, contain in embryo the major thematic and structural elements of Ibsen's artistic evolution.

The first half of Ibsen's career opens and closes with dramas on classical themes, the Roman world of Catiline, the Greek world of Julian. The second play, *The Burial Mound*, introduces the antinomies of the southern and northern worlds, the pagan and the Christian, which are to undergo such signficant developments in the later work. What is particularly interesting about these early plays is that we can watch Ibsen mapping out his spiritual terrain, setting up the terms of his great poetic argument. The many themes of this argument will intertwine polyphonically in the succeeding dramas, until the dramatic writing achieves the fugal intricacy of

Emperor and Galilean. For all their apparent clumsiness, these early works are the efforts of a serious and imaginative artist who is laboring to make his art form—the drama—capable of the most ambitious achievement.

CATILINE

Ibsen's debut as a dramatist, with *Catiline*, at age twenty has none of the precocious mastery of Marlowe's *Tamburlaine*, Schiller's *The Robbers*, Buechner's *Danton's Death*, or Brecht's *Baal*, all written at a comparable age and all unmistakably announcing the arrival of genius. *Catiline* is compelling only to the reader or viewer aware of Ibsen's later mastery and of the way in which the play prefigures his later works. The drama seems at once conventional and fumbling as it attempts, with painfully inadequate artistry, to fulfill the terms of the German fate-tragedy and of the Romantic, i.e., Byronic, drama (in the manner of *Manfred*) of the lonely, blasted hero bringing himself to destruction.

In a book on Ibsen that takes its title—*Catiline's Dream*[1]—from this play, James Hurt argues that *Catiline* establishes the essential and unchanging drama, or psychic myth, discoverable in all Ibsen's work. Noting the incongruity of the play's classical subject matter with its luridly Gothic form and substance, Hurt interprets the play as a schizoid myth or allegory. However, even the oddest and most "archetypal" aspects of *Catiline* can be traced to the Romantic movement which was Ibsen's immediate cultural inheritance.

In 1848, when *Catiline* was written, the Romantic movement was still active, though in a more extravagent, reactionary form than previously, as Georg Brandes records in his account of Young Germany.[2] It is not difficult to see in the play its prototypes in the Byronic hero and in such *Sturm und Drang* plays as Schiller's *The Robbers*. (Karl Moor and his band, and Catiline and his followers differ mostly in costume.) The subject of the play, probably accidentally, resembles that commended by Hegel in his comments on the early plays of Goethe and Schiller:[3] that of the rebel who attains to a form of spiritual unity by opposing the totality of his fragmented society at a moment of momentous historical transition. In Goethe's *Götz von Berlichingen* this is the moment when the old heroic individualism of the aristocratic feudal class gives way before the inimical new mercantile and bourgeois order. In the greater *Don Carlos* of Schiller, it is the moment when the entire Spanish and Catholic world order is about to go into decline before a newly emergent Protestant and freedom-seeking world order.

Catiline takes place (if "place" is not too emphatic a word for the vague setting of the play) at the time when republican Rome is about to collapse before emerging Caesarism, and Catiline himself, in his disgust at the decadence of republican Rome and in his fiery ambition for preeminence, is a harbinger of this very Caesarism. This pattern, of momentous individual development occurring symptomatically and paradigmatically as a huge cultural development, was to be one of Ibsen's most basic actions. He was long to retain this dialectical, rational, and historical content of his writing, expanding it into the elaborate cultural/historical modalities of *Emperor and Galilean.*

The other pattern, which Ibsen soon was to abandon, that of the Byronic hero, blasted, moody, disenchanted, cut off from his fellowmen and responding only to abysses within himself and to the more awesome and exalted aspects of Nature, was to find *its* parodic apotheosis in *Peer Gynt* and its parodic reduction, perhaps, in Stensgaard of *The League of Youth.* For a very young, very lonely, and very ambitious poet such as Ibsen in Grimstad, the sheer imaginative bravado of impersonating the long-dead, much maligned rebel and scourge of his society who terrified a whole civilization must have represented a welcome means of exploring his own potential spiritual rebellion and of defining, tentatively, his artistic identity vis-à-vis society. His problem, for some years, as a poet in a cultural backwater of Europe, without the established native traditions which English, French, and even German dramatists could adapt or rebel against, was to discover the artistic forms that still had relevance to the conditions of the present and to adapt these forms to his individual, national, and artistic needs as the dramatic poet of Norway. To this end, he was forced to draw upon forms that had not sprung from the cultural traditions in which he lived but from different and even alien ones. "It is only through some national *form* that national *themes* can fully reveal themselves,"[4] he wrote in his essay on the heroic ballad; and the early plays are searching as much for the suitable national *form* for a modern Norwegian drama as for the suitable *themes.* The great uncertainty of Ibsen's lengthy apprenticeship in his art can be seen as deriving from his need to take up already existing, foreign, dramatic forms only to discover their inadequacy for his purposes as the national dramatic poet of Norway. The conspicuous presence of highly derivative Romantic themes and conventions in his early work is, therefore, neither surprising nor blameworthy but part of his necessary self-education and his exploration of the cultural realities to which he sought to direct the consciousness of his Norwegian audience. Ibsen's nationalism seems never to have been a chauvinistic turning inward, in Wagnerian fashion, to the exclusively Scandinavian or Teutonic spirit, but the lifting of the Norwegian consciousness to an influential and honorable place within the established culture of Europe.

Ibsen's most ardent admirers must concede that the youthful Grimstad poet's knowledge of the world is painfully insufficient for the grand-scale story of individual rebellion, political conspiracy, military strategy, and social decadence that he has chosen to tell. The play's somewhat startling and claustrophobic emphasis upon the subjective, psychological drama of Catiline, which has impelled interpreters like James Hurt to detect a strong unconscious compulsion behind the writing (as if, in this play, Ibsen's id is nakedly exposed), might be due as much to the poet's ignorance of the objective world he proposes to present. Unable to supply rich external detail to his dramatized "Rome," Ibsen would be forced to concentrate upon the subjective drama of Catiline. However, the subjectivity of *Catiline* is too startling for this to be a wholly sufficient explanation. It also is obvious that the subjectivity of the play is a conscious intention on Ibsen's part, that, in keeping with the other Romantic elements of the play, the hero's subjectivity with its attendant symbolic and archetypal aspects is the play's *subject.* It is therefore a mistake to see the play as an almost uncontrolled upsurge from the maelstrom of the poet's emotions and impulses or as an unconscious reversion by the modern young poet to primitive and archetypal psychic realities.[5]

The historical fate-tragedy, then, serves highly personal, but still conscious and controlled, themes and purposes. The light-darkness, height-depth, inner-outer symbolic dualities, the Nature imagery, the characterization of the rebel-hero alienated from a degenerate reality and flanked by contrasting and competing female forces, and the theme of redemptive death — all are major elements of Romantic symbology, that is, of Ibsen's immediate cultural inheritance. The influence of Schiller's *The Robbers* and Byron's *Manfred*, two of the most enthusiastically admired Romantic works (Hazlitt recorded the impression of *The Robbers* upon the imagination of the young, and Robert Schumann approached the task of composing incidental music to *Manfred* with awe), seems most evident, whereas many other details in the play are part of the general stock-in-trade of Romanticism.

Especially attractive to a youthful poet, one imagines, must have been the permissiveness of Romantic dramatic structures, whose free, fluid, "organic" forms allowed the poet to pursue the most profound, sublime, and occult regions of the spirit without any inhibiting need to conform to a plausible or even recognizable reality.

The Romantic subjectivity of *Catiline* weakens its dramatic impact. The characters, overcharged with immediate symbolic and archetypal implication, belong less to the realm of drama than to that of opera. At its most extreme and most successful, (as in the music-dramas of Richard Wagner, where major psychic themes and archetypal figures are linked in an action that pays no great attention to the laws of time, space, and elementary physics), this Romantic subjectivity can create the impression of a cosmos of profound feeling but of very little thinking. In Wagner's operas the elements of earth, fire, flood, and air and the most gigantic acts of creation, transformation, and devastation build up a symbolic drama that has totally detached itself from the realm of human society and of rational history. Extreme Romantic art, reversing the work of the Enlightenment, sought to subdue all objective reality to subjective reality and then to extend this subjectivity into the cosmos; *Tristan and Isolde* is the exemplary statement of this endeavor.

Historical fate-tragedy with its rationalistic emphasis, the category to which *Catiline* also aspires to belong, cannot compete with Wagnerian music-drama either in power or in scale of feeling. The pre-eminence of nonmusical drama over opera lies in the realm not of feeling but of thought: in the scale, complexity, subtlety, and accuracy of its *concepts*. Although it does not look for conceptual novelty or even conceptual validity, for these are the concern of philosophy, dramatic dialogue, whether in verse or prose, seeks authenticity of expression through verbal precision as well as depth of feeling. Implausibility of situation is far less damaging in opera than in drama, for in drama, however deeply felt the subjective emotion, it has to be expressed in the context of a plausible human reality. If, for example, one required Wagner's music-dramas to be dramatic poems conveying the full substance of human life, building up structures of such subtlety and complexity that all our faculties, intellectual as well as emotional, will be roused to heightened awareness and discrimination, and if we experienced the librettos alone, we would be scandalized. The librettos are preposterously implausible, ill-organized, prolix. They actually *diminish* our aesthetic and critical awareness by their recourse to magic potions, supernatural powers of movement and of appearance, disappearance and disguise, obtusely mistaken motives, overblown loves and hates, and so on, evincing a radical absence of dramatic integrity and of dramatic finesse. It is only the music that transforms the Wagnerian pantomime into artistic structures of immense power, complexity and subtlety—a persuasive theater of authentic feeling. *Catiline*, which actually reads much like an opera libretto, has nearly all the deficiencies of the opera form without the one ingredient, music, that could give it artistic unity and authenticity.

The flight from Reason, which so much Romantic art embodies, found its perfect haven in opera. Hence opera was immensely popular in the nineteenth century, an age which, as Georg Brandes documented in his *Main Currents of Nineteenth Century Literature,* had turned its back, in fear, on the rational principles of the revolution. Opera, ballet, and the well-made play of the boulevard theaters were the major theatrical arts of the nineteenth century, and in each we find a maximum of theatrical excitement combined with a minimum of conceptual danger. Drama was to return to preeminence in the theater, making the modern age one of the three or four great periods of dramatic art, by once again becoming intellectually significant and daring, and it was Ibsen who re-created this idea of the theater. His future as a major dramatic poet could lie only in the greater intellectual (conceptual) extension of his basic, archetypal subject matter as it is expressed in *Catiline.* Scarcely a year after composing this play Ibsen, in an article on the use of ancient myth in modern writing, argues for the dredging up of ancient myth from the sea depths to study it upon the plane of speculation. In this article a tough Hegelian artistic theory is brought to bear upon the prerational substance of myth. What is important is not only the meaning, the implications of the article, but also the fact that Ibsen should have written it at all, that he should embark upon such an intellectual journey at the beginning of his dramatic career. Each of Ibsen's plays, like each of the plays of Shaw or Brecht, Beckett or Handke, is a dramatized *concept,* but this is most evident in the early plays, in which the concept often is too apparent. The greater plausibility and affective power of the later plays merely represents the fine and more intricate extension of his concepts within the realm of human experience.

The setting of *Catiline* is a vaguely indicated area of republican Rome in decadence. We never *see* this Rome (as we see the Paris of *Danton's Death*) and we hear of it only through Catiline's disgusted rejection and the accounts given by the feebly individualized coconspirators, so that Catiline's rebellion seems at once fiercely emphatic and completely undefined. Like Karl Moor in *The Robbers,* he is greatly superior to his comrades and remains spiritually aloof in his relation to them, yet, also like Karl Moor, Catiline finds his rebellion degraded in every particular until the noble moral rebel becomes the moral criminal—a theme of much Romantic and post-Romantic writing from the time of Schiller and Byron to that of Dostoevsky and, in our own day, Camus.

Ibsen's use of his stage space is as conveniently undefined as is his fictional locale. Characters enter and exit entirely according to thematic convenience and without any attempt on the author's part at significant or even plausible motive. They can retire backstage to overhear conversation and "step forward" to reveal themselves with maximum stage effect. This permits the dramatist an entirely unhampered poetic and histrionic rhythm which serves further to heighten the subjective nature of the psychic drama by minimizing the presence of any countervailing objective world (even that of dramatic plausibility) whose reality and whose laws the action would need to take into consideration.

The words that open the play, "I must! I must!" announce that this is a drama of the will, of its inward pressures, its aspirations, and its engagement with the world—a subject that Ibsen, much later, triumphantly established as his own imaginative domain. This first unrest of the will, felt by Catiline, is the primal psychic energy out of which Ibsen's long procession of agitated heroes and heroines will be born. They too will feel, even if obscurely, Catiline's sense of a call from "deep within the soul," and they too will share his disdain for a life with no aim, no aspiration to realize one's best self.

The first speech in the play is a long soliloquy, a meditative self-revelation in the manner of Manfred which, with the least artistic complexity, provides the reader with a maximum of information about the hero's character. Two Allobrogian ambassadors (from *northern* Gaul, thus incidentally or coincidentally anticipating Ibsen's recurrent north-south dualism) appear with their followers and, not seeing Catiline, who "overhears" them, usefully inform each other, the unseen Catiline, and the theater audience, of who they are and why they are there. At this point Catiline "steps forward" to reveal to these total strangers his highly ambitious and criminally rebellious attitude toward Rome[6] (thus putting himself utterly in their power). The scene ends with Catiline's apostrophe to the city of Rome seen in the glow of a setting sun (visually foretelling decline and perhaps fiery destruction).

Detailed characterizations are rare enough in youthful work—even *Danton's Death* fails to bring Danton's companions to life—but Catiline's fellow-conspirators are, more so than usual, a mere cloud of unindividualized forms hovering around the Byronic hero. Furia, as her name all too resonantly proclaims, is merely incarnate fury and revenge; her lack of substantial reality creates an impression of operatic hysteria (of a *femme-fatale* without qualities) somewhat like that of the incongruous Electra in Mozart's youthful *Idomineo*. Aurelia, similarly operatic, is hardly more than a symbol of gentle femininity appearing onstage at the thematically appropriate moments to articulate her themes of love, peace, and self-sacrifice. Continually, one feels that the characters onstage should be *singing* (the conspirators, who so resemble an operatic chorus, do, at one moment sing), and, in fact, as an opera libretto *Catiline* would be acceptable and effective. Verdi could have made the story musically compelling.

The lack of objective content in the play allows us to see its "drama of consciousness," or psychic drama, with a clarity somewhat at odds with its dark and vague setting, and there is a distinct fascination at seeing the perennial Ibsen themes in naked embryo form, without any obscuring subtlety or complexity. For example, at her first entrance Furia, emotionally pent-up, trapped in a situation not of her own choosing, despising the world she finds herself in, is already an Ibsen heroine, a prototype of Hedda Gabler. In this play she clearly is invested with semi-mythic powers and with a strength driving from her entombment and resurrection to the world of life and action, qualities more concealed in the heroines of the realistic dramas. She is made to act with more than human effect, her proclivity for making frenzied appearances at implausibly appropriate moments having a devastating effect upon the plot's claim to serious attention. (In what almost is a masterstroke of dramatic bathos which Henry Fielding, one fears, would delightedly have parodied in *Tom Thumb,* she pops up in one scene, like a demented Jack-in-the-box, to frighten away the entire Allobrogian army.)

The dark underworld that is Furia's realm is established, with interesting ambivalence, as that which the heroic will both needs and fears: it seems to be identified with the buried forces within the psyche and, more objectively, with the traditional lower "cthonic" supernatural realm of the furies which Hegel, anticipating Nietzsche here, as elsewhere, saw as quite as necessary to tragedy as the realm of Apollo and the sun. The presence of this underworld of both the individual and the racial psyche will be a recurring theme of Ibsen's art, as in the spirit world of *Emperor and Galilean,* the troll worlds of *Brand* and *Peer Gynt,* the ghosts of *Ghosts,* and the fearful "helpers and servers" of *The Master Builder.* The powers and energies that derive from this underworld are necessary for great actions within the objective world, but, like the powers that Macbeth calls upon, they are ambiguous and can turn upon the hero and destroy him.

Aurelia, in schematic contrast to Furia, belongs to the upper, conscious world of light, innocence, and peace: the realm of aspiration to the highest and holiest, uncontaminated by the darker strategies of the human will. This aspiration, unless it can successfully engage with and surmount the forces of the nether world, is particularly vulnerable. As a lure, also, this "Aurelian realm" can be as treacherous to the heroic will as the nether realm is. (One is reminded of Blake's dualism of Innocence and Experience, of Heaven and Hell.) The attempt to attain the holy without acknowledging as one's own the darker aspects of the psyche (an ethical evasion attempted by not only sentimental melodrama but even much Elizabethan drama) is based on a desire to retreat from full moral adulthood, and Aurelia actually conjures up for Catiline the picture of an infantile, pastoral peace and innocence free from the knoweldge of "alienation" and from the conflict and danger upon which, alone, the heroic will can thrive. Although Aurelia desires maternally to protect the hero and to be protected by him, to support and to be subordinate to him, this Aurelian lure (which will recur throughout Ibsen's dramas) must be rejected by the hero if he is to achieve heroic independence. Aurelia offers a heaven attained without struggle and conflict, a state of grace free of passion, experience, and intellectual effort. The necessity to reject such a lure is one of the major themes of Romantic literature and philosophy, which took up and greatly elaborated the idea of *felix culpa,* or the fortunate fall from innocence. Just as within the destructive vindictiveness of Furia lay the "good" of a challenge to heroic growth, so in the protective love of Aurelia lies the "evil" of an attempt to thwart this growth and to proclaim the beneficence of regression.[7]

Aurelia and Furia, therefore, each contain positive and negative aspects of the feminine maternal figure who stands in the way of the emerging heroic male. Yet each, in a way, is a helpmate, companion, and comrade of the hero (as Hedda and Thea are both designated "comrades" by Lövborg), and can share the hero's aspirations and enter into battle with or against him. Aurelia wishes to lure Catiline toward unheroic, infantile pastoralism, but she also shares the hero's disgust with the corrupt "parental" Rome. Furia, as priestess, inhabitant of the lower realm, and avenging fury pursuing Catiline, is a classic example of the destructive, antimasculine, matriarchal, and cthonic power that Eric Neumann[8] sees as the agency surrounding and imprisoning the male ego in the early stages of psychic growth. But at the same time Furia alone fully understands Catiline's heroic aspirations, his own fascination with the darker powers, and she unites her voice with his in ambitious aspiration and in scorn of the established world of Rome.

Aurelia and Furia also divide between them another important ingredient of Ibsen's idea of reality—the past. Aurelia represents the memory of Edenic innocence and childhood, in Romantic terms, the unalienated or "naive" and Rousseauist idea of humanity before there was knowledge of alienation and evil begot by the process of history, whereas Furia resurrects from the past Catiline's consciousness of crime and guilt. Each, equally, is a fundamental component of the hero's consciousness and is equally intrinsic to his identity. This dual nature of the past and of the hero's struggle to establish his identity and his purpose by means of it, similarly will undergo rich variations up to the end of Ibsen's career. The theme reflects a major dilemma of much Romantic writing. Such writing looked to the past for examples of human greatness or justice or freedom unknown in the present in order to establish a basis for a new and revolutionary consciousness—"a revolution in the human spirit"—and to end modern man's alienation from both human institutions and from Nature; nevertheless, it was forced to recognize within the past the record of human error and evil. "The world's great age begins anew," sings the Chorus from Shelley's *Hellas,* joyfully predicting the regeneration of the world, "The golden years return . . ." and the Chorus ends, after predicting that greater deities than the Greek gods or Christ (what Ibsen is to call "the third empire") will appear and imploring fearfully that the darker and more painful substance of the past be not resurrected also:

> O cease! must hate and death return?
> Cease! must men kill and die?
> Cease! drain not to its dregs the urn
> Of bitter prophecy.

> The world is weary of the past
> Oh, might it die, or rest at last.[9]

The Aurelian lure, with its sexual and spiritual yearning upward and outward to innocent pastoral community, also is a Rousseauist retreat from the complexity and guilt of modern, "alienated" reality, a common Romantic theme that we will find variously modulated throughout Ibsen's later writing: in Rosmer's dream of a utopia of happy, noble, innocent beings which crumbles before his first intimations of personal guilt; in the desire of Alfred Allmers, in *Little Eyolf,* to preserve such a childlike peaceable kingdom, not subject to "the law of change" in his relation to Asta. In Romantic philosophy and art, this lost innocence can be regained only after acknowledging the necessary fall of the human spirit into alienation and self-division, and it will be regained only after a "circuitous journey" involving the knowledge of guilt and suffering. Yet this recovered innocence will be at a "higher level" than Edenic innocence—as adult innocence is higher than that of the child. The retreat that Aurelia proposes to Catiline is to an infantile state of nature before there was knowledge of good and evil:

> Have you forgot our little homestead where,
> I lived my childhood and where we later, glad
> In love's first season of pure happiness
> Have lived so many joyous summer days?
> Where was the grass more green that it was there?
> Where greater coolness in the forest's shade?
> The little white house midst the darkling trees
> Peeped out and beckoned to its peaceful ease.
> Thence shall we flee and dedicate our lives
> To rural tasks and quiet peacefulness.
> There shall a cheerful wife enliven you
> Whose kisses all your sorrows will dispel . . .
>   (Smiling)
> And when, with meadow-blossoms at your breast
> You come to me, your sovereign lady fair,
> I shall proclaim you as my prince of flowers
> And bind the laurel wreaths upon your brow.[10]

This version of pastoral, drawing upon a long tradition that goes back to Hellenistic literature, calls to mind Perdita's tribute of flowers to Florizel (*her* prince of flowers) in Shakespeare's *The Winter's Tale.* Aurelia and Perdita offer their heroes refuge from experience and from the world of knowledge of suffering and evil, so that even the infatuated Florizel exclaims, "What, like a corse!" as Perdita verbally smothers him with flowers; for such love, which is based on natural innocence, is a threat to the aspiring heroic will. Pastoral literature, as an evasion of the serious conflicts upon which dramatic art depends, is a literary genre that Ibsen himself, as an aspiring *dramatic* poet, would have to reject, so that one might say that Ibsen's relation to Aurelia and Furia resembles that of Catiline! Catiline's declaration that life is a ceaseless struggle between hostile forces in the soul is an early version of Ibsen's famous description of the poetic life as a war against the trolls that infest the heart and mind. Therefore, for the poetic life, Furia is at least as necessary as Aurelia. The gentle, maternally solicitous figure who winds flowers around her prince in their mutual bower of bliss might well be preparing him for a form of sacrifice (as in the ambiguous festival of roses in Kleist's *Penthesilia*). It is Catiline's *adult,* developed, guilty identity and his heroic will that prevent him from accepting the Aurelian lure of a return to Eden, from giving up dialectical struggle and retreating into a lotus land of unheroic consciousness. In the later realistic plays we will encounter three notable figures, Lona Hessel, Gregers Werle, and Hilde Wangel, who enter households to arouse those who have withdrawn to nonheroic retreats.

The alternative to this community of innocence is the exploration of one's inner and more alarming powers, one's energies, appetites, and desires. Such an exploration, which involves the loss of innocence, represents the stage of individual self-assertion that must involve separation and isolation from one's former community, for there are few links between the inner psychic powers by which one now lives and the community "outside." The modern artist attempts to link his or her community with these powers by investing images of the community with archetypal and mythic content—hence the mythopoetic work of so many modern authors, including such realists as Ibsen and James Joyce. The community that refuses such links, whether through intellectual laziness, moral outrage, or philistinism, becomes a community in which the poet or the exceptional individual cannot participate. So the gallery of Ibsen characters who are given to wrestling with the trolls that infest the heart and mind are singularly lonely—as was Ibsen himself. The attempt to reintegrate the fragmented and diminished human community with its total human identity (which must include the acknowledgment of semi-conscious, inner, and often tabooed energies and powers, the darker aspects of the psyche, as well as the conscious, "spiritual," and intellectual development of these into a free and authentic human community) will be the themes of *Brand, Peer Gynt,* and *Emperor and Galilean,* the great trilogy in which Ibsen's long artistic and intellectual odyssey finds its first adequate poetic/dramatic definition.

Catiline is isolated and surrounded by "communities" competing for his allegiance. The first such community, that republican Rome against which Catiline rebels, might be seen as the parental community and Catiline's rebellion as a form of filial revolt. To further this revolt, he joins an alternative community, a masculine, rebellious band of comrades or fellow conspirators of which he, like Karl Moor, will be the somewhat aloof leader. Using Eric Neumann's scheme of the emergence of the heroic will from the repressive parental authority, Catiline joins what Neumann (in *The Origins and History of Consciousness*) would designate the "homosexual" bonds of the brotherhood and then proceeds to such further strategies of ego liberation as the rape of Furia's sister. The conspirators themselves, with their corrupt sensualism, their invocation of Bacchus, and their debased facsimile of Catiline's discontent, represent the lower and more dubious appetites and desires of Catiline himself, necessary stages from which his tentative ideological rebellion struggles to emerge and define itself. Erotic rebellion, linked to what Ibsen will later designate as *"livsglede,"* or "joy-of-*life*," will play a major role in his analysis of cultural and psychic repression and liberation.

Against the two debased communities of conventional but decadent Rome and the equally decadent band of malcontents who are Catiline's companions, alternative spiritual communities are offered by Aurelia's invitation to retreat to infantile innocence and by Furia's lure toward an underworld of darker powers and energies. Catiline's vacillation between these latter alternatives is a more powerful source of his actions than the very nebulous objective rebellion and battle that he perfunctorily engages in. (The entire, supposedly crucial, battle against his Roman opponents is a brief off-stage action carrying nothing like the weight of his psychic struggle between the ambiguously good and bad angels, Aurelia and Furia.)

Believing Furia to be dead (she *has* been entombed), Catiline encounters what he believes to be her spirit, which, since her death, has undergone a transformation. This spirit now loves him and wishes to ally itself with his ascent to greatness—as if his ambitious project can be fed only by his acknowledgment of his darker, guilty past. Furia's language, for all its duplicity, *is* one of death and rebirth, of a habitant of the dark underworld who is a "familiar" of Catiline's secret inner life; and she decisively impels him into rebellion and conspiracy. Although he is somewhat clumsy at handling his themes of the psychic energies that go into the projects of the will, Ibsen does locate deeper sources of psychic life and attempts to delineate them more precisely than does Buechner in his far more accomplished *Danton's Death*. Whereas Furia represents the guilt, but also the energetic and adult aspect, of Catiline's past, Aurelia offers a version of the past that is sealed off from the corruptive world, a past that can be seen as a welcome and familiar friend:

> You dig the ground and I shall till the soil;
> Around our home will spring a floral beauty,
> A hedge of roses, sweet forget-me-nots,
> The quiet symbol that the time is near
> When you can greet each memory of the past
> As a friend of childhood visiting your soul.[11]

Catiline, however, insists that such a time "belongs still to the distant, unknown future." What, for Aurelia, is an innocent past that can be returned to, putting aside knowledge of later history, for Catiline is a condition that has yet to be attained, a *recovery* of innocence, resembling the painfully attained innocence, after the overcoming of alienation, of Romantic thought.

With a single exception (and *that* is a "phantom"!) we find no compelling male counterparts to the two female influences upon Catiline's spirit, for the hero remains aloof from his fellow conspirators. Curius, who does duty in the play as Catiline's young friend, is the merest cipher of male friendship, a pale shadow of the deeply emotional attachments of Carlos and Posa in Schiller's *Don Cardos* or of Ferdinand and Egmont in Goethe's *Egmont*. Curius's love for Catiline (who, to be sure, extends no energetic friendship to Curius—indeed Catiline never speaks to him in the play until the last act when he crushes him with magnanimous forgiveness) collapses instantly before his fatal love for Furia. This absence of male friendship indicates what will become the curious isolation of the Ibsen hero, his lack of "playfulness" and his inability to extend, creatively, into the world surrounding him as Carlos and Posa are able to do by means of a passionately shared ideological project. This heightens the impression we get from Ibsen's dramas that, to the hero's spirit, the surrounding world is alien and hostile, forcing him, as it does Catiline, to draw upon his own, inward resources. Since his "companions" Aurelia and Furia are, essentially, extensions or aspects of Catiline's own spirit, the community of consciousness depicted by the play is highly solipsist, with no very convincing movement outward to a world of actual loves and allegiances.

The predominance of the psychic and subjective content of *Catiline* over any plausibly objectified reality prevents the emergence of an interesting plot. The perfunctorily rendered "Roman" setting really is not necessary at all—hence the almost ludicrous paucity of objective details. On the other hand, the archetypal action is reduced to the barest bones of basic Romantic myth. A contrast with *Danton's Death* is instructive. The equally youthful Buechner presents us with a brilliantly rendered social context represented by the cynical Danton on the one side and the fanatic Robespierre and St. Just on the other, between which two extremes of political temperament the suffering and angry mob of Paris is buffeted. Beyond these three embodied elements of fanatic idealism, cynical resignation, and, in between, the victimized community there is no very profound or convincing characterization. But the world of Paris, with its starving crowds, its beggars, prostitutes, agitators, executioners, bourgeoisie, and politicians, is vividly presented to us, as is the gruesome presence throughout of the guillotine whose falling blade practically terminates the play. We see a whole world betrayed equally by Danton's irresponsible cynicism and by Robespierre's merciless fanaticism. Like the later *Woyzeck,* the play presents a sharply and sardonically observed surface of fragmented modern reality that is totally credible in its multiple and vivid detail, as Ibsen's world, in *Catiline,* all too glaringly is not.

But the exploration of the hidden and mysterious origins and contours of the psyche and the depths of its subjectivity, which Ibsen conducts in his first play, is missing from the world of Buechner. The cynical Romantic rhetoric of Danton, spoken in the context of gaming houses, brothels, and prison, contrasts with the rationalist, abstract rhetoric of Robespierre and St. Just spoken in isolation or before the Assembly. The disjointed utterances of Woyzeck are the bizaare surface expression of a psychic and a cultural breakdown that Buechner presents but does not identify and explore, does not "get inside" and analyze. The surface details of *Catiline,* on the other hand, are the most meager and perfunctory mask for an actual reformulation and extension of the conventional Romantic psychic drama.

The young Ibsen already has at hand a Romantic metaphysical vocabulary which his naive art ardently embraces as expressive of his spiritual condition. Thus he is able, as a poet, to leap from the extremes of personal to universal meaning, and back again, while taking only the scantest notice of that intricate, historically determined, rationally as well as irrationally evolved, interpersonal and objective world through which, alone, the nature of our human condition can be seen, evaluated, and at least partly understood. Ibsen's later problems in achieving an adequately complex dramatic form can be predicted from the romanticism of *Catiline,* for if the leap from subjective and psychological to metaphysical and universal meaning can be effected so early and so easily (the goal arrived at without the process of getting there, as Hegel would say), what is left for dramatic art to encompass? The answer of course is, everything of significance. The model of Byron's *Manfred* might have tempted Ibsen to this exercise in the immediate possession of the sublime, and the later plays represent an arduous search for both a more adequate content for the dramatic form to encompass and a more substantial dramatic form to express this content.

An indication of the strange insubstantiality of *Catiline* is the fact that the two most vivid events in the play are Catiline's account of a dream, and his later meeting with a "phantom." The account of the dream is a highly conscious, literary exercise and not an uncontrolled eruption from Ibsen's unconscious. It is, in fact, the sort of "set piece" or obligatory signaling of the more fantastic and fearful areas of the mind that we find in so much Romantic writing. It begins in a setting of darkness and chaos, a vaulted underground chamber of tomblike obscurity—similar to the vault in which Furia was imprisoned—filled with swirling visions, clouds, and phantoms. This dark chaos is penetrated by light, as in a psychic repetition of the cosmic creation myth of the Old Testament. Beautiful (angelic?) flowered children sing of a half-forgotten home, suggestive of the lost paradise, and they surround a pair of contrasting women, one fair as the fading light of evening, the other severe and dark as night. The fair figure is maternally benign in her smiling aspect, and the dark women has eyes that flash like lightning, filling the hero with dreadful pleasure. (Curius feels the same dreadful pleasure in the presence of Furia.) The two women are seen playing a game of chess, still surrounded by crowding visions and forms, until the fair woman, apparently defeated, fades away. With her departure, the fair children vanish also. Now from the tomblike darkness two eyes burn with the joy of victory and fix themselves on the dreamer. The hero becomes dizzy, and the dream ends.[12]

Whatever Ibsen's inner promptings might have been, the subjective drama he describes by this dream is made up of elements that derive from common Romantic metaphors. The dream tells us nothing about Catiline's situation vis-à-vis Aurelia and Furia that the objective action of the play has not told us already, and all the details of the dream have been consciously articulated by the various characters at some time. Its real significance, therefore, must lie in Ibsen's desire to signal to his audience that the action of the play is as emphatically within his hero's subjective mind as it is within the objective world of external characters and events. The narrative poet can have his hero brood "onpage" before us and thereby unfold his subjective drama, as is true of Childe Harold; but drama does not permit this device, and its equivalent, the long soliloquy, lacks dramatic impact. To project the life of the subjective spirit onstage, Byron and others resorted to visionary experience and dream, with Goethe's *Faust* (both Parts One and Two) being the most ambitious example.

In the plays that follow *Catiline* Ibsen will create dramatic metaphors involving both visionary experience and dream in *St. John's Night*, *Olaf Liliekrans*, *Brand*, *Peer Gynt*, and *Emperor and Galilean* as he seeks to develop dramatic actions that fully integrate subjective and objective realms of human reality. Peer's descent to the troll kingdom and the great last act of *Peer Gynt* in which the hero walks through a spirit-filled landscape encountering the fragmented aspects of his psyche are the finest dramatic renderings of this subjective world in his poetic drama; and the integration of the two realms that he effects in his dramatic art goes a long way toward establishing the profoundly explored realism of the great cycle.

By thus "signaling" the presence of this subjective realm, Ibsen can show that Catiline's "fate" is as much built into the structure of his consciousness as it is built into the structure of the objective world against which he rebels. Although this idea is handled somewhat naively, it is highly sophisticated. Halvdan Koht mentions that at first the play was to "dramatize Catiline's ambition as something actually prompted by an idealistic desire for social revolution" and that it was only later that the dramatist decided to focus on "the moral and psychological conflicts within the man himself."[13] If this revision of intentions did occur during the writing of the play, it reveals to what degree Ibsen developed his idea of reality as he reflected upon it further. The conscious, objective drama of politics and passions between factions within republican Rome is, by means of the dream (and the later meeting with the phantom), reestablished within the realm of the heroic psyche independent of any particular time and place; at the same time, the archetypal stature of Furia and Aruelia is reinforced by their oneiric parallels.[14]

The dream describes an evolutionary, fluid movement of the mind; out of its dark and swirling energies emerge more distinct and brighter forms, childlike and radiant and gentle, singing of some half-forgotten home. A conflict between darkness and light, dark *energies* and radiant *forms,* grows into a fiercer struggle in which the darker and more destructive energies alarm and fascinate the dreamer, whose fate seems to depend upon the outcome of a contest between two aspects of the female: the benign and the terrible. These aspects, which struggle for predominance as Aurelia and Furia, have openly contested for Catiline's soul in the objective drama. The dream, which ends with the victory seemingly going to the terrible aspect of the female, merely elaborates, in Romantic and occult terms, what the action of the play has established; but it thereby insists that we read this drama as a pattern of inward events.

The encounter with the Phantom almost immediately follows the account of the dream, and we see that the Phantom seems to be the masculine counterpart to the powerful female images of the dream. He is an archetype of power and ambition who has stamped his image upon history (in the 1875 version he is identified as the ghost of Sulla) and who therefore represents Catiline's ambitions within the objective world. His criminal traits imply he belongs to the creatively negative aspects of the world-spirit, as do the ghosts of Cain and of Judas in the séance scene of Act 3 of *Emperor and Galilean.* Thus the Phantom is the objective equivalent of Furia, for both figures draw upon that in the hero which represents his darker energies and ambition. The Phantom might be seen as an alternative "paternal" archetype (as Lucifer is to God) to the paternal Rome against which Catiline rebels. Through the agency of the Phantom, Ibsen fuses the objective and historical action with the subjective and psychological. The Phantom is the reproachful paternal archetype seeking to prevent Catiline from eclipsing his fame which would constitute his continuing existence in the world, but he also is an earlier example of the ambition by which Catiline is now driven and he makes evident the suffering and guilt attendant upon that ambition.

In spite of the misdirections and fumblings of this and other early plays, there was always in Ibsen's work a sense of certainty about his spiritual quest, a certainty which he finally converts into aesthetic assurance. Because the spiritual subject matter he sought to bring under artistic control was so urgent and compelling, it prevented Ibsen from early finding, and then dissipating, his great talents. The archetypal content of his work, which is announced all too clearly in *Catiline,* forced the dramatist to organize his later structures into forms of significantly balancing and contrasting forces, to mold his fictions to this archetypal structuring thus giving to even his most sophisticated modern plays the spare symbolic symmetry that one finds in ritual art. From this archetypal foundation, he developed an intellectual, dialectical, and genuinely modern drama in which the underlying archetypal forces are evolved to their rational fulfillment, as in that further development of mythic material which Ibsen saw as a function of poetry.

If we valued archetypal content in literature the most and found the presence of compelling archetypes sufficient to guarantee the worth of a work, *Catiline* would be Ibsen's most valuable play, for it contains hardly anything but fervidly archetypal and mythic content, whether we see this as public and Romantic or private and subconscious. But to be truly important, a work of art must significantly objectify its form and content. What so obviously is missing from *Catiline* is not only a subtly felt, rational, objective, and fully human content but also a clear conception of the nature of the conflict it is dramatizing. In 1875, Ibsen recounted that the play was written in response, in part, to the 1848 uprisings in Europe, so it is all the more surprising that instead of creating, as one might expect, a young poet's excited drama of revolutionary enthusiasm he created almost its opposite: a drama of ambivalent ambitions, guilt, self-doubt, and unhappy fate with the lines of social and psychological motive so intricately crossed and baffled. Although the result is a work of some confusion, the ambiguities provide the greatest source of interest in the play.

Catiline, though dying with his subjective drama unresolved, does arrive at a crucial perception:

> Is not life then a ceaseless battle
> Between the hostile forces of the soul
> A battle that is the very life of the soul... [15]

In this passage (which Ibsen, strangely, omitted from the revised version of 1875) we find the poet's whole future subject: that the life of consciousness is a dialectical struggle whose conflict of mutually hostile forces enables the restless aspiration of consciousness to rise to higher and higher forms of self-determination. The life of the mind, of Reason or of Spirit, does not depend upon retreat into the subconscious or escape into peaceful innocence but upon engagement with the forces within the self and within the world. One must struggle to attain and to sustain one's human identity in order to realize it fully, and upon this struggle the whole enterprise of human liberation within civilization will be built.

THE BURIAL MOUND

After the dark confusions of *Catiline*, the limpid ideological simplicities of *The Burial Mound* (1851) seem a drop in Ibsen's dramatic aspirations. It is not a very difficult task to deride the play's sentimental, chauvinist, and utterly implausible depiction of the Viking past, its romantically yearning heroine in Christian Normandy dreaming of the north and of its blond and blue-eyed heroes, and its facile pairing off of the characters at the end of the play when the northern Gandalf appropriates the southern Blanka and the southernized Bernhard-Audun acquires the northern scald, Hemming. The formalism of the character-pairing reveals the naive dialectical aesthetic of the play in which thematic considerations take precedence over individual character. The poet's concentration upon his southern-northern, pagan-Christian, male-female dualities prevents him from endowing his figures with much human or dramatic life.

As a stage in Ibsen's artistic development, however, the play is important. It represents a major poetic breakthrough in his dramatic method which is to have immense consequences not only for Ibsen's later career as a dramatist but for the development of modern drama itself. And much of the too neatly balanced dialectic will enter into the vital substance of the later work to become an important motive in his depiction of characters and conflicts.

The artistic innovation is introduced so simply and directly as to belie its actual importance: it is the central visual symbol that draws into itself the dominant meanings of the play. The symbol focuses our visual attention, at the same time becoming a center, itself, of dramatic action and conflict. It is a mute, physical thing, yet the human spirit is drawn to it, discovers itself in it; nevertheless, the symbol remains an independent object and even can reflect ironically upon the characters and events that occur around it.

The idea of a central, cohering visual symbol catching up all at once in a memorable image a cluster of meanings probably derives from Ibsen's "other" art, painting. Such a device is as much a feature of Romantic painting as it is of Renaissance painting (whose complex symbology has been investigated by Erwin Panofsky), and we find it developed to particularly telling effect in the work of the Dresden artist Caspar David Friedrich, who might well have influenced Norwegian painting through his close working association with the Norwegian painter Johann Christian Dahl. In many of Friedrich's paintings an isolated object, such as an old ruined chapel, a cross in the mountains, a tree, a rock, or a distant sail, is the hieroglyph for a cluster of symbolic meanings. For example, a critical account of one of Friedrich's paintings, *The Watzmann,* reads:

The high mountain is a symbol of God, and the snow on the glacier, which never melts, alludes to his eternal nature. The salient crag in the middle-ground (a motif from the Hartz mountains) combines the ideas of faith and death. The fir tree on the rock directly beneath the peak of the Watzmann stands for the believing Christian; the birch trees are symbols of resurrection.[16]

It is unlikely that Ibsen employed so elaborate a symbology of visual detail, although the idea should not be dismissed out of hand. In *The Burial Mound* he did develop a new, visual, "objective" symbology that is able both to encapsulate and to extend the metaphor developed by the human action of the play. What is more, the objectively existing symbol (for it *is* an "object") firmly relocates the play's action outside the subjectivity of its main characters. It is impossible to see the action of the play as, for example, the dream of Blanka, for the meanings that the play enacts exist for *us,* objectively, there on the stage in the form of the visual symbol. Ibsen's own landscape paintings employ what seems at least a rudimentary symbolic method in the manner of

Friedrich, for some paintings have foregrounds of intensely color-
ful foliage and flora and backgrounds of majestic but inhospitable
snow peaks, setting up a contrast between the cyclically renewing
forms of life in the foreground and the eternally abiding, distant
forms of the mountains in the background.[17] In *The Burial Mound*
the cohering, objective visual symbol gives the play its title, for
this symbol is the burial mound itself, centrally placed onstage.

The pagan-Christian details of the burial mound contain, in
their stillness, the same dialectic of opposites struggling toward
synthesis that the action of the play will work out dynamically. As
in *Catiline*, we find the theme of a historical dialectic emerging at
a moment of consequential spiritual *transition:* here the transition
of the northern world from paganism to southern Christianity.
Even in so primitive a play as *The Burial Mound*, we find Ibsen's
argument intellectually developed beyond that of a mere exciting
clash of opposites. In fact, the themes of the play are the embryos
that will evolve into the rich, subtle, and wide-ranging argument
of *Emperor and Galilean*.

As in the opening of *Catiline*, the time of the play is evening,
indicative of the end of an era. The play opens with Bernhard's
reflection that only after the wild forces of humanity have been
stilled by Ragnorök (signaling the fiery end of Germanic paganism)
will Odin, Baldur, and Freia, gods of wisdom, beauty, and love,
rule over men in peace. The play will close with Blanka's prediction that the warrior Viking spirit now will engage solely in "purer
strife on silver seas of thought."[18] The action of the play lures the
Viking warriors into this dialectical development (by a form of
"cunning of Reason") and then works upon their spirit so that
they fulfill Bernhard's prediction and are ready for Blanka's challenge. Her exhortation, obviously addressed to the Norwegian
audience, that Norway's future lies in friendly *intellectual/spiritual*
combat with its neighbors (one is reminded of the "mental fight"
of Blake's *Jerusalem*) is a theme that recurs continually in Ibsen's
writing—indeed it is the overriding purpose of his art. It is the new
struggle to which Brand attempts to rally his uncomprehending
countrymen, which Peer Gynt warily evades, and which Julian
dreams will be the glorious sublimation of the violent conflicts
within his empire. It is as though, in this play, revised from the

52 *Catiline/The Burial Mound*

earlier *The Normans* for presentation in the Norwegian capital, Ibsen is anxious to proclaim himself the poet of this intellectual evolution.

The central onstage symbol, the burial mound, signifies the dead Viking culture, and the altar of flowers, to which it has been converted by Blanka's ample strewing of flowers upon it, represents the new compassionate order of Christianity to which her own spirit is loyal. The mound is earthen and dead, the flowers fresh and alive. The living strength of these lovely, delicate things reflect the deceptive strength of Blanka who, by her gentleness, already has overcome the murderous nature of Audun (Bernhard) and who will conquer the seemingly unyielding warrior spirit of Gandalf.

Blanka is a typical Romantic heroine, dreaming of the north and its blond heroes who will elevate her life to vivid purposefulness, much as Richard Wagner's Norwegian Senta dreams of her flying Dutchman who will arrive to lift her out of her petty, everyday existence. Blanka and Senta are examples of that yearning, subversive, impossibly aspiring Romantic spirit (dramatized by Ibsen in *The Lady from the Sea*) found in so many of the European bourgeoisie in the nineteenth century.

The "Norwegian myth" launched into dramatic service in this play and destined to carry a heavy cargo of cultural implication in the plays that follow is, it is true, an example of the conventional chauvinism of the time. But we should also realize that it represents a welcome extension and objectification of Ibsen's dramatic material beyond the mostly subjective confines of *Catiline*. For the time being, this extension beyond subjectivity takes on only a nationalist-historical form, but it will develop into the "positive world philosophy" of *Emperor and Galilean* when Ibsen becomes the poet, not just of Norway, but of modern European man. Therefore, though the characters of *The Burial Mound* (Bernhard, Blanka, Gandalf, and Hemming) are "merely conventional signs," as the crew in pursuit of the snark would say, standing for Old Man, Ardent Girl, Warrior Hero, and Scald, they are to be welcomed as advances leading to the creation of "objective correlatives" for contending forces within Ibsen's imagination.

Bernhard and Blanka, after the briefest dialogue, exit "to walk in the woods" and gather fresh flowers for the already amply bestrewn mound. At this moment, Gandalf and his picturesque Viking companions appear onstage, "armed for the battle, with sword in hand." The Vikings represent what Heinrich Heine described as "that ancient German eagerness for battle which combats not for the sake of destroying, nor even for the sake of victory, but merely for the sake of combat itself," and Heine warned his readers that this German spirit would one day reawaken and shatter the world. "Christianity," Heine added, "subdued to a certain extent the brutal warrior ardor of the Germans, but it could not entirely quench it."[19] "What would this life be, if not for battle?"[20] Gandalf asks. The Viking warrior ardor *is* a virtue, but only if it is sublimated (*aufgehoben*) into mental fight, and Christianity has to teach the pagan Vikings this lesson. In her dialogue with Gandalf on her return from the woods, Blanka takes up this theme in answer to his rhetorical question:

> Ah yes, the inner battle, the spirit's fight,
> And light's decisive victory over darkness.
> Such battles give to life its truest purpose.[21]

Blanka is the new *spiritual* warrior confronting the older, epic culture of *physical* warriorship, and her war against spiritual darkness—what Ibsen will call a war against the fiends that infest the heart and mind—will first oppose, then merge with, and finally sublimate the Viking warrior spirit: an example of the dramatic action as a dialectical process. Although outwardly weak and helpless, Blanka undermines and weakens her young conqueror. His simplistic warrior code becomes confused, infected with the "pestilence and poison" of her message, which infiltrates him like the scent of the flowers on the burial mound. In good dialectical fashion, the transition to the higher spiritual life for which the whole north is destined already is "built into" (or in modern terms "programmed" into) the spirit of the northern world, for its myth of Baldur the beautiful inaugurating, after his resurrection, the regeneration of the world anticipates the Christian victory. One might protest that Gandalf's interest in the new Christian order all too patently is connected with the very evident physical charms of Blanka and therefore hardly constitutes a test case for the new Christian dispensation; such confusion of doctrinal with erotic attraction is not unique in literature. But this, after all, is the old ladder of Eros of Plato, and Ibsen will incorporate it, profoundly, in his scheme of things in the later plays.

A rudimentary use of dramatic suspense in *The Burial Mound* marks yet another advance in dramatic technique over that of *Catiline*. Bernhard, who actually is Gandalf's long-presumed-dead father, Audun, teasingly and dangerously delays this revelation and, by this delay, impels Gandalf to a crisis of decision (whether or not to avenge according to the warrior code), a crisis which further urges him toward the new Christian order since he spares and forgives the man he believes killed his father. So far, indeed, has Gandalf journeyed toward Blanka's values that he agrees to kill himself, as the supreme act of pagan sacrifice, out of Christian reluctance to shed his enemy's blood. Gandalf's willingness to commit suicide to escape his dilemma testifies to the depth of his inward struggle at the same time that it catches up the best elements of both pagan and Christian culture preparatory to their merger in the future marriage of Blanka and Gandalf. Only at this moment does Bernhard reveal he is not the killer of Audun but Audun himself, long since converted to Christianity by the infant(!) Blanka.[22]

The play ends with a *tableau* in which Blanka and Gandalf unite, "joining northern strength with southern mercy."[23] Hemming joins old Audun to become his now Christian scald, and Blanka, like a Brechtian heroine, seizes a banner, "steps forward," and exhorts the theater audience to resurrect the Viking and northern spirit "to purer strife on silver seas of thought."[24] In this exhortation, as in Catiline's late insight that true life is "an unending battle/Between the hostile forces of the soul...,"[25] Ibsen's reaffirms his commitment to an intellectual and a dialectical dramatic art and, through Blanka, clearly invites the people to enter into the wider intellectual and spiritual community of Europe. It is easier to deride the naiveté of *The Burial Mound* than to try to detect the core of genuine intellectual commitment that it represents.

When he revised *The Burial Mound* for performance in Bergen in 1854, Ibsen made its dialectical thrust more emphatic. There is some slight further development in character portrayal, but it is the argument of the play that he most sharpens and clarifies.

The north-south polarity is emphasized by setting the scene in

Sicily, which, as J. W. McFarlane observes, is more "languidly and lushly Mediterranean."[26] The play opens with a new soliloquy in which Blanka contrasts the decadent, attenuated culture of the south with the vigor and vitality of the north; themes Ibsen was to develop in his essay on the heroic ballad. McFarlane sees in these changes of emphasis a somewhat pathetic attempt by the poet to ingratiate his chauvinist Norwegian audience; but the change is thoroughly in accord with his later development and therefore probably represents his sincere beliefs at the time. Whereas the 1850 version gave the ideological advantage to the Christian south and showed the north in spiritual dissolution, the 1854 text shifts the advantage to the Viking north which, in spite of its greater vigor, still is destined for conversion by Blanka. The description, in the new soliloquy, of a culture whose decay is represented by its crumbling statues of pagan gods is repeated in the powerful opening scene of *Emperor and Galilean,* and this defunct culture of dead stone gods is contrasted with the "godlike" and living warriors of the Viking north. This is an early and artlessly direct statement of one of Ibsen's major themes: the contrast between the merely traditional and dead in our spiritual and cultural life, and the living, spontaneous joy of *life* forces in which the new directions of the world spirit will be found.

In the new version, the character of Blanka has been radically changed. Now she is more ardently a Scandiaphile, and the Romantic aspects of her earlier identity have blossomed into the Romantic convention of the ardent, responsive, feminine imagination whose inward dreamworld is a sentimental education that builds up her spiritual reserves, enabling her to rise to the challenge of her fateful encounter with her Viking counterpart. Such an encounter pits the deeply subjective and inward against the effectively objective and outward—that is, the maiden against the warrior. Blanka represents a central doctrine of Romantic lore: that in the inward, submerged life of the spirit and the imagination one can enter into areas of reality as genuine as that provided by engagement with objective life. This inwardness, which was obviously a useful consolation to the bourgeois (and in particular the feminine) spirit denied access to power in the actual world, was to become the most notable aspect of bourgeois literature, especially in the novel, separating it unmistakably from the more objective art of the eighteenth century. Although this theme of spiritual inwardness and its resources is presented somewhat unsubtly by Blanka, it is the germ of what will be one of the most fascinating aspects of the "Ibsen heroine," the inhabitant of an inward psychic realm as impressive as the external world from which she is excluded to such a great extent.

But it is not only this subjective and imaginative realm that is more firmly delineated in the later version of the play; the objective, external, and historical reality also is more firmly rendered. It is true that the "Norwegian myth" is still there and will remain with Ibsen for some years, impelling him to create an ideal, imaginary realm of heroism, but, later, when the remoteness of this ideal from actual reality becomes clear to the poet, the travestied or betrayed ideal will continue to function as a subversive criticism of the present.

The naive Romanticism of the play, especially in its later version, is obvious. Blanka too patently is a nineteenth-century poetic sensibility transplanted to the twelfth century to appreciate Nature in the modern manner and to admire the unspoiled energy of Viking life at first hand. Gandalf, too, although no intellectual heavyweight, is a most articulate Norseman aware that, in good Hegelian fashion, the north is undergoing a transition to a higher phase and that his own self-doubts, rudimentary as they are, are a symptom of that transition. The stage conventions are as permissive as those of *Catiline*. When Gandalf, after delivering a long soliloquy to the surrounding air, hears Blanka approach, he steps aside to listen, unseen, to *her* soliloquy in which she utters the themes of the power of art to redeem and consecrate past life and the power of the imagination to transport the dreamer to another realm. The soliloquy is operatic in its high, lyrical, arialike strain that is meant to stir the theater audience into rapt inattention to the wildly improbable situation: for we confront a Norseman, in Sicily, unsurprised at hearing his own language fluently spoken by a native who, like himself, is given the habit of addressing, at length, no one in sight. As Blanka throws an oak wreath to the ground, calling upon a hero to appear, Gandalf, of course, "steps forward," revealing himself and seizing the wreath. Even more than in *Catiline* we are in unconditioned stage space only, not in any conceivable actual space. This is purely escapist theater which has neither the discipline imposed by the need to simulate a plausible reality nor that imposed by a demanding theatrical convention.

The revised version makes more of the struggle within Gandalf's soul, in which his epic and objective nature attempts to absorb the "lyric" subjectivity of Blanka. This struggle is paradigmatic of the transition from the old epic and objective world order of the pagan, Viking culture to the new subjective and lyric order of Christianity. There is thematic subtlety in the contrast of the northern, masculine weakness beneath the outward strength of the pagan hero and the feminine strength beneath the outward weakness of the Christian heroine. The considerable extension of Ibsen's thematic material beyond that of *Catiline* may be missed if we consider only the all too evident crudities of the play.

The dramatist is far less fortunate that the musician or the visual artist. The earliest sketches and unsuccessful attempts of a great painter are valued and respected; but a play, if it is not performable, is likely to be totally eclipsed. *The Burial Mound* marks an artistic breakthrough as significant, in its way, as the innovative yet not wholly realized breakthroughs of a Cezanne or a Picasso. Ibsen has created the method of a new dramatic symbology in terms of the thematic visual object, and we will see this device grow more searching, more profound, and more all-encompassing in the evolution of his art until, in the plays of the realistic cycle, his characters move in a uniquely fateful symbolic space. In *The Burial Mound* he also far more successfully balances inner psychological and outer historical actions, while a distinctly dialectical rendering of reality, already apparent in *Catiline,* now takes on a clearer and firmer objective shape.

THE RECOVERY OF THE PAST
St. John's Night
to The Vikings at Helgeland

With the completion of *The Burial Mound*, Ibsen tentatively had created a dramatic form that was able to portray, simultaneously, forces within the psyches of individuals and forces corresponding to them within an objective, historical world. This dramatic interaction between the intersubjective and the objectively historical realms of reality marked a great advance over the more subjective method of *Catiline*, however inauspicious the naive and inartistic handling might be.

After *The Burial Mound* Ibsen seeks further to enlarge the areas of both the subjective and objective realms. Blanka had responded ardently to the world of nature and to the power of the inner imagination to inhabit a world as rich as the objective world; but the world of nature and the world of the imagination in *The Burial Mound* were decorative appendages to the ideological drama rather than being instrinsic to it. In the unfinished sketch of a play, *The Grouse in Justedal*, Ibsen goes on to experiment unsuccessfully with the Romantic themes of the relation of the natural to the supernatural and of the chosen and "awakened" imaginations that are able to respond adequately to both. Set in medieval times with the Black Death as a recent memory, the sketch makes fairly straightforward use of the Romantic dualism of the wild, untamed, innocent, and natural aspects of the human spirit, found in the heroine, Alfhild, and the unresponsive, imprisoned, unnatural world of guilty social involvement and obligation. These themes, which are a further version of the Schillerian contrast of naive and sentimental natures and which go back to Rousseau's *The Social Contract,* are clumsily handled, but one can see their inherent seriousness and the manner in which they expand the circumference of reality beyond the bounds of *The Burial Mound.* Through the figure of Harald the minstrel, Ibsen articulates the values of the awakened imagination and its responsiveness to the natural and supernatural and to the past within the present. However, the main vehicle of this natural consciousness, Alfhild, is an impossibly "fey" creation, an embarrassing example of the brainless heroine so dear to nineteenth-century readers and so difficult for the modern sensibility to tolerate. She is counterbalanced by the equally impossible, "roguish" Mereta.

One understands why Ibsen abandoned this sketch, but, surprisingly, he was to toy with it in various forms for a number of years, keeping the main themes for *Olaf Liliekrans,* written seven years later. Many of the details and themes were worked into *St. John's Night* in which Alfhild becomes the fey Anne, who is also responsive to the supernatural; Alfhild's lover, Björn, becomes Anne's lover, Johannes Birk; and the contrasting pair, Mereta and Einar from *The Grouse in Justedal,* are transmuted into the less sympathetic Juliane and Julian. This latter pair are the first example we have yet seen (apart from the squib *Norma: or a Politician's Love*) of the strong satiric tendency of much of Ibsen's writing. In *The Grouse in Justedal* the supernatural world simply is an extension of the natural world, the latter shading off into the former, whereas in *St. John's Night* it is far more decisively an extension of the imaginative world, a neglected inheritance consciously alluded to, which, like the old trunk with its secrets of Birk's material inheritance, needs to be reclaimed for the present by the responsive consciousness. As with Shakespeare's *Love's Labour's Lost,* the literary quest of the play becomes it dramatic subject, for Ibsen is attempting to extend his dramatic medium to encompass the supernatural while the characters of the drama, in particular the hero Johannes Birk, are engaged in a similar quest in their fictive situation.

The series of plays that Ibsen now writes, from *St. John's Night* to *The Vikings at Helgeland*, form in reverse order a chronological sequence as Ibsen, beginning with his contemporary world, removes layer after layer of the past until he reaches the "epic" Viking and pagan substratum of the Norwegian consciousness. In *St. John's Night*, set in the nineteenth century, the past is an inheritance that must be recovered by the imaginative spirit; it is as if Ibsen was here setting forth the program he was to follow with the succeeding plays. The next drama, *Lady Inger of Østraat*, takes place in the sixteenth century, at a time of decisive change in the political fortunes of Norway, and the form and the atmosphere of the play are appropriately Renaissance and Shakespearean. *The Feast at Solhoug*, which follows, goes back farther into the past to the medieval period when a new chivalric order begins to tame and civilize the rough Norwegian spirit. Set in the same period, the next play, *Olaf Liliekrans*, dramatizes the medieval sense of magic, enchantment, and the supernatural. *The Feast at Solhoug* traces the development of the national spirit from the "epic" mode of the ballad into a new "lyric" consciousness, whereas *Olaf Liliekrans* attempts to remain within the balladic consciousness itself—hence the great problems in the *dramatic* form of the play. This series ends with *The Vikings at Helgeland*, which re-creates the purer epic world of the Viking saga—the bedrock of the Norwegian consciousness upon which, in succeeding ages, the whole superstructure of the modern consciousness will be built.

There is no evidence that Ibsen explicitly intended to create this reverse chronological sequence, from memory-filled present, through the past, to the Viking consciousness. But Ibsen's critical writings, which insist that the structure of the modern mind has evolved dialectically from the past and that the modern poet and his or her audience should recover their full inheritance (the theme, also, of *St. John's Night*), should make us consider at least the possibility of some such purpose. This, also, would explain why he occupied himself with such uncongenial forms (for drama) as *The Feast at Solhoug* and *Olaf Liliekrans* for these might then be seen as essential stages of the gradual restoration of the past. We know that Ibsen set aside *The Vikings at Helgeland* after completing *Lady Inger of Østraat* and that he used much of the plot of the Viking and "epic" subject for the medieval and "lyric" *The Feast at Solhoug*. In his essay on the heroic ballad Ibsen argued that the romances and ballads were later historic/cultural developments from their mythic sources, and this suggests that he thought it necessary to dramatize an intermediate, medieval, and romance phase between *Lady Inger of Østraat* and *The Vikings at Helgeland*.

ST. JOHN'S NIGHT

St. John's Night, containing a parody of the excesses of cultural nationalism, marks an advance in Ibsen's *self-critical* literary sensibility, but it pays the price of structural awkwardness: contemporary intrigue plot, fairy-tale fantasy, literary satire, and romantic love story intertwine incongruously. The Schillerian theme of the contrast between naive and sentimental or alienated consciousnesses undergoes a more open and more complex literary development than in Ibsen's earlier work. The naive heroine, Anne, will be educated in the ways of the alienated world while the sentimental or alienated hero, Birk, will rediscover his forgotten, native, naive, and true roots through the agency of Anne's love. Ibsen's own criticism, in an 1851 review, of what he felt was a spuriously nationalistic play, *The Hulder's Home*, is our best guide to his intentions in *St. John's Night*. Attacking the "tawdry nationalism" that seemed to think "verse-making contests, folk-dancing, swear words and dialect expressions" were the elements of nationalistic drama, Ibsen urged that "the truly national author is the one who knows how to impart to his work those undertones which ring out to us from mountain and valley, from meadow and shore, and above all from our own inner minds."[1] In *The Grouse in Justedal* and *St. John's Night* he evidently was attempting to find the right dramatic expression for this truer, deeper nationalism.

In *St. John's Night* the genuinely responsive characters, Anne and Birk, are depicted as being in touch with the "undertones" of the national spirit and its past, and they are contrasted with the sophisticated and superficial enthusiasts for the folkish and the natural, Julian and Juliane. The attack upon this false cultural nationalism does not imply an attack upon the genuine article.[2]

The theme (and major metaphor) of *St. John's Night* is that of inheritance, whereby the modern intrigue plot revolving around the material inheritance of Birk counterpoints the romantic plot of the spiritual inheritance of Norway, maintained by Anne and her grandfather. With the union of Anne and Birk the two inheritances merge. Birk had been denied both his material and his spiritual inheritance, for just as his material patrimony has been concealed and kept from him, so his modern education, away from home, has cut him off from his deepest cultural roots. Anne will be the agent through which both inheritances will be recovered.

Inheriting from her grandfather a store of folk-legend with which her imagination is filled, Anne, unsurprisingly, is considered "strange" by the unimaginative people around her; but the well-educated and citified Birk is drawn toward her despite his engagement to the more sophisticated and artificial Juliane. Anne and her grandfather spend much time in a picturesque old log house that stands *behind* the modern house, an emblem of the way in which the past of folk memory stands behind the modern consciousness. One sees, here, the further elaboration of Ibsen's use of the visual symbol, for whereas the burial mound of the previous play had been a central, static symbol around which the characters grouped, the two houses of *St. John's Night* — one foreground, the other background, one representing prosaic modern reality and the other a hidden, imaginative reality filled with memories from the past—are far better integrated into the action of the play. Characters move from one location to the other, signifying their commitment to conflicting realms of value, while one of the objects within the background log house, the old chest of secrets and its key, decisively changes the situation that has been created by the modern house.

In this way Ibsen transforms a hackneyed, mechanical convention of the well-made play, the missing documents in the locked chest, into a metaphor. In fact, the metaphors of *St. John's Night* will undergo a superb transmutation in *The Wild Duck.* The stage division of *The Wild Duck,* with its foreground of the Ekdal photography studio, or prosaic reality, and the loft in the background with *its* chest of treasures (left by "the flying Dutchman") and its characters similarly moving between the two realms as between two forms of spiritual life, is a more deeply poetic and more disenchanted rendering of the visual symbolism of *St. John's Night*, and Anne and her grandfather have evolved into the poignant characters Hedvig and old Ekdal.

There may be an element of cautionary self-satire in Ibsen's portrayal of Julian Poulson, but we should see that the hilariously pretentious jargon Poulson is given to utter is utterly unlike the determinedly objective and even pedantically conscientious terminology of Ibsen's critical writings. "I will immerse myself in immediacies, that is to say, the higher... the artistic immediacies,"[3] Poulson declares, anticipating by travesty Walter Pater's subjective and impressionistic aesthetics. Poulson's intuitional approach to art and reality, comprising *attitudes* rather than *concepts*, is placed within a play that is itself a dramatized concept.

Poulson, it is to be noted, is anti-intellectual, starting his education in "aesthetics and criticism" but soon giving up these disciplines for enthusiastic nationalism. The superficial nature of this nationalism actually shuts him off from the deeper sources (presented as both natural and supernatural) of his nation, sources which the play is seeking to locate within the present as an aspect of the modern mind's heritage. Where Birk and Anne, at the celebration of midsummer eve, see spirit forms from folktale, Julian and Juliane see only peasant folk, being unable imaginatively to "get behind" prosaic everyday reality. Birk, engaged to Juliane but drawn toward Anne, and Juliane, engaged to Birk but drawn toward Julian, are, by a process of elective affinities, led to compatible unions. The process by which Birk and Anne discover their value for each other involves suffering: Birk must experience the despair of having, honorably, to uphold his unenthusiastic attachment to Juliane, thereby losing Anne, and Anne, for her part, must undergo the pain of loss of innocence for the experience of "alienation" in the painful severance of her instinctual from her moral life. This critical point is reached in act 3 when Anne, heartbroken at learning that Birk's love for her cannot remain innocent but must conflict with his honor, takes back the flowers (*natural* objects) with which she had recently sealed her compact of innocent love for Birk. She then undergoes the painful but necessary "fall into the alienated world of experience when she tells her first lie to Birk, who himself has lied to her about his feelings for Juliane.

The play swiftly and artlessly resolves its intrigue plot and its romantic plot by the revelation of concealed documents which give to Birk his rightful inheritance and by Birk's union with Anne which reunites him with his cultural inheritance. Artless though this resolution is, we should note the increasing thematic and structural complexity of Ibsen's dramatic writing. He attempts to grasp a larger and more problematic reality than he has hitherto embraced and to grasp it by means of a more diversified and multi-layered art. The use of visual symbolism is ambitious, looking forward to the considerable mastery of this device in the first three acts of *Lady Inger of Østraat* where, it seems to me, Ibsen creates a whole new language for modern drama. No one will claim that *St. John's Night* is major drama. The abstract and dialectical aspects of the play are more readily apparent than any compellingly rendered life. But the theoretical structuring of the play is *conceptually* significant and, though not shown to great advantage here, will turn out to be a major source of strength in Ibsen's later artistic development.

LADY INGER OF ØSTRAAT

Even though its construction is very badly flawed, *Lady Inger of Østraat* is the first work in which Ibsen reveals himself as a major dramatic presence. The play is his "first symphony," the Rubicon that must be crossed by all authentic artists even at the cost of badly overreaching themselves, as Ibsen does here. With this provision in mind, one can be free to admire the development of a formidable technical skill and to appreciate the depth and variety of the ideological and psychological themes that the drama encompasses. In all of Ibsen's early plays one is always aware of a large mind that is clumsily taking up the often fragile and inadequate dramatic conventions of the day, and this is particularly true of *Lady Inger of Østraat*. One senses that the poet's imagination descends with self-conscious awkwardness into the theatrical machinery of the period, that he is not happy with what the public wants. The public seemed to understand this and did not take to him even when he made concessions to its nationalist and aesthetic sensibilities—though he made fewer than interpreters have claimed. The awkward titanism that continually reveals the large human being in Ibsen is one of the winning aspects of these early plays.

The revealing clumsiness of *Lady Inger* compels us to protest that the machinations of his fiendishly well-made plot—where individuals are made to meet by accident just the people they should not and not to meet just the people they should, and to impart just the information they should not and withhold just the information they should impart—violates the human rights of the dramatis personae. On reflection, however, this complaint contains a tribute. No one could possibly worry about the human rights of the characters of Scribean drama because the characters never are permitted to be human; whereas Lady Inger, Eline, Nils Stensson, and Nils Lykke are impressively or poignantly or charmingly or intriguingly human, and the suffering of such characters at the behest of a totally unfeeling, implausible infernal machine of a plot becomes intolerable to us because we are made to feel a genuine concern for them. Lady Inger may err and deserve, in dramatic terms, to be punished, but she should not be pitted against a contrived theatrical world in which coincidence and the most unlikely chance are the instruments of an unfeeling laboratory experiment—a world in which uncompleted, misconstrued, or unspoken phrases can bring down the most appalling consequences. The more we grant life and substance to Lady Inger and the other characters, the more we are repelled by the spectacle of their attempts to extricate themselves from a lethal theatrical machinery whose levers are being pulled by a playwright who has forgotten that he has granted his characters compelling life. In other words, there is a discrepancy between the suffering and the means by which it is brought about whereby this *unfairness* of dramatic situation does not lead to tragic purgation and insight but to frustrating indignation.

Indignation at the merely arbitrary can be a legitimate dramatic response evoked by the poet. Lessing, in *Emilie Galotti*, increases our indignation at, and contempt for, arbitrary autocracy by having the Galotti family, whom we have come to know with some intimacy, destroyed by the frivolous whim of the prince and the petty malice of his minister. The incongruity between the frivolous cause and the harrowing effect serves Lessing's purpose of stirring up bourgeois and enlightened contempt for a social order whose power of life and death over its subjects does not have the dignity of tragic guilt. The audience has been led to recognize that such an order needs to be swept away for being ridiculously offensive to reason, so that the disparity between the human dignity of the victims and the arbitrariness of their fates is a telling propagandist point in enlightenment's fight to create a social order more consistent with human reason. This is not a *tragic* insight, however, but closer to the "alienation" devices of the propagandist theater of our own time.

Ibsen clearly intended *Lady Inger of Østraat* to be a tragic drama, and therefore it has to create a consonance between cause and outcome if it is to realize this most difficult of dramatic genres. Not only must the characters be heroically conceived, impelled by substantial motives, and engaged in a significant action of considerable scope, but the tragic denouement must be seen as the inevitable result of the interaction of these elements. Ibsen was practically the only major modern dramatist who was concerned with creating full-scale tragedy throughout his career, and he declared that with *Emperor and Galilean* his thinking had become "fatalist"—which is a very different thing from pessimistic thinking. Tragedy of fate perceives rational, even inevitable, reasons for tragic events and reconciles our human reason to their inevitability, whereas pessimism sees no such *rational* inevitability and so denies that reason can reconcile itself to necessity. *Lady Inger* is conceived by the young poet as a tragedy, with Lady Inger meeting her nemesis; however, because the means by which this nemesis is brought about is offensive to our reason, the play lapses into melodrama.

Hegel distinguished between ancient and modern ("modern" meaning from the time of Shakespeare) tragedy, observing that the subjective nature of the tragic characters, "the various descriptions of the human heart and personal character [and] the particular complications and intrigues" of their motives had no place in ancient tragedy, because the protagonists of this early phase of tragedy were identified solely with "essential powers that rule human life and [with the conflicts] between the gods that dominate the human heart."[4] In modern tragedy, however, the subjective life, the individual passions and motives and the human idiosyncrasies that make up a recognizably modern character, does have its place. The modern tragic individual must possess "formal greatness of character and a personality powerful enough to sustain everything negative and, without denying its acts or being inwardly wrecked, to accept its fate."[5] The character must be involved in substantial and fundamental ends, "country, family, crown and empire," but these form only the "specific ground on which the individual stands with his own subjective character and where he gets into a conflict, instead of providing him with the proper ultimate object of his willing and acting."[6]

This subjective aspect of modern tragedy can include "a spread of particular details concerning both the inner life and also the external circumstances and relations within which the action proceeds."[7] This leads to an art in which every detail need not be devoted to furthering and keeping clearly in view the tragic argument:

Therefore we find legitimately in place here, in distinction from the simple conflicts in Greek drama, a variety and wealth of dramatis personae, extraordinary and always newly involved complications, labyrinths of intrigue, accidental occurrences, in short all those features which, no longer fettered by the impressive and substantial character of an essential subject-matter, are indicative of what is typical in the romantic, as distinct from the classical, form of art.[8]

Lady Inger is meant to be a tragic heroine in this modern sense, unlike the characters of the later The Vikings at Helgeland who are closer to the ancient type. The crossed purposes of her subjective life and its inner divisions, the intrigues by which she outwardly operates and by which she is destroyed, her alienation from the world she finds herself in are features that Hegel sees as modern, and her daughter, Eline, and her opponent, Nils Lykke, share these qualities. Lady Inger's present identity as the shrewd politician who has survived and prospered by successfully engaging and compromising with the world of intrigue of the oppressors of her country is at odds with her earlier identity as the heroic young woman who stirred her countrymen by courageously resolving to liberate her country. The end for which Lady Inger now works is "substantial," involving the destinies of three kingdoms, and in her drama her identities as mother, patriot, politician, and shaper of the future are intertwined yet at odds with each other. In terms of his central dramatic character, the motives by which she acts, and the larger ends in which she is involved, Ibsen has created a play of genuinely tragic implications in the modern sense, approaching the Schillerian model in scale of action and even surpassing it in depth of psychological portraiture. But for her daring yet vacillating spirit to be brought to fully tragic action and insight, the world against which she engages and within which she is enmeshed should have equal ethical value—as it does in Schiller's best tragedies. That is, if the processes of the world are tragically to bring her down, they must do so honorably, as an equal ethical combatant. Hegel noted that this was a particular problem for modern drama which, even in Shakespeare, did not satisfy the "pressing demand for a necessary correspondence between the external circumstances (of the plot) and what the inner nature of those fine characters really is."[9] In Ibsen's play the disparity between the nature of the characters and the external circumstances from which they suffer so terribly is extreme.

To realize the tragic view of life as dramatic form in the modern world, Ibsen would have to see how this tragic view was built into the structure of reality through objective, substantive content as well as through subjective character. In *Lady Inger* one feels one has tragedy by personal disposition. Lady Inger is disposed to act in the high tragic mode, and the world obliges, going to some effort by means of the intrigue. Somewhat hard pressed, the world must even cheat a little and resort to extraordinary coincidence, critical failures of common sense at crucial moments, and suicidal reticence or communicativeness so that, at last, Lady Inger can mount the tragic stage with full dramatic honors.

The play, therefore, is manufactured tragedy, springing not from a tragic view of life but from the dramatist's desire to bring off tragic effects which then have to be contrived externally instead of emerging inevitably from the nature of the reality presented.

The compulsion behind the writing of the play seems primarily aesthetic. The story is a good subject that can be worked up for tragic effects; one feels that the final scene was conceived before the rest of the drama and represented the ambitious goal the plot tried to reach. Once again one finds the convention, commended by Hegel, of a historical period undergoing *transition*, in which the individual dispositions and destinies of the protagonists exemplify a larger historical/cultural turning point, here the moment before Norway decisively enters its long period of historical darkness. Lady Inger sees herself as once having been given a great and sacred mission to fulfill, the God-given task of working for her people's freedom. She has had to betray this mission by compromise until her entire life's purpose has been redirected to intrigue and selfish ambition. She desires to see her son, brought up as a stranger to her, crowned king of Sweden, and this love for her son becomes the strong subjective driving force of her actions. For the betrayal of her earlier mission she will be terribly punished by being brought, mistakenly, to murder her son. To effect this piece of enormous tragic irony, Ibsen confronts Lady Inger with her masculine counterpart, the machiavellian Nils Lykke, whom chance supplies with the one secret that can destroy her. So far the plotting, though in the "old" style, is excellent: Lady Inger has betrayed her sacred mission through intrigue, and intrigue will be her nemesis.

Her ingenuous young son, Nils Stensson, has been brought up in total ignorance of his identity and without the skill of reading whereby he can discover his identity from the letter he is delivering to a complete stranger. At this point the plotting goes badly off the track. Stensson must deliver a letter, the contents of which he cannot read, to a stranger whose name he does not know but who will be waiting for him at his mother's house. The stranger, Skaktavl, likewise does not know the name of the man (Stensson) he is to meet, and mistakes Nils Lykke for Stensson. Stensson, similarly, jumping through a window of Lady Inger's house, naturally encounters no one but Nils Lykke, whom he takes to be the man he is supposed to meet. There is nothing inevitable—or even probable—in all this, so that Lady Inger's plans go astray owing to circumstances so freakish that they could be tolerable only in farce. What should be the soul of drama, its plot or argument for which the characters and details are conceived, is being sacrificed for such considerations as character. And on his characters Ibsen lavishes a great deal of rewarding attention; they are the best he has yet created.

The great advance in technical skill and artistic sophistication is evident in that central, defining symbol which Ibsen introduced into his art with *The Burial Mound* and which he elaborated still more effectively in *St. John's Night*. In *Lady Inger* this visual symbol still is a single object—the Great Hall. Although it is not yet the omnipresent symbolic world of the later plays, it is used with richly elaborate and highly dramatic effectiveness. The entire play takes place at night, indeed within one night, which itself becomes a metaphor for Norway's darkest hour. We first see the Great Hall moonlit and mysterious, the light that illumines it fitful because of a storm. The foreground room is lit mainly by firelight, which would create a flickering, burnished glow on the objects of armor and weaponry that hang on the walls or that are being polished by the servants. These glowing pieces of metal lying about the stage set at first seem only decorative, a pretext for theatrical genre-painting as in such historical-picturesque works as Goethe's *Götz von Berlichingen*. But Ibsen soon begins to extend this visual imagery beyond the picturesque into a tellingly functional and accurate metaphor for the entire spiritual condition dramatized by the play.

Without heroes to wear and wield them, the pieces of armor are merely decorative appendages to the empty, moonlit, and somewhat ghostly Great Hall, just as the hall itself is an anachronistic survivor of vanished heroic times. Whether the armor we see glowing on the stage so picturesquely is to remain no more than decorative, like the harp of Tara in the Irish ballad, or whether it will be taken up for heroic purposes is a focal issue of the dramatic action. With a renaissance of heroism, the Great Hall, too, would be transformed from a place evoking memories of guilt and loss to one of heroic life. Very likely Ibsen is drawing an analogy between the condition of the Great Hall, which awaits a resurgence of heroism, and the condition of his own theater, whose histrionic heroism is merely decorative but could be the expression of a new and authentic heroism. The whole scene, therefore, is in search of heroes and a heroic cause to reawaken it and lift it from the indignity of decoration to the vitality of heroic life.

The dialogue of the two servants, Finn and Bjorg, which opens the play while plausibly providing necessary exposition, also continues, verbally, the visual metaphor. The helmet Finn is polishing is "an empty shell," like the Great Hall and like Norway which is "bright on the outside but worm-eaten inside." The sword's rust needs scraping off, for the sword has hung on the wall of the Great Hall instead of "rusting in Danish blood." The themes of brightness and of rust are ambiguous: brightness as polished readiness for battle and brightness as mere decorative polish; rust as the effect of cowardly disuse and rust (blood) as the result of heroic use. We hear that the last knight (*riddersman*) has died, so that Norway now is a land without heroes, left with only the nostalgic and decorative emblems of past heroism. There are many elements of Elizabethan drama in *Lady Inger*, which would be appropriate for the period the play is dramatizing, and this ingenious wordplay, between two servants filling us in with essential information, seems to derive from Elizabethan practice.

This complex of meanings inhering in a carefully created structure of setting, characters, actions, props, and dialogue reveals how far Ibsen has advanced in making the theater both intellectually and sensuously expressive. The visual symbolism, developed beyond the thematic "statement" of *The Burial Mound* and the demonstration of the dualism of *St. John's Night*, now totally dominates the action, defining and extending it. Ibsen is able to displace much of the function of language onto a poetry of visual suggestion that amplifies the action without any loss of poetic control. In so doing, he creates a dramatic method more richly detailed than Schiller's rhetorical poetic method and far more metaphorically "loaded" than the well-made plays of the boulevard theaters. This intellectual element of Ibsen's art amplifies and renders more subtle the aesthetic experience of his dramatic argument and forces upon the viewer a vigilance at least equivalent to that required by verbal poetry.

The servants' dialogue turns to the superstition of the ghost of a lady that is believed to haunt the hall—an appropriately "Gothic" detail for such a setting which broadens into the idea of the ghosts of past heroism reproachfully haunting the present imagination. The steady development of a *concept* (here the dialogue between the past and the present) neatly continued and amplified, little by little, by means of scenic detail, props, action, and dialogue might seem at first *too* intellectually manipulated, "not inevitable enough." But we should realize that the youthful Ibsen is evolving a very subtle and increasingly more adequate dramatic language and that the very excesses of virtuosity in this play are positive stages of his self-apprenticeship.

It is a sure artistic instinct that drives Ibsen toward the difficult disciplines of greater realistic plausibility combined with greater *conceptual* implication, for these were the areas in which the dominant theatrical art form of the nineteenth-century — opera — was weakest. In Ibsen's theater the audience's attention is heightened, intellectually and sensuously, to extreme acuity and vigilance, a discipline that imposes notable rigors upon the poet, demanding authenticity of expression from him. This is the complete opposite of the attention demanded by the Wagnerian *Gesamtkunstwerk* in which great depth of feeling, allied with the "magical" effects of theatrical trickery, overcomes the audience's critical resistance to implausibility of situation and fuzziness of concept. Lacking the rich adornment of Wagnerian music or Shakespearean eloquence, the action of the Ibsen play is naked and exposed, but it is precisely here that it must satisfy the most stringent aesthetic and intellectual demands. This is an aesthetic puritanism in which evident inauthenticity or implausibility will be cruelly revealed. The reward for an audience capable of perceiving the stringencies of this art is participation in a discipline as rich, distinguished, and rigorous as that of Sophoclean drama, where the reduced terms, like the leanness of functional architecture, carry the greatest weight of conceptual implication. The intrigue plot of *Lady Inger of Østraat* is no more implausible than that of many of Shakespeare's plays, but the realistic convention it is operating within makes its implausibilities more painfully obvious.

Eline, Lady Inger's daughter, overhears the servants' account of her mother's nightwalking, the symptoms of uneasy conscience over her betrayal of her mission. Like Anne in *St. John's Night*, Eline longs to hear the fables from the past, as told by the servant,

Bjorn. But Eline is in many ways a composite of Ibsen's previous heroines. She is the romantic yearning heroine, similar to Blanka, who finds she has outgrown her attachment to the nostalgic legends of past heroism and who wants to participate directly in present heroic action—somewhat like the Clara of Goethe's *Egmont*. Like Blanka, she dreams of her hero, this time Nils Lykke, but her feelings are ambivalent because he has a reputation as a seducer. With a dead and unavenged sister, betrayed by Nils Lykke, she repeats the relationship of Furia to Catiline, and Lykke himself resembles the Byronic Catiline with his wordly cynicism that thaws before the nobility of Eline's proud nature.

The "machiavellian" aspect of Nils Lykke is a Shakespearean motif in this play, as is the character of Lady Inger herself. Her first appearance, flitting like a ghost almost somnambulistically in guilty unrest through the Great Hall, recalls the sleepwalking of the guilty Lady Macbeth. Feeling that the eyes of the portrait of Knut Alfson reproach her, she turns the picture to the wall—an action, like Lady Macbeth's washing of the invisible blood from her hands, that is an attempt to exorcise the ghosts within the subjective spirit by external means. No sooner is the Great Hall forcefully established as a place of guilty memory than it suddenly and startlingly comes alive within the present, for a group of rebel farmers bursts in, confronting Lady Inger and demanding that she help their rebellion against the Swedes. When she perceives that their plan could further her own ambitions for her son, Lady Inger encourages them to take weapons from the Great Hall, and the many lighted candles that the crowd brings into the hall make it burst with light, which also is reflected by the weapons and armor that the crowd is taking down from the walls and flourishing. The metal now is gleaming functionally, for heroic use, just as the hall is transformed from a dimly moonlit receptacle of the guilty past into busy, active, luminous life.

We detect how thoroughly the *scene* of the play has been thought out in terms of a brilliant metaphor, how richly, subtly, and suggestively it had been waiting for just this "epiphany." Richard Wagner creates a similar theatrical symbolism; one recalls, for example, the moment in Hunding's hall when the sword Nothung (already mentioned significantly by Sieglinde) suddenly flashes into Siegmund's view. But in Wagner the visual symbolism is too patently a theatrical "poetry" that is not realized in terms of plausible human reality. The Wagnerian symbolic effects are attained by holding in abeyance our critical control over the reality, or even the plausibility, of the events, so that we escape into a realm other than that of our experience of reality without forcing that realm to stand the test of truth. Ibsen wants the same poetic meanings as Wagner—wants somewhat more, in fact—but he insists that they be demonstrated as capable of plausible human embodiment, a requirement that might, to the romantic, seem unpoetic when actually it is the highest form of poetic truth.

We have watched the Great Hall first in its aspect as a repository of nostalgia and guilty memory and now, with the metaphor of the darkness giving way to brilliant light, as the manifestation of heroic purpose flaring up again in Norway to restore the fortunes of the nation. After the crowd leaves and the hall darkens again, Eline reproaches her mother for betraying the great task God had laid upon her, that of leading the nation from darkness to light. "It is still night" (*det er ennu natt*), Eline exclaims as she stands on the darkened stage.

The true distinction of the young dramatist's imagination emerges here. The play may manipulate the specious dramatic tricks of the Scribean formulas, but the poetic core of the play, with its themes of spiritual darkness and enlightenment, sleep and awakening, and of the interplay between the past and the present, is rendered with poetic depth and brilliance as human drama and as telling theatrical metaphor—the evidence of a first-rate dramatic mind intent upon "the best and master thing." In intellectual reach and in poetic audacity *Lady Inger* is of a much smaller order than Schiller's *Don Carlos*; nevertheless, Ibsen is searching out, gradually, a new and subtle theatrical language that ultimately will encompass more than the Schillerian method. Ibsen's method will expand the human condition to the widest terms of time (history) and space (nature) while exploring a larger inward psychic landscape than that of Schiller's plays.

The whole first act of *Lady Inger* is masterly. The situation of the nation, Norway, is mirrored, in miniature, in the situation of Lady Inger's household and is developed extensively as historical drama and intensively as psychological drama. The national, social, familial, and individual destinies are intertwined fatefully as Lady Inger is forced to confront the demands made upon her by her daughter and her people; at the same time she must navigate the dangerous waters of international intrigue created by Nils Lykke and by her own counterclaims for her son. Until now, and until the plotting goes badly off the track, one would not think of the play as Scribean; one has only to compare the ideologically serious and poetically and theatrically realized themes of *Lady Inger* with a Scribean historical drama like *A Glass of Water* and its trivial (but dangerous) thesis that Chance alone decides all events in life to perceive the great difference both in purpose and in accomplishment. The first act of *Lady Inger* has laid out the foundation for the intrigue plot. Far more consequential, it has also set forth the terms of the human, ethical, and ideological argument, and it is this aspect of the play that is, in Henry James's phrase, "the distinguished thing."

The development of the play after the second act, however, advances the intrigue plot at the expense of the deeper argument. Not until *The Vikings at Helgeland* is Ibsen able to present an interesting, adequate, objective plot development which is at the same time the perfect expression of the play's argument, and after *The Vikings* Ibsen will always make the dramatic structure and its story the human and aesthetic embodiment of the play's total meaning. An indication that, from about the middle of the second act, Ibsen is not engaged in his drama at the deepest levels, appears in the great slackening of the visual metaphors used so richly earlier in the play. (A similar falling off in the imaginative creation of visual metaphor occurs in the second part of *Emperor and Galilean*.) It is as if the argument of the play is fully developed halfway through the play's action, so that the rest of the action has to proceed on the more superficial level of intrigue plot, a level which provides Ibsen with no compelling creative purpose. The setting of act 3 of the play is the Great Hall itself, arranged for grandeur, feasting, intrigue, and Lady Inger's final melodramatic "obligatory scene" of personal devastation and madness. Portraits of knights and ladies now are seen to adorn the walls of the hall, and a prominent seat of honor is prepared. Outside, the storm continues.

The scene presents Lady Inger's inheritance and her purposes at their most imposing, and we will watch these become entangled and endangered as Lady Inger's two children, Eline and Stensson, fall into the hands of Nils Lykke. Eline, with her nobility and ardent patriotism, represents the best in the past of the great house; Stensson, young, ingenuous, an energy yet to be channeled into an intelligent direction, and easily moved by others, represents the treacherously tentative future that Lady Inger hopes to build upon.

Unfortunately, from the moment young Stensson appears, the implausible contrivances of the well-made plot subvert the higher dramatic interest. Stensson, engaged in the most dangerous state matters, has received no instruction regarding his mission and has no idea of the identity of the stranger to whom he is supposed to entrust the most far-reaching secrets. Ignorant not only of writing but also of his own identity, Stensson has been placed in this incredible predicament by the dramatist so that he coincidentally can encounter and confide in just the man (Nils Lykke) he should avoid. We protest against such plotting because the issues clarified earlier, and the characters as we have come to know them, mean too much to us for us merely to sit back and enjoy a deftly mechanical Scribean intrigue. The result is that the play becomes one exasperating experience after another. In act 5, for example, when Lady Inger at last meets young Stensson, believing him to be her lover's legitimate son Count Sture (who is coincidentally the same age as Stensson), she is totally unmoved by the appearance of the boy who is, we hear, the faithful image of the one great love of her life. Instead she is totally indifferent toward him, seeing in him only the rival to the son she has not seen since his infancy.

Stensson had been enjoined by Nils Lykke, on the flimsiest grounds, not to reveal his relationship to his mother and, even when driven to the utmost limit of danger, when speaking of this relationship would be the most natural and intelligent thing to do, he keeps to his oath, only blurting out words of sufficient ambiguity to convince Lady Inger that he is her deadly enemy, and thus driving her to murder him. This implausible piece of stage trickery, relying on the tedious device of mistaken motives and misunderstood speeches (a device Ibsen was to employ too frequently in his early plays), is contrived so that the last scene of the play can be staged as grand tragedy, with tragic irony and harrowing effects. A semi-demented Lady Inger now turns all the pictures to the wall (visually extinguishing the line of ancestors), beginning with that of her lover, Sten Sture, whose son (and hers) she has just unwittingly murdered. She then mounts the scene of honor ready to receive the final tragic information (conveyed by that stalest of devices, the telltale ring) that will bring her swiftly to the ground, imploring to be buried.

Plot, in *Lady Inger of Østraat*, has been an attempt to arrive at tragic irony and tragic effects by external means. The major poetic effort has been to create tragic characters in the modern manner—characters driven by strong subjective impulses toward criminal actions, driven by guilt and a sense of betrayal of higher purposes, and finally destroyed by forces that lack the objective ethical substance of Greek tragedy. One senses the power of the dramatic talent at work, misdirected and clumsy though it is, and the original and explorative nature of the poet's talent which does not permit itself the facile borrowings of, for example, Shelley's *The Cenci*. The poet is probing a humanly and aesthetically consequential reality and devising his own artistic means of revealing it. The painful discrepancies between theatrical effect, dramatic method, and thematic content reveal that Ibsen is at least facing the right problems in his quest for a new dramatic form.

THE FEAST AT SOLHOUG

In the interesting and amusing Preface to *The Feast at Solhoug* Ibsen writes that, while at work on *Lady Inger of Østraat*, "I tried as far as possible to live myself into the ways and customs of that period, into the emotional life of the people, into their patterns of thought and modes of expression."[10] This, of course, is an impossible endeavor and that Ibsen should consider it artistically desirable, reveals what importance he attached to the act, on the part of the poet and his audience, of living through past phases in the life of the race. We noted, in *Lady Inger of Østraat*, the great discrepancy between the Scribean form of the play and its historical and tragic argument. In *The Feast at Solhoug* Ibsen attempts a closer consonance between form and substance. To dramatize "the literary romanticism of the middle ages,"[11] he creates what he terms "lyric drama" in which the plot, taken from the earlier, *epic*, and objective phase of Viking culture, is transmuted into terms of chivalry, sin, subjective guilt, and miraculous salvation. The fierce saga-story is toned down and softened in *The Feast at Solhoug* "to harmonize with its nature as drama and not tragedy."[12] The distinction between "drama" and "tragedy" seems to follow Hegel's distinction between the purer classical division separating tragedy and comedy and the modern form of "drama" which lacks the precondition of an objective, ethical order suitable for tragedy. Medieval culture strictly adhered to could not admit tragic consciousness, so for Ibsen to write as if he were within that culture, within "its patterns of thought and modes of expression," he had to forego the tragic form that had been imposed externally and unsuccessfully upon *Lady Inger of Østraat* and which was to be more effectively realized, although in uncomfortably stark terms, in *The Vikings at Helgeland.*

The possibility of *lyric* expression in art arises, in Hegel's aesthetic theory, only after the individual has severed himself from "the concrete national whole, with its conditions, modes of opinion, exploits and destiny; it is only, further, after the division in man himself between his emotion and volition..."[13] *The Feast at Solhoug*, we will see, depicts a culture in a period of momentous transition in which an earlier and simpler "epic" consciousness is developing into a more problematic spiritual condition of individual emotions and wills at variance with "the concrete national whole" and at variance with each other within each individual.

The play dramatizes the medieval-chivalric spirit's idea of itself rather than offering a modern perspective on the past action. The movement of the play, like its story, evolves from wild, Viking-derived passions and conflicts through romantic and lyric expression to a new moral percipience and self-knowledge which begins to transcend the lyric consciousness of the play and to augur a new spiritual phase. Thus Margit, the central consciousness of the play, whose experience of the moral depths into which her passions plunge her, creating a shattering of her old self, anticipates the more complex cultural and psychological condition already dramatized in *Lady Inger of Østraat.*

The term "lyric drama" is something of a contradiction for, as Ibsen himself noted, drama is the achieved synthesis of the epic and lyric modes, combining the objectivity of epic, where the individual author's voice is subordinate to the national theme he or she is relating, and the subjectivity of the lyric poet. Where a predominantly lyric expression prevails in the play, the form is only very uneasily dramatic. Ibsen faces the problem of creating drama while "miming" a phase of consciousness that in itself could not give rise to drama. He encounters a similar difficulty in the Viking play *The Vikings at Helgeland*, where the epic naiveté of the characters makes them unsuited to dramatic art. Whereas in *The Feast at Solhoug* the characters seem overloaded with lyric expression, in *The Vikings at Helgeland* the characters are insufficiently endowed with psychological complexity to sustain much dramatic interest. Hegel observed that the nature of the northern (i.e., non-Mediterranean) Europeans was predominantly lyric and that this lyric expression infected the categories of epic and drama, making it doubtful which class their writings belonged to. *The Feast at Solhoug,* which dramatizes this northern lyric consciousness, has a similar indeterminacy of form.

The use of highly lyric, rhymed verse gives to the play a remote, exalted, and self-consciously literary quality. We notice that this verse is spoken only by the three "exalted" characters, Margit, Signe, and Gudmund, who form a trinity of lyric consciousness above the level of the cruder (epic) characters who speak only prose. The conceptual intention that the higher and advanced lyric consciousness should stand out against the earlier and cruder epic consciousness from which it has evolved seems clear. This higher consciousness also is more complex and, in the person of Margit, undergoes a painful process of self-knowledge more profound than is possible for the "lower" characters. Such a hierarchy of consciousness, analogous to the hierarchy of rank in Elizabethan and neoclassical tragedy, suggests a new "spiritual aristocracy." The same hierarchy of consciousness will be present in Ibsen's modern bourgeois plays, creating a mental heroism in which the spiritually "advanced" individuals, those in whom the drama of human consciousness has evolved most profoundly, often undergo a suffering and sacrifice of which the "lower" characters are incapable.

Already in *The Feast at Solhoug* we encounter Ibsen's paradox that tragedy is the privilege of the fully human.

Acts 1 and 3 take place in a stately room whose scenic details indicate a historical/cultural conflict. On the right of the stage, by a bay window with lead panes, stands a small table with a collection of feminine ornaments, indicating social, civilizing, and female values at work upon the house but perhaps (in the detail of those lead bars on the windows) also suggesting constraint and imprisonment within wealth — themes that are stated directly in the dialogue. On the left side of the stage is a larger table, with silver tankards and goblets, indicative of a coarser (and masculine) lifestyle which, in the play, will degenerate into unruly drunken feasting. The door in the background opens onto a gallery through which is seen a wild fjord landscape. This purely natural, pre-civilized realm corresponds to the freer, passionate, and uncivilized reality underneath the tenuous cultural order and to the wilder areas of the individual psyche, as in Margit's passionate journey from the civilized and cultivated restraints that she attempts to impose upon reality to the frightening and murderous desires that lie just beneath.

If one were to describe the overall "concept" that the play is acting out, it would emerge as that of a painful dialectical upheaval, on many levels of existence, from the natural and unreflective and violent to the self-constrained, self-reflective, and "sublimated," a dialectical action undergone by a whole culture and, most intensely, by a representative individual. At the simplest level, we have the action of Knut Gjaesling's evolution as his unruly appetites give way to an acceptance of social law and decorum. At a higher level is Gudmund's civilizing sojourn in France and his importation into Norway of a new knightly chivalry that will enable the nation to take its place in the cultural community of Europe. At the most painful and profound level we have the drama of Margit's discovery of her own capacity for evil leading to her difficult renunciation of her passionate self for a morally and spiritually "higher" self when she decides to enter a convent. The new spiritual order that will emerge out of this painful dialectic is represented (not too vividly, it must be conceded) by Gudmund and Signe who have witnessed and understood

Margit's descent into crime and guilt without being compromised by it. It is Margit, however, who strikes one as best anticipating the more complex world that is evolving from this one. Therefore, whatever the defects of the play (and they are many), it does seek to create drama out of a serious concept, to create a dramatic form in which the working out of the fictional story and the dramatic "complications" is at the same time the working out of the concept.

The period of the play, the early fourteenth century, is one in which the earlier, "wild" Viking culture has only very recently and very uncertainly been subdued by the Christian and chivalric culture of medieval Europe — a cultural condition mirrored in the microcosmic situation of individual consciousnesses. The fjord landscape, all the time within view in act 1, keeps in mind the wild natural world from which the human community has evolved into social and civilized order, and in the linguistic structure of the play the more evolved "lyric" voices of Margit, Gudmund, and Signe continually "lapse" into balladic echoes of an earlier cultural phase. The lyric speeches, in fact, frequently are reformulations of or developments from the balladic material, revealing how close this lately attained subjective lyric voice still is to the objective and epic mode of Viking culture. The *subject* of the play, namely, the painful evolution to a higher phase of human consciousness, therefore, is reflected in the linguistic structure of the play as well as in its setting, characters, and actions. The play begins with the crude eroticism of Knut Gjaesling's bid for Signe, modulates through Margit's devastating jealousy and anguish, and ends with the attainment of the refined love of Gudmund for Signe. The dialogue, between Knut Gjaesling, Bengt, and Margit, begins in prose but as Margit's opposition to Knut increases in feeling (and thus in "subjective" content), she modulates to rhymed verse, to which the others reply in prose. Grasping the conceptual intention of this contrast removes much of its awkwardness for the reader. When the others leave, Margit's subjective exaltation is even more apparent, for she then delivers a long soliloquy in rhymed verse and goes on to sing a ballad whose story of a young girl, Kirsten, imprisoned in wealth and jewels by a mountain king, matches her own situation, as she is well aware. She expresses this awareness in the form of a pun. Young Kirsten's waist *(liv)* is encircled by a silver girdle just as Margit's life *(liv)* is imprisoned in an unhappy marriage. This is the first instance of a process that the three lyric characters undergo: of singing "epic" ballads and then adapting them to their individual, subjective situations in more complex "lyric" speeches. Hegel noted of this period in the northern world that its insistent subjective and lyric nature continually infected and distorted the often objective and nonlyric forms it attempted,[14] and something of this process is observable in the play.

Gudmund, the companion of Margit's youth and the man she truly loves but has betrayed by her marriage to Bengt, arrives from France where he had helped transact a marriage between Norway's king and the French princess, an alliance that will bring Norway into the circle of civilized Europe. But the chivalric culture of civilized Europe also is more ambiguous and with the complexity comes evil. The French princess, in the manner of Iseult with Tristan, falls in love with Audun, the king's ambassador, and plots with him to kill the king with a vial of poison. They are interrupted in their plotting by Gudmund and implausibly abandon the vial of poison which Gudmund takes up and reveals to Margit, who finally will gain possession of it. Although crudely introduced, the metaphor is that of poison and corruption in foreign and high places filtering down into the house of Solhoug and into the consciousness of Margit — the seemingly exotic, alien, and sinister which comes to be recognized and acknowledged as one's own. The psychological drama of Margit and Gudmund is linked to the national and cultural drama, implying that both individual and universal processes are taking place, simultaneously.

In the ensuing dialogue of crossed meanings between Gudmund and Margit, we see how far Ibsen has advanced in devising a multilayered dramatic technique. Pretending to be content with her loathed marriage and to be indifferent to Gudmund whom she still loves, Margit receives him coldly in front of her husband who, in turn, is delighted by what he supposes is a display of wifely devotion. Gudmund, meanwhile, is mortified and engages in a strained dialogue with Margit, and the give and take of this dialogue is both good theater and excellent character protrayal. Margit's pride forbids her to reveal her true feelings of humiliation, while

Gudmund's pride is offended by Margit's display of cold civility and artifice, a false civility which is the negative aspect of her cultivated mind. The dialogue of reciprocal shocks expresses the psychological drama within the minds of the protagonists; though not yet fully developed, this is the poetry of an "inner" dimension of reality which we can detect "between the lines." The naive awkwardness of so much of the play should not blind us to the very real advances in his art that Ibsen is making and that evolve into the later mastery. In the little exchange between Gudmund and Margit one can see the beginnings of the new dramatic language that Ibsen will create. This is a language of the subjective and even subconscious movements of individual psyches, a notation of shocks, recoils, half-suppressed rushes of emotion, half-finished sentences, pauses, and silences, and it achieves in prose a delicacy and accuracy as fine as anything in verse.

Soon after his return from France, Gudmund recounts, he was victimized by the guilty chancellor Audun (who realized Gudmund overheard his plotting with the French princess). He has had to live as an outlaw in the wild landscape that has served him as a refuge from the corrupt civilized world, for, with typical irony, the wild and savage that needs to be tamed by culture is also the natural, uncontaminated by corrupt culture. Signe, who seems to us a more insipid object of Gudmund's affections than Margit, is, I believe, meant to represent the synthesis of the natural and the civilized that has eluded Margit and that is the ideal of the play's argument.

Gudmund sings to Signe and Margit a song that describes two aspects of love, one joyful, the other sorrowful, and each woman repeats the lines appropriate to her own situation. The two women thus repeat the Furia-Aurelia duality, but here the urgent tensions of the earlier play have been softened considerably into literary and aesthetic symmetry and contrast. The act closes with the chorus singing in praise of hospitality and blessing the house of Solhoug — a reminder of the civilizing ideal of this play.

In act 2 we move closer to the natural world. The setting is a birch grove adjoining the house, and into this grove runs a waterfall from the wilder hillside. This is perhaps a visual analogy to the human situation, where emotions and passions from "nature" have entered into the constraints of civilized life. The house (left), the birch grove (center), and the waterfall (right) create a visual progression from the social to the purely natural realms, and vice versa — a further elaboration and subtilization of Ibsen's scenic symbolism. The action opens with the chorus singing in praise of music, dance, and young eager love, blending the civilized and aesthetic with the natural and instinctual. Knut Gjaesling and Eric enter, debating whether to capture the outlawed Gudmund and so obey the king's law which, we learn, operates only feebly in the countryside; this is another indication that the period is a time of cultural transition from the primitive and natural to the civilized. Gudmund and Signe enter, their declaration of mutual love, in its reticence and naturalness, contrasting with both the barbarous nature of Knut Gjaesling's eroticism and the civilized perversity of Margit's. The lovers' evocation, in their speeches, of the elfin and natural-picturesque may make us impatient, but we should note that Ibsen intends the lovers to represent an innocent yet delicately responsive sensibility.

On Signe's exit Margit enters and the innocence of the earlier dialogue now gives way to her darker consciousness, where thoughts of love for Gudmund are linked with thoughts of murder of her husband. Margit is haunted by the image of the vial of poison which already has poisoned her imagination, a heavy signaling of the events to come in act 3. The vial is being built so obviously into the play's argument at this point that its forceful use later becomes inevitable. This is, it is true, a "Scribean" use of the stage prop, but whereas Scribe's purpose was to displace the burden of dramatic significance from *language*, with its ideological risks, onto neutral *things*, thus creating a dramatic excitement free from conceptual danger, Ibsen was to see in "things" vehicles of metaphoric and conceptual implication matching, and supplementing, that of language. The *formulas* of the well-made plays of Scribe, Dumas *fils*, Augier, and Sardou created a purely materialist world, safely inexpressive of ideaological or metaphysical content. Objects, like a glass of water, a locked bureau, a sealed envelope, a vial of poison, might be employed for deadly or comic effect according to the chance of the action, but their properties never were allowed to embrace more than materialist significance. The playwrights, seeking to excite and please a materialist bourgeois audience while trying not to offend the Bourbon censorship, were careful *not* to let their stage worlds take on the dangerous coloring of ethical, ideological, or metaphysical realities. By banishing these rational dimensions of reality, such seemingly innocuous entertainments, like those of Broadway and Hollywood today, actually served a harmful political purpose.

But Ibsen perceived that objects, things, could be made into metaphors for the excluded ethical, ideological, and metaphysical dimensions of reality, and thus could restore rationality (in the Hegelian sense of that term) to the theatrical image of the world. It was Ibsen's genius to see that through the symbolic shaping of scene and objects the theater could regain what modern discourse had lost.

A scene of multiple misunderstandings between the four lovers now follows as Knut and Signe, Margit and Gudmund, in a series of half-finished sentences and "asides," speak totally at cross-purposes, enabling everyone to draw the wrong conclusions. The conscientious technical virtuosity of this leaves the reader cold, but the action does at least place the four lovers in contrasting roles for the audience's contemplation. Knut Gjaesling threatens bloodshed, and we detect the underlying theme of the passions in conflict both with love and with civilized community, an ironic contrast to the opening words of the chorus. Margit painfully struggles with her clashing inclinations and her sense of duty. Her long speech (after which she collapses), is a more poignant retelling of the ballad of young Kirsten and the mountain king, now rendered far more directly and subjectively in terms of her own personal situation, so that she exhibits that subjective lyric consciousness working upon objective and epic ballad material which Ibsen described in his essay on Paludan-Müller's poems. She now weaves into the story of Kirsten the theme of the minstrel and his harp, representing Gudmund, and emphasizes the total desolation of the unhappy wife.

The third act opens with another long, passionate soliloquy by Margit, in which she first relates a conventional tale of a child born blind, then freely applies its example to her own situation. The painful self-knowledge and turmoil revealed by this speech, which concludes with her hesitating to poison her husband, show how far Margit has traveled in psychological self-exploration and self-knowledge. It is as if we were witnessing one of the births of a new form of consciousness — or self-consciousness — that succeed each other so momentously in Hegel's *Phenomenology.* The transition from this speech to the heavy and contrived business with the goblet and the vial of poison is something of a hard jolt, but the goblet scene, bad as it is, is doing more than a first view would suggest. The goblet is given weighty symbolic significance so that it is used for more than merely melodramatic purpose. It is the one treasure from Margit's happier past that has been brought into Solhoug, a treasure, also, with which Gudmund was directly linked. It represents to her the nature of her sacrifice, and her husband's boorish unawareness of that sacrifice is evidenced in the way in which he greedily drinks from the goblet. Raymond Williams's complaint, in *Drama in Performance,*[15] that the goblet has taken over the center of the stage as "the principal actor" and that, unlike the duel scene in *Hamlet,* the scene fails to enact the complexities verbally established, is only partly correct. It is true that in this scene language is used at times mainly to keep up the confusion, but the scene is loaded with more ironies, carefully established, than Williams allows, ironies inhering in the intricate symbolism of the goblet and in its various uses by Bengt, Margit, Signe, and Gudmund which further clarify the nature of their interrelationship. The scene is heavily handled, but we should see that in his use of the stage prop Ibsen is attempting something more consequential than merely resorting to a hackneyed melo-dramatic device. The symbolic fatefulness of objects on the stage will later be a major source of Ibsen's poetic strength, so it is not difficult to view sympathetically his apprentice work in this field.

The play's emphasis upon the transition to a gentler, chivalric condition perhaps accounts for the strange squeamishness (strange for the period dramatized) over *killing* that the characters express. Such squeamishness indicates that the old, heroic, warrior, and Viking culture is being left behind. Bengt is killed, and Margit thereby freed from her hated marriage, but he is killed in the dark, by accident, by Knut Gjaesling who is deeply penitent. Not only Margit, therefore, but the whole culture, is moving to a "higher" stage of consciousness. Margit, having felt "the deep remorse, the frantic fear/Which comes on those who risk their soul"[16] resolves to enter a convent. Gudmund is pardoned and rewarded by the king so that his chivalric honesty is honored at court — although there may be an ominous aspect in the fact that Gudmund's enemy, Audun, is beheaded for offending the queen who, we remember, plotted with him to murder the king. The transition is not entirely to sweetness and light and the cultural phase that is to succeed this medieval one, that of the renaissance (the period of *Lady Inger of Østraat*), will give rise to more problematic concepts of individuality and personal guilt. For the present, however, Gudmund and Signe can celebrate their innocent love while the sun rises on the scene. Margit's wonderful delivery from evil and Gudmund's no less wondrous delivery from outlawry and disgrace perhaps represent the sense of the miraculous and marvelous that is inherent in this cultural phase, a theme to be explored more fully in the next play, *Olaf Liliekrans*. The faults of *The Feast at Solhoug* are not difficult to detect (although they hardly are grosser than those of *Titus Andronicus*); more difficult to detect, but more interesting, is the serious *concept* that the play represents. It is the simplest thing in the world to dismiss the play as a "failure" but much harder, and more rewarding, to applaud the great increase in conceptual and formal mastery as Ibsen seeks to make his art responsive to an ever increasing grasp of reality.

OLAF LILIEKRANS

In *The Feast at Solhoug* the consciousnesses of the individual characters in the play and the consciousness of the cultural phase to which they belonged were shown undergoing a transition from the balladic to the lyric form. The main characters, Margit, Gudmund, and Signe, stood at only a short remove from the realm of balladic expression; they continually recited or quoted from ballads and adapted balladic themes and stories to their own condition. Ballad, one might say, was the imaginative form that the characters had only recently left behind. *Olaf Liliekrans*, on the other hand, is rooted directly in the balladic consciousness; the play is, in fact, a dramatized ballad, and this accounts for the unusual simplicity or naiveté with which the story is told. Unlike the lyric conscious-ness, that of the ballad lacks the quality of self-reflection; charac-ters express their thoughts and feelings with naive, forceful, and unreflective directness. In his essay on the heroic ballad, which can be taken as the theoretical "ground" for both *The Feast at Solhoug* and *Olaf Liliekrans,* Ibsen puts the ballad in the same (Hegelian) category as the epic. It is an essentially "objective" form because "literacy subjectivity has no significance for the people; they do not care about the poet, only about his work insofar as they recog-nize in this a particular aspect of their own personality. . . ."[17] Yet the ballad is closer to the lyric form than is the epic and so is more suitable than the latter for dramatic treatment. This suggests that whereas *The Feast at Solhoug* is a drama of the lyric conscious-ness looking back to its recent balladic past, *Olaf Liliekrans* is a drama of the balladic consciousness looking forward to its lyric future. This, in fact, does seem to be the nature of the latter play, in which a balladic naiveté is continually straining toward lyric expression.

Lacking the subjectivity of the lyric mode, *Olaf Liliekrans* is bound to lack the dimension of "inner" drama that characterized *The Feast at Solhoug.* More drastically than the earlier play, *Olaf Lielikrans* depicts a phase of violent *transition.* In his article on the heroic ballad, Ibsen notes how strongly heathen elements are present in the ballads but "on a quite different and higher level than in the mythic stories, and it is by reason of this that the poetic offshoot of Christianity, romanticism, manifests its influ-ence on the ballad."[18] The dismayingly extravagant romantic aspects of *Olaf Liliekrans,* in which the wild, natural, semi-heathen, and mantic surround, like an aura, the characters Alfhild and Thorgjeir, would seem to be a deliberate artistic (and thematic) choice on Ibsen's part as he tries to re-create the spirit of the period, in which a still pagan consciousness was being "tamed" by Christianity.

With a rare lack of critical skepticism Ibsen presents a number of basic themes of Romantic doctrine: the contrast between un-corrupted Nature and corrupt human society, between imaginative and prosaic reality, and so on. Some faint dialectical element is introduced through the fact that both natural innocence and corrupt culture are extremes that must meet for mutual qualification, so that Alfhild, the naive inhabitant of wild nature, must take on the "alienated" knowledge of guilt and suffering whereas her lover, the "alienated" Olaf, is led to rediscover a lost purity and strength to be found only through his vision's awakened response to the splendid realm of Nature. Alfhild's father, Thorgjeir, is a Romantic convention: the wanderer, outcast, and seer, in communion with both Nature and the supernatural. He very likely derives from the original wanderer, Odin, for, as Ibsen notes in his essay on the ballad, the old pagan and mythic figures, with the legends surrounding them, were transmuted into the more romantic themes of the ballads. In terms of thematic composition, therefore, *Olaf Liliekrans* is substantial. It is Ibsen's decision to re-create the naive directness of the balladic imagination by means of an equally naive dramatic method that makes the play so unacceptable to modern taste, although one can understand how, at the time, when the Norwegian nation was re-creating its identity as it prepared to become one of the modern community of nations, this aesthetic re-creation of its past possessed great interest.

Through visual details the play draws a contrast between magnificently spacious natural scenery and the confined, cramped, and unsatisfactory human community. Acts 1 and 3 are romantically splendid scenes of Norwegian landscapes, perhaps reflecting Ibsen's recent tour, in 1856, of the Hardanger area. One also is reminded of Ibsen's paintings of the Norwegian landscape. So overwhelming is this natural setting (very similar to that employed by Schiller in *Wilhelm Tell*), which is seen first in the red glow of sunset, then bathed in moonlight, that the extravagent claims the play makes for the natural and naive almost become acceptable. The action of the play similarly is devised to bring out the contrast between the natural and the "alienated" conditions. All the evil action takes place in act 2, the setting of which is the cramped, confined social enclosure of house (right), church (back center), and large storehouse (left), with the three buildings contriving to shut out the natural vistas. This setting represents a society that has turned its back upon the natural and instinctual world, fearing it as a place of heathen enchantment, and that looks instead to a God it encloses in a ludicrously small stave church.

In the world of human society, all relationships have become problematic and mutually damaging. Arne is tormented by his headstrong and willful daughter, Ingeborg, who, in turn, cruelly torments her young servant, Hemming, by alternately encouraging and snubbing him. Olaf is dominated by his snobbish mother, Lady Kirsten, who has persuaded him to enter into a disastrous relationship with Ingeborg to save her economically vulnerable estate. Unsatisfactory relationships of parent-child, husband-wife, master-servant, and higher and lower classes are all presented in act 1 in swift review — an image of a multiply alienated society. In the past, we learn, there was quarreling and fighting between the two neighboring estates of Arne and Lady Kirsten, and this conflict could flare up again at any moment. Surrounding this unhappy community, at a remove, is the vast landscape, unexplored by the socially constrained characters who fear it as a realm of dangerous magic. The Black Death has swept through the land in the recent past, decimating its inhabitants and leaving behind a few, strange, outcast survivors like Thorgjeir and Alfhild who live in the natural world, cut off from communication with human society.

A major weakness of the play is the distinctly operatic nature of its compositon (Ibsen was to begin a revision of the play as a Romantic opera), which accounts for the extravagent implausibility of many of its situations. Opera audiences are trained to pay careful inattention to wild implausibilities of stage situation which exist only to provide the occasion for extravagent lyric expression, but the dramatist does not enjoy this privilege (if it *is* one). *Olaf Liliekrans* contains more music than any other Ibsen play as it seeks to create a balladic mood; but, unlike opera, which is consistent in the musical convention it is employing, the musical elements of *Olaf Liliekrans* merely add to the stylistic confusion. The play open with two choruses alternately singing. The first, Lady Kirsten's retinue, is searching for Olaf who has disappeared from home on the eve of his wedding. The second, Arne's retinue, is on the way to the wedding feast, singing in celebration of the event. The first chorus calls out to Olaf, warning him against the dangerous and treacherous world of heathen enchantment in the countryside, for the Christianity of this society still is fighting against the native spiritual traditions. The heathen and natural is

contrasted with the Christian and social. Alfhild declares the
Christian church too small and derides its claim to be the house of
God; it is the huge and splendid house of nature that is God's
true home (a theme that is more consequentially developed in
Brand). At the end of the play, however, having come to know
pain, suffering, and guilt, Alfhild invokes the angelic retinue of
God, in penitence, suggesting her advance from pagan innocence
to the fallen estate of Christianity.

The period of the play is the same as that of *The Feast at Solhoug*, but it deals far less with the historical and social aspects of
the time. Instead, it takes up the medieval-romantic aspects of
magic and fantasy as found in the ballads — including the ballad
Olaf Liliekrans on which the play is partly based. Alfhild herself
first appears by moonlight to Olaf and, for much of the play, is
viewed as supernatural by him, enchanting him to new visionary
understanding. Thorgjeir, Alfhild's dismayingly mantic father, has
preserved the tales and songs of the past and has educated his
daughter in this heritage. As in *St. John's Night*, the past is seen
almost entirely as a rich and beneficial heritage qualified only by
Alfhild's realization that her father's account of life in the valley
does not square with the facts of her experience there. In Alfhild,
the innocent, visionary, and idealistic spirit longs to take part in
life and is lured toward the human community and its problematic
realities. Olaf, by contrast, struggles against the coils of this community's hold upon him and yearns to be lifted up to the visionary
realm of Alfhild. The account of this visionary realm as elfin,
magical, and picturesque, enthusiastically transmitted to us
through the wild poetic outbursts of Thorgjeir, is difficult to
tolerate. Ibsen nevertheless is depicting a serious spiritual division,
similar to the "unhappy consciousness" in Hegel's account of the
Christian-medieval world, in which the actual realm on one level
and the idealistic on the other have developed into mutually antithetical extremes that only the most drastic action can overcome.
Thorgjeir's disastrously inadequate notions of the nature of life
and death in the actual world — pretty fantasies that Alfhild's
first encounter with human reality will contradict — are the result
of an idealism that keeps itself totally undefiled by reality. Similarly the narrowly social and materialist concerns within which the

spirits of Lady Kirsten and Arne remain confined represent a spiritual darkness desperately in need of an active idealism. The strongest emblem of this materialism is the loveless arranged marriage between Olaf and Ingeborg. To the Romantic spirit, such a marriage (which even Peer Gynt rejects when it is offered him by Ingrid) would be a crime against the most sacred of human relationships. A drama of such drastic dualisms must lead to extremes of action, which it does with Alfhild's frenzied attempt to burn down the entire community.

For a dialectic of such extremes, the highly wrought, vividly immediate presentation of events derived from ballad or rendered in terms of balladic simplicity is appropriate though it hardly encourages dramatic subtlety or complexity. In an attempt to offset the too evident simplicity of the play, Ibsen once again resorts to a passage of strained ingenuity in which Lady Kirsten and Hemming, each assuming the other knows what he or she means, feel totally unobliged to express themselves in a manner by which they can be understood, thus allowing for the most radical misunderstandings. This, however, is only a token attempt at dramatic virtuosity and complexity of situation and is, mercifully, short-lived.

Like Anne and Birk, Alfhild and Olaf receive an education in sorrow and guilt before they attain a happy union. Somewhat like the daughter of Indra in Strindberg's *A Dream Play* and Hilde in *The Master Builder* (which repeats many themes of *Olaf Liliekrans*), Alfhild descends from her innocent "heaven" into the hell of human life, taking on the experience of misery, guilt, and painful separation, an experience that shatters her naive idealism. At the end of the play she accepts and blesses this experience and permanently joins the human community, thanking the "angels" who have guided her steps to this destination. This acceptance of the human community and of the process by which she became integrated into it marks a new strength in her own spirit while it initiates a spiritual advance within the community, which had turned away from the ideal and visionary realm. Thorgjeir refuses to settle in the community, but Olaf promises he will build a hut (strikingly similar to the "hermit-grottoes" of fashionable country estates in eighteenth-century England) in which the wandering seer can visit the young couple from time to time, presumably to help them maintain links with the natural and visionary realm.

Olaf Liliekrans is without doubt Ibsen's weakest play. But it marks the darkness before the dawn, for the plays that follow, beginning with *The Vikings at Helgeland,* show an increasing dramatic power and a widening range of conceptual implication. And the intellectual forces that are so misapplied in the creation of *Olaf Liliekrans* are substantial and in one sense mark a real advance over *Lady Inger of Østraat,* since the dramatic plot is constructed as an argument as well as an aesthetic design. Apart from a small amount of superfluous confusion between Hemming and Lady Kirsten, Ibsen dispenses with the tiresome devices of the well-made play. The baldly presented supernatural elements of the story remove it from the realm of serious drama, but the metaphysical dimensions of experience that they symbolize were to remain vital elements of Ibsen's later and greater dramas.

THE VIKINGS AT HELGELAND

In the swift, highly charged dramatic opening of *The Vikings at Helgeland* (1858), the old Viking, Ørnulf, encounters and challenges the young Viking, Sigurd, while the followers of both prepare for battle. That the whole tense situation is built up and completed within twenty lines of dialogue indicates how far Ibsen has advanced in dramatic artistry since *Catiline,* written only eight years earlier. The same opening scene, however, points to a major flaw in the play, in the way Ibsen has conceived his form and subject matter, for passions and sentiments of such stark simplicity, nobility, and ferocity lack the dimensions of human complexity and subtlety that alone make for interesting dramatic life. The opening scene is a superb painter's composition, with its rival factions grouped at opposite sides of the canvas and its center occupied by the two leaders of the groups. But this vivid pictorial effect has been gained by means of an aesthetic externality, an aesthetic manipulation and "composition" of elements which, though extraordinarily deft, prevents us from becoming deeply involved with the events dramatized.

So epic and one-dimensional are the major characters, in fact, so singly the embodiment of the particular point of honor they defend or feel has been offended, that one somewhat guiltily warms to the villainous and cowardly peasant, Kaare, for at least briefly introducing a degree of psychological multi-dimensionality into the play's texture. In spite of its considerable formal beauty, *The Vikings at Helgeland* compels one to conclude that Ibsen's earlier doubts about the suitability of saga material for dramatic treatment were justified. For all its saga-fierceness, the play is a "version of pastoral," since the characters and the world they inhabit are the naive objects of our more sophisticated attention. They live, if at all, across a gulf, in a world that has no connection with our own. A reviewer of the first London performance likened the characters to creatures from another planet, and one can see what he meant. Characters who can be roused so unreflectingly to passion and murder, to feeling the deadliness of insult or wrong to the exclusion of any other emotion or thought, do not invite or sustain our interest, however consistently, within the terms of their own world, they may act. One admires the skillfulness with which Ibsen has created a world so distant and alien from our own, giving it laws that its characters obey down to their logical conclusions; but the result is somehow only distantly instructive. If authors create characters below their and their audience's intellectual level, they at least need to surround them with authorial irony, so that we may find something of ourselves in the drama. However, any breath of irony would kill off Ibsen's Vikings immediately, for they exist in a pure ether of aesthetic "epic" atmosphere sealed off from contamination by humor, irony, or common sense.

This is not to say the play is a failure. It works impressively and is Ibsen's first wholly successful play, but it is successful in a way singularly unhelpful to the development of a modern dramatic art. We have already suggested what may have been the compulsion behind Ibsen's resolve, after *St. John's Night,* successively to "mime" more and more distant epochs of his nation's history — or identity. Nevertheless, the great amount of dramatic and imaginative skill that has gone into the play's construction, testifying to an imposing dramatic talent, seems to us, today, somewhat pointlessly expended, and reveals what a long way there is yet to go before modern drama, through Ibsen, will discover its form and subject. A major problem Ibsen faces and does not solve in *The Vikings at Helgeland* is that the cultural phase he is portraying could not give rise to a *dramatic* art (for during the cultural phase of the "objective" epic individuals do not exist at the level of self-reflection nor at that of civic, ethical conflict out of which a truly dramatic conflict arises. Characters and their actions are consequently "below" the level of the art form in which they are depicted. The world of the story is disjunctively different from the world in which the theater exists, and to render this world convincingly, the theater has to negate itself and its audience rather than address itself and its audience. All major theater, however, always dramatizes itself and its own cultural conditon. The conventions of classical Greek, Elizabethan, and French neoclassical theater always kept in mind the world in which the theater and its audience existed, maintaining an interplay between the myth or fiction being related and the contemporary sensibility observing it. In Ibsen's modern realistic plays the characters onstage conceivably could be in the audience: Nora and Torvald Helmer or Hedda Gabler could have just returned from seeing a play like *A Doll House* or *Hedda Gabler* as the curtain rises on their drama. The lack of such an interplay between the world on the stage and that of the auditorium is, of course, a problem with historical drama generally, and the gulf between the two worlds is usually bridged (in Shakespearean and Schillerian historical drama) by fairly blatant anachronism. The public's increasingly sophisticated historical sense in the nineteenth century made such anachronism less acceptable (although Ibsen was to resort to such a device in Bishop Nicholas's return from the dead to address the audience in *The Pretenders*), so that, paradoxically, with the better understanding of history, historical drama became more limited in its scope. In *The Vikings at Helgeland* the conscientious resolve to be faithful to the spiritual phase being dramatized, even to the extent of creating an archaic language for the characters, locks them in their alien world where there is no possibility of communicating to us.

Similarly, what at first looks like a real advance in dramatic technique — the abandoning of the "operatic" quality we found in the lyric drama *The Feast at Solhoug* and the balladic drama *Olaf Liliekrans,* and the absence of asides to the audience — very likely is due to the fact that the objective saga material, with its "epic" nature, denies the characters the subjective consciousness from which lyric speech and the aside derive. Another paradox, then, is that though the characters of *The Vikings at Helgeland* are more primitive than their counterparts in the lyric drama *The Feast at Solhoug,* they also are the products of a higher order of dramatic artistry. The play, in fact, is a literary *tour de force.* One is once again aware of Ibsen's somewhat poignant situation of having to create his national dramatic tradition rather than inheriting it. For he was not living at a time of excited rediscovery and invention of dramatic form, like the Elizabethan age, but at a time of great cultural sophistication where an awareness of highly evolved dramatic forms already existed. In Norway itself, however, these forms had not taken root. Much of Ibsen's preoccupation with the cultural past in the early plays that follow in sequence from *St. John's Night* to *The Vikings at Helgeland* may be due less to nationalist pride than to his concern with creating a collective artistic identity, a spiritual heritage, which then could be drawn upon and developed. The intention might have been less to depict "how great we were and, by implication, are" than to depict "what we were and, by implication, are." Thus there need be no quarrel among nationalism, aesthetics, and philosophy such as we found in the character of Poulson in the play inaugurating this series of explorations of the past. Poulson is absurd precisely because he cannot synthesize these aspects by thinking them through to the point where their apparent comic contradictions are adequately overcome. In Poulson, "aestheticism and nationism fought a life and death struggle in my breast,"[19] but in *The Vikings at Helgeland,* far from their being at odds, the aesthetic purpose of the play is perfectly fulfilled by the nationalist purpose and vice versa. This means that the effectiveness of the play depends upon a limited idea of dramatic adequacy whereby the consistent sustaining of illusion in the archaic fiction, by means of a highly artificial and literary idea of Viking life, takes the place of the truly artistic compulsion to reveal reality by means of artistic form. *The Vikings at Helgeland* is the perfect aesthetic rendition of Viking themes, an extremely skillful shaping and plotting that is performed with a remarkable suspension of rational-critical vision. The play operates, as it were, by means of strained artistic faith on both the author's and the audience's parts, and the great effort needed to sustain the fiction cannot permit a critical commentary upon the reality purportedly offered. To attempt to write as if within the Viking spirit means not to examine critically a character such as Hjordis; yet a character so appallingly destructive, so solely preoccupied with wrongs done to herself and so indifferent to wrongs suffered by others is, unless critically presented, only irritatingly repellant. Her motives for action seem dictated by incessant hysteria deriving from a megalomaniacal conception of self-worth. There is no way one can get "near" such a character, and the characters surrounding her, who are grievously affected by her, seem unable to react reasonably and firmly to her. Normal responses and reactions are abandoned for a scale of "heroic" acting that, to succeed, would have to be grandly theatrical and external in the High Victorian mode.

Yet within this antiquated tradition Ibsen creates the most assured dramatic structure of his career to date. The very limitations of the epic and objective reality being dramatized, free of all multilayered subjectivity, help create a tense and urgent action not unlike the very lean realism of the sagas. The coincidences upon which the plot rests are artistically unobtrusive. The one sequence of mistaken meanings (the last appearance of this device in Ibsen's drama), young Thorolf's ambiguous references to his father's pursuit of Egil, does cause a catastrophe but it is plausibly rooted in its situation, for this time the verbal ambiguity is deliberate. Thorolf wishes to wound his enemies and speaks in a way that will alarm them, so that the catastrophe is a nemesis attendant upon the Viking spirit of sensitive honor.

The aesthetic emphasis of the play is evident in the symmetry of its plotting. The two outer acts, 1 and 4, represent a complementary pair, being set in desolate coastal scenery and beginning and ending in storm and human conflict. The two inner acts, 2 and 3, similarly balance each other, being set in the banquet room of Gunnar's house as they proceed to explore the crossed relationships of the two pairs of lovers. Beginning and ending thus in battle and winter storm, the play throughout sustains an action of high, urgent conflict.

The opening contest, between the old and the young Viking, is over the space (the boat house) each seeks to occupy, resembling the struggle of two male animals for territory. The conflict then becomes that of securing the safety of the woman, Dagny, against that of the men, Ørnulf's followers. Sigurd's chivalric higher estimate of the woman's value is perhaps the first slight indication of his conversion to Christianity until he reveals this fact at the end of the play; for the pagan, warrior culture is depicted as contemptuous of women. Thorolf, Ørnulf, and Hjördis all speak scornfully of women, and this devaluation may be a judgment on the masculine warrior culture. Ørnulf, the old representative of this warrior culture, ends up alone and childless; Sigurd's friend Gunnar and Gunnar's son, Egil, seem in their gentler natures to prefigure the new order. When the boy, Thorolf, whose high warrior spirit contributes tellingly to the most dramatic scene in the play, is killed by Gunnar at Hjördis's instigation, Egil, on hearing of his death, exclaims: "If Thorolf is dead I won't get my fighting men,"[20] a comment that seems to hint at the extinction of the old Viking culture, as does the conversion of its greatest warrior, Sigurd to Christianity.

That it should be the bold warrior Sigurd, and not the rational and gentler Gunnar, who is Christianized seems at first an anomaly. But Ibsen's procedure, here as in the earlier plays, is to link the personal drama of individuals with the drama of a larger cultural/ spiritual transition; only through a figure such Sigurd, who, like Gandalf of *The Burial Mound,* sums up the Viking spirit at its best, could the conversion to the new spiritual order gain such significance. Through Sigurd, also, we see how elements within the Viking and pagan culture are evolving into the new Christian order: the pagan compact of blood-brotherhood between Sigurd and Gunnar, which causes Sigurd to act with such mildness under almost intolerable pressure, anticipates the ideal of Christian brotherhood and Christian mildness that will be the aspiration of the later spiritual phase.

The spirit of the old order that must pass away is manifested

in its simplest, most poignant form by old Ørnulf and his youngest
son, Thorolf. In Thorolf we see the proud, high-spirited, and masculine basis of the Viking culture at its most attractive. His death
at the instigation of Hjördis (who, though hardly representative
of the female principle, *has* been wronged as a woman by Sigurd
and Gunnar) leaves the childless Ørnulf devastated and seems to
portend the passing of the Viking world itself.

Hjördis also is the incarnation of the warrior spirit, but, because
she is a woman, she is excluded from the realm of significant warrior activity. Such sexual one-sidedness would need to be overcome by recognizing that women's participation in the culture
demands equivalent recognition. A Hedda Gabler without Hedda's
subtlety, Hjördis is an unremittingly quarrelsome nature destroying spirits finer than herself. Her fierce pride, so totally uncompromising, strikes one, finally, as unintelligent, and one is somewhat
exasperated at the way the milieu of the play literally lets her get
away with murder. Her enormous vindictiveness, before which the
other characters are so helpless, makes her a northern Medea without Medea's more substantial cause of grievance. Ibsen's determination to take her seriously harms the credibility of the play.
The exalted perspective from which the characters view themselves
denies them the quality of humor — the generous-spirited rough
humor that is a redeeming characteristic of many of the sagas and
of the warrior type. This absence of humor disqualifies the play's
claim to be truly representative of the Viking spirit.

"The humanization of the mythic figures," which, Ibsen explained to the readers of the German edition of the play, he had
undertaken, led to the creation of characters with realistic attributes responding to events that have supernatural and superhuman
origins. Hjördis is a Valkyrie who is given a specific situation within a network of merely human characters whom she then finds
wanting owing to their less than superhuman traits. Viewing
Hjördis, one is put in mind of Jack's comment, in *The Importance
of Being Earnest*, that Lady Bracknell was a monster without
being a myth, which was not fair. A heroine whose bedroom is
guarded by a great white bear which has to be overcome by the
young man destined to be her mate — a task no young man has
been able to fulfill — is a figure of pure myth, in the same league

with Turandot and the many *femmes fatales* of legend who set their suitors lethally impossible tasks. Such a mythic figure can only incongruously complain of injuries to her *human* feelings, yet Hjördis massively and monotonously complains about this and murderously holds others accountable. The mythic aspect of her identity cannot be assimilated satisfactorily into the human world in which Ibsen places her. She remains a "great part" for a tragic actress, but it is a part calling for sonorous external versatility rather than inward authenticity. A German actress did have great difficulty understanding the motives from which Hjördis acts until Ibsen provided her with a reason: that because Sigurd did not make love to Hjördis on their night together, she doubted that he really loved her. But this hardly reconciles us to her vindictiveness and reduces her moreover to the tiresome cliché of the woman scorned compared with whom hell hath no fury.

One dwells thus on the character of Hjördis because the problem with Hjördis vividly exemplifies the problem with the play generally. The characters and events are seen and created with an admirable definiteness and vividness, but it is the definiteness and vividness of fantasy. There is no compellingly rendered intervening realm between the stark conflict of ego with ego and the exaltedly mythic and universal level to which this suddenly is raised. Greek drama, employing myth, was at the same time ethically and philosophically substantial. One feels that a solid, diversified as well as intellectually subtle *contemporary* world is implicated in the actions of an Orestes, an Oedipus, or an Antigone, that a brilliant and subtle civic community, Athens, finds its most immediate as well as its most universal interests involved in the dramatic ritual. The Norwegian audience viewing *The Vikings at Helgeland*, on the other hand, could only find its fantasy-reflection, the most flattering and unchallenging idea of its Viking past, embodied by the glamorous devices of the theater. One understands why, later, Ibsen made such a point of having finally freed himself from "aestheticism" for, although *The Vikings at Helgeland* is the most perfect of Ibsen's early plays, the artistic perfection entails the sacrifice of art's most serious purposes.

With *The Vikings at Helgeland* Ibsen concludes the series of plays whose major purpose seems to be progressive exploration, in dramatic form, of past phases of the Norwegian consciousness, finding forms of expression and juxtapositions of "epic," "lyric," and "dramatic" structures that were meant to reproduce what he felt was the essence of these phases. Björnson's criticism of the artificially archaic language of the play, and Ibsen's concession that the more contemporary language of Björnson's *Sigurd Slembe* (1862) was more suitable to the age, seems to have prompted Ibsen to abandon the finally self-defeating attempt to mime the imagined spiritual forms of the past. Ibsen was to write two more historical plays, *The Pretenders* and *Emperor and Galilean,* and in these he allows his plays to speak directly to the present in the language of the present. The play that follows *The Vikings at Helgeland, Love's Comedy,* deals, for the first time since *St. John's Night,* with contemporary reality. The break is not as radical as it seems, because Ibsen's present now will be filled with these layers of the past that he had explored so conscientiously; only when Ibsen recognized that the heroic past in its original form was lost forever could he begin to rediscover its transmutations into the multilayered life of the present.

THE ACHIEVED ART
Love's Comedy
and *The Pretenders*

Catiline and *The Burial Mound,* at the beginning of Ibsen's career, exhibit, separately, the embryonic forms of opposite aspects of Ibsen's later development as a dramatist. *Love's Comedy* and *The Pretenders,* embodying Ibsen's artistic mastery, present two contrasting strengths of Ibsen's art: the creation of dramatic structures that are at the same time poetic arguments, and the creation of a completely convincing dramatic realism. For those who believe that Ibsen's "poetic ideology" (as Bjorn Hemmer has termed it)[1] is the main thing, *Love's Comedy* will hold the greater interest. Those who are most enamored of Ibsen's ability to present us with the illusion of "real life" will prefer *The Pretenders.* The predominantly psychological and moral interpretation of Ibsen in recent times has meant that *The Pretenders* generally is held in higher esteem. My own preference for *Love's Comedy* no doubt reflects the emphasis of this book.

Whereas the argument of *Love's Comedy* is fully explored through scenic and character-type metaphors, which sustain a clear pattern of imagery and action that all the time illuminates the evolving thought, the argument of *The Pretenders* is limited by the nature of the historical subject matter which the dramatic fiction must adhere to. It is the modern discussion drama in verse

102

rather than the historical drama in prose that most clearly points to the great achievement of Ibsen's mature work. *The Pretenders,* though possibly a better *play* because its themes have been translated into theatrical actions, is less impressive in terms of its total argument. It is with *Love's Comedy* that Ibsen first marks out for himself the dramatic world that he was to master so incomparably: the dialectical drama of characters of the modern age, yearningly or fearfully, consciously or unconsciously, responsive to the huge legacy of the spiritual past and to the surrounding cosmos, yet inplicated urgently within the little community of present-day society. This may be why G. Wilson Knight, in his admirable book *Henrik Ibsen,*[2] decided to treat *The Pretenders* before *Love's Comedy* and to reserve the latter for a new chapter, "Poetic Quests," that also includes *Brand* and *Peer Gynt,* since these plays have affinities and common purposes which *The Pretenders* does not share. *The Pretenders,* indeed, makes us aware of the inescapable limitations of historical drama as an adequately poetic form, for the author's development of his dramatic idea cannot proceed from the inevitability of its dialectical logic but must to a great extent be circumscribed by the nonartistic and nonlogical business of sticking to the historical facts.[3]

In *Love's Comedy,* on the other hand, Ibsen can freely develop his dramatic argument, invent for it the appropriate characters, and give them the actions and speeches whose conflicts will illuminate the argument. Thus he creates an artwork whose "facts" are not to be discovered outside the play but only within the composition itself as elements of the total artistic structure.[4]

LOVE'S COMEDY

When two beings fall in love with one another and begin to suspect they were made for each other, it is time to have the courage to break it off, for by going on they have everything to lose and nothing to gain.

Kierkegaard, *Either/Or,* Vol. I

Two lovers stand locked in an embrace. At a short distance is a busy, gossiping, inquisitive group of citizens, mostly female. But in the far distance, beyond and above the young couple, stretch the fjord leading out to the great ocean and the mountains leading upward to the very limits of the earthly terrain. The intense anguish of the lovers as they separate, finally, from each other is a microcosmic convulsion whose waves of energy reverberate to the farthest distance, just as in Edward Munch's landscapes with lovers we sense the continuation of lines of energy and feeling from the human figures into the surrounding landscape.

Ibsen has "arrived" as a dramatist, and *Love's Comedy* is his first assured masterpiece, the brilliant culmination of a long and awkward apprenticeship. It is no accident that it is also his first wholly contemporary play (for *St. John's Night* was seriously compromised in this regard by its recourse to romantic and folkish fairy-tale elements), and it indicates where Ibsen's strengths as a dramatic poet of the modern world really lie.

The scenography of *Love's Comedy* is a further development of the impressive spatial metaphors for the human condition that were in *Olaf Liliekrans* and that will be extended so consequentially in *Brand, Peer Gynt,* and the plays of the realistic cycle. We find a sharply observed, constricted, and constraining human community, fiercely watchful of any transgression of its conventions, and, surrounding this little community, an expansive landscape whose vertical extremes of sea depths and mountain heights suggest freer or profounder extensions of the human spirit to which finer-natured individuals, like Falk and Svanhild, are responsive. The conjunction of sharply rendered bourgeois realism and the most ambitious Romantic scenography (as if the forces of Jane Austen and Lord Byron were united) will be the chief source of Ibsen's power as a modern dramatist.

In addition to this *spatial* extension from the little community and its intense center to the great surrounding cosmos, there is, in *Love's Comedy,* a temporal extension that stretches back through history to the prehistorical and legendary and to which, again, the finer-tuned characters of his plays will be responsive. From *St. John's Night* to *The Vikings at Helgeland,* we saw, Ibsen had undertaken a long journey into the past of his nation. The contours of this "temporal landscape" were made up, layer upon layer, of a past whose spiritual convulsions, begetting new phases of mind and culture, are like the volcanic and seismic convulsions that shaped the layers beneath the surface of the earth.

Falk and Svanhild, placed in these huge spatial and temporal perspectives, inaugurate a long series of such fateful couples. The artist, Falk, accepts the loss of his lover, Svanhild, and at the end of Ibsen's career artist and lover, Rubek and Irene, meet again in an identical landscape to regret just such a separation.

The emphatically Romantic use of time and space in a play whose playful bourgeois parody of heroic archetypes resembles Alexander Pope's *The Rape of the Lock* signals a unique presence in nineteenth century theater. The parody is the subversive consequence of Ibsen's long commitment to the heroic past as a source of his dramas. Now, in a mood of post-Romantic disenchantment, Ibsen contrasts the heroic archetypes with their debasement in the petty present while indicating, at a deeper level of Romantic commitment, that these archetypes can and must be recovered for the life of the present.

Love's Comedy is a work that one imagines Byron, who so admired Pope, would have liked to have written; and G. Wilson Knight, in fact, commends "the glinting Byronic satire" of the play.[5] It is also, in many ways, Ibsen's most Shavian play, and one catches echoes of the text in a number of Shaw's dramas, notably *Candida, Getting Married,* and *Man and Superman. Candida* recreates the plot of the young poet whose rejection by his lover for a more prosaic husband is a form of liberation, whereas *Getting Married* and *Man and Superman* recreate the satiric contrast of love and marriage as conventional social institutions, with the potentially subversive, anarchic nature of romantic love. *Love's Comedy* also most fully realizes Shaw's ideal of the "discussion play," for the play is virtually nothing but brilliant discussion from beginning to end. This had led some critics to pronounce the work undramatic, but it might well prove highly effective in the theater if performed with the brio that can make a play like *Getting Married* so dramatically delightful.

The setting on which the play opens is an attractive floral garden, tastefully laid out but fenced in, its gentle, attractive, and pastoral quality constituting a dangerous "lure" to the rebellious spirit, in the same way that Aurelia, in *Catiline,* offered a pastoral regression from the world of heroic conflict. The scenic opposition to this domesticated nature is the background of fjord and islands, with their great sweep of vertical levels indicating a freer, more exhilarating, but also potentially more desolate expression of the human spirit. Scenically, therefore, the stage already contains an "argument" between tamed and untamed nature, constriction and freedom, precise social reality and the timeless natural realm.

The opening lyric, sung by the rebel, Falk, who is accompanied by a chorus of young men, continues, by its ambiguities, the tensions suggested in the scenic contrast:

> Solglad dag i hegnet havet
>
> skaptes deg til lyst og lek;
>
> tenk ei paa at höstens gave
>
> titt nok vårens løfter svek.[6]

The sun-joyful (*solglad*) day in the fenced-in (*hegnet*) garden moves one — or makes one ready to be moved (*skaptes deg*) — to desire and play. The sexual desire implied is curiously imprisoned and artificial. The sun, that constant Ibsen emblem of the burning spirit of life, quickens the little human community with desire, but the desire is constrained and perhaps a little false. The next two lines tell us not to consider that the "gifts" of autumn are often betrayals of spring's promises. The overt message is that of *carpe diem*, to make most of the moment and not to think that the consequences of spring's passion, pregnancy, will be a perhaps unwelcome gift of autumn; but it equally can mean that the "matured" relationship of the married couple, in autumn, may be a far cry from the values ecstatically affirmed at the height of passion. The rest of the lyric is similarly ambiguous, seeming to continue the *carpe diem* theme so familiar to love-poetry but also perhaps giving us a first idea of a love value that the little community will not be able to tolerate, however it may thrill at its *poetic* expression.

The imagery of the lyric, while conventionally that of a flower garden and of songbirds, will develop richly in the play in terms of the garden and nature, and flowers and birds. The hero, Falk, and the heroine, Svanhild, are named after the hawk and the swan, emblems of freedom and beauty, and the names of other characters in the play are derived from birds, plants, and minerals. Guldstad and Styver (gold and farthing) are earthbound metals; Lind (linden), Mrs. Halm (straw), and Straamand (strawman) are earth-rooted or earth-derived plants, and Miss Skjaere (magpie) is a bird, like Falk and Svanhild, but a notoriously ignoble bird who has snapped up the bright farthing, Styver!

After the lyric, the assembled company discusses poetry, and we note that Ibsen has developed a new kind of poetry that is jaunty, filled with what the Elizabethans called "conceits" (from *concetti*, or concepts), which, in their ability to make the most banal or familiar objects into pregnant metaphors, already look forward to the transmuted poetry of the realistic cycle. Styver, for instance, once was visited by the poetic muse in his government office and wrote reams of poetry on unstamped (private) and stamped *(stemplet)*/(official) paper, managing to break into the muse's temple *(templet)* with love's jimmy *(brekkjern)*. These conceits sometimes are jaunty Byronic responses to the possibilities invited by the rhyming verse *(stemplet-templet)* and sometimes full-blown conceits in the mode of Jacobean metaphysical poetry, as in the famous analogy between love and tea. The Ibsen conceits, it is true, lack the often darkly tense drama of the best metaphysical conceits which make one feel that the Jacobean poets defensively and desperately are yoking violently together areas of experience that threaten to split apart in a disintegrating culture. But Ibsen's conceits spring from a dialectically freer culture, in which the dramatist can set concept against concept, playfully, or seriously as when Svanhild takes up Falk's conceit of the poet as a hawk, refutes it, and replaces it with the conceit of the poet as a paper kite. In such encounters, Falk and Svanhild are an intellectual Benedict and Beatrice: that is, more so than Shakespeare's contentious lovers, their "wit" and their argument are seriously conceptual, and from their inevitable encounters a new concept of the nature of love will emerge.

The discussion on poetry between Falk and Styver, with the watchful Guldstad intervening, sets up poetry and idealism against conventional and practical reality. At this stage of the play, Falk's conception of poetry, which he pits against the careful, calculating world of society, is that of a reckless abandonment to the truth of the moment. Society, in its institutionalized organization, would prevent the possibility of any such freedom, needing, in fact, positively to protect itself against such alarming activity. Idealism in conventional society is not active and alive but is frozen, stabilized into dogma. "He who does not believe that revelation is continuous," Shaw wrote, appropriately in *The Quintessence of Ibsenism*, "does not believe in revelation at all."[7] Just as an emerging prophet, armed with new religious revelation, would be most unwelcome precisely to those conventional believers who have safely codified past revelation, so Love as a soul-shaking revelation cannot be contained by a society that at the most allows Love to be a somewhat impractical sentimentalization with which society can live;[8] and so the assembled ladies now tell the moving story of Pastor Strawman and his ideal love, carefully building up the sentimental details at the expense of the practical facts as Guldstad, to their irritation, points out.

Strawman's love is the perfect idyll for conventional society because it is sentimental and totally nonsubversive. It represents the kind of self-sacrifice that most conventional young people would be willing to undertake and which will never actually challenge the social order that has tamed and emasculated eros to such an extent.

Falk's friend, Lind, reveals that he has succumbed to the love-virus so prevalent in the Halm house, and in Lind we see the early stages of that now famous "sacrificial" love which Strawman had felt. Because of his new love, Lind now will not take part in the projected trek up into the mountains with the quartet of young free men (who seem a charming emblem of Young Norway). He declares he now can breathe "mountain air" in the valley with its flowers and singing birds — again, this is the "Aurelian lure" against which the heroic will should be on guard.

Conventional love, even Lind's ardent passion, reconciles the individual to insidious forms of compromise. The contrast, here, between mountain freedom and valley love-compromise will become a significant part of Ibsen's extension of the human gesture through his vertical scenography. *Brand* is one long, slow, agonizing ascent from the valley to the mountain peaks; in *Peer Gynt*, mountain freedom and solitude (in Peer and Solveig's outlaw hut and the draft dodger's mountain home) are played off against the valley and its conventional life (the Hekstad farm and the conventional marriage that Ingrid offers Peer); and in the later plays the mountain regions, with the sea, are always associated with a form of freedom inimical to the relationships of conventional society.

The oddly bitter conclusion to *Love's Comedy*, therefore, in which Falk renounces the Aurelian lure of love for mountain freedom, is not the result of a passing pre-occupation on Ibsen's part; the action is anticipated in *Catiline* and was to be built permanently into his later work. *Love's Comedy* is useful to our understanding of Ibsen's dramatic vision — the total metaphor established by his lifework — because its vertical contrast between the realm of spiritual freedom (habitable, if at all, only with courage and difficulty) and the cozy realm of petty conventional society is so starkly clear. The same contrast is present or implicit in all his subsequent plays. The world of *Pillars of Society*, for example, with the sea on one side and the mountains on the other (travel and communication across both being avidly discussed in the play), gains its intense moral coloring from the fact that here an entire representative human community (it could as well be London or Paris if we adopt the cosmic perspectives of the play) is juxtaposed against the huge impersonal perspectives of the natural landscape. The moral life of the characters, their human posturing no doubt revealing the "dear old domestic animals" beneath the human masks, is so vivid to us as satiric portraiture because we sense the greater impersonal forces surrounding the human community. It is as if the world of Dumas *fils* and Augier were surrounded by, and permeated with, the metaphoric landscape of Wordsworth. Ibsen's use of sea and mountains as emblems of spiritual liberty, in fact, recalls Wordsworth's sonnet:

> Two voices are there; one is of the Sea,
> One of the Mountains; each a mighty voice:
> In both from age to age thou didst rejoice,
> They were thy chosen music, Liberty!

The smallness of the little human community in contrast to the immensity of nature impels Falk to describe it in terms satirically miniscule. He tells Svanhild how he saw her, standing out, at a "tea-time Saturnalia" in which the eminently respectable com-

pany crowded round the table to celebrate the decent joys of tea
and domesticity. Falk, however, had noticed Svanhild's name, the
one anomaly in this "orgy of froth," for it called into the consciousness of the present a memory of the Volsung saga with its
"long tale of fallen kinds." Svanhild mildly chides Falk for "hearing the voice of spirits where the spirit is silent," but Falk continues with the old legend, seeing the modern Svanhild "trodden
down and trampled into undistinguished clay" (in McFarlane's
translation) — the original suggests even more an obliteration of
the archetypal form — by a world that always will plagiarize
(plagierer) the Creator's work and remake it in its own image. The
action of society, in refashioning God's work, is highly blasphemous, but the same society would consider highly blasphemous
any attempt to realize, in freedom, the Creator's idea.[9] From a
free spirit Svanhild will become a "quite normal" woman who fits
in well with the decorations of the room, the remade artificial and
fine lady feeding on the death of the free one.

Falk holds out to Svanhild a "higher destiny": her response to
the call of freedom will be the inspiration for his poetry. In free
association with him, and in defiance of society, she will share in
the creation of his songs — until he has exhausted his need for her
or she for him. (Again we are reminded of the Rubek-Irene relationship.) Scornfully rejecting this destiny, Svanhild takes Falk's
metaphor of himself as the falcon born aloft on the breeze of
Svanhild's spirit and converts it into that of a flapping paper kite,
a thing of words instead of deeds. Only living deeds have the
"right of way" *(ferdselsrett)* to the heights.

The exchange between Falk and Svanhild is the climax of act 1.
It pits poetry against life and gives the victory to life, a victory
reinforced when Guldstad, the intelligent merchant, enjoins Falk
to use his talents in *living*. Falk ardently assents and determines
the next day to become engaged to Svanhild. The act closes with
the quartet of young men singing of the dangerous joys of freely
putting out to sea.

In act two, the opening chorus sings encouragement to the
conventional new lovers, in an ironic salute to their *legitimacy*.
The action develops a sharply satirical turn as the ladies crowd
round Lind and Anna in a ritual sacrifice of Lind's freedom. He is

"measured," embarrassed, and humiliated, and Falk, observing him, likens him to a sacrificial beast needlessly tortured and likens the whole scene to a "slaughter" of the poetry of love. The image is not an empty conceit; as in *The Rape of the Lock*, a sublimated savagery is detected beneath the decorous modern conventions just as, in the last scene, Svanhild will be "trodden underfoot" by the same gathering of ladies.

The whole company is thrown into the greatest confusion by the news that Lind has resolved to take up a ministry in the new world, and they exert all their powers to crush this last vestige of freedom in the young man. Lind already has conceded so much to the world of conventional duties that he very easily is persuaded to give up his great calling, and after only the briefest complication, Lind and Anna subside into a totally conventional pair of smirking lovers received enthusiastically into the society of the aunts.

The company now settles down to discourse on the nature of love, in a decorous modern way that is far from the dynamic and alarming discourse of the guests in Plato's *Symposium*. Each member of the company offers a more or less conventional simile or conceit until Falk submits his famous conceit of love as tea. Love, like the finest tea-tips, originates from a fabulous celestial kingdom, and only the highest spirits are allowed to taste this; but it filters down to modern society through institutions, laws, and regulations so that only the stalks and dust are available for consumption. As Falk's attack upon the lie of conventional love increases, his audience is more and more enraged and the little drawing room becomes a place of open battle (something of a Homeric battle of frogs and mice) and Falk is ordered out of the house — the natural consequence of his turning from poetry to deeds. Svanhild now joins him, willing to embark with him upon a war against society.

Act 3, which is to see Falk's ejection from the bourgeois garden of Eden, presents the garden at its most alluring. Lights from lanterns, soft piano music from the house, sounds of festivity — all present in the most attractive terms the world the hero will give up for the discipline of rebellious solitude. Falk has given up his books and burned his poems — the opposite of Ibsen who remained a poet but who always admired the poetry of lived heroism.

Falk greets Svanhild in a beautifully lofty speech of spiritual emancipation, and she responds at the same level, contrasting the new height of freedom they have gained with the glittering pleasures of the scene around them — the sounds of merriment and celebration and feasting that are really the knell of spiritual defeat for Lind and Anna. This superb dialogue between Falk and Svanhild indicates the true Ibsen "note": the contrast of the exalted loneliness of a hard-won rebellious authenticity and the Vanity Fair of socially approved, inauthentic happiness where the spirit is caught in a platonic cave of illusions. Falk develops the contrast: of the "friendless pair" *(vennelose to)* who are the richest and who have the "bright lamps of the sky," and the others who circle in dance around the lights and music of the house.

The contrast between the love that is attuned to and serves the truer purpose of the cosmos, and the love that is the distorting conventional fiction of a blundering society, is as explicit in this scene as in *Man and Superman.* Falk, moreover, is a John Tanner who does not capitulate, who, unlike Tanner, refuses the commonsensical surrender to social norms, and who, by his continuing rebellion, insists on the reality of an absolute valuation of love unassimilable by society. The whole scene between the two militant lovers, falcon and swan, is set against the background of domestic coziness, yet, through their speeches, it soars outward to the mountains and stars. The scene is an emblem, not only of impossibly idealistic love but of the human condition itself, which is trapped in a *conditioned* time and space but which consciously and unconsciously is responsive to and lured by the vast surrounding time and space.

As Falk and Svanhild resolve to leave society, converting social ostracism into a positive action of rebellion, three "tempters" appear in the forms of Strawman, Styver, and Guldstad. Strawman *(Straamand)* the priest offers as temptation the realities of *family* life and its virtues and riches, which entail a sacrifice of idealistic love, and he pleads with Falk not to dishonor family life and so make his own great sacrifice worthless. Strawman's speech poignantly reveals the pointlessness of such a sacrifice: in order to secure the future for his children — who *may* carry forward a more ideal way of life and love — he has created around these children a way of life that is a perpetual sacrifice of idealism. The new generations that will emerge from such a sacrifice will be hopelessly blighted by it. This theme of inherited misery will be taken up in more somber terms in *Brand.*

Styver, the civil servant, now offers the *social* temptation of maintaining social harmony in order to make bearable the *poverty* of marriage. Romantic idealism, seriously pursued, cannot be reconciled with a life pursued between the home and the office; it is irreconcilable with good citizenship. In a pair of lines worthy of Schiller, Falk proudly replies:

> en man skal vaere borger av sin tid,
>
> men adle tidens borgerlige gjerning.
>
> A man must be a citizen of his age,
>
> Yet raise the age of which he would be citizen.[10]

Styver's view is the commonsensical one (like Relling's idea of love, whereas Falk's is closer to that of Gregers Werle) in which two less than ideal lovers have established a harmony by which to live life in its inevitable drudgery. Falk refuses to live in eccentric and inactive isolation with his claim of the ideal, as Strawman and Styver inplore. Instead he insists on tormenting society with this claim, even at the cost of society's happiness, a stance reminiscent of Kierkegaard.

Contemplating Styver, Strawman, Lind, and the aunts, Falk sees them imagining themselves in bliss though they really are damned, imagining themselves gods while actually in hell surrounded by devils. Shaw was to repeat this idea of hell as fashionable society in *Man and Superman,* but Ibsen's expression of this idea is even more forceful.

It is Svanhild who likens Strawman and Styver to two "evil tempters" *(onde fristere),* each a spokesman for half the human race, one denying that ideal love can survive the material riches of the world, the other denying it can survive life's unceasing penury. As she pledges to stand with Falk against the world, the third "tempter," Guldstad, appears. Like the Fourth Tempter in *Murder in the Cathedral,* he is totally unexpected and more terrible than the other tempters. As if he were an agent from hell, he tells the lovers that he has come to cast off his "disguise" *(hammen)* in order to speak out to Falk and Svanhild. The other tempters had accepted the fact that love as an ideal cannot be maintained without harm to ordinary life. Guldstad, Falk's true dialectical opponent, announces that he does not wish, like the others, to save life by sacrificing idealistic love, but to save idealistic love by rescuing it from commonplace life. Because Guldstad, in his way, has never compromised, being as impatient as is Falk with the sentimental cant of love in conventional society but from an opposite standpoint — the pragmatic — he alone has the stature to measure up to the young rebel. Guldstad is factually honest where Falk is idealistically honest; his pragmatism is the genuine dialectical antithesis that Falk's idealism must confront if it is to remain genuine.

Guldstad asserts that he wishes to save *three* lives, so that Falk the idealist, Guldstad the pragmatist, and Svanhild the spirit searching for direction make something of a living syllogism between them. Under Guldstad's promptings, the syllogism will be completed when Svanhild synthesizes the two opposites: she will preserve, in its pure state, the *memory* of ideal love, within the context of a loveless practical marriage. This somewhat sour dialectical joke has discomfited many critics, but it is the perfectly logical outcome of the argument. There is no *practical* place for idealistic love. It can remain idealistic, and so exert a salutary transforming force upon conventional and compromised society, only if it itself remains uncompromised. Falk's "love," in fact, is not so unlike the true Christianity of Kierkegaard and Brand which had to keep itself free of the compromised "Christendom" of the established church. The argument is disconcering in its paradoxical insistence upon its extreme dialectical terms, and one feels the discomfiting force of that relentless logic which is one of Ibsen's sources of greatness.

Falk and Svanhild are devastated by Guldstad's argument that, no more than the other lovers they have hitherto scorned, will they be exempt from the world's process that gradually turns ideal love and all its high intentions into decent, practical, uninspiring marriage. Svanhild therefore decides to accept Guldstad's offer of a practical, loveless, but companionable marriage with him. These extraordinary lovers, Falk and Svanhild, join in ecstatic renunciation, with a leave-taking as ardent as their earlier love-declaration and union. In order that their love for each other remain the precious thing it is, uncontaminated by the process of the world, they will part and go their own ways, each holding, as in a private shrine, the memory of their unsullied, perfect love. In the final paradox of the play, love is rescued by being renounced, its beautiful life on earth ensured for the future by two lovers who part, unconsummated, from each other. Svanhild will marry Guldstad while Falk, released, will forge a future poem of life, beginning by traveling "in young Norway's chorus" up into the mountains.

The firm undeluded separation of the ideal from the real which the play insists upon is disturbing to a world that likes to imagine itself adequately appreciative of the ideal while still keeping its practical affairs in order. We pay for art so that artists will supply us with cheap excursions to the realm of the ideal, and we are not unnaturally discomfited, even infuriated, as Ibsen's contemporaries were, when the artist whom we expect to be our tour guide in the ideal realm suddenly turns out to be a Gabriel with a flaming sword of idealism ejecting us from the paradise. Shaw's account of Ibsen, in *The Quintessence of Ibsenism,* as the resolute demolisher of idealism is closer to the nature of his achievement than the more fashionable psychological expositions of his art today, for the sentimental, convenient, and compromising idealism of the nineteenth century was a major object of Ibsen's satire. But Shaw saw only this major aspect of Ibsen's artistry, saw only the demolition and not the concurrent art of spiritual reclamation that is going on in the plays. The inauthentic idealism is demolished so that the authentic can be established. Otherwise, *Love's Comedy* would be only a bitter paradox instead of a tragi-comedy of idealism.

Svanhild's saga archetype, we learned, was crushed to death under the hooves of horses. The modern Svanhild renounces freedom (her *friluftsliv*) and, observing that the leaves are falling, she allows the "world" to take her. A dance starts up, champagne corks pop, and the ladies come in, stop for a moment looking fearfully at Svanhild, then suddenly rush forward in gleeful triumph, surrounding her, crushing her out of sight — a visual equivalent of the grim saga punishment. This action tells us that Svanhild's renunciation also is a painful sacrifice to the savage, crinolined fetishes of her culture.

THE PRETENDERS

The character dualisms of the early plays from *Catiline* to *The Vikings at Helgeland* seemed to involve alternate heroines struggling for the hero's allegiance, but in *The Vikings at Helgeland* a dualism of masculine consciousness, that between Sigurd and Gunner, emerged to parallel that of the feminine consciousness, Hjördis and Dagny. This masculine dualism now becomes an equally important structural principle in Ibsen's writing, from Haakon and Skule, Brand and Peer Gynt, up to Rubek and Ulfheim at the end of Ibsen's career. The contrast between the "lucky," confident, "naive" Haakon Haakonson and the vacillating, doubting, self-reflective Skule expresses an opposition between types of consciousness that we noted from Ibsen's earliest critical writings: that contrast between the naive and the self-reflective which was a feature of Romantic thinking from Rousseau to Nietzsche and beyond.[11] It seems inevitable, therefore, that Ibsen would set out this dualism forcefully, as he does in *The Pretenders*, irrespective of his musings on the contrast between his own baffled, self-doubting, relatively unsuccessful artistic career and the blithe and confident progress of Björnstjerne Björnson's literary career then enjoying immense prestige with the Norwegian public. The biographical fact of Ibsen's friendly rivalry with Björnson (the two friends had shared the platform at a national festival in Bergen in June 1863) is therefore of somewhat limited interest and usefulness as a tool for understanding the nature of Ibsen's shaping imagination and the substance of *The Pretenders*. The creation of contrasting characters whose opposite natures represent opposing life principles is as old as literature and can be traced to the quarrel between Agamemnon and Achilles without any need to speculate on Homer's possible rivalry with a more popular poet. When the subject of the play becomes the contest for a kingdom and the examination of fitness for power, such an illustrative dualism becomes almost obligatory. *Richard II* creates a sharp contrast between the opposite characters of Richard and Bolingbroke; *Julius Caesar* contains a series of such contrasts: Pompey and Caesar, Brutus and Cassius, Octavius and Antony. In *Mary Stuart*, where the power is disputed between two women, we find a similar contrast, between Mary and Elizabeth. When the dispute for power is idealogical and not monarchical, a similar dualism emerges, as with Danton and Robespierre in *Danton's Death*. In all these plays, psychological character type is bound up with the requirements of political-national destinies and frequently, as in *The Pretenders*, the weaker, or defeated, nature contains qualities, lacking in the victor, that the play honors.

Bjorn Hemmer, for example, interprets *The Pretenders* persuasively in terms of its Christian argument.[12] Haakon, the "positive" hero, possesses a God-given destiny — to bring unity to Norway — which he fulfills. Skule sets himself against this destiny and, opposing the divine plan, falls into the satanic service of the "negative" Bishop Nicholas. Skule fails to overcome "existence" and live according to the "essence," whereas Haakon stands for "essential" values and thus overcomes the worldly values of "existence." Only at the hour of his death does Skule truly recognize his criminal error in opposing the divine plan embodied by Haakon. Through this redemptive insight Skule is able to humble himself, be at one with God's purposes, and be rewarded, not with the worldly crown he errantly sought but with a divine crown.

The Christian themes of Hemmer's thesis obviously are present in the dramatic argument, but I believe that Ibsen evolves them further in terms of a Romantic and Hegelian historical drama. Schiller's Wallenstein, Mary Stuart, and the pretender, Demetrius, are depicted in situations similar to that of Skule, and Mary's redemptive death, in particular, anticipates Skule's. The Christian elements of *The Pretenders*, it seems, are transmuted into a more elaborate and less doctrinal dialectic. Skule, it is true, goes to his death acknowledging the presence of the divine plan from which he had swerved, and he and his daughter, Sigrid, envisage his redemption in specifically Christian terms: But this is the historical world view in which they live, the sole manner in which such a dialectical process would evolve. We have noticed that from *The Burial Mound* on Ibsen always attempts to write as if he were within the cultural period he is dramatizing; though in *The Pretenders* he no longer attempts an archaic style, he is still faithful to the *Zeitgeist* he is bringing to dramatic life.

Haakon's embodiment of the divine purpose and Skule's opposition to it, to the point of serving the diabolic purpose of Nicholas, might be seen by us as the theistic "mythic foundation" on which the more elaborate historical and dialectical structure is built. A cultural period that lived within a Christian interpretation of the world and its teleology would then find reality on all levels revealing a Christian dialectic, although "for us," as modern readers, the dialectic would extend to further dimensions.

Haakon Haakonsen is the "naive" character who, by a special grace that spares him self-doubt, can step into his appointed role in the world order over a rival equally gifted and more complex. Haakon is a clear example of a character type designated by Schiller "die Kinder des Hauses" — the children of the house — whose legitimacy to the titles to which they lay claim is borne out by a conjunction of physical and moral grace. In fact, the theme of "die Kinder des Hauses" is indicated in the Norwegian title, *Kongs-emnerne,* the stuff of kingship, and the theme will occupy Ibsen again in his last and greatest historical drama, *Emperor and Galilean.* It is a theme that is bound to give rise to searching dramatic portraiture, and the psychological depth and substantiality of the three main characters, Haakon, Skule, and Nicholas, derive from the degree to which characters are judged by their fitness for *vocation* — the main theme of *Brand.* This character portrayal marks a great advance over the more superficial Romantic and satiric portraiture of *Love's Comedy:* If *The Pretenders* nevertheless seems, to the present writer at least, a lesser *poetic* achievement, this is due to the inevitable limitations of the *genre* of historical drama. Georg Brandes's shrewd comment on the historical novels of Sir Walter Scott applies with equal force to historical drama:

. . . the historical novel, with all its merits, is a bastard species — now it is so hampered with historical material that the poetic development of the story is rendered impossible, — again it is so free in its paraphrase of history that the real and the fictitious elements produce a very discordant whole.[13]

Just what constitutes a "historical" drama is difficult to define. If one uses the criterion of the degree of liberty taken with the historical facts, Aeschylus's *The Persians*, Shakespeare's History Cycles, Schiller's *Don Carlos* and *Mary Stuart*, and Brecht's *Galileo*, all manifestly plays about historical processes and conflicts whose outcomes have decisively affected the world, are hardly more historical than the *Oresteia*, *Macbeth*, *William Tell*, or *Mother Courage*, plays that one would not term "historical." One feels that in the latter group historical concerns are transcended so that the characters and actions are obeying a nonhistorical dramatic logic and aesthetic in which the historical actuality is forgotten. What Brandes calls "the poetic development of the story" is freed from the requirement of being true to history because we feel that the drama is being responsive to a higher and more demanding truth — tragic truth, perhaps. In his fascinating account of the archetypal, mythic, and "primitive" imagination, *Cosmos and History: the Myth of the Eternal Return*, Mircea Eliade argues that when the prerational, prehistorical imagination is faced with events that threaten to break free of the circle of archetypal explanation, to become historical, and thus to create an uncontrollable chain of cause and effect, this imagination alters the events, denies their historical uniqueness, and returns them to the realm of archetypal explanation.[14]

It is possible that what we consider satisfactory aesthetic form, as in authentic tragedy, performs a similar function. It returns potentially inchoate historical events to the decorum of archetypal form and meaning. Historical events then are reinterpreted, made to obey completely nonhistorical patterns, as in *Lady Inger of Østraat*, and we assent to this process because we perceive the archetypal significance of the dramatic patterns.

Strictly historical drama seems to suffer from the same liabilities Brandes observed of the historical novel. It has to satisfy four competing requirements: historical actuality, the sensibility of the modern audience, the dramatist's idea of reality, and the demands of the dramatic form. Hegel had commended the youthful works of Schiller and Goethe for creating one form of historical drama: the history of the rebellious or tragic individual whose personal actions and crisis were the symptoms of a moment of significant historical change and even contributed to that change. Hegel did not offer this as a model for modern historical tragedy — it was not Hegel's procedure to legislate to artists — but this model was, in fact, taken up by Hegelian aestheticians, including Johan Ludvig Heiberg who introduced his own interpretation of Hegel to Scandinavian aesthetics. John C. Pearce, in his pioneering article "Hegelian Ideas in Three Tragedies by Ibsen," describes the Hegelian "formula" for historical tragedy:

(1) historical plays should dramatize the conflicts and reconciliations marking the progress of human history toward the ultimate higher synthesis of antithetical forces; (2) protagonists of historical drama should symbolize the ideas that are in opposition to each other; and (3) the tragic protagonist's free subjective choice to oppose a rising order in the continuing movement toward synthesis brings catastrophe to him with the downfall of the old order.[15]

This 'Hegelian' formula ignores Hegel's own clear distinction between ancient tragic art, in which the ideas in opposition are completely embodied by the protagonists, and modern tragic art, in which there is no such consonance between the subjective drama of the protagonists and the objective ethical order in which they find themselves, and Pearce notes that Kierkegaard attacked the Heibergian aesthetic as a distortion of Hegel.[16] The disciples of Hegel simplified his *Aesthetics,* as well as his other philosophical writings, and the philosopher was later held accountable for this simplification.

Armed with such pseudo-Hegelian formulas, the modern poet could roam through history searching for an appropriately decisive turning point, select the characters that best exemplified its dialectically opposing forces, and render all this in dialectic dramatic form. One sees there are far too many conveniently "given" entities in this procedure: the subject, the interpretation, the formal conflict, and its dramatic expression are all readily available without any need for the critical exploration of reality that alone can lead to truly original art. Ibsen, we have seen, did employ this formula and his historical dramas reveal its structure; but he loaded the formula with sufficient individual, critical content, pushing it to its limits, that, in his best writing, he was forced to transcend it. *Emperor and Galilean* probably never will receive the high valuation that Ibsen placed upon it, as his greatest work; it remains, however, a fascinating and greatly significant work because in it, as artist-thinker, Ibsen existentially and not facilely attempted to experience, and make us experience, the nature of the dialectic-historical process.

The more facile dramatic rendition of the historical dialectic, an intellectual exercise that could not draw upon the deeper sources of art, was devastatingly impugned by that most disturbingly percipient artist, Richard Wagner:

The end results of history we posited as the cause of its movement, or as the goal toward which a higher, conscious spirit had therein striven from the beginning. Led by this view, the expounders or setters-forth of history believed themselves justified in deriving the seemingly arbitrary actions of its ruling personages from "ideas" in which was mirrored back the inputed consciousness of a governing world-spirit: they destroyed the unconscious necessity of these rulers' motives of action, and, so soon as they had sufficiently accounted for those actions, they displayed them as arbitrary out-and-out.

Through this procedure alone, whereby historic actions could be disfigured and combined at will, did the romance succeed in inventing types, and in lifting itself to a certain height of artwork, whereon it might seem qualified anew for dramatization. Our latter days have presented us with many such an historical drama, and the zest of making history in behoof of dramatic form is nowadays so great, that our skilled historical stage conjurors fancy the secret of history itself has been revealed for the sole benefit of the playmaker. They believe themselves all the more justified in their procedure, as they have even made it possible to invest history's dramatic installation with the completest unity of place and time: they have thrust into the inmost recesses of the whole historic mechanism, and have discovered its heart to be the antechamber of the prince, where man and the state make their mutual arrangements between breakfast and supper. That this artistic unity and this history, however, are equal forgeries, and that a falsehood can have only a forged effect — *this* has established itself plainly enough in the course of our present-day historic drama. But that true history itself is no stuff for Drama — this we know also; since this historical drama has made it clear to us, that even the romance could reach its appointed height, as art form, only by sinning against the truth of history.[17]

The formula that Wagner here effectively derides did come to life when passionately employed in the service of, for example, Schiller's idealism, in which the poet actually created archetypal and semi-mythic figures from the historical material. The network of symbolic contrasts that Schiller sets up in *Don Carlos*—between Posa, the light-bringer, and the blind Grand Inquisitor who maintains Spain in darkness, between the life-affirming Prince Carlos and the death-creating Duke of Alba, between the self-repressive Phillip and his queen, the warmly expressive Elizabeth—creates a dramatic-spiritual *rhythm*, a ritual of the idealist spirit, sustained by the rhetorical verse, that has all the heightened tension, the *intensity*, of the best dramatic art. This aesthetic intensity, controlling the choice of each detail of scene, character, action, and language, because each of these details is an indispensable moment in the unfolding of the total argument, seems lacking in the more diffuse dramatic method of *The Pretenders*. The realistic method Ibsen chose for the play employs the dramatist's very impressive skills in the convincing depiction of the given characters and their conflicts rather than in the shaping of a symbolic poetic world into a single, unified, original artistic endeavor, as in *Love's Comedy*. "I cannot write it in verse," Ibsen said of this play,[18] and there is indeed a prosaic quality in the more relaxed artistry of the play which is different not only from Ibsen's great verse plays but also from such urgently conceived and shaped plays as *Emperor and Galilean*, part 1, and the plays of the realistic cycle.

In Ibsen's greatest work every detail of scene, time of day, season, weather, character, speech, gesture, object, movement, confrontation or juxtaposition vitally contributes to a dramatic rhythm whose tension, density of implication, and consequentiality of step-by-step unfolding are thrillingly felt by the audience. In the more expansive "mental dramas" intended for reading, there is a larger-scaled but similar shaping of a symbolic reality, a symbolic cosmos, even, in the interconnection of all the details. When Ibsen is not writing at this very difficult height, as in the second part of *Emperor and Galilean* and in *The Pretenders*, we detect the slackening of this dramatic tension, with the narrowing of the spiritual import. The very virtues of *The Pretenders*, the rich character portrayals unfolded in extensive soliloquies, the great variety of scenes, are atypical of Ibsen's best realism which always has the spareness, the economy of symbolic art. The relaxed, more easygoing method of the play, in fact, is what many critics expect—and want—of realism.

One indication that, in *The Pretenders*, Ibsen is not engaged at the highest level of creative intensity is the absence of that symbolic stage set, that subtle and vital visual symbolism which, we saw, the poet had devised and refined from *The Burial Mound* to *Love's Comedy*. The scenes that Ibsen devises for *The Pretenders* are not negligible; they are impressive historical recreations, visual substantiations, as it were, of the human situations, but they do not seem to be elements of a developing symbolic pattern such as we find even in the realistic settings of *Emperor and Galilean*.

The play opens, for example, with an imposing tableau. The scene is the Bergen churchyard with Christ Church in the background. In the foreground, a crowd is assembled for a major national and state action: the (presumably pagan) test of red hot iron which Haakon's mother must undergo to prove her son's legitimacy to the crown. The spiritual life of this nation is grandly institutionalized and represents a powerful background against which the political drama will be played out. This institutionalizing of the spirit has led to its corruption, as we will discover in the figure of Bishop Nicholas, so that it meddles, destructively, in national affairs. Haakon and his followers occupy the left-hand side of the stage while Skule and his followers are on the right. The whole tableau announces the main themes of the play and the immediately succeeding actions and speeches fill in the details of this historical reality.

The conflicting groups in front of the church, who contest the right to kingship, reveal the spiritual and national forces in discord working upon this historical moment—a discord which Haakon, in advance of his time, already seeks to overcome and which Skule, the embodiment of this condition of discord, will develop dialectically so that its defeat will be final and national unity permanently achieved.

From Skule's irresolution and Haakon's confidence we see that the right to succeed to the throne is both an external matter (legitimacy) and, even more, an internal right, for Haakon alone can envision and bring about the cultural unity that must emerge from this division.

In the next scene we see the contest for kingship within the domestic setting of the palace where Skule's wife, sister, and daughter anxiously await the outcome of the test. When Skule and Haakon enter we understand the nature of their different characters in relation to the intimate world of family loyalties. Haakon, under advice, resolutely banishes his mother (who had undergone the painful ordeal for him) and as resolutely proposes marriage to Skule's daughter, Margrete. He astonishes Skule by also banishing his young mistress, Kanga. In everything he does, Haakon is firm, assured, resolute, and ruthless, very similar to Strindberg's Gustav Vasa, and we feel the painful impact of this man on the destinies of those closest to him. By contrast, Skule makes a relatively weak impression in this scene, acquiescing, merely, in his daughter's betrothal and adapting himself to the startling policies initiated by Haakon.

In act 2, the theme of the "children of the house"—the specially chosen—is taken up in the dialogue between Skule and Bishop Nicholas. Haakon has just left the banqueting hall in Skule's palace in Bergen, and Skule remarks on how quiet it has become. "The king has gone," the bishop answers, and the two reflect on the power of kingship. Skule repeatedly has had the opportunity to seize power and has repeatedly lost the opportunity from one scruple or another. He has never dared "burn all bridges but one" upon which to hazard everything. (Later Skule will be defeated in battle because he hesitates to break the bridges of Trondheim.) Yet Skule is not lacking in courage. What, then, makes the "greatest man"? "The most courageous," answers Skule, and the bishop replies:

Thus speaks the warrior. A priest would say: he with the greatest faith,—a philosopher: the most learned man. But it is none of these, earl. The most fortunate [*lykkeligste*] man is the greatest man. It is the man of happy fortune who achieves the greatest deeds; he who is possessed by the yearnings of his time as if by a passion, begetting ideas that he himself does not grasp, pointing to him that way which will carry him he knows not where but which he yet follows and *must* follow until he hears the people shout in joy and, looking around him with sparkling eyes is astonished to see he has achieved a work of greatness.[19]

The word "lykkeligste" means both the *happiest* and the *luckiest*. Its possessor is suffused with the sense of personal power without being aware of where it comes from, and Ibsen uses the imagery of sexual potency as a metaphor (and perhaps also a symptom) of this power. The time's craving (*krav*) overwhelms (*kommer over*) the hero like sexual longing (*liksom i brynde*) guiding, as it were instinctively, the hero's movements to their outcome, impelling him to beget (*avler*) the ideas that will become the vital life of the age. The imagery of sexual potency linked to the gestation of the ideas that continue the life of the spirit in the world implies that the hero is in mysterious union with the world spirit at a level he himself does not understand, although he is happily conscious of possessing this power. In the opening scene of the play, when Haakon is urged by one of his followers to "pray to the Lord thy God," Haakon replies, "There's no need. I am sure of Him." It is as pointless to protest against the unfairness of possessing this potency as it is to protest against the possession of human beauty, that "natural superiority," as Plato, with typical Greek mercilessness, termed it. We will meet the same linking of "lykkelig" with sexual potency much later in *The Master Builder* where Solness combines the figures of Haakon and Skule into one: the great achiever upon whom luck/happiness attends but who still doubts, who can burn bridges, like Haakon, but can suffer from the scruples and remorse of Skule.

Haakon's luck/happiness is not merely a good fortune from without which therefore looks for omens and signs of assurance, as does Skule who hoped that God would intervene to place him on the throne. It is a confidently felt and experienced power, and, as with an Alexander, a Julius Caesar, and a Napoleon, the world-will seems to work through Haakon, giving him the uncanny ability of knowing exactly what to do at the right time and place when other men, as gifted and even more subtle and clever, are helpless. Haakon is Ibsen's only portrait of such a "man of destiny" and he seems to have had less enthusiasm for this type than did Strindberg who devoted a trilogy to the very similar Gustav Vasa. Yet it is fascinating that Ibsen incorporated elements of Haakon into his later major male characters, who otherwise have more of the qualities of Skule. Brand, Julian, Bernick, Stockmann, Lövborg, Solness, Borkman, and Rubek all in some way possess—or have possessed in the

past—Haakon's potency, but, with the exception of Thomas Stockmann (who is the happy doubter that the skald Jatgeir describes),
they are Haakons who have developed into Skules, because their
great powers have led to terrible consequences.

Skule concedes to Bishop Nicholas that Haakon is one of the
lucky/happy ones, for whom all things prosper magically. By what
right, the bishop insinuates, does Haakon and not Skule have this
magical "right"? Haakon *believes* himself to have the right, whereas Skule doubts. The bishop reveals that Haakon, too, might have
cause to doubt and thereby lose his serene confidence. For Haakon
may not be the son of Inga of Varteig and of Haakon Sverresson,
may not be a true "child of the house" and heir to the throne.
When the son was born, Nicholas, as priest, ordered that he be
exchanged for another to escape his enemies. The man who carried
this out left the country and died abroad, but a letter exists that
can clear up the whole matter. At first sight this looks like a relapse
to the old device of letter-intrigue—the menacingly written, cunningly hidden, sensationally discovered, fervently pursued, and
triumphantly flourished letters of the well-made play. But here
the device is used appropriately and subtly. The presence of the
letter indicates that the reality that Haakon so serenely commands
is more problematic than he is aware, so that the actual disunity in
reality is contrasted with the harmony of Haakon's spirit, a harmony he seeks to assert over reality. Skule, more aware of the disunity of this problematic reality, seeks not to overcome it but to
exploit it for his own ends and thereby never attains to Haakon's
power over it. Skule feels that if the evidence of the letter should
prove him to be the more legitimate claimant to the throne, he
would be able confidently to assume kingship; but this is just another instance of Skule's seeking external assurances to make up
for his lack of inner certitude.

Nicholas, the most interesting character in the play, thrives in
disunity as in his natural element. He is the first in Ibsen's long
procession of "satanic" characters, possessing, like them, a sar-
donic, blackly humorous attitude toward reality. The disharmony
and disquietude he creates, like that of Goethe's Mephistopheles,
is ultimately beneficial; it forces the good to emerge dialectically

from conflict in spite of himself. It is probable that he is partly modeled on Goethe's character.

The complications and intrigues that the impotent Nicholas creates, and which ensnare the uncertainly potent Skule, constitute the medium of conflict and challenge through which Haakon's confident potency develops into true, humane kingship. In the marvellous scene of the bishop's death chamber (strongly reminiscent of Browning's "The Bishop Orders His Tomb"), Nicholas calls for more and more light against the gathering darkness of his vision; the choristers in the background are exhorted to louder and louder efforts to save his soul while the bishop himself, outrageously, funnily blasphemous, continues to intrigue up to his last gasp. Particularly fine is the manner in which Ibsen presents the human intensity of the situation—the bishop's alternating terror and malice; Skule's mounting anxiety and Haakon's proud indignation—and at the same time controls the whole scene with some of the deepest humor in modern drama. The bishop's desire to bequeath to Norway a future of ceaseless power conflict, a plan in which Skule will abet, will be defeated by Haakon's profound commitment to the principle of national unity.

After the bishop's death, Skule urges that the best national policy is to set group against group, to maintain power by keeping the country disunited and weak. Haakon loftily opposes to this his vision of Norway as a nation and a united people.

To Skule and his followers, reality is fixed for all time. Their total reliance upon the past and its example makes them unable to conceive the dialectical process whereby the new emerges from the conditions of the past. "Norway's saga has never dreamt of such a thing," Skule exclaims to Haakon, and this is the refrain with which Skule and his followers reproach the new. A united Norway is unthinkable; it even is unthinkable to Paul Flida, Skule's follower, that the Birkbeiners can be defeated twice, "because such a thing has never happened before in Norway's saga." Skule, more intelligent than Flida, gradually sees the merit of Haakon's concept, but he cannot *embody* it. He thus is in the predicament of many Ibsen characters (Mrs. Alving, for example) whose *intellectual* emancipation is contradicted by a deeper conservatism and by hopelessly divided loyalties between past and future.

The disunity of Norway, which the bishop had exacerbated, reaches its climax when Norway finds itself with two kings and two hostile armies entering into open battle. Haakon's legitimacy seems confirmed by the "omen" of the birth of a son to succeed him; Skule, with no heir, is visited by the mistress of his youth who presents him with their bastard son, Peter, a devout novitiate who now links his young and innocent life to that of his father. Peter's fortunes now drastically follow those of Skule and involve sacrilege, the contemplated murder of Haakon's infant son, and, finally, redemptive death when on the brink of hell.

Before he is defeated in battle, Skule is visited by the ghost of Bishop Nicholas—a recollection, perhaps, of the visit by the ghost of Caesar to Brutus before Phillippi. This visit, as Hemmer notes, confirms the satanic aspect of the bishop; but it can only be considered a blemish for there is no way of accepting the episode, theatrically, within the convention of realism that the play otherwise sustains. Compounding the stylistic awkwardness, Ibsen ensures that we do not pass off the haunting as a figment of Skule's disordered imagination by having the ghost step forward to address the audience, an impossible incongruity which had better be dropped from performances of the play.

Defeated, and appalled at the degradation he has instigated in Peter, Skule at last humbles himself, acknowledges Haakon's divine legitimacy and his own readiness for death in order to ask mercy from "the king of kings" and be pardoned for his "life'swork." The play closes with Haakon's epitaph on Skule: "Skule Baardson was God's stepchild on earth: that was the riddle of him." He was the stepchild, only, because, while possessing the richest gifts of courage and wisdom he lacked legitimacy or grace and therefore was destined not to attain kingship. The idea suggests both that of "die Kinder des Hauses" and the medieval-Elizabethan concept of divine right. It is not a mere matter of blood—for, as Miranda (surprisingly wise in such matters) observes in *The Tempest*,"good wombs have borne bad sons"—but of inner potency and grace, a spiritual legitimacy which is the mark of the modern leader in contrast to the divine right of the old hereditary leader. Whether the letter

Bishop Nicholas dangled before Skule proved or disproved Haakon's blood ties almost was irrelevant, for Haakon had the higher and more effective legitimacy of spiritual grace. Haakon, however, remains something of an abstraction in the play, for it is impossible for the author or the audience to "get inside" him. Confronted by him, one is impressed but somewhat chilled as one is when confronting someone who is convinced he or she has "found the faith" —the Christian or Marxian, for example,—someone whose shining-eyed confidence seems not fully human. Haakon possesses a faith that does not need to be "proved" upon the pulses" (in Keat's phrase) or tested on every level of experience of life including an agonizing doubt as to the validity of the faith itself such as is suffered by the hero of Ibsen's next great play, *Brand*. Such faith, to our deepest level of reflection, is really the possession of an illusion. It is the need to escape from one's own doubts, the inability to live in uncertainty, that impels people to be impressed by such illusory qualities as the "charisma" of a leader or the certitude of a faith or dogma. Ibsen was too deep and independent a poet, too committed to integrity of will and intellect, to need the simplifying allegiances upon which dogmas and demagoguery thrive. So it is not surprising that Haakon, the man of destiny presented without irony, is unique in his gallery of portraits.

Skule's conflict with Haakon served the purpose of bringing to an ultimate crisis the legacy of disunity that Haakon had to overcome. If Haakon was to evolve a new unity from the old conditions, they had to be "worked through" dialectically to their logical outcome, and it was by representing the old condition of disunity at its most challenging that Skule, a victim of "the cunning of Reason" (*die List der Vernunft*), ensured that Haakon's victory would be final. Ibsen was to write one more historical drama, and in it he explores Skule's dilemma and the irony of his contribution to the processes of history to its deepest and furthest reaches. Julian, the far more brilliant prince of a far more brilliant culture, also is God's stepchild on earth, and round his body, too, the other characters gather to contemplate the mystery of his existence and his purpose.

BRAND
The Tragedy of Vocation

I am not one of those taking part in the strife, but I am both the combatants, and am the strife itself. I am the fire and the water which touch each other.

> Hegel
> *Lectures on the*
> *Philosophy of Religion*

In *Love's Comedy* Ibsen tentatively created a scene that was both an extension of the range of human gesture into cosmic space and, at the same time, the metaphoric expression of the human spirit's highest and deepest levels of experience. This was achieved by an emphatically vertical landscape, from sea to mountain heights, surrounding the little human community in the valley. Used as a symbolic frame of reference, the landscape put into perspective the larger human drama that would have been lost sight of had the scene been restricted to the world of the community alone. Thus the scenography of the play records the Romantic movement's exploration beyond the social scene of eighteenth-century drama. Yet, by taking into account the world of civic community, the play rejected the tendency of Romanticism to bypass the social world altogether and to present its spiritual heroes and heroines as isolated characters communing only with the world of nature. The finer elements in the human community, Falk and Svanhild, were shown to be lured toward the immensity of the natural world, and it, in turn, seemed to act upon them, influencing their responsive spirits. The play closed with the rebel hero, Falk, determining to travel up to the mountain peaks.

In *Brand* an even more immense landscape surrounding the

human community is not only indicated but actively explored by the central heroic consciousness, Brand himself. In his address to the reader of the narrative poem *Brand,* Ibsen described his "song" as resembling a landscape, rising by easy gradients from the peasants' ground to vistas of snow-clad peaks. In the final, dramatic form of the poem, this ascending landscape, stretching from its sea depths to its mountain peaks, is all the time present as a vital space of action, defining the levels of that action. Once before, in *Olaf Liliekrans,* Ibsen created a symbolic landscape that was metaphorically explored by its major characters: Olaf's ascent from the valley and Alfhild's descent from the hills clearly defined contrasting levels of spiritual reality. Alfhild will "become" the much more disturbing mountain dweller, Gerd, in *Brand,* with the idealist remoteness from reality that she represented now looked at far more critically. There is a far greater degree of conceptual complexity in the metaphoric landscape of *Brand* than in that of *Olaf Liliekrans,* and the fact that all its levels are not divided between separate characters but can be found within the spirit of one character, Brand himself, makes far a more decisive engagement with the natural world.

The peasant valley, which also is the scene of Brand's origins, hidden from the sight of the sun and of the peaks, is the "fallen" or "alienated" scene for the lowest level of spiritual action; the level of material needs and social conformity. At the opposite extreme is the ice-church, the domain of the totally anarchic and manic Gerd—an extreme to which, by painful logic, Brand heroically is driven. It is not just that the symbolic natural setting and its levels *define* human actions; the levels seem to be spiritual *lures,* often begetting the actions, somewhat like a sublime Snakes and Ladders where certain spiritual "moves" lead to alarming vertical consequences. We should look at the landscape of *Brand* as if it were a Romantic landscape painting that had the ability to change seasons, weather, light, and darkness; this drama of the huge landscape being a visible extension of the drama of the human figures who can be seen struggling within the landscape. This also will be the landscape of the realistic cycle of plays, from *Pillars of Society* to *When We Dead Awaken,* an ambient spiritual environment expressed through natural details, to which the human figures are variously attuned.

Looking at *Brand* as if it were a living, peopled landscape, we almost can define the characters by asking where they "stand" in the total picture, how adequately they are aware of, and respond to and explore, its immensities. Different scenes in the play create different scenic compositions, with some of these strongly calling to mind the subjects of Romantic painters and engravers. One such scene which, in the book, cries out for a Gustav Doré illustration is in act 2: Brand and Agnes cross the stormy fjord as the townspeople huddle fearfully on the shore; meanwhile, high above from a cliff, the fantastic, manic Gerd shrieks and hurls stones down on the pair.[1]

The scenography explored by Ibsen in *Brand* is a fusion of the Schillerian and the Wagnerian landscapes. We find, as in Schiller, an objectively observed landscape in which events, however appropriate to the human drama, occur through natural causes; but we find also, as in Wagner, a landscape that is the direct symbolic expression of the human and spiritual drama. In Schiller's *William Tell* the gorgeous natural settings are not strictly essential to the drama because the struggle for liberty against alien historical injustice does not require the dramatic verticals and impressive shifts in light and weather that Schiller lavishes on his play so effectively. These are the perquisites the playwright enjoys from the Swiss setting of his drama, and he uses the landscape skillfully to reproach the pettiness of human injustice with the majestic indifference of the natural world; or he reveals the natural setting to be one in which the Swiss, unlike their oppressors, are "at home" and which they can use to their advantage. In the superb scene of act 2, scene 2, Schiller presents us with a magnificent natural spectacle. The Swiss rebels have gathered in the open air to unit against tyranny. The scene is a meadow surrounded by high cliffs and woods:

On the cliffs are paths with railings and ladders by which the countrymen later are seen descending. In the background appears the lake, over which a moon rainbow is seen as the scene begins. The view is closed by lofty mountains, behind which ice-covered peaks tower higher. The scene is dark, but the lake and the white glaciers gleam in the moonlight.[2]

The purpose of the setting is to give heroic definition to the idea of liberty for which the conspirators gather, to suggest a huge sphere of reality free of human tyranny which therefore makes all the more "natural" the rebels' indignation at the petty tyranny of Gessler and the political forces behind him. But Schiller is too good a Kantian to invest nature with moral or spiritual value. The realm of moral and spiritual value is that of the human community and its ethical, political, and religious life whose institutions can and must be made responsive to moral law. When the rebels' meeting in the meadow closes on a note of heroic affirmation, the scene directions tell us:

As they go away in three different directions in profound silence, the orchestra strikes up a splendid flourish. The empty stage remains open for a while and shows the spectacle of the sun rising above the glaciers.[3]

We see the wholly *aesthetic* nature of this setting. We, as audience, are meant to contemplate it, stirred by the musical accompaniment, and to see in the splendid landscape an *analogy* to the spiritual freedom that the play proclaims. But this is all that the landscape does. It is not symbolic, and its verticals are not explored by the essential action of the play as they are in *Brand. Brand* recovers for modern drama, in even more extensive and profound terms, the natural metaphors of the Shakespearean drama. In *Macbeth*, the natural world is part of the same continuum of spirit in which the human world exists, and a convulsion in one part of the structure—the murder of the king—begets a convulsion throughout the whole, from the world of external nature agitated by storm, to the internal nature of Macbeth who can no longer distinguish dream from reality.

Richard Wagner created a wholly "subjective" symbolic cosmos in which the landscape was only the landscape of the soul; its depths and heights, from the Rhine depths to Valhalla, were shadowy embodiments of states of mind. In *The Ring of the Nibelungs* the Rhine maidens swim, singing underwater, pursued by the spiritually and physically deformed Alberich—symbolic of the primitive lust that turns into compensatory greed for the gold shining in the deeps. An underground world of dwarfs becomes enslaved by this material greed derived from Alberich's thwarted passion. At the other extreme is the castle of Valhalla, representing Wotan's realm of divine intellect. The theater stage magically lightens and darkens, flashing its symbols at the appropriate moments in defiance of all laws of nature and of physics. Fire and flood rise in response to the human drama and valkyries fly through the air. It is a great spiritual pantomime in which everything serves a subjective allegory more extraordinary and fantastic than the great objective allegories of Dante, Spenser, and Bunyan. It is a landscape of the spirit, from infantile watery depths to the heights of Wotan's intellect comprising power and empire. It also is a world strangely denuded of human, historical, and rational content: a landscape almost polar in its nudity, so that the Wieland Wagner scenic innovations at Bayreuth, where the figures sing and gesture against a background seemingly composed only of northern lights, are tellingly appropriate. Not only does the prehistoric, prerational cosmos of *The Ring* deny the relevancy of history and rationality; it denies the objective reality of nature. Instead of encountering alienated reality, Wagner simply bypasses it and puts in its place images and actions that are the expression of nothing more than the subjective drama which the poet believes he has discovered in the subconscious (and therefore authentic) life of the race.

The great achievement of *Brand* is that its symbolic landscape is expressive of the spiritual drama, as is Wagner's, but at the same time it recognizes the objectivity of this landscape, as does Schiller. All the events of this landscape, from the first storm to the final avalanche, have objective, natural causes, yet they are the symbolically apposite extensions of the human drama, not pictorial embellishments of it. At times the action of the play seems conventionally allegorical in the manner of Spenser or Bunyan, where scenes and events are tied to a given structure of meanings. At other times actions within the natural world are explored in terms of a Romantic and subjective parable, as in Melville's *Moby Dick* or the novels of Hawthorne. A metaphysical symbology is revealed by actions within the natural world; indeed, Melville's symbol of Captain Ahab's fanatic quest — the white whale — and Ibsen's symbol of Brand's quest at its most extreme and abstract — the remote, glittering, white ice-church — are very similar in meaning.

The opening scene of *Brand* reveals the way its scenography serves multiple purposes and how Ibsen's creation of a visual symbolism has evolved from the single, central symbol of the burial mound to a totally symbolic setting, an ambient symbology. Brand, accompanied by a peasant and his son, is risking all their lives to cross a treacherous mountain plateau riddled with fatal crevasses. He insists on the overriding importance of the crossing, and his heroism is reproachfully contrasted with the pusillanimity of the peasants, who finally will not risk their lives to bring comfort to a dying girl. The action of crossing the treacherous plateau, while having a realistic motive (bringing absolution to the dying girl), also performs the same allegorical function as Dante's finding himself in the darkling wood, Spenser's Red Cross Knight on the plain, or the wood in which Christian, in *Pilgrim's Progress,* discovers himself.

The scene is meant to represent an actual landscape in which the danger of losing one's life is a literal possibility, but at the same time it is evident that the landscape is allegorical, that its verticals, from seadepths to glacier, is the theatrical or fictional equivalent of a mental landscape such as that described by Gerard Manley Hopkins:

> O the mind, mind has mountains; cliffs of fall
> Frightful, sheer, no-man-fathomed. Hold them cheap
> May who ne'er hung there.[4]

This, however, is extremely difficult, if not impossible, to translate into *theatrical* action. Although *language* is able to maintain a series of links between natural and mental processes (by investing human emotions with nature-derived images and investing natural forces with imagery taken from human emotions), it is not easy to transfer the same emotions onto visually presented objects of nature or to invest human gestures with superhuman significance. This required a far more precise visual notation—of props, sets, and actors' gestures—which Greek drama no doubt possessed, which Elizabethan theater possessed to a degree, which we find in Japanese theater, both Noh and Kabuki, and which Ibsen finally evolved, in realistic terms, for his cycle.

The visual notations in *Brand,* with a few exceptions, are not of this precise order, and it is hard to see how an actor, performing the scene described above, can embody the symbolic as well as the literal meaning. This is not a defect of the play for it was written not to be performed but to be read, and it is the reader who surrounds the human gestures with their symbolic equivalents. There is a major difference in the nature of the attention we give to a theatrical performance, at which we vigilantly "see" what is presented to our eyes, and the attention we give to a "mental drama" like *Brand* or *Peer Gynt,* for which we translate the words we read on the page into an inner fictive world where we can invest the gestures with larger symbolic resonance than an actor and his props could supply. *Brand* and *Peer Gynt* are such impressive reading experiences that we naturally assume they will be equally successful theatrical experiences, more successful than individual plays in the realistic cycle. Yet this, I believe, is not correct, for the reasons already mentioned, and directors in fact find they have to supply many imaginative theatrical additions to the texts to make them work. Directors love to do this, of course, and therefore are likely to pronounce a play such as *Peer Gynt* "greater theater" than *Ghosts.* [5]

Another episode in the play that, one feels, cannot be enacted with any adequate expression of its symbolic meaning is Brand's encounter with Einar and Agnes—at this stage a pair of "aesthetic" and hedonistic characters—who are cheerfully running, dancing, and laughing on the edge of a precipice, holding their danger cheap because they have not fathomed it. *Reading* the poem we can supply the obvious allegorical meaning; but were we watching *Brand* in the theater, their action would be one of simulated physical danger only, for that would be our visual experience of the situation. All of this merely indicates that whereas, in *Brand,* Ibsen has fully created his total metaphoric "world" and its symbology, he has not yet created its *theatrical* expression.

The levels of the poetic world of *Brand* reach from seadepths to mountain heights. This is what Rolf Fjelde, in his essay "The Dimensions of *Ibsen's Dramatic World,*" has termed a "scenography of nature" which can stand comparison with the total worldviews of Greek and Elizabethan drama.[6] (see facing page)

There is no direct statement in the play that Brand's parsonage is a little *above* the village, but the evident remoteness of the parsonage from the village, the fact that visitors to it are seen from a distance, that it is bleak and exposed, and that Gerd and the

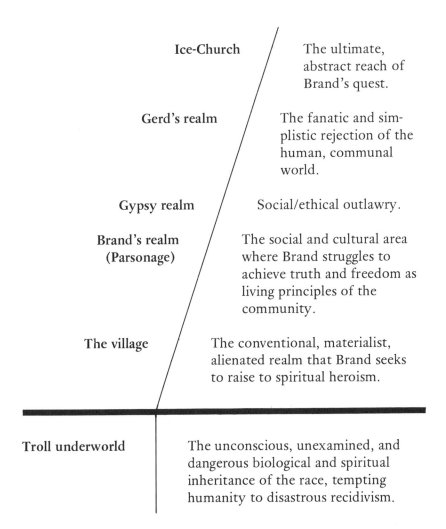

Ice-Church	The ultimate, abstract reach of Brand's quest.
Gerd's realm	The fanatic and simplistic rejection of the human, communal world.
Gypsy realm	Social/ethical outlawry.
Brand's realm (Parsonage)	The social and cultural area where Brand struggles to achieve truth and freedom as living principles of the community.
The village	The conventional, materialist, alienated realm that Brand seeks to raise to spiritual heroism.
Troll underworld	The unconscious, unexamined, and dangerous biological and spiritual inheritance of the race, tempting humanity to disastrous recidivism.

gypsies who inhabit the heath and the hills visit it, suggests it is situated on higher, remoter ground than the village. The lowest realm of this scenography, the troll underworld, represents regression to an alarming recidivism, a startling animality beneath the conscious surface that can burst into the open at any time. This is explicitly stated in Gerd's speech in act **3** when she believes Brand is about to abandon his struggle with and for his community:

"Have you heard? The priest's absconded!"
From the hills and from the barrows
Swarm troll-shapes and apparitions
Dark and hideous, large and small.
Ugh! how viciously they're clawing,
Almost taking out my eyeball;
Snatching out half of my soul . . .
. . . Listen! all the bells around us
Ring together down the heathlands.
Can you fathom why these myriads
Travel down *that* chapel way?
Can you see the trolls in thousands
Whom the priest to the sea depths banished?
Can you see the thousand dwarf shapes?
Until now they lay fast-buried
With the priest's seal heavy on them.
Sea and grave no longer hold them:
Out they're swarming, cold and clammy,
Troll-babes, seeming dead, rise, snarling
Rolling back the rocks behind them
Screaming, "Hear us, mother, father,"
And human parents give them answer!
The parishioner walks proud among them
Like a father with his sons
And women take these risen corpses
And feed their dead mouths with their breasts.[7]

In this nightmare, which seems to express the most primitive of terrors, that of the *gengangere* or risen dead returning to plague the living, the landscape bursts open in a hellish eruption, and swarms of hideous and monstrous figures, hitherto lying dormant and uneasily subdued by Brand's unwearying battle with the trolls that infest the mind and heart, take possession again of the human community, like the forces of a terrifying subhumanity repossessing a whole nation that has unlearned the painful lessons of hard-won civilization. This frightful atavism is a spiritual or mental event, but it also occurs as an external event in the world of nature which acts out the human drama on a vast scale, involving both the sea and the land. This primeval underworld (we meet it again in *Peer Gynt*) seems to consist of man's biological and spiritual past; the animalistic and primitive strata of his identity still exist beneath his modern persona and are kept in abeyance only by mental fight. We see how the mythic and subconscious areas of psychic and cultural life, in this passage, are extended into the natural terms of an objective landscape. This seething underworld of monstrous forces seems the opposite extreme of the static, frozen, overhanging, and equally menacing ice-church with *its* accumulations of century after century of slow and glacial activity. The extremes are of a horrifying animality at one end and of a terrifying, chill abstraction at the other. This is very similar to Julian's account, to Basil and Gregory, of his tranced experience of hovering over a terrifying abyss between a slimy seabed, far below, and the silent arch of the sky above.

The village, lying so dangerously near this threatening subhuman world, has compromised drastically with the "ideal" realm which should shape its vision, and has settled, instead, for a way of life limited to immediate material needs and to the comfortable but soul-stifling debasement of its rich spiritual inheritance. This inheritance has been reduced to a sentimental travesty that can only debase the spirit further. Brand is a Moses descending to a people who are bound to the golden calf, and his first opponent, the sheriff, seems a version of Aaron, worldly and benignant, who has utterly turned his back on the life of the spirit.

Brand and Agnes establish their home somewhat apart from and higher than the community, and it is here that they fight their own higher and more tragic drama, which results in the death of the couple's infant son, then of Agnes. In the last act Brand descends to the village again and attempts to lead his people up the mountainside to a new promised land of authentic spiritual life. The whole community mounts toward the deadly ice-church and even when they finally turn back, it seems they are involved in the disaster that overtakes Brand and Gerd, just as Captain Ahab's crew perishes with their leader; for the ending of the play implies that the avalanche which "fills the whole valley" wipes out the community too.

At the end of act 1, Brand, in a soliloquy, had declared the falsity of the ice-church after encountering its frenzied guardian, Gerd. He then proceeded to define three types of spiritual error: the frivolous courage that did not understand the danger it was in (Einar and Agnes); the dull slothfulness of the unawakened people imprisoned in degenerate conventions; and the mad fantasizing that could not distinguish between good and evil, fair and foul (the manic vision of Gerd). Each of these "three trolls" is a "deadly enemy" to the suffering world, against which Brand sees he has to struggle. Together they constitute a "triple alliance" against humanity.[8]

In the poem *Brand,* Einar was to be given a far more prominent place as representative of the "aesthetic" vision which, as in Kierkegaard's *Either/Or,* was to be superseded by the "ethical" vision of Brand. By the time he came to write the play Ibsen either decided that it would be an undramatic situation or he no longer accorded to the aesthetic vision so prominent a place; and it was at about this time that he wrote to Bjørnson that he had freed himself from the aesthetic creed. The second element of the triple alliance, the earthbound vision unable to raise its eyes beyond its immediate and customary round of narrow action, engages much more of Brand's attention (for Einar's "frivolous" concept of God is fairly swiftly dismissed), and the representatives of this material-ist vision, the sheriff, the schoolmaster, the dean, and the doctor, obviously maintain a far stronger hold over the popular imagina-tion than does the artist. Furthermore, the sheriff and the doctor are formidable intellectual opponents. They present to Brand the identical argument the Grand Inquisitor presents to Christ in Dostoevsky's lurid fable, the argument Relling will repeat against Gregers Werle in *The Wild Duck:* that, because common humanity is incapable of the heroic individualism and idealism required by Brand, such a humanity is best served by wise and humanitarian leaders who satisfy the material and spiritual hunger of their flocks with the minimum of spiritual danger.

The third member of the triple alliance is the fanaticism of Gerd and her ice-church, a fanaticism which is deadly because Gerd's "shortcut" to the spiritual sublime evades the complex, chastening, tragically painful *human* experience out of which, alone, the spirit can grow authentically and establish its fully human values. Gerd's fanaticism is in many ways Brand's most deadly opponent. For although the other two aspects of the triple alliance were external opponents against which he could do battle, Gerd's fanaticism is an extreme to which Brand himself might succumb. His painful, reluctant ascent to the ice-church is filled with human involvement and suffering: his spiritual drama is fought on all levels, from the atavistic realm of the subconscious, symbolized by the underworld and the seadepths, through the immediate personal realities of painful parental and familial conflict and suffering, to the wider circle of citizenship within the community and its history. Brand could echo the words of Falk:

> A man must be the citizen of his age
>
> Yet raise the age of which he would be citizen.[9]

Only by experiencing tortuous human realities can Brand liberate his spirit, transcending the alienation of the world in order to serve God and be his priest. That his quest ends in tragedy and in painful paradox is no refutation of his endeavor for, as Kierkegaard asserts at the conclusion of *Either/Or,* "Against God we are always in the wrong":

Though you were to knock but it was not opened unto you, though you were to seek but you did not find, though you were to labor but acquired nothing, though you were to plant and water but saw no blessing, though heaven were to remain closed and the witness fail to appear, you are joyful in your work nevertheless; though the punishment which the iniquity of the fathers had called down were to fall on you, you are joyful nevertheless, for against God we are always in the wrong.[10]

Brand moves through "alienated" space and time: through a harsh and mostly sunless landscape to which he is reluctantly bound and which actually destroys him ultimately; and through a present time in which the accumulations of the past, of personal, familial, and communal guilt and betrayed values, decide the nature of the present. All the while, there is maintained, in the play, a close correspondence between Brand's inward, personal progression and his exploration of the outward world and its history in which he finds himself, from the darkened valley of his mother's sunless home to the deadly ice-church that perpetually hangs like a nemesis over the scene. The great reach of Brand's spirit, which always tests the human and the ideological implications of his quest in terms of existential experience, means that Brand is the outstanding spiritual explorer of his world. With *Brand,* there no longer existed for Ibsen a separation between the subjective, inner world and the objective outer world; the mind was a cosmos extended in time and space, and the exploration of this cosmos was the exploration of mind or spirit. This will give Ibsen, later, the notation for a new and authentic theatrical poetry, because situations within the human mind can be translated directly as situations within a landscape, and, conversely, the delineation of a landscape and the changes that occur in it, such as light and shadow, height and depth, seasons, weather, can be the notations of spiritual change. This is not the "pathetic fallacy" in which nature takes on the coloring of human qualities but the creation of a mental landscape, a means of objectifying what Ibsen sees as the structure of the mind into the largest possible terms as the structure of the cosmos.

A method that is both symbolic and realistic, both a metaphysical allegory and an intensely felt human drama, is one that, for the modern reader who is used to the two modes being decently separated, is difficult to grasp. Something of the same situation is found in the American writers Hawthorne, Melville, and, to a greater extent than is realized, Henry James. One is reminded, also, of the paintings of Caspar David Friedrich, in which allegorical meanings are conveyed by the most meticulously observed and carefully rendered realistic details.

Just as the scenography of the play is part of the concept that is to be dialectically developed by the hero's actions—a *space* to be filled by the human spirit's aspirations—so the surrounding *time* is a medium in which the human spirit extends itself, finding in the past, and the contrast of the past to the present, signposts pointing to the future goal of its own prospectively achieved identity. Both the surrounding space and the surrounding time can be seen as a series of expanding symbolic circumferences through which the hero pushes, seeking the ultimate circumference represented, perhaps, by the ice-church: a cold, remote abstraction that has existed long before, and will continue long after, human history.

Not only is the past a medium in which Brand's spirit extends itself; in its negative aspect it rises up before him as a barrier preventing his moving onward, south, to the virgin land which, in

Agnes's vision in act 2, waits for him to fill it with new life.[11] In this scene, Brand has just emerged from the cottage where the father murdered his own child and killed himself. Brand reflects on how this action will reverberate through the future generations of the family, setting up an inescapable pattern of guilt and retribution like the curse on the house of Labdacus or the curse of Original Sin which, in Christian mythology, lies upon the human race. Brand hopes to escape the curse by traveling to a new land, and he rejects a villager's plea to remain behind in the sunless valley. Agnes presents to Brand an image of his life in the new land:

> I can hear a voice proclaiming
> Thou shalt people this new earth!
> Every thought that shall be spoken,
> Each act to be undertaken
> Waken, whisper, breathing, calling,
> As if their birth time was arriving ... [12]

In excited response to this, Brand cries out:

> Within! within! There's the summons!
> There's the path that we must follow.
> In each heart the new world's fashioned,
> Shaped for a new life with God.
> There the will-devourer's vanquished,
> There, reborn, is the new Adam.
> Let the world continue moving
> In slavery or jubilation.
> But if as enemy it meets me
> Seeking to destroy my lifework,
> Then, by heaven, to death I'll fight it.
> The world's whole space at least is needed
> For the self's complete fulfillment.
> That's the lawful right of mankind.
> Less than this I will not ask for.[13]

In this speech is contained the Romantic revolt against a world whose institutionalized conventions and values deny the potentialities the Romantic rebel felt to be his birthright. Brand's desire to go out into the world and create a new intellectual kingdom recalls the aspirations of the early Wordswroth, of Blake, and of Byron and Shelley. But, reflecting on the father's murder again, Brand falters before this vision of spiritual freedom and asks:

> To be oneself entire; but how, then,
> Can we loose the debt of guilt.[14]

At this moment, Brand's mother appears, blinking uncomfortably in the light of the sun. Here is the first "circumference" of the multilayered past, the circumference of Brand's immediate parental origins. Persuaded to renounce love for wealth and a loveless marriage (an action, it is startling to reflect, that was given approvingly to Svanhild in *Love's Comedy*), Brand's mother has led a life that has been one long betrayal of her soul, a betrayal that Brand inherits as his first burden of guilt.

The mother's renunciation of love has led to Brand's involvement in Gerd's frantic condition. In a somewhat tortuous explanation, the sheriff tells Brand that the latter is related to Gerd because his mother's rejected young lover turned for consolation to a band of gypsy women and fathered a brood of anarchic gypsies including Gerd. This detail we will discuss later, for it seems an important, if perplexing, element of the total metaphor of the play. In the figure of the mother, therefore, the past already has loomed up problematically before Brand, creating a barrier between himself and the new realm of intellectual freedom he had envisaged. From this immediate, familial past of guilt by blood association, Brand also will explore the whole alienated past of institutionalized society and of degraded and guilty historical tradition, all of which act as barriers against spiritual truth and freedom. The self can be freed only if it conquers this past, breaking the "mind forg'd manacles" that imprison the spirit. There is, however, no magic formula to cut the Gordian knot of alienated reality. The problem, here, is that which haunted Romanticism from Blake on and which the betrayal of the French revolution made all the more evident. How is one to create a world conforming to the highest human ideas of truth and freedom when the legacy of untruth and unfreedom lies within our blood, within our language, within our most intimate individual and interpersonal modes of speech and action, as well as in the history that defines us and the institutions under which we live? We cannot trust our very self-communings, because they are infected with this inheritance, unknown to ourselves. We understand why more than once Ibsen insisted that external liberties, external revolutions, were irrelevant, that what was needed was "a revolution in the spirit of man." The old, confident days of rational progress, when one could proclaim, "We hold these truths to be self-evident...," seem like the childhood of thought—when it was believed that the mere proclamation and dissemination of "self-evident" truths would bring about a Golden Age of justice. The awareness in the nineteenth century of the hold of the past upon the present, of the ghosts (*gengangere*) that infect every area of human life (an awareness that was to lead to the depth psychology of the present age) places a huge gulf between itself and the age of enlightenment.

The institutionalized past has travestied its spiritual inheritance so that its traditions have become the acceptable and sentimentalized past of which the sheriff can approve. Ibsen's own earlier connivance in the creation of sentimentalized heroics in historical drama (although, as we saw, his exploration of the past has a serious, conceptual purpose) makes him now acutely conscious of this form of inauthenticity. This was to lead not to Ibsen's abandoning his belief in the past's grip upon the present but to his seeing this in far deeper and more complex terms. The past was a rich inheritance that had been betrayed, yet it also was a legacy of error and guilt whose stranglehold upon the present everywhere prevented the emergence of truth and freedom. The old *heroic* past, such as that of *The Vikings at Helgeland,* to which the poet and his audience made gratifying excursions from the present, now was descredited; but a new and problematic past, which *reproached* the present and which contained realities whose revelation was unwelcome, now became the disquieting realm into which Ibsen would lead his reluctant audience.

The sentimentalized spiritual past has produced the emasculated God of Einar's art, the drunken and maudlin recollection of the Viking heritage of "King Bele's days," the cramped church and its god-concept, and the dispirited life of the community which has lost sight of its birthright of spiritual freedom and so is unable to lift its eyes "upward" to the spiritual vistas which Brand believes it can come to see and to claim. The sheriff, good-natured and benevolent, as Brand concedes, is yet, he avers, an agent of spiritual death, reconciling the community to its fallen condition. By invoking and attempting to awaken the *subversive* rather than the comforting aspects of this past (as Kierkegaard sought to subvert "Christendom" by resurrecting the uncomfortable identity of Christ), Brand endangers that spiritual sleep of humanity over which the sheriff, schoolmaster, and dean preside. These worthy officials of institutionalized tradition wish only to lead their "sheep" in docile ignorance through a half-life to death, believing, with the Grand Inquisitor, that common humanity is incapable of the heroism of spiritual individualism. One sees the spiritual radicalism of Brand's (and Ibsen's) idealism. Ibsen is not interested in creating a Wagnerian hero, a Siegfried, to whom the rest of humanity must do homage; he wishes to resurrect the heroism within each and every individual.

In Schiller's splendid historical dramas, the great forces of historical and institutionalized tradition versus the forces of freedom, forces of superstition against those of enlightenment, of love against repression, had taken on archetypal life and power in such oppositions as the Grand Inquisitor and the Marquis of Posa, the Duke of Alba and Prince Carlos, King Phillip and Queen Elizabeth. In plays like *Don Carlos* and *Mary Stuart,* the reader or viewer has the exhilarating sense of seeing great world-historical forces taking on palpable, glamorous identity while being ranged in conflict in a splendid rhetoric of words and actions. In *Brand,* the same forces have dwindled to the conflict between a village priest and the village's petty officials, but the great conflicts of Schillerian drama are present and are localized so that their operation upon our experience of everyday life can be more accurately understood. In Schillerian drama these forces for good and evil had been kept at a rhetorical distance, where they could be affirmed or denied in a glow of liberal righteousness; in *Brand* they are brought uncomfortably close to home, and neither affirmation nor denial is quite so easy to achieve—a highly discomforting process which Ibsen was to develop to its ultimate in the realistic cycle.

The typical Romantic hero was portrayed as a wanderer: Words-worth's wanderer figures, Byron's Childe Harold, Manfred, and Don Juan, Goethe's Faust (a wanderer through time as well as space), Wagner's Flying Dutchman, Lohengrin, Wotan, and Parsifal, and Ibsen's Peer Gynt. These heroes detach themselves from their communities, often travel immense spans of time and space, live in an imaginative medium of lofty generalization and sometimes of lurid fantasy. Finding any human community too small for their wideranging thoughts and feelings, they generally are at home in only the wildest and grandest of natural settings. Not wanting to do battle with institutionalized reality, yet feeling hostile to the historical processes that have given rise to the conditions of modern society, they simply, in Arnold's phrase, "put it by."[15] Brand shares much of the Romantic spirit of rejection of alienated social reality, but Ibsen's hero fights his battle within the community. His contempt for the social forces represented by the sheriff, school-master, and dean equals that of Byron and Shelley for institution-alized law, learning, and religion but, more radical than the two English poets, he wishes directly to transform this alienated histo-rical and social reality into vital spiritual reality. Peer Gynt, on the other hand, who best performs the Romantic roles of wanderer, seer, and rebel, betrays Romantic aspirations the most.

Ibsen, who admired Byron, seems nevertheless to have detected the lack of substance, the evasion of direct dialectical conflict, in the Romantic gesturing; he must have seen that truly to establish Romantic ideals meant making them seriously take on ordinary life at its most intractably ordinary. The way in which *Brand* locks Romantic idealism into the world of class conflict and of personal and social actuality is reflected even in the language of the play. The clenched and constrained nature of the octosyllabic verse suggests an almost unbearable constriction of the spirit; in contrast to the looser, freewheeling, and shifting verse form of *Peer Gynt.*

All of history turns upon the inward decisions of a country priest in a remote Norwegian village. Because each modern indivi-dual consciousness is the heir to, and the product of, all human consciousness, each individual inherits the entire human history of achievement and loss, glory and guilt, and, if he or she is to be "awakened," must confront the demands implied by this past immediately in his or her personal life and, above all, in his or her vocation.[16] We see how this essentially Romantic concept in many ways resurrects, in secular and larger terms, the drama of consciousness of Christianity, in which each individual inherits the history of the Fall and at the same time inherits the means by which to overcome it.

Brand's identity, his relation to his world, is not a "given" but something that must be painfully realized through a tremendous act of will: a heroic rejection of all that is inauthentic in his world and an equally heroic attempt to establish the authentic. It is in his *vocation* as priest that Brand is able to realize authentic identity; that is, vocation is the way of salvation. For this reason Ibsen insisted his hero might have had some vocation other than priest, such as sculptor—or poet. As long as the hero strove to realize his authentic identity through his vocation, whatever its form, he would face the same struggle as Brand. Furthermore, the attainment of heroic identity by means of vocation is a possibility for each one of us. The hero, in other words, is not a select individual, with god-given or magical or mysterious sanctions, but each one of us who performs the willed action of choosing, then authentically living up to, a vocation. In *Brand* the tragic hero is finally and forever removed from his special "grace" and remoteness and becomes a reproachful paradigm of our own possible best self. The requirement upon the individual, again, is not unlike that upon the individual member of the Christian community. The major difference is that the identity of "Christian" is "given" whereas that of vocation has to be personally chosen by a wholly individual act of will. As Jean Paul Sartre stated:

Not only is man what he conceives himself to be, but he also is only what he wills himself to be after this first thrust towards existence. Man is nothing else but what he makes of himself. Such is the first principle of existentialism.[17]

As there no longer existed a system of valid sanctions guiding man to the realization of his true identity, he would need to discover and maintain this, existentially, minute by minute. He could allow no compromise, for this would endanger the identity he was maintaining with so much effort. Brand is not trying to be a perfect Christian; he is trying to be a perfect priest, and it may be that the vocation of priest, if pursued with absolute integrity, must exclude the elements of mercy and love that would soften the terrible demands of God. The doctor can soften these demands, for that is admirably within the nature of his vocation as doctor, but the priest cannot, without compromising the office of priest. He is to bear witness to his people of the terrible and unforgivable nature of spiritual blindness, and such a Savanarola cannot weaken the force of this idea by lapses into kindly indulgence. Brand must be a totally uncompromising priest no matter what the cost to himself or others, and it is for this reason that he is led to tragic, honorable inflexibility.

It therefore is irrelevant to the argument of the play to question whether Brand is right or wrong as a Christian; one can argue only whether he is true to his vocation as priest and whether he carries it to its ultimate conclusion. If the identity of priest is to be valid in the world, it requires someone to prove it, to take it on totally, for to be a part priest, a priest *almost* totally, with some kindly backsliding, is not to establish the validity of the identity of priest in the world. This probably is the "syllogistic" or logical aspect of the play to which Ibsen referred, and, in fact, the play really only makes sense as a tragedy of vocation, of chosen identity.[18]

Brand chooses his identity of priest, then strives to realize this identity in terms of his vocation, existentially proving it upon the world and upon himself. The stringency of Brand's quest for authentic priesthood derives not from personal psychological idiosyncrasy but from the need to define, by living experience, what relation to the world is entailed by priesthood. He discovers that it is one in which no compromise can ever be allowed between the priest's authentic relation to his conception of God and the bearing witness of this relation to his community. If the effort of realizing this identity is not the greatest and highest, it is better not to attempt it at all; if it is not "all," it is better that it is "nothing" for as nothing it does not compromise and debase the idea of priest. If Brand ever yields and compromises, he has put into danger the idea of priest and the idea of God which the priest serves: not only has he endangered his own chosen identity, he has endangered the "archetypal" identity of priest and passed on a debased inheritance to the future.

Although Brand tests it existentially in terms of harrowing self-sacrifice, such a concept, both of priest and of God, is chillingly above most human experience, as coldly remote as the icechurch that hangs over the community. Brand is as determined to be a priest as Antigone was to be a sister or Creon to be a ruler, and the result, as in Greek drama, is far more uncomfortable to the human community than the lurid villainy of a Richard III. It is because the play is about vocation rather than about character that the hero is led to the paradoxical conclusion of attempting to save humanity by an ideal no humanity can be expected to adhere to. *Brand*, in fact, rediscovers the *paradox* of heroism that Greek tragedy explored, for the Greek hero, wonderful and admirable as he is, also is an alarming and often disastrous presence in his community. The hero of Greek tragedy pushes to extremes from which the community, symbolized by the chorus, fearfully and wisely shrinks back, yet, at the death of the hero, of an Antigone, Ajax, Oedipus, the community also feels it has been in touch with a presence resembling the divine. Heroism is tactless, awkward, alarming, but it dares to test an aspect of life to its limits—fidelity with Antigone, knowledge with Oedipus, honor with Ajax—thereby forcing the integrity of these concepts upon a community that would prefer to compromise them. In the modern world, chosen vocation is the only equivalent to the Greek concept of heroism, and Brand resembles his classic prototypes by the manner in which he pushes the essence of his vocation to the extreme of perverse heroism.[19]

In *Brand*, for the first time in drama, a bourgeois hero attains a stature equal in tragic dignity and force to that of the heroes of Greek, Elizabethan, and neoclassical tragedy, and he attains this stature through *intrinsic* greatness, through "authenticity." The extrinsic heroic sanctions of heritage and rank were discredited in post-revolutionary Europe, and the attempt to revive such extrinsic heroics, as in grand opera or such vapid enterprises as Victor Hugo's *Hernani*, only confirmed their irrevocable demise. Brand is heir to the great Romantic exploration, in art and thought, that discovered "within" the only authentic as well as the most profound and sublime spiritual realities—the *potential heritage* of every modern man and woman irrespective of rank or class. Brand's speech beginning "Within! within!..." explicitly affirms that it is within each individual spirit that the world can be made new.

The modern hero is a "mental traveler," in William Blake's phrase, "voyaging through strange seas of Thought alone," in Wordsworth's. M. H. Abrams, in *Natural Supernaturalism,*[20] shows how the image of spiritual development as a "circuitous journey" in which the hero ascends a spiral pathway of despair, finally overcoming alienated reality and regaining innocence at a "higher" level, is a constant theme of Romantic thinkers and artists, attaining its ultimate and definitive statement in Hegel's *The Phenomenology of Mind.* The landscape of the mind in which the mental hero is both explorer and conqueror is as strange and dangerous as the external landscape through which a Herakles once journeyed, humanizing the world by defeating its monstrous forces. The historian Herder drew an analogy between Herakles and the modern mental hero when he wrote:

Men who succeed in removing wants from the creation, falsehoods from our memory, and disgraces from our nature, are to the realms of truth, what the heroes of mythology were to the primitive world? they lessen the number of monsters on the Earth.[21]

The modern mental hero does not enjoy metaphysical aid, need not attain to high rank, but, instead, must by his own labors become the vehicle of authentic and significant spiritual power. Frequently in Romantic writing the hero's power comes from an aloofness and often from specifically antisocial situations: he has committed some unmentionable crime, or is an outcast or outlaw, or great suffering has made him remove himself from his community. From this situation of isolation from his fellowmen, and gifted with unusual capacity for profound reflection, he ponders the human condition—in soliloquy—with far greater depth and insight than other men. He has become a hero of thought, and his painful isolation is the price he must pay for his heroism, the equivalent of the heroic isolation of the Greek hero, from Achilles to Philoctetes. Frequently the modern hero finds that his only adequate companions are Nature and History, for in them alone, and not in debased and alienated society, he finds equivalents, on a suitably grand scale, for his own mental landscape. Childe Harold travels a landscape of awesome nature and of countries and cities filled with the ghosts of the past ("Stop! For thy tread is on an Empire's dust!"),[22] Manfred personally confronts and addresses an entire cosmos, speaking directly to the spirit of:

> a star condemn'd,
>
> The burning wreck of a demolish'd world,
>
> A wandering hell in the eternal space . . .[23]

Wordworth's spokesmen, the persona of himself that he creates in *The Prelude,* or his Wanderer figures in reflective poems like the exquisite *Margaret,* are men withdrawn from community, nursed in unusual suffering which they either have experienced or have witnessed. By the sublimity and profundity of their reflections, these men and women become spiritual kings and aristocrats, capable of tragic experience.[24]

Brand is a tragic hero because he explores his world to its limits, so that, with his "fall," a whole spiritual world order falls too. To the frequently muddled question of whether the "common man" can be a tragic hero, the answer must be that, insofar as he is common, he cannot. A tragic hero is as great as the issues he chooses to confront. If the issues are not great, or are not greatly conceived, one may have poignant drama, as in *A Streetcar Named Desire,* but one does not have tragedy. If the hero does not consciously confront the issues, but is a helpless victim of them, as in Buechner's *Woyzeck,* one does not have tragedy, however interesting the play. When neither the issues are great nor the characters intelligently conscious of them, but when the gesturing has all the scale and urgency appropriate to matters of great significance, one has melodrama, as in *The London Merchant* and *The Death of a Salesman.*

Authentic tragedy is the most difficult of dramatic forms, and success in it is far less likely than in other dramatic *genres,* or in such modes as the pathetic, the satiric, or the tragi-comic. A victim is far easier to conceive of than a hero, for the former need not be significantly or daringly articulate, need not act consequentially. Evasive, "indirect" incongruous speech and action are far easier to achieve than tragic speech and action, because the tragic hero must raise greatly conceived and authentic issues — a profound and moving argument—and greatly work them out to their logically inevitable conclusion. This produces an art which, because its eye is on the main thing and cannot be diverted from it, can appear naive and crude when compared with less rigorous methods. Classic severity is not a popular taste because it is concerned with essentials, only, forcing the audience to "see" these essentials and not letting it pleasantly indulge itself with peripheral speculation. Tragedy also is the *genre* in which inauthenticity on the poet's part is most likely to be cruelly exposed.[25]

The greatness of *Brand,* which overcomes the play's faults of prolixity and occasionally too humdrum satire, comes from its *overall* concern with essential issues; it is able to perceive such issues and compellingly follow through the consequences of this perception. The rigors the play sets itself, in its restricted verse-form, its almost perversely unglamorous scene, characters, and actions, and its obstinate and resolute pursuit of its great argument, give the play much of the severity of classic drama. In the little provincial setting, with its humdrum bourgeoisie and peasantry, a drama is taking place which has all the tremendous intellectual import of such overtly world-historical works as *Don Carlos, Mary Stuart,* or *Emperor and Galilean.* All world history is involved in the present actions of Brand, both the conscious inheritance of the race and the subconscious which make up the structure of dialectically conflicting forces in the modern world.

Brand is a great parable forcing us to interpret its details not only on the literal level of humans in conflict but on the philosophical level also, as a criticism of life, and on the allegorical level where the whole drama attempts to be a moving image of the total human condition, from the basest instincts to the most chilling spiritual abstraction. This simultaneous seeing of more than one level of reality within each event is what gives the play (and all of Ibsen's subsequent work) a scale, and a density of texture, similar to that of Greek drama, Also reminiscent of Greek drama is the striking theological boldness of the play, its freedom from the obligation to reflect a dogmatically "given" structure of reality, a freedom deriving from the Romantic movements philosophical independence from orthodox ideology. In *Brand* Ibsen creates a fiction that is the fully adequate expression of his intellectually and imaginatively free argument, and we are expected to "read" that fiction as an argument as well as a story.

Reading the play in such a multilayered way, however, does create difficulties when we encounter details that Ibsen has deemed important enough for his argument to include in his fiction but which do not sufficiently "account for themselves." What, for example, is the reader meant to make of the story of Gerd's parental origins? Her father was the rejected lover of Brand's mother; and the sheriff, straining the fact somewhat, suggests Brand is somehow implicated in Gerd's engendering and madness. One sees the relevance to the theme of a complex heritage of guilt in which any one member is implicated with the entire community; but what is the signficance of the fact that the young lover was a "brilliant scholar"? With strict naturalism one need not consider this overmuch, though one still would deplore an extraneous detail that was not functioning significantly. There is no source that Ibsen is drawing upon (as in historical drama where one has to include details not strictly essential to the argument, but too familiar as historical fact to be left out) to explain the detail. *Brand* is a closed system, a world invented by Ibsen whose details are there by his own choice. In a work that the author himself described as a syllogism and whose intention is to create a great metaphor, nothing is there because, as in a stew, it merely adds a piquant presence. The interpreter is confronted with a riddle to be solved if he or she is to declare the artwork finally coherent; he or she confronts a fragment like a piece in a jigsaw puzzle which, when fitted into its rightful place, not only clarifies its own identity but also clarifies the total design.

That Gerd's father should have been a brilliant young scholar, a stranger to the area, driven half-crazy from rejected love, taking up with a band of gypsies (outcasts) and fathering children upon them, children who now roam the land disturbing conventional society by their anarchic actions and life-style, is too vivid a component of the total design to be set aside except by those who cannot distinguish between art, with its organizing principles, and "real life." If we reflect on the whole argument of the play, the image of the total human condition that it creates, possible meanings suggest themselves. On the most literal level, we are bound to speculate whether the brilliant young scholar from outside the area was not also Brand's father, accounting for Brand's anomalous intellectual power. Brand and Gerd then would be brother and sister, and his mother's crime, of rejecting her young lover and marrying an older man for his wealth, would be all the greater. Since Ibsen does not clear up this matter, it has to remain an interesting speculation only. On the metaphoric level, the detail of the young lover and his progeny does enrich the argument. To the little, closed community comes a brilliant scholar from the west coast. Brand's mother is untypically agitated by love for him but rejects him for local wealth and respectability. He lives wildly, consorting now with the most anarchic inhabitants of the landscape, the gypsies, begetting children on them before dying. These children, later in the play, will confront Brand and Agnes, in the person of the gypsy woman and her child, and will demand the last belongings of *their* child, Alf. This wilder, anarchic world, therefore, seems significant in the great spiritual journey of Brand. After the loss of Agnes, for whom the sacrifice of the last idolatry of her love for her dead child proves fatal, Brand will attempt to lead his community upward through the landscape inhabited by Gerd and the gypsies, toward a vague territory higher and farther off. The pieces seem to fit into a pattern of meanings in which intellect, wild nature, anarchy, idolatry, renunciation, sacrifice, and transcendant affirmation combine, and though it might be dangerous to try to interpret these pieces of the puzzle, it is more respectable than to ignore them. There seems to be a history in which intellectual emancipation (the brilliant young scholar) seeks out the community, is rejected by conventional society, then leagues itself with the anarchic, antisocial elements of humanity and with the world of nature, creating a whole new "wild" area of mental life with which Brand's responsible intellect must grapple. It almost seems like a capsuled account of the Romantic movement itself and probably represents Ibsen's desire to maintain an important part of his total argument as well as to add human interest to his fiction.

Ibsen has succeeded in restoring to the modern theater the metaphysical dimensions of the Greek and Elizabethan stages, and has done so by means of a metaphoric landscape; but the realm of society, in *Brand* and *Peer Gynt*, remains obstinately "secular" and alien. Not until *Emperor and Galilean* does Ibsen actually integrate the social realm fully into the metaphysical drama. He will do this by seeing human institutions as extended, metaphysically, in time, as spiritual history. In *Brand* the relation of the hero to the realm of the state, of society, and of the institutionalized history it represents is one of hostility and alienation, and society is depicted purely in terms of satiric rejection. The play does not seem to envisage any change or revolution in this sphere, yet neither can the author's spirit accept it as it is. The significant and compelling relations in the play are those of the individual with his own spirit, with other individuals, and with the realms of nature and the spirit's universal history. The social world, in other words, is not a medium through which personal salvation and the divine purpose are to be found. The "folk" are to look to Brand as their spiritual leader without mediation through the realms represented by the sheriff, dean, schoolmaster, and doctor. As in T. S. Eliot's *Murder in the Cathedral,* organized society and worldly processes are derided whereas an alternative order of allegiances, derived from an alternative concept of the past (the history of the church and its martyrdoms in Eliot's play, the spiritual-cultural history of the race in Ibsen's) is proferred by the leader to the folk. In *Brand* it is only when the play is not dealing with the social realm that we find a poetry that successfully engages the deepest and most complex feelings and conflicts. When, however, the play deals with social themes, as with Brand's dialogues with the sheriff, dean, and schoolmaster (law, church, and learning) or when these three argue among themselves, the poetry often drops to a level of dry, one-dimensional satire and polemic. At this stage in his career it seems that Ibsen cannot see how, in his social relations, man can be deeply or inspiredly engaged, and so he cannot make his representatives of the social order carry anything like the poetic "weight" of a Creon, Tiresias, or chorus; nor can his social conflicts give rise to the deeply charged ethical problems of, for example, *Measure for Measure.*

Ibsen's "poetic ideology," Bjorn Hemmer notes, requires a singular loneliness of the hero. Rather than try to restore to the state its lost metaphysical value, this ideology bypasses the state and asserts its values above and beyond it. What is noteworthy (and what was to draw a reprimand from Georg Brandes) is that this ideology, so frequently sentimental and histrionic in earlier Romanticism, is here pursued with the most thoroughgoing integrity, logic, and tough-mindedness, bringing the whole idealistic enterprise into question.

In Marxian theory, the humane and "progressive" capitalist who seeks to alleviate the brutalities of capitalism is more of a menace than the unashamably brutal capitalist who fights for his right to employ child labor, pay minimum wages, and maintain intolerable working conditions, for only the existence of the latter conditions will goad the proletariat into revolution. Similarly the idealistic dialectics of *Brand* sees the good, humane, and efficient characters, such as the sheriff, dean, schoolmaster, and doctor, as enemies that Brand must unremittingly oppose; and because Ibsen at this stage shares Brand's contempt for these social roles, he cannot invest them with the capacity for genuinely moving conflict and genuinely poetic "presence" which, in the later realistic cycle, he will discover.

The most deeply felt and most successful scenes in the play are those of Brand's self-communings, his dialogues with his immediate relations to mother and wife, and his commitment to his vocation and its aspiration beyond the social realm to universal spiritual values. It is obvious that Brand will not be deeply engaged in the little town, therefore, and his final ascent of the landscape to the peak of the ice-church seems inevitable from the beginning. In a play like the *Antigone* of Sophocles, the scenes of social conflict, between the ruler and the chorus, the guards and the priest Tiresias, are as charged, poetically, as the scenes between Creon and Antigone, Creon and Haemon, and the scene of Antigone's dirge as she reflects on her fate. We do not feel, as we do in *Brand*, that in these social scenes we are responding to a lower order of poetic creation. Unlike the hero of Greek tragedy, Brand finds communion with his fellowmen, deep involvement in the "fate" they have in common, difficult to effect, so that his whole perception of reality, and his vocation, involves him in a different, "higher" drama, higher than they are capable of participating in. Sophocles can give, even to the insignificant guard who first brings news of the body's burial, then, half-joyfully, half-sadly, brings in Antigone as prisoner, his significant moment in the tragic pattern that has woven itself around the entire community. The guard feels his moment intensely, and because of this, we are able to see in the ironic disparity of his good fortune and Antigone's tragedy the way in which the argument affects everyone in the state. But the dean, schoolmaster, and sexton in *Brand* are satirically depicted as unable to understand or be significantly involved in Brand's spiritual situation. They uncomprehendingly follow him, with the rest of the mob, then turn upon him, with the mob; we do not see them as individual characters caught up in Brand's drama but more as aspects of his experience of that drama. When the play removes itself from this social realm, however, it achieves its poetic intensity.

The scenes with Gerd, for example, are passionately charged because Gerd's outcast condition is a more extreme version of Brand's own hostility to the alien social realm. Similarly the conflicts caused by his mother's guilt or his wife's suffering, because they do not involve social relations at all, are rendered with the intensest feeling and deepest perception. One remembers, for example, the scene in which Brand's mother appears, a figure from the past, hostile to the light of the sun, who in a moment blasts Brand's dream of traveling south to a new land and a new creativity; or the famous scene in act 4 when Agnes brings in the Christmas candles while the dead child, Alf, lies buried under the snow-covered earth. Agnes wipes the streaming windowpanes, likening the moisture to tears shed by the house which prevent the child from looking in and sharing the warmth and light of the room. The feeling, here, is far too deep for sentimentality, and the last example alerts us to the complexity of Ibsen's theatrical and verbal poetry. The Christmas candles, for example, are a throwback to pagan winter celebrations, signaling Agnes's essentially pagan nature which Brand has "lifted up" but also violated with his Christian absolutism. Her "idolatrous" refusal to accept the finality of her child's death (so that she imagines Alf, in the grave, actually watching the house and seeking to return to it) and the notion that the house is itself "weeping" at the separation belong more to pagan than to Christian thinking, to the idea of a numinous cosmos where the spirits of the dead still benignly haunt the earth — an idea that returns in *Little Eyolf.* The warmth indoors clashing with the harshly cold outdoors causes the condensation that makes the windows "weep," and in human terms this also signals the clash between the warmth of Agnes's love and the cold removal from that love that Alf suffers and which Brand enforces. By a tremendous discipline, Agnes herself does not weep; but she manages to displace this necessary action onto the house itself and wipes away the window's tears so that the exiled child might be able to see and share the warmth within. In a telling reversal, the "eye" of the house must be wiped clear in order that the child outside can see more clearly. By this action, the grave outside becomes clearer and more vivid (the house sees better, too), and light is thrown from the house across the grave like an embrace, an embrace that Brand ends by closing the shutters on the window, separating the house from Alf.

The whole scene, indeed the whole of act 4, is intensely poignant drama, but its intellectual content steadies this emotionally charged situation, which easily could become mawkish, and thereby increases the poignancy, for so many more human implications are revealed in it. It is precisely when the *argument* is dialectically extreme, as in this struggle between pagan and Christian values, of idolatry (as when Agnes, like a superstitious Catholic, wishes to keep the *relics* of Alf) versus authenticity, that Ibsen finds his deepest poetry.

Brand is led, through extremes of suffering, to the very heart of loss, a "soul's agony" or "dark night of the soul," at which point he is suddenly rewarded. With Falk and Svanhild, he sees that life lived in the valley, unilluminated by authentic spirit, is hell, and, in a remarkable soliloquy, he imagines the future world blackened and polluted from the soulless materialism of Britain's "smoke-clouds." The idea looks back to Blake's recoil from the "dark satanic mills" of industrial Britain to the vision of a new Jerusalem created by a revolution in the spirit of man. Out of this satanic materialist world emerge only stunted human forms who are incapable of that spiritual battle which, from his earliest writing, Ibsen saw as essential for human wholeness. Such stunted individuals protest that they are too "small" for the great battles of the world and that it was not for them that Christ underwent the agony on the Cross. This new race, therefore, willingly relinquishes its great spiritual birthright, the heroic identity that Ibsen for so long has been struggling to recover for his art.

Thus justified in his mission to his community, even though it has turned upon and stoned him, Brand now undergoes a more agonizing self-justification as his own inward doubts and fears become projected as an invisible choir offering the "Aurelian lure" to give up heroic struggle; for he is of the earth, merely, and is not destined to share in divinity. He now sees a phantom of Agnes who offers to restore the earlier days of love and happiness if Brand will only relinquish his uncompromising demand of "all or nothing." But Brand insists that the struggle to realize authentic life, against the hell of inauthenticity, is its own justification and that he would have to undertake the same stairway of despair all over again, even to once again losing his son and wife. This is the paradox of Brand's martyrdom. The claims of spiritual truth and freedom — or the divine "call" — override those of happiness, and only the great and authentic individuals, like Brand, are capable of living at this tragic level. Their reward is that they suffer at a height far above and with a lucidity far beyond that of the valley-dwellers, and they are incapable of relinquishing this agonizing authenticity for the dulled vision of the valley. (In the next play, *Peer Gynt*, the Troll King actually offers to perform an operation on the eyes to cure humanity of this inconvenient clear-sightedness.) The image of Agnes vanishes with the cry, "Die! The world has no use for you!" and this indicates another paradox of Brand's heroism: that, pursued to its logical limits with complete integrity, it redeems the human spirit by recovering the greatness upon which the community had turned its back, yet at the same time there is no place for this heroism in the actual structure of the world.

At this moment Brand is joined by Gerd. These two will die together on the heights just beneath the ice-church, which strongly implies that their spirits will merge. Gerd, we saw, never had compromised with the valley world and so was free of its corruption. Nevertheless, she never had encountered it existentially, had never been implicated with it at the human level, so that her visionary nature was an "empty height" not arrived at by the heartbreaking, and therefore self-validating, fully humanized struggle of Brand. Gerd now exalts Brand as the Christ figure, kneeling before him and the stigmata of his wounds, but against this Brand insists he is "the meanest worm that crawls." Both ideas of him are correct: he has undergone an agony, a dark night of the soul, that is equivalent to the agony on the Cross, but his own spiritual redemption must require his sincere total abasement so that he is not guilty of that subtle and ultimate *pride* in martyrdom which T. S. Eliot's Beckett, also, must overcome. At this moment of greatest self-abasement and desolation, as Brand pleads to be allowed to clasp just one fold of the gown of salvation *(frelsens-kledet),* he at last weeps, and the spectacle of the tears streaming down his face moves Gerd to proclaim that not only her own glacier (of memory) is melting but that of the ice-church, too, so that the landscape thaws with the spiritual thawing of Brand.

The scene directions point to a transformation within Brand. He suddenly is radiant, clear, and rejuvenated; his reward has arrived as a mysterious bursting forth of joy out of his agony, like the blooming of the rose within the Cross. He feels the landscape of his soul turn from winter to summer with "warm and rich" flowing streams from the melting ice. At this point the shadow of the falcon, already identified as the spirit of compromise, falls upon them both. This can be interpreted as indicating either that Brand's "thawing" is a form of compromise or, as I believe, that the pattern of temptation to compromise is about to resume. Firing at the falcon with her rifle, Gerd dislodges the avalanche and the play ends on a final riddle as Brand, about to "plunge into death's night," pleads for a final assurance. A voice calls through the sound of the avalanche, but Brand already is buried in it so that it is the reader, and not Brand, who is left to ponder the meaning of the Voice's words — "He is the God of Love!" *(Han er deus caritatis!")* — and to reflect upon the riddle of the hero's fate.

To be called upon to act heroically in Greek drama (which, after all, was an event not so distant from the actual experience of the warrior-citizen) was to be involved in the paradox of spiritual elevation through suffering. Everything we know of Greek culture in the classic period proclaims that this paradox was understood and respected. Ibsen's tragedy of vocation revives this paradox. Simply by being who he is, Brand cannot help but respond to the divine "call" that inevitably lures him on to ever higher and ever more painful spiritual conflicts, and to an ever greater alienation from his world. Once raised to spiritual authenticity, the hero finds compromise impossible, for it is a form of death. The consciousness of participating in the life of the spirit and not in its death is the hero's great reward, his heavenly crown, although, ironically, this makes the hero all the more vulnerable to suffering. Just as the audience in Greek drama observed with respectful awe a level of tragic experience that raised the hero, however aberrant, above his fellows, so the reader of *Brand* feels the higher truth and logic of the fate to which the hero agonizingly assents.

The different and discordant levels of poetic writing that we noted in *Brand* are due to the many more levels of human reality, from animalic to divine, that Ibsen is attempting to structure into an artistic unity. The artistic unity of *The Vikings at Helgeland* was achieved by a style and subject matter that evaded awkward reality, so that the simplistic histrionics and stylistic remoteness as well as the purely theatrical formalism of that play represents a far smaller artistic achievement than the less smoothly integrated *Brand*. *Brand* is one of those immensely important, even epoch-making, but awkward transitional works, typical of many great artists, which might even represent the major creative effort of the artist but which is not as satisfactory as later, less strenuous, and more assured works. The creation of a symbolic landscape that is as much a mental as a natural scene is brilliantly and profoundly sustained throughout the drama so that from its underworld to its ice-church this world is an embodied concept. Less successful, I think, are the hawk and dove metaphors. The shooting of the hawk whose black shadow across the snow is converted into the dove of the falling avalanche is a brilliant image, but it is distracting. Remembering that Falk had been the model of the uncompromising spirit in *Love's Comedy,* it is difficult to see the appropriateness of this fierce predator as the very image of the spirit of compromise, in *Brand.* Other details, such as the history of Gerd's father, are difficult to bring into the desired unity of the poem. We have noted that the poet's inability to invest the *social/political* realm with any intensity of feeling allows the verse of these scenes to drop to an uncomfortably low level.

Nevertheless, the spiritual Prometheus in the dress of a modern Protestant parson that Ibsen has created, the symbolic world with which he surrounds him, the archetypal levels of the action (the Babel myth, Moses and Aaron, the Christ story, Abraham and Isaac, and so on), and the great tragic drama to which Ibsen subjects his hero make up a decisive and impressive "moment" in the history of drama and of literature. *Brand* fulfills the goal of a "mental drama" which Byron had sought and at the same time fulfills Blanka's prophecy, in *The Burial Mound,* that future conquests by mankind will be on "silver seas of thought."

THE PARABLE OF *PEER GYNT*[1]

> MRS. ALVING: *Well, what do you think of him, Mr. Manders?*
> MANDERS: *Well, I must say—no, but—is it really—?*
> OSVALD: *Yes, really—the prodigal son, Pastor.*
> MANDERS: *But my dear boy—*
> OSVALD: *Well, the homecoming son, anyway.*
>
> Henrik Ibsen
> *Ghosts*, act 1

In *Dyret i Mennesket* (*The Beast in Man*), a very provocative study of *Peer Gynt*, Asbjorn Aarseth notes the immense and international scope of the critical commentary on this play, which testifies to the strong hold it has taken upon the modern imagination.[2] Bernard Shaw, long ago, declared that Peer had entered that rare company of recognizable archetypes, like Oedipus, Hamlet, Don Quixote, Don Juan, or Faust, figures who project brilliantly essential aspects of our total humanity. It is difficult to bring to mind any other figure from Ibsen's time—or subsequently—who has attained this status. English scholars may proffer Leopold Bloom, but only English scholars would agree. The great appeal of this character whom Ibsen is determined to condemn creates a highly ambivalent response from the reader (as do the other archetypal figures with whom he joins company), and we cannot help but feel that the author, also, shared this ambivalence.

For whereas *Brand's* earnest integrity of purpose and depth of tragic feeling command our respect rather than our enthusiasm, *Peer Gynt* triumphs by the very arts of shameless ingratiation that it sets out to indict. Just as one feels that Ibsen's honesty and in-

164

tegrity compelled him to explore the dilemma of Brand's idealism to its most discomfiting conclusion, so one feels that the subject of *Peer Gynt* led the poet beyond the moral judgment he intended.[3] Apart from the prolix act 4, the drama is superbly realized in unforgettable scenes, characters, and actions. Many regret that Ibsen abandoned the form he brought to such mastery in this play, particularly when they proceed from its free and imaginative artistry to the constrained and overingenious mechanics of *The League of Youth. Peer Gynt*, however, for all its virtues, still is "literary" and "mental" drama. We are greatly moved when reading it, but, in the theater, it has none of the almost unbearable closeness of *Ghosts*, the fine subtlety of *Rosmersholm*, or the exhilarating sense of *our* world being lifted into the magical and fearful that we experience from the last four plays in Ibsen's realistic cycle, plays which "read" less well than *Peer Gynt* but which are more consequential as theatrical art.

Brand and *Peer Gynt*, it is generally conceded, were conceived as dialectical opposites, the Norwegian version of the thesis-antithesis of galilean-emperor, and at the center of the two plays are equally opposite heroes. Brand is all integrity and authenticity, Peer all expediency and inauthenticity. Brand stays rooted in one place of painful ascent; Peer roves the world in a circle of repetitions. *Brand* depicts a small drab community overshadowed by the vast, challenging landscape; *Peer Gynt* displays a continuously changing world peopled with fantastic and grotesque characters. As Brand climbs his winding stairway of despair, he is all the time achieving his true identity by slaying false selves; Peer, for all his greater mobility, is spiritually static, his identity tragically unevolved as he fails to advance dialectically. Brand is the quintessential tragic hero, holding onto absolute values so imperative that life itself can willingly be sacrificed for them; Peer is the archetypal comic hero, brilliantly adapting himself to changing circumstances, celebrating the determination to survive, to *live* at all costs, and vigilantly to escape the snare of deadly absolutes.

Tragedy clarifies values so demanding that we feel, at least for the moment, that the claims of mere life are secondary—that Antigone must not yield even to avoid death. Comedy performs the opposite function, vigorously defending life against its enemies, often mercilessly exposing and punishing them. The villains of comedy, such as the Socrates of *The Clouds*, Shakespeare's Malvolio, Congreve's Lady Wishfort, and so on, frequently are not wicked in the manner of Jonson's Volpone or Molière's Tartuffe; but they do stand in the way of freely functioning life. Such enemies often are old, possessing the power and material wealth that should serve younger life, and they often prevent young lovers from uniting and gaining possession of this wealth. The comic hero sometimes rescues the heroine from the threat of a grotesquely false marriage with an older man or a buffoon who, by his clumsy behavior, implies he is impotent—and this will be Peer's first vivid comic action when he rescues Ingrid, briefly, from Mads Moen.

Peer's comic aspect is revealed in his infinite adaptability which contrasts so strongly to the unyielding constancy of Brand. This adaptability was a salient characteristic of the comic slave of ancient drama and the comic servant of European drama, characters who often were more resourceful than their masters. Like Peer, they are given to exaggeration and boasting; they overvalue life by pretending, and partly believing, that its possibilities are more numerous, various, and exciting than they actually are. Holding the value of life itself as a supreme good, the comic hero will do anything to continue living—and Peer is the most resourceful of them all. Because mere actions themselves cannot possibly sustain the value such heroes claim for life, these heroes are given to fantasy, storytelling, and lying.[4] Peer's lying stands in strong contrast to Brand's painful struggle toward authenticity of expression, but one detects beneath this lying a genuine "joy-of-life" (*livsgleden*) pursued with an energy that must command our grudging admiration. For Peer *is* a hero, however misguided: he is uncommon, far above the level of his fellows, and he enhances our idea of life by the high value he places on it even as he betrays its highest values. For one thing, whereas Brand drastically narrows life's possibilities to one path of authentic action, Peer opens up various vistas of possible human activity. In a later play Ibsen will contrast the two conceptions of life, terming Peer's the "emperor" nature and Brand's the "galilean". We already have noted how each of Ibsen's three heroes, Brand, Peer, and Julian, envisage creating a new human order: spiritual for Brand, physical for Peer, and the third-empire integration of both in Julian's Heliopolis. Aarseth demonstrates the prevalence of the "emperor" *motif* in *Peer Gynt*, from Peer's early daydreams of imperial power to his final realization that he is a mere emperor "of the other animals." In our account of *Brand* we suggested that Gerd's vision of Brand as Christ, with his wounds as the stigmata, was justified.

The impulse to conquer *this* world, the emperor impulse, which delights in the physical manifestation of life in all its forms is, for Ibsen, as necessary and as noble as the galilean impulse which, striving for spiritual authenticity, is prepared to renounce this world and all its beauty and potentiality for a higher *jenseits,* or beyond. At the conclusion of *Brand* the painful and clenched logic within which Brand is honorably imprisoned suddenly bursts, and Brand at last feels able to embrace, and to participate in, a warm and brilliant world that hitherto had eluded him. Similarly, at the conclusion of *Peer Gynt* Peer, confronting Solveig, sees the light break over the confusion of his misspent life as the higher meaning and purpose of his life, preserved by Solveig, is revealed. Both moments seem to be mysterious syntheses in which the excluded values briefly join with their opposites before they engage in the more searching dialectic of *Emperor and Galilean* and the realistic cycle. Peer's dizzy career is a total misdirection of his energies but those energies are honored by the play, and the world in which Peer delights, and from which Brand tragically was excluded, is not despised by Ibsen. There is a tragic hollowness at the center of the comic energy, but the play's compelling re-creation of great archetypal fictive forms reminds us that the values Peer is traducing *are* values that once were and might again become living principles.

The most obvious fictive form the play is parodying is the Romantic hero who, as outcast and wanderer, communes only with himself and with the grander manifestations of nature and history as he travels across the world. Childe Harold traverses Europe, musing on the contrast between present pettiness and vanished past grandeur, and Peer parodies this action in act 4 with his own remarkably unobservant journey from West to East across the north African desert. The most flagrant example of Peer's desecration of the life of his Romantic prototype is when he reverses

Byron's sacrifice of his life for the Greek cause by sacrificing the Greek cause for personal profit.

The Romantic convention of the heroic journey of discovery of the world and of the abysses within the self recovered one of the oldest of fictive forms: the quest myth. According to this myth, the hero leaves his home, travels through the world to perform great heroic actions, encountering human, monstrous, and divine beings, descending to the underworld, and journeying across the sea, and finally returns to his native land, often with some magic knowledge or possession that might redeem the wasteland that his home has become. The hero then dies with great honor among his people. This is the basic plot of such variant forms as *Gilgamesh*, *Beowulf*, the Grail legends (especially *Parsival*), and countless other myths and legends from many cultures. The greatest version is *The Odyssey*. Odysseus journeys over sea, land, and the underworld (the Book of the Dead) meeting men, gods, and monsters, finally returning to his patiently waiting wife, Penelope (whose weaving loom reminds us of Solveig's spinning wheel), to put right the accumulated evils of the wasteland created by the suitors. Allegorical versions of the quest myth are works like Dante's *Commedia*, Spenser's *The Faerie Queene*, and Bunyan's *Pilgrim's Progress*, with the journey now being internalized as that through a mental landscape.

In drama, the quest myth classically is represented by Sophocles' treatment of the Oedipus myth. Oedipus leaves his home (Corinth) for Thebes. On the way he encounters a violent opponent (Laius) whom he slays and a monster, the Sphinx. He solves the riddle of the Sphinx (the answer to which is "man") and so brings prosperity to his new community only to discover, later, that there is the more terrible riddle of his own identity to be answered. This version of the quest myth is acknowledged by Ibsen when he has his hero, Peer, meet the Sphinx right before he collapses over the riddle of his "self." Discussing the many forms of the "circuitous journey" that Romantic thinkers and artists like Hegel, Schiller, Wordsworth, Byron, Shelley, and Keats variously employed, M. H. Abrams notes that one such model was the Prodigal Son:

The Bible also contained an apt, detailed, and impressive figure for life as a circular rather than a linear journey, which had been uttered explicitly as a parable of man's sin and redemption, and by the authoritative voice of Jesus himself. This was the story of the Prodigal Son (Luke 15: 11-32) who collected his inheritance and "took his journey into a far country, and there wasted his substance with riotous living"; then, remorseful, made his way back to his homeland and the house of his father, who joyously received him, clothed him in the best robe, a ring, and shoes, and ordered the fatted calf that they might "eat, and be merry: For this my son was dead, and is alive again; he was lost, and is found."[5]

This plot, in fact, precedes Romanticism in Henry Fielding's *Tom Jones*, whose hero has much in common with Peer; and in Fielding, as in Goethe *(Wilhelm Meisters Wanderjahre)*, the riotous journey will prove to be an ultimately salutary self-learning. Abrams discusses the way in which this tale of the Prodigal Son, and other myths and legends of the circuitous journey, were taken up by Romantic writers and applied by them to a world in which they felt themselves homeless:

This sense of being an alien in a world which had been made by man's own unhappy intellect also manifested itself in a widespread revival of the traditional plot-form of the wandering of an exile in quest of the place where he truly belongs; although . . . with differences that demarcate sharply the various Romantic quests both from the Plotinian odyssey and the Christian pilgrimage.[6]

The presence of the parable of the Prodigal Son in the story of *Peer Gynt* was indicated by Theodore Jorgenson in his study of Ibsen,[7] and much of the power of the play is derived from this employment of such archetypal plot forms together with Ibsen's awareness of the philosophic implications of the Romantic revival of these forms. The sources feeding into *Peer Gynt* are, I believe, many, but the play is unique in its very thorough exploration of the many aspects of the quest myth. Peer leaves home, is outcast, travels over an extensive landscape and sea, journeys underground, speaks with monstrous and phantasmal figures, confronts the Sphinx, and returns home, in old age, to a wasteland where a faithful wife is waiting; and this homecoming is the possible redemption of his misspent life.

In act 5 the play also takes on aspects of the Christian morality play — a play like *Everyman*, for example.[8] Peer's final journey through a landscape that itself reproaches his former life, a landscape peopled by such fantastic figures as the Strange Passenger, the Troll King, the Button Molder, the Devil, and the patiently waiting Solveig, has become a journey through a landscape of the mind, as in Christian allegory.

These layers of literary structure, from quest myth, through folktale, epic, drama, Christian allegory, and Romantic journey, to modern satire, give *Peer Gynt* its great richness of texture and represent a culmination of the process of spiritual evolution, from mythic foundation to modern mind, that Ibsen so early articulated.

It is difficult not to conclude that the play quite consciously resurrects its great archetypal and literary models to reveal their devaluation by the modern spirit. Peer's journey above and beneath the earth and sea is not a heroic quest but a lifelong evasion. He encounters enemies and monsters, yet flees conflict with them. When he meets the Sphinx he does not answer it but questions it without waiting for response, as Rolf Fjelde observes in his foreword to *Peer Gynt*. Rather than bring home to his people and the wasteland healing wisdom and powers, Peer is washed ashore on the wasteland materially and spiritually bankrupt, desperately seeking help instead of giving it. Unlike Everyman, and the heroes of morality drama, Peer does not learn from the allegorical figures he encounters, and it is uncertain if he finally understands Solveig's answer to the riddle of his identity.

The male-female identities of *Brand* are reversed in the two main figures of *Peer Gynt*, another indication of the thesis-antithesis relation of the two plays. Whereas Agnes is the pagan nature trained in the hard Christian discipline of Brand, Solveig is the Christian nature whose faith is the still center, like the fixed foot of the compass, of Peer's roving, pagan, masculine, and animal energies. Whereas Brand's severe Christianity honorably forfeits a whole area of spontaneity and warmth which the young Agnes had possessed, Peer's pagan spontaneity and genuine, though unreflective, warmth clearly lacks the willed *direction* that prompts Solveig's boldly irrevocable ascent to Peer's outlaw hut. As with Brand, the scene of the play is an extensive landscape whose verticals, from depths to heights, are extensions of the spiritual drama;

and in *Peer Gynt* the heights and depths, sky and underworld, desert and wilderness, sea and storm, function even more brilliantly.

As in *Love's Comedy* and *Brand*, the landscape makes up a metaphoric notation in which heights represent freedom, the valley is restricted and "fallen," and the underworld (the troll world) suggests the subconscious — *mentioned* by Gerd in *Brand* but now audaciously presented in terms of direct actions and figures. Storm and shipwreck are metaphors for spiritual convulsion, and the desert scenery of act 4 suitably mirrors Peer's spiritual sterility. Physical and spiritual conditions intricately parallel each other as when Peer, in complementary scenes in act 5, encounters first his material identity, his past, scattered into the remnants of the auction (scene 4), then his disintegrated and scattered spirit in the Onion episode (scene 5) and the burned landscape that reproaches him (scene 6).

Such parallels alert us to the fact that the seemingly improvisational nature of the play actually conceals very careful structuring. Asbjorn Aarseth, as we note on p. 173, demonstrated one constantly repeated archetypal pattern in the play, that of Peer as animal, as centaur, and as the horseman who continually "falls." Bjorn Hemmer notes in his study of *The Pretenders*, *Brand*, and *Peer Gynt*, referred to previously how the first "fall" — in the Christian sense — of Peer's bride rape is repeated in the play; and Rolf Fjelde, in his foreword to *Peer Gynt*, greatly expands this theme of repetition to cover almost all aspects of the play. Peer and Solveig, we suggested, are the pagan-Christian dualism at the center of the story, a dualism further extended in the contrast between Peer's recklessly extravagent parents and Solveig's frugal, pious parents. The Hegstad farm and its wedding guests represent the conventional "valley" world that will outlaw Peer, whereas the trolls' feast is, as Rolf Fjelde comments, the Hegstad wedding and its guests internalized (and diabolized). In the outer world, the international forces of finance and power are represented by Peer's mutually destructive business partners on his yacht, and the intellectual/spiritual confusion of this world is imaged in the Cairo madhouse, where Absolute Reason, on which the whole system of reality depends, has died.

Solveig, Peer's true princess *(kongsdatter)* whose spiritual father is God, is the apex of a whole female pyramid at the base of which is the troll-woman, daughter of the diabolic Troll King and, therefore, Peer's false *kongsdatter*. Ingrid, from Hegstad farm, is woman as Fallen Eve. Her "property and honor" represent conventional society's reward to the male energies that capitulate into conformity — as with the conventional couplings in *Love's Comedy*. The further debasement of Eve in the saeter girls and Anitra becomes an un-Faustian descent that is summed up in Peer's famous misquotation of Goethe which degrades the elevating power of the eternal feminine into mere sexual attraction. Beneath the superficially chaotic appearance of *Peer Gynt* lies an almost inexhaustible wealth of such significant parallels and contrasts.

One of the major achievements of the play is the creation, once again for the theater, of directly symbolic and metaphoric figures, the equivalents of the Greek gods and the Elizabethan ghosts, witches, fairies, and so on. Here, of course, Ibsen is indebted to Goethe's *Faust;* but Ibsen's employment of such supernatural figures is more notable as a theatrical symbology, possible on the stage, of the *modern* world. Lessing, in a trenchant passage in *The Hamburg Dramaturgy,* devastated with ridicule Voltaire's frigid employment of a ghost in his *Semiramis,* and Lessing left the reader with the conclusion that the time for employing supernatural machinery in drama was over — particularly in a drama of modern times. *Peer Gynt* uses the supernatural so successfully (more so, I think, than *Macbeth* its witches) because the supernatural figures are perceived by us to be aspects of the disordered subjectivity of Peer *and* presences revealing forces within the universal human mind. As consequential spiritual forces they cannot be treated lightly — they carry the chill of real terror — yet they also are highly enjoyable theatrical presences. They have serious objective identity as emblems and forces in the spiritual drama, and it is because we see that they are conceptually authentic that the trolls, the Boyg, Memnon's statue, the Sphinx, the Strange Passenger, the Devil, and the Button Molder are so effective.

Since Ibsen by now imaginatively inhabits a "numinous" world, *believes* in it (e.g., that there are universal forces operating on human life), he can create these supernatural beings with artistic authenticity. In Ibsen's later realism, although spirit suffuses, works upon, and transforms everyday reality, it does not violate it in the way that T. S. Eliot's Eumenides violate the world of *The Family Re-Union;* and the fantastic elements of *Peer Gynt* were an important stage in the development of Ibsen's later, subtler method.

For a reader's drama, the play contains an astonishing amount of *physical* action paralleling, and, we will see, complementing, its equally amazing verbal fluency. Aarseth made this physical, or animalistic, aspect of the play the major theme of his study of *Peer Gynt,* and this emphasis upon the physical, upon the body, which is so striking, is appropriate to the comedic form. Samuel Taylor Coleridge observed that whereas "the tragic poet idealizes his characters by giving to the spiritual part of our nature a more decided preponderance over the animal cravings and impulses, than is met with in real life: the comic poet idealizes his characters by making the animal the governing power, and the intellectual the mere instrument."[9] The animalistic in Peer, therefore, might be not so much the negative judgment upon him that Aarseth sees, although I agree this is present since it is the expression of Peer's comedic identity; yet the animalistic, in Peer, is also very clearly related to positive (and pagan) energies. In his very different way Peer is as remote from and "above" the valley dwellers as is Brand: if he is an animal, he is wild and free whereas they are tamed and limited. Like Brand, Peer is a paradox rather than a moral cipher. The play as much honors as it condemns Peer's extraordinary mental agility that can play any role, chatter away on any subject without understanding, like a facile actor; and, in the same way, it is ambivalent toward Peer's amazing physical agility. This conjunction of verbal facility and physical agility is a profound insight of Ibsen's. The number of physical actions given to Peer exceed, I think, that of any fictional hero with the possible exception of Odysseus, who also was a consummate liar. Peer walks, runs, jumps, carries his mother, wrestles, rides a reindeer through dizzying space (in imagination, where the lie and the physical agility coalesce), climbs, carries off a bride, a troll-woman, and an Arab girl, dances, has sex, rides various steeds, swims, crawls on all fours, and, finally exhausted, sleeps in

Solveig's arms. Similar to Odysseus, Peer is the archetypal male celebrated also by Sophocles in the famous Ode to Man from *Antigone*. He is infinitely resourceful, and the actions given to him make up virtually the entire range of the human body. It is impossible to view this only negatively.

Nor can we judge Peer's fantasies and lies only negatively. In *After Babel*, George Steiner suggests that lying might be a fundamental purpose behind the invention of language, even more so than the communication of "truth". Not only is lying a useful device by which to deceive opponents and preserve against intruders the things the tribe wishes to possess alone (a water hole, for example), but it is also a device by which man can create illusions to overcome the terror of actuality, especially the actuality of death. Steiner quotes with approval Nietzsche's aphorism in *The Will to Power:* "There is only *one* world, and that world is false, cruel, contradictory, misleading, senseless. . . . We need lies to vanquish this reality, this 'truth,' we need lies *in order to live.* . . . That lying is a necessity of life is itself part of the terrifying and problematic character of existence." The paragraph in which this appears ends with Steiner commenting, "Ibsen's phrase pulls together the whole evolutionary argument: man lives, he progresses by virtue of the life-lie."[10]

As Steiner points out, Greek culture in particular greatly valued verbal adroitness — lying — and Odysseus himself is especially loved by the goddess Athene for almost matching the divine facility in mendacity. Pertinent to the history of dramatic art, it is worth noting that whereas the epic poet Homer approved of this mendacity in Odysseus and delighted in it, Homer's tragic hero, Achilles, despised it, preferring honorable inflexibility. The later Greek tragedians, especially Sophocles, shared Achilles' distaste, and Odysseus appears in their tragedies almost always negatively. In fact it is Achilles' son, Neoptolemus, who is rescued from the lies of Odysseus by the inflexibly honest Philoctetes. Lying, however, was to return to drama as a triumphant facility in the comedies of Aristophanes where it is wedded to a hilariously varied physical expressiveness. Although Ibsen obviously does not share this admiration for lying, he responds, imaginatively, to its vital aspects. The contrast between the painfully honest hero Brand leaving in his wake a trail of honorable devastation of the lives of others and Peer's reckless, unreflective, and more superficially destructive course seems to act out, among other things, the paradox of language itself: saving truth and saving illusion; destructive truth and destructive illusion. Ibsen, as a poet, must have been acutely conscious of this dilemma, and it is worth noting that the play in which he formulates the concept of the "life-lie" as opposed to the lie of "ideals" presents, in reductive terms, Brand and Peer Gynt as Gregers Werle and Hjalmar Ekdal, respectively.

For all the variety of speech and action, however, the play shows us Peer caught in a hell of repetition, the repetition the individual is doomed to who evades *dialectical* evolution — the slaying of lower and false selves to attain to the higher and truer self. Because, unlike Brand, Peer never confronts his "self" in any of the crises in which he is caught, he is incapable of development so that, however varied and extensive his speech and actions, he does not advance. In acts 4 and 5 he becomes dimly aware of this dilemma. "Where have I heard that before?" is a typical question which, of course, he never stops to answer. Instead of the "circuitous journey" on the spiraling advance to higher levels, Peer returns home having learned nothing, in danger of descending below even the animal and vegetable realms to a form of Ur-stuff to be recycled as bungled material, and looking only to others for illumination.

In acts 1-4 Peer set out, ambitiously, from his mother's home and the height of the outlaw hut into the wide world, fleeing from his self and being crowned "emperor of self" by the deranged inhabitants of the Cairo asylum. In act 4 we see Peer going in the reverse direction: fleeing from a world emptied of meaning, burdened with confused consciousness, and encountering the scattered fragments of his lost unity (the "wholeness" that Brand had sought) as he approaches confrontation with the evaded self to which Solveig has been faithful. His erratic life is contrasted with that of the peasant boy who cut off his finger to evade conscription and who remained home, battling nature and establishing his family. Peer, who overhears the priest's eulogy over this now-dead peasant, applies the text to himself. The contrast is instructive. On one side we have the stubborn, heroic clinging to life under even the most appalling physical conditions, forcing upon the natural world the human right to exist within it; and, on Peer's side, the audacious, irresponsible adventuring, physically and mentally, which opens up more possibilities than Peer is able to establish. Neither mode is lifted into the spiritually exalted mode desired by Brand. The narrow stubbornness and persistence is as animalistic as Peer's riotous journey, establishing nothing in the spiritual sphere. On one side we have the son who stayed at home, on the other, the prodigal who wasted his inheritance.

We first meet Peer as the adolescent whose physical and mental energies are explosively at their peak but who cannot channel these energies into an intelligent or meaningful course of action. Having run from home when it most needed his attention, he now has returned only to evade responsibility for his actions by lying. Both methods of evasion, physical flight and imaginative fantasy, will become a lifelong pattern in Peer and, though they point to a disastrous weakness in his character, they also indicate more positive and unusual qualities.

Unlike his fellows, who resemble the dull and slothful valley dwellers of *Brand*, Peer at least can perceive that given, alienated reality is unbearable, and his desire to escape it *could* become a desire to transform it, as in the actions of Falk and Brand. If, ultimately, we condemn Peer for wasting the divine spark within him, he at least had that spark to a notable degree, as Solveig clearly sees, and it sets him above his fellows. Apart from Solveig, we will meet no one in the play whom we would put "above" Peer—at least if we keep to the strictly human characters. And it is Peer's lying and fantasizing that marks him as superior. I would agree that Peer is no *poet;* at best, he is a pseudo-poet, so that it is not his weakness for fantasy which Solveig responds to. But the lying and the fantasies are indications of energies and desires that cannot find their equivalents in the fallen world around him (he will reject Ingrid and her farm) any more than Solveig's desire to commit herself to a supreme object of her love can find any equivalent—apart from Peer! Peer's unusual gifts and energies make him the object of dislike of the villagers (a sure indication of his value) and create in him the awkwardness and sense of alienation, evident in the Hegstand scene, that lying helps alleviate.

We encounter the first example of his facility for lying in his brilliant account of the reindeer ride, an account of an exhilarating leap into space and a dizzying fall. Aarseth points out that this is the first in a whole series of such rides and falls, and links the theme to the traditional metaphor of the horseman as the intellect in control of his passions.[11] In Greek mythology, Aarseth reminds us, the battle between the Lapiths and the centaurs (the subject of many temple friezes, including that of the Parthenon) represents the overcoming of the animalistic by the human,[12] and the half-human, half-equine centaurs signify the passions controlling Reason. Aarseth relates Peer's drunken quarrelsomeness and the bride rape at the Hegstad wedding feast to the occasion when the centaurs drunkenly attempted to rape the Lapith women and boys at a wedding feast to which they were invited, causing the Lapiths to set upon and kill them, as Peer is set upon and outlawed by the community.[13] Peer, in effect, remains a centaur in many respects and never achieves the human victory over the animalistic. This metaphor is to be found in another famous Greek image, Plato's account of the charioteer (the mind) who must control the horses (representing the will and the passions) and who will be disastrously upset if he fails to control them.

Peer's account of the exhilarating reindeer ride and its climactic and explosive conclusion primarily represents the eruption of adolescent sexual energies. But the imagery that accompanies this account—the journey through a sublime landscape of mountaintops, glaciers, suns flashing between the peaks, the ptarmigan bursting into squawking flight beneath the reindeer's hooves, then the great still depths mirroring the fall—brings together major themes of Romantic poetry. The passage is a tour-de-dorce of the Romantic poetry it is debunking, reading, in fact, like one of the more memorable passages from *The Prelude*. It concludes with one of the most brilliant images of all: the reindeer and rider plunge down through the air into the fjord and the fjord reflection of reindeer and rider rushes upward to meet the falling pair in a blinding explosion. Aarseth notes that Peer's variation of Gudmund Glesne's story makes the rider helplessly controlled by the mount, the mind by the body, as it were;[14] but one also notes the imaginative brilliance and depth of Peer's account.[15]

The image conveys the idea of an overwhelming union of higher and lower, conscious and unconscious energies and powers. The rest of the play, in fact, will be the repetition and elaboration of this theme of the integration of higher and lower selves—of primal unconscious energies and the demands of loftier, conscious purposes. Peer, we learn, is the heir to three heritages, each of which he has the opportunity to control and convert to better purposes. The first is his material inheritance, the ruined farm, left by his profligate father in a state of poverty and disrepair, which Peer could set about reclaiming, in the manner of the draft dodger, or, like Brand, converting to the service of God. Peer merely abandons this inheritance and it is confiscated, serving no useful purpose, for we encounter the property again, in act 5, in a condition of total devastation.

Peer's second inheritance is cultural: the legends and folktales his mother told him to compensate for their mutual misery, tales which, like the fiction of Europe, supply a wonderful escape from reality. Much of Peer's life, as commentators note, follows the pattern of the *eventyr,* or folk legend, in more somber terms, especially that of the male Cinderella, Askeladd, who is the Prodigal Son in reverse. Peer's life traduces that of Askeladd, for when the latter leaves home he proves masterful in performing difficult tasks, vanquishes trolls, and wins the hand of the true king's daughter, with half the kingdom. Peer, we noted, gains the false king's daughter (and, in act 4 is willing to sacrifice half his kingdom for a horse). Peer confuses these two heritages—the material and the fantastic—retelling legends as if they were actual events in the world while fantasizing his degraded condition into legendary glamour. Faithful neither to the world of imagination nor to that of reality and unable to distinguish between them, he will invent no new songs or poems and will transform neither the world of mind nor that of material reality.

This confusion between material and imaginative reality renders Peer all the more vulnerable before his third heritage: the long biological/historical identity, evolved over millions of years, that he has inherited from the race. The stages of this evolutionary inheritance are "there" in the world Peer will explore, and he will fail to define his human essence in relation to it. The stages also are within him, in the impulses, passions, desires, appetites—what he self-damningly will term his "Gyntian self"—which, as Plato warned, if not subordinated within a truly human hierarchy, would make one the most miserable of men. When impulses and forces from this heritage erupt into his present life, like the upward-rushing reindeer and rider from the lake depths, Peer neither understands nor can control them but is himself controlled by them. The climax of Peer's journey through his subconscious is his meeting with the Boyg in pitch darkness, where he fails to solve the riddle of selfhood; the climax of his superficial journey through the external world is his meeting with the Sphinx whom he addresses as the Boyg, where, again, the riddle of the self defeats him, after which he enters the madhouse. In *Brand*, Gerd declared that the priest's spiritual battle had kept down the monstrous, subhuman forces of the trolls who would repossess the human community if he relinquished his struggle. In Peer we see the human approximating the condition of the troll by failing to unite conscious and subconscious energies in a compelling *human* synthesis.

Although Peer, unlike Ibsen, is not a poet, he is at least an *actor*, facilely playing at roles he does not comprehend. One can imagine a production in which Peer frequently addressed the theater audience while being watched, perhaps, by the characters before whome he will have to appear for judgment: the Strange Passenger, the Troll King, the Devil, the Button Molder, and Solveig. Because Peer's purely external role playing never has communed with inward spiritual reality, all his roles have been as empty as costumes to be taken up and discarded. Identity is that which one establishes by effort within the world, but Peer has abandoned this identity, leaving it in the custody of Solveig, and has squandered his spiritual heritage in the poor performance of empty roles. He is a bad actor who, at the end, is likely to be hissed off the world stage.

Ibsen's most Norwegian hero is also a modern Everyman, heir to great cultural and spiritual riches which he prodigally squanders, being willing to lose his soul to gain the world. He shares modern man's belief that the universe—God—has a destiny for him which he need not struggle to comprehend and attain, and that the universe will not allow him to go the way of the brontosaurus or megatherium. It is typical of Ibsen that he should employ topical Darwinism—which most of his contemporaries were wont to interpret flatteringly as meaning that man, the highest being in the chain of evolution, was proceeding to new triumphs—to draw the opposite conclusion: that, as any earlier species, man is most likely destined to perish, not from external causes but from inner hollowness, from lack of integrity of identity which alone can generate faith in living. For, Ibsen asks, why should the universe be concerned with man's survival unless, by his own intrinsic qualities, he makes himself invaluable? If he does not, extinction would be the most merciful respite from the hell of eternal repetition. At one point, in act 4, Peer even is willing cheerfully to slide down the evolutionary tree again when he is willing to take on the identity of the monkey. Peer plays at all the once-positive and vital roles of Romanticism—rebel, outlaw, wanderer, dreamer, adventurer à la Don Juan, prophet, and thinker—but just as easily slips into the negative roles of slave owner, idolater and purveyor of idols, merchant, antirevolutionary, epicure, miser, and murderer, sliding from role to role with the amazingly energetic and restless pace of the nineteenth-century bourgeoisie itself.

Acts 1-3 set out the drama of Peer's adolescence in terms of the Christian parable of the Fall. Until the end of act 1, Peer is all innocent energy and potentiality, a young Adam without a serious anticipative destiny or like the pagan world, according to Christian accounts, before contact with Christianity. His fervid imagination attempts to contain the world, from depths to heights, entirely in terms of excited sense-impressions as he fantasizes the sensation of an almost cosmic ride on the reindeer and as he dreams cloud formations into the images of pagan-imperial pageants with himself as emperor. In these sequences Peer is the isolated ego, the Adam without Eve, but then he journeys to the wedding feast at Hegsted. Marriage is the institutional union of ego with ego, and Ingrid and Mads Moen are celebrating one idea of marriage of which society approves but which is a violation of Romantic concepts of love. Marriage comes in for such severe treatement in Ibsen's works because it is a metaphor for the union of spiritual forces, and its failure or debasement indicates a deep flaw in the spiritual reality depicted by the play. Through sexual union one's self-awareness is increased by the awareness of the significance of an other, with the self and the other complementing one another and drawing out the deeper and higher elements of each other. This awareness can be the basis of new growth, but, if *used* to serve the conventional and baser purposes of society (i.e., the preservation of property, as in *Olaf Liliekrans*), it will lead only to mutual diminishment—as Peer sees when he rejects Ingrid. Ingrid and Mads Moen are willing to neglect each other's value in order to serve the interests of the social group: they marry for the sake of property. As in *Love's Comedy, A Doll House,* and *Ghosts,* the social norm is a spiritual aberration.

However, two marriages take place at the Hegstad wedding, for Peer and Solveig, like Romeo and Juliet, "change eyes" as they flash recognition of each other's value. This second marriage will be unconventional, nonlegal, a social aberration which will result in outlawry for them both, but it is the true marriage because Peer and Solveig need and complement each other. Peer's uneasiness and awkwardness at the marriage feast, his boasting contempt for the company and its reciprocal hostility to him are signs of a superiority that Solveig perceives.

Peer's rebellion against this society, the abduction of Ingrid after his rejection by Solveig, is an erotic rebellion, and in Ibsen, as in Plato, the erotic is the foundation of subsequent structures of identity. Ibsen's analyses of aberrant society have at their base a condition of sick eros, most forcefully stated in *Ghosts,* and his rebel figures, like Falk, as well as his victims frequently feel a frustration or betrayal of erotic values—a frequent theme of Romantic writing. The erotic is the very life-impulse itself, *livsglede,* and the truth and freedom of its expression will decide all subsequent truth and freedom.

At the conclusion of act 1 Peer has emerged as rebel and social outcast, the wild animal hunted by the tame pack, offending his entire society by an act of erotic rebellion. For the first time, to his mother Aase's astonishment, he has shifted drastically from fantasy to a consequential action that will decide the rest of his life. Peer, the young Adam born into a fallen world, sins with his Eve (Ingrid) but will perceive in Solveig's madonnalike identity a way of salvation.

Act 2 is filled with the imagery of "after the Fall," and the sequence of action makes up a complete time cycle, beginning in the morning, proceeding through day and evening to night, climaxing in pitch darkness in the encounter with the Boyg, and ending with the sunrise of the next day. References to the Fall color the text of scene 1. It is the morning following the night of the abduction, and Peer and Ingrid confront each other in recrimination, like the original guilty pair in the Garden. In act 1 Peer boasted of ensnaring the devil in a nutshell; in act 2 Peer realizes that he has become ensnared by the devil when he exasperatedly repeats, "the devil lies in everything I remember, the devil lies in all women."[16] Peer's "fall" brings him down to the level of the conventional world he had despised, and its representative, Ingrid, understands this and offers absolution from the guilt of the Fall. Sex was the sinful bait luring the sinner, but Peer can atone through respectable marriage with Ingrid with the attendant rewards of "property and honor" by which his potential rebellion will subside into domestic and social conformity. *Not* to capitulate means ostracism and punishment, even hanging; one sees how the menace underlying the code of conventional love in *Love's Comedy* now comes unambiguously to the surface. Peer refuses the bait, declaring he "cannot afford it"—one of the moments when Peer does glimpse that he has a soul the loss of which connot be made good even if he should win the whole world.

This scene is an excellent example of Ibsen's ability to create penetrating and compelling human drama which is at the same time an emblematic and almost allegorical *argument,* an argument that contains the critique of the reality it is presenting. Throughout the brief scene the memory of Solveig flashes potently, in poignant contrast to the sullen exchange of the fallen pair.

Even more emblematic and allegorical is the next scene, where Aase, Solveig, and her parents "search for the lost Peer," introducing the theme of the Prodigal Son. Solveig leaves the side of her father, whose harsh pietism would gladly sacrifice Peer's body in order to save his soul, and joins Aase, whose conceptions of reward and punishment are wholly physical and who is concerned only to save Peer's body. The life-denying pietism is as deficient as Aase's soul-denying attitude, and Solveig's desertion of her parents exposes the inhumanity of their beliefs: their Pauline indifference to the beauty of the flesh and of the world. Aase's beliefs essentially are pagan and folklorical, the basis of Peer's pagan energies and imagination, and Solveig's attraction to this aspect of Peer implies the value inherent in him. The emperor-galilean theme is present in Ibsen's mind.

Without Solveig (whose name phonetically suggests "sun-way"— one of Ibsen's perennial sun metaphors), Peer's rebellion lacks all direction and can dissipate itself utterly; thus scene 3 opens with Peer as the glorious Romantic rebel exulting in his freedom and degenerates into the orgy with the three saeter girls who themselves have associated with the subhuman, troll world. The saeter girls, like the similarly anarchic gypsies in *Brand*, live outside the bounds of conventional society. They are not rebels and the level of sexuality they offer Peer is an animalism incapable of assimilation by society rather than a courageous alternative in the manner of Solveig's later willed, unlawful ascent to Peer's outlaw hut. The descent from Solveig to Ingrid, the saeter girls, and the woman in green (troll-woman) is a reversal of the platonic ladder of eros described by Socrates in *The Symposium*.[17]

Scene 4, following the saeter orgy, presents one of the most splendid natural settings in Norway, and Peer's speech, as the sunset gilds this scene, is a mixture of genuine Romantic nature imagery of aspiration—mountain peaks, soaring eagles, the clean air of the peaks—and of his own internal growing pains as his consciousness attempts to contain this sublime external scene. Visually the "high point" of Peer's rebellion and spiritual expansion, it will lead to his most drastic descent and degradation. The stages of Peer's collapse into the underworld are worth noting. He begins with a wild and distraught speech that typically confuses natural scenery and fantasy, while his head feels as if squeezed in a clamp. He hears bells chiming in the distance (they are ringing for him, to ward off evil spirits). These bells, rung at the behest of Aase and Solveig, will punctuate the entire night-world sequence, creating the one contact between his dissolving consciousness and the outer world, that prevents him from sinking completely in the darkness of this mental underworld. As he hears the bells he angrily attempts to suppress his own subjective fantasies and, catching sight of two eagles, yearns to leave the filth of his own condition and follow them upward. Again, however, the impulse outward and upward is confused with fantasy; Peer retreats inward and downward under its spell and relives in imagination the past splendors of his life in the valley. At this point he falls unconscious to begin his abrupt descent into his own spiritual underworld. The failure to move outward and upward, to sublimate his physical energies into spiritual energies—which has been the theme of all of Ibsen's work—is a failure of *will*. Peer by now habitually surrenders to the dreams and impulses, built up through his past, that act as a lure away from his mastery of the present. In *Catiline* the heroic will could be compromised by succumbing to the lure both of the darker, underworld powers (Furia) and of the pellucid but infantile realm of nonheroic innocence (Aurelia), and Peer, it would seem, succumbs to both at once. The descent into the troll world is the submergence of the will in the dangerous labyrinth of prerational, animalistic forces and, at the same time, a relapse from difficult reality into the fairy-tale (*eventyr*) fantasies with which Aase and Peer had evaded dialectical conflict.

The journey through the troll underworld of scenes 5-8 has many parallels in underworld sequences in world literature: *Gilgamesh, The Odyssey, Beowulf,* Dante's *The Inferno,* and the many examples in folklore and myth that testify to the potency of the action. One can find parallels to Peer's descent to animality in the Circe's island episode of *The Odyssey,* in the Walpurgisnacht of Goethe's *Faust,* in the Nighttown sequence of James Joyce's *Ulysses,*[18] and in the many underworld sequences of modern writing where the lower depths of a Paris, London, Berlin, or Moscow mirror tabooed areas of the modern psyche.

The trolls, almost all commentators agree, represent humanity's possible lapse into the subhuman. To be fully human, to be true to one's highest potential, is to struggle to realize this potential in the individual, as in Pindar's phrase, "You shall become who you are."[19] To be a troll is to evade this struggle and to be content with given reality. The trolls are neither civilized nor revolutionary. They fear light, struggle, and conflict, which, as we will hear from Memnon's statue as the light of the sun strikes it, are the necessary conditions of life of the spirit. Moreover, while lacking fully human qualities, the trolls also lack animal grace and innocence, for animals are never *less* than their true selves. "Only the animal is truly innocent," Hegel wrote at the beginning of his *Lectures on the Philosophy of History.* Man, on the other hand, has to accept the fortunate fall from innocence and to recognize dialectical conflict as the healthy and indispensable disquietude from which, alone, the human spirit can grow. Being neither innocently animal nor aspiring to full humanity, the trolls are a constant reminder, in the manner of Swift's Yahoos, of what humanity might sink to. The troll motto, in contrast to the human "To thyself be true," is "To thyself be sufficient"—that is, do not attempt to realize your full humanity but be content with the identity and reality in which you find yourself. Against this, the heroic will in life and thought, since the time at least of Homer (as Julian, later, will recall), has preferred to immerse itself and its community in pain and suffering. Thus Odysseus drove his weeping comrades from the land of the lotus eaters knowing they would have to endure suffering when they left this sanctuary; thus Christian refuses Vanity Fair and Brand brings conflict and discord (in the manner of Christ) to the one-dimensional community he lives in. Unlike the animal, man has innocence as a *goal:* a higher innocence than that of the animal or of Eden before there was knowledge of good and evil. To accept, complacently, the condition of the Fall, to exploit it without understanding or attempting to overcome it, is to live the life of the troll.

Peer's abduction of the troll-woman, mounted on a pig as he descends into the troll kingdom, establishes the pattern of repetitions that will dominate his life. The ride on the pig repeats the reindeer ride; the wedding with the troll-woman repeats the abduction of Ingrid whom he had carried "like a pig." The troll wedding guests will set upon Peer as the Hegstand guests had done, and, after the troll sequence, Solveig and her sister Helga will search out Peer as Aase and Solveig had done after the Hegstand episode. This pattern of repetition can be made clearer in productions of the play, with the same actress playing Ingrid, the troll-woman, and Anitra and the same groups representing the Hegstand guests, the trolls, the monkeys, and the madhouse inmates. Repetition is the punishment that those who will not dialectically advance (slaying false selves) must undergo.

The troll-woman who promises Peer the property and honor that would come with marriage and who later turns on him for his betrayal of her is the underworld version of Ingrid; but as the princess (*kongsdatter*) she is also the "diabolic" version of Solveig. Just as the memory of Solveig flashed through Peer's quarrel with the "fallen-Eve" figure of Ingrid, so Peer remembers and calls upon Solveig in his struggle with the troll world. The parallels between the two marriage feasts indicate the interplay of inward and outward, higher and lower realms of action that occurs throughout the play. For events in the outer world are repeated as inward events just as Peer's experiences in this inward underworld will return to plague him in the outer world when the troll-woman establishes herself as the diabolic antithesis of Solveig in Peer's outlaw home, sharing in their lovemaking.

From the moment Peer joins forces with the troll-woman to take part in the troll wedding feast, he allows forces from his inward world—what we might call his subconscious—to take control of him, just as he had allowed himself to be controlled by, rather than controlling, the consequences of his rebellion in the external world. From now on, Peer will be a playboy of the western world, running from his inner and his outer identities until he comes up against the wasteland of his final homecoming.

The details of the troll-descent are all, as Aarseth notes, animalistic—but with a particularly nasty (Yahoolike) blend of the animal and human in which both are debased. Peer rides with the woman on the back of a pig, in the Dovre hall agrees to eat and drink animal excreta, sees the two dancing girls as a cow and a sow, allows a tail to be tied to him (in a reversal of the legend that a troll, when married to a Christian, loses its tail), and engages in a bestial battle with the trolls. The scene is built around the *eventyr* situation of the boy who must answer riddles and undergo tasks to win the princess and half the kingdom. But Peer proves his fitness for trolldom by failing to answer the riddle (what is the difference between man and troll?) even as he rejects the troll princess and refuses the final test (to alter his vision). Peer is saved, at the climax of this encounter with the trolls, by the sound of the church bells (coming from his highest conscious life, for they are rung by Solveig and Aase) as the conscious and external world struggles against the unconscious and inner. But first Peer must journey to the very heart of darkness: he has an encounter, in "pitch blackness," with the Boyg, suggestive of the utmost reaches of Peer's subconscious. The Boyg is difficult to define because it is the very riddle of the subconscious, the matrix, like the Freudian id, of the energies and powers that the individual must harness and control to attain individuality. As the all-conquering, nonfighting, enveloping, and smothering power that outwaits and wears down all opposition, the Boyg is the ultimate enemy of the will, Brand's "will-devourer" who, Brand declared, could only be defeated "within." The Boyg is Peer's worst enemy, as he concedes, and is surely the most brilliant dramatization of the interior of the mind. As Peer is almost overwhelmed by his invisible opponent, the sound of the church bells become louder and louder, drawing Peer out of this dark innerworld and into the light of the dawning day.

Waking in the light of the dawn, Peer is gently led back into the external world of consciousness. We notice that Solveig does not appear to him. She remains hidden but sends, as an emissary, her sister Helga (whose name has associations of holiness). More than one commentator, including Aarseth and Hemmer, have noted aspects of the Virgin in Solveig, which does not lock the play into Christian allegory but draws upon this as upon many other archetypes within the European memory. Solveig's invisible communing with Peer—in which he at first is impenitent then, under her gentle reproach, implores her to remember him—as well as his giving the token of the silver button to Helga, has much of the divine-human relationship between the sinner and the Virgin. It has been suggested that the silver button, given to Helga, is symbolic of Peer's best self, now placed in Solveig's custody.[20] In act 5 the Button Molder will tell Peer that he was destined to be a silver button on the vest of the world but that his loop gave way. In act 3, scene 3, the casting ladle, with which Peer once played button molder, is one of the few objects remaining in Aase's house. The ladle, in the care of the mother, would be an appropriate "womb" for the button that is then given over to Solveig's care.

The sequence of act 2, from rebellion and outlawry, through imaginative exaltation, freedom, physical debauchery, and the descent into the underworld of the subconscious, is the most momentous single movement in the play, and we have noted the careful structuring beneath the appearance of loose and free improvisation and the very careful deployment of temporal and spatial metaphors. Peer might be improvising, but Ibsen is not; the disordered and directionless hero is being presented to us by means of finely controlled artistry.

The meeting with Solveig temporarily exalts Peer, and as act 3 opens he is building his outlaw hut and attempting to exorcise from his mind the impulse to escape into fantasy. It is now that he encounters the draft dodger who cuts off his finger to disqualify himself for military service. This action causes Peer to shrink back in horror as he similarly had balked at the little operation on the eyes in the troll kingdom, for both forms of maiming represent irrevocable commitments. Act 3 is divided into two areas of possible commitment on Peer's part, and we will see him evade responsibility to both. One area is the outlaw hut and its rebel height to which Solveig climbs; the other is the mother's hut in the valley with the dying Aase. The division is between the future and the past, the bride and the mother, the difficult new life and the discredited old life, future truth and former fantasy. The outlaw altitude, however, will be invaded by creatures from Peer's uttermost depths, the trollwoman and her offspring, so that the purity of the heights is endangered by the filth from below, a problem with which Peer should wrestle but from which he flees. To the modern reader, the implications of psychological meaning are obvious: of conscious and subconscious, ego and id; but we have seen that Ibsen's height-depth metaphors were part of the Romantic vocabulary.[21] In Romantic lore the "higher" gestures of freedom and rebellion must battle the lower, darker forces within each individual and within the repressive world. Shelley, in 1819, had banished his tyrannous God and all he stood for to the depths of Demogorgon's dark realm (in an audacious reversal of God's banishment of the Romantic hero Lucifer-Satan) while the entire universe celebrated a new golden age of universal love. But by 1866 it was obvious that the gates of this hell swung both ways, and the infernal brood had almost effortlessly repossessed the world. If we see *Peer Gynt*, as I am sure we should, as not just the study of an individual mind, nor of the Norwegian consciousness, but that of the European mind as well, these extensions of the circumference of range of meanings in the play are not only defensible but obligatory.

Thus the once glorious but now degraded and discredited inheritance of Peer would be that of any free individual, and the outlaw hut with its tentative and difficult future and its new spiritual value (Solveig) would be that facing any modern rebel in life or art. Peer movingly responds to Solveig's courageous act of love as she joins him on the heights, and, for a moment, the two are a Falk and Svanhild who have turned their backs on the discredited valley world with the high-minded fervor of so many idealistic Romantic lovers. "My princess!" (*Min kongsdatter!*) exclaims Peer, and, immediately, the other *kongsdatter* appears, the troll-woman with her hideous child. The allegorical import of this juxtaposition must be that Peer's new commitment to the highest values will entail a strenuous struggle against the lowest. The troll-woman warns that she will always be present with Peer and Solveig, that when the lovers make love the woman will join them in their lovemaking; the "highest" and "lowest" are now inextricably interwoven in Peer's consciousness. Peer's act of tragically renouncing Solveig and exiling himself may seem noble, but it is an evasion and, in fact, without Solveig he falls into the power of the troll world. The contrasting scene in *Brand* is the moment when Brand's mother appears, blasting his hopes of creating a new life in a southern world with Agnes. Brand decides to stay his ground and wrestle with the past and its heritage of guilt; this is the act of will of which Peer is incapable.

Peer's last major youthful evasion also forms a contrast with a similar situation in *Brand*. Descending to his mother's home, not only does he refuse to face up to the spiritual realities of her dying; he prevents Aase from facing those realities. Brand, in order to save his mother's soul by attaining authentic consciousness, had refused her the deathbed sacrament unless she relinquished all her sinful wealth. Poor Aase has no wealth to relinquish but she has a soul to be saved: the right to a final enlightenment as she collects her consciousness before the fact of her death. The playfulness and tenderness of Peer's act of evasion, in which he reverses their old role of fable-telling parent and child, hides the fact that Peer ensures that Aase dies in ignorance and illusion. With Ibsen's stern Brandlike eye upon us, we must beware of succumbing to the tenderness of the scene, and to fortify our wavering disapproval, Ibsen makes Peer indulge in a last, outrageous evasion. For Peer exits nobly, enjoining Aase's friend Kari to see that his mother is "buried with honor"—a clear impossibility in the light of the economic and social situation that Peer has brought about!

By the close of these first three acts of the play we have seen the adolescent Peer gradually being molded half-helplessly into his future identity, evading the dialectical conflict upon which, alone, his considerable gifts could have grown into authentic achievement. While conceding his infectious charm and energy as a comic hero and noting the aspect of him that is capable (alone in his community) of recognizing the value of Solveig, we note, too, the disastrous corruption and degradation of his spirit. He is the Prodigal Son who squanders his material and spiritual birthright to become the hollow man of the modern world, filled with only feeble, because uncomprehended, echoes from the past. In many ways Peer is Schiller's "naive" consciousness gone astray; he is unwilling to recognize and take on the burden of the alienated consciousness (what Hegel terms the "disintegrated consciousness" of modern culture)[22] and hence is incapable of learning. Instead, he unsuccessfully attempts to remain in an innocent state of nature, a condition possible only for animals.

Acts 1-3 provide us with a good illustration of Ibsen's dramatic method: a poetic and at the same time *conceptual* art that is striving to be not just a good poem nor just an absorbing human story but also a "great argument" about the human condition. Ibsen had no given, conventional world view such as Shakespeare still (uneasily) possessed; he had to create it and its poetic expression for himself, drawing upon the great legacy of Romantic thought and art which itself had transmuted its heritage. The achievement of Romanticism had been to provide the secular imagination with a conception of reality at least as wide-ranging, deep, and comprehensible as the Christian world view it supplanted. What gives both this play and *Brand* the quality of a great philosophical parable, such as one detects in Aeschylus's *Prometheus Bound*, is Ibsen's way of synthesizing by imaginative apprehension a rich and diverse intellectual heritage derived from the accumulated resources of European art and thought. This well-reasoned use of the cultural past to create authentic new artistic expression makes Ibsen, the genuine modern poet, the opposite of Peer, the superficial traducer of the past who becomes, consequentially, its victim, not its shaper.[23]

Act 4, by common agreement, is the least satisfactory in the play, and Ibsen himself suggested replacing it with a musical interlude or tone-picture for the first performance of the play. Peer has degenerated into garrulous middle age to become a superficial world traveler, chattering endlessly and ignorantly on everything under the sun. The portrait is appropriate but, as with the portrait of Julian declining into pettiness and pedantry in the second half of *Emperor and Galilean*, the situation makes for low-keyed drama.

Peer's mind, as shown in his speeches, is filled with superficial quotations and misquotations from the cultural past as he becomes a mere tourist of the world, seeing everything and understanding nothing. Appropriately for such a condition, he is shown traversing a desert, the scenic equivalent of his spiritual sterility. But Ibsen cunningly counterpoints his unobservant progress with a historical/philosophical commentary of which Peer is unaware. In the course of the act Peer travels from the West (Morocco) to the East (Cairo), which takes him against the course of the sun (sol-veg). In his *Lectures on the Philosophy of History* Hegel likened the progress of the spirit in history to the course of the sun, rising in the Orient and its spiritual conceptions and then progressing westward through Egyptian, Persian, Greek, Roman, Christian, Mohammedan, and Germanic phases (Germanic, it must be noted, includes all northern Europe), with the whole progress being the gradual realization, in terms of world history, of the principle of spiritual freedom. Peer, we notice, reverses this rational development (for Hegel, the progress is the work of Reason), traveling from the West to the East and taking up, as he does so, in totally superficial form and in reverse order the spiritual roles analyzed in such depth by Hegel. He lands on the West African coast as modern Germanic and Americanized entrepeneurial man, plays at being Mohammedan prophet, resolves to live "a Christian life," fancies the idea of being a (Roman) Caesar (*keiser*) of human life, stands before the Greek statue of Memnon and fails to understand a song with a riddle from Zeus, meets the Sphinx, and finally ends up in an Egyptian insane asylum whose inhabitants, taking on the identities of animals and animal-derived objects, fit Hegel's description of the Egyptian religion. By journeying against the progress of spirit, or reason, Peer ends in a house of unreason governed by a keeper suddenly gone mad—Begriffenfeldt ("field of concepts"). Rolf Fjelde has seen the satirical use of this Hegelian term as Ibsen's attack upon the Hegelian system on behalf of Kierkegaardian existentialism;[24] but, as Aarseth points out (and as we have suggested in terms of the *Lectures on the Philosophy of History*), Ibsen makes serious use of Hegelian themes and ideas, especially from the *Aesthetik*, in the sequence from Morocco to the Cairo madhouse.[25] Aarseth suggests that the Hegel parodies in the text are at least double-edged—directed as much at Peer as at Hegel. In this connection we might recollect Hegel's famous apothegm: "He who looks at the world rationally, to him the world looks rationally back." To look at the world rationally is to undertake the strenuous intellectual labor that Peer evades (and even reverses), so that his world looks back at him as an insane derangement of the reality rationalized by Hegel.

As traveler across this uncomprehended external world, Peer has gone as far as possible (from Norway to San Francisco, taking in China and Africa) and has desecrated both human and divine images by trafficking in slaves and idols. Spiritually vacuous, he crosses the desert, encountering its half-buried history but failing to read the "signs" it presents to him: the prophet's role, Memnon's statue, the Sphinx. Peer, therefore, lives in empty time and empty space and has lost his own specific identity which a meaning-filled time and space would have defined. The modern human, to Ibsen, is thousands of years old (at least) in a world much older than himself. No man is born yesterday, like Adam, freshly prepared for a pristine world; man is born with physical and mental endowments that have long evolved in time, and everything he subsequently acquires, language, interpersonal relationships, loves, customs, morals, opinions, tastes, beliefs—in fact his entire mind—are historical products. Much as one may peel layer after layer of these accretions away, one does not come to a self independent of history. Plato taught that all learning is remembering, the spiritual equivalent, perhaps, of the animals' reacquiring in their lifetimes the complicated instincts of the species. In modern jargon one might say that each man is "programmed" to attain a certain identity which his deep and authentic comprehension of his time and place will help realize. He is free, however, to fail, in which case he will be recycled (the Button Molder's image) to repeat the individual experiment within the universal plan. But Peer acts continuously as if he were born yesterday, delightedly observing everything afresh, noting it superficially, taking up one exhausted role after another as if it still were new, and seeing only the external aspects of things and never their essences.

Peer continually loses ground from the promise of his youth. To his international business friends he describes his "Gyntian self" as a maelstrom of appetites and desires, none of them subordinated to higher ends, and it is this chaotic self that Peer wishes, futilely, to command into the identity of "emperor." Peer's associates are all negative aspects of the modern world: Teutonic aggression, Anglo-Saxon philistine mercantilism, French chauvinism, and Scandinavian pusillanimity (Ibsen has not forgiven what he believed to be the betrayal of the Danes in the Dano-Prussian war)—all existing under the masks of good intentions and fine feelings. We meet these characters again, I think, under different names and localized in provincial Norway, in Bernick and his business friends in *The Pillars of Society*.

In a succession of episodes Peer takes up one empty identity after another. He is willing to live as an ape (scene 4), then, in his Germanic role, he reverses Faust's resolve to reclaim land from the sea by envisaging bringing the sea to the land to found a new city, Peeropolis, peopled with the Nordic race, crossing the dalesman's blood with Arabian. This is a purely animalistic conception[26] of the spiritual regeneration envisaged by Brand and, later, by Julian. Peer then proceeds to the Mohammedan role of prophet which he swiftly debases through his infatuation with the Arab woman, Anitra, to whom he significantly misquotes Faust on the eternal feminine, thereby reducing Goethe's idea of the attractive power of the feminine to lift up the spirit (as Solveig had done) to mere animal attraction. Thus the eternal feminine in Anitra quickly drags Peer down into the follies of middle-aged infatuation, transvestism, and masochism (scene 8), and, following Anitra's treachery, Peer resolves to leave this "Mohammedan" phase to "live a Christian life," to become a wandering scholar and superficially trace the course of history without the discipline of any difficult groundwork (scene 9).[27] He will "own" the past and become "emperor of human life" (*menneskelivets keiser*). But following this Roman imperial resolve he arrives before the statue of the demigod Memnon just after conceding, "Hellenism I will have to set aside" (scene 11). Before Hellenism is set aside for the Egyptian phase, however, it challenges Peer. In the preceding scene the image of Solveig suddenly and briefly appeared before us (but was unseen by Peer), bathed in sunlight, singing of her waiting for Peer and sending her blessing out to him: "God give you joy if you stand at his throne." Sunlight now touches the statue before which Peer stands as Memnon's mother, Aurora (the dawn), appears and, in accordance with the legend, music sounds and the statue sings to Peer the warning song:

> From the demi-god's ashes rise, youth-renewing,
> Birds brightly singing.
> Zeus, the All-knowing
> made struggle their longing.
> Wise Owl, among
> birds, is sleep so much safer?
> You must die or decipher
> this riddle in song.[28]

Asbjorn Aarseth devotes a number of pages[29] to a discussion of the significance of the Egyptian figures of Memnon's statue and the Sphinx, and he cites the work of previous scholars who have demonstrated the presence of nonparodic Hegelian elements in Ibsen's depiction of what Hegel sees as the "animalic" spiritual conceptions of the Egyptians. Hegel's account of Egyptian art, which he sees as belonging to the phase of symbolic art he designates "Unconscious Symbolism," pays particular attention to the

Memnon statue and to the Sphinx. (The latter, Hegel wittily calls "the symbol of the symbolic itself."[30])

Symbolic art is, for Hegel, inherently defective and is struggling to evolve to the later (Hellenic) phase of classical art. It is defective because it "stops short of free individuality," which, for Hegel, is the condition of human wholeness. Peer, we noticed, decided to postpone his Hellenism to attain to free individuality (i.e., *humanity*). It is worth quoting Hegel's account of the Memnon statues because (if the reader will forgive the metaphor), the passage throws light upon the figure of Peer:

Just as on one side the Egyptian superstition has an inkling, in the animal form, of a secret inwardness, so on the other side we find the human form so represented that it still has the inner element of subjectivity outside itself and therefore cannot unfold itself into free beauty. Especially remarkable are those colossal statues of Memnon which, resting in themselves, motionless, the arms glued to the body, the feet firmly set together, numb, stiff, and life-less, are set up facing the sun in order to await its ray to touch them and give them soul and sound ... taken as *symbols*, the meaning to be ascribed to these colossi is that they do not have the spiritual soul freely in themselves and there-fore, instead of being able to draw animation from within, from what bears proportion and beauty in itself, they require for it light from without which alone liberates the note of the soul from them. The human voice, on the other hand, resounds out of one's own feeling and one's own spirit without any exter-nal impulse, just as the height of art in general consists in making the inner give shape to itself out of its own being. But the inner life of the human form is still dumb in Egypt and in its animation it is only a natural factor that is kept in view.[31]

Hegel describes the "dumb" and stony rigidity of the statue in terms that Ibsen echoed in his Memnon poem of 1855 (the light awakening the unliving, giving it "soul and sound"), and he con-trasts this with the free spiritual expression of the human voice that does not need liberation from without. It is Solveig, *singing,* who possesses this freedom whereas Peer needs to be awakened and given soul by the light of Solveig who was, as we noted, bathed in sunlight immediately before Peer confronted the Memnon statue. The Memnon statue was awakened to the life of the soul by the maternal Aurora, or Eos, and Solveig, at the end of the play, again in the light of the rising sun, perhaps saves Peer by preserving the soul's life he had evaded.

The song insists that the demigod (*halvgud*) lives a life of struggle and conflict; and the birds, rising and fighting from the flames like phoenixes, are images of the warring aspects of dialectical conflict, reminding us of the hawk and swan in *Love's Comedy,* the hawk and dove in *Brand,* and the soaring eagles that the young Peer gazed at.[32] Julian, later, will see rising like a phoenix from the flames of his burning fleet the united spirits of the warring emperor and galilean, and this notion of the necessary conflict between warring aspects of the soul is, we have seen, Ibsen's "program" since *Catiline.* Birds symbolize aspiring spirit but the song asks why the owls of wisdom are sleeping, *Visdomsugle/hvor sover min fugle?* This suggests that Peer is like an unawakened Memnon statue. By dying in and rising to new life from the flames, the birds exhibit that paradox of being oneself by slaying oneself with which the Button Molder will confront Peer.

But Hegel-Ibsen has not yet finished with Peer and, following the pages of the Aesthetic, our hero proceeds from the Memnon statue to the Sphinx (a journey of just two pages, in fact!):

The works of Egyptian art in their mysterious symbolism are therefore riddles; the objective riddle *par excellence.* As a symbol for this proper meaning of the Egyptian spirit we may mention the Sphinx. It is, as it were, the symbol of the symbolic itself.... Out of the dull strength and power of the animal the human spirit tries to push itself forward, without coming to a perfect portrayal of its own freedom and animated shape, because it must still remain confused and associated with what is other than itself. This pressure for self-conscious spirituality which does not apprehend itself from its own resources in the one reality adequate to itself but only contemplates itself in what is related to it and brings itself into consciousness in precisely what is strange to it, is the symbolic as such which at this peak becomes a riddle.[33]

Unlike Begriffenfeldt, Hegel deprecates riddling art for he sees the task of art as attaining full "self-conscious spirituality"—the great achievement of Hellenic culture. And in the Greek myth of the Sphinx, Hegel notes, the monster is linked to this higher spiritual destiny:

The Sphinx propounded the well-known conundrum: What is it that in the morning goes on four legs, at mid-day on two, and in the evening on three? Oedipus found the simple answer: a man, and he tumbled the Sphinx from the rock. The explanation of the symbol lies in the absolute meaning, in the spirit, just as the famous Greek inscription calls to man: Know thyself. The light of consciousness is the clarity which makes its concrete content shine clearly through the shape belonging and appropriate to itself [the human form] and in its (objective) existence reveals itself alone.[34]

Ibsen adds to the Sphinx's riddle by having Peer address it as the Boyg, just as he likens Memnon's statue to the Troll King, and this has generated an academic discussion over which Begriffenfeldt is the appropriate presiding genius. Since Ibsen's mentor Hegel insists that riddling art is inferior art, the fact that Peer now is plunged into a context of riddles that he fails to answer shows how far he is from the Hellenic goal "Know thyself!" which, as Hegel demonstrated, his heroic predecessor Oedipus achieved. One reason for the riddling identities in *Peer Gynt,* such as the Boyg, the Memnon statue, the Sphinx, the Strange Passenger, and so on, is to portray the disordered subjectivity of Peer who has not overcome the contradictions of his spirit to achieve clarity. In *this* sense, Aarseth is correct: Peer remains an animal, in the "Egyptian" phase of consciousness. In his struggle with the Boyg Peer had been saved by external means, and the identity of the Boyg remained for him an unsolved riddle. The Boyg, as the "will-devourer," is the riddle of Peer's inner world; the Sphinx (who devoured her victims) might represent the riddle of humanity itself: its need to overcome its animalistic nature and to struggle for authentic humanity.[35] It is with difficult self-knowledge ("know thyself!") that one transcends the Sphinxlike condition for that of the fully human. But Peer does not answer the Sphinx's riddle. Instead he asks it to reveal its identity and then endows it with precisely the unity and wholeness which, Hegel demonstrated, it so notably *lacks.* "He is *himself,*" Peer tells Begriffenfeldt,[36] whereas Hegel had described it as "confused and associated with what is other than itself." Peer's misconception is total. Just as he claims for the Sphinx the unity it lacks, so he applies the same quality to himself. "I've always sought to remain myself . . ."[37]

Begriffenfeldt's ecstatic reaction would be less lunatic were Peer speaking the truth, and we will find other of Begriffenfeldt's comments to be more cogent than insane. For example, his account of the condition of the asylum inmates, as utterly sealed and enclosed in "self" and unable to feel for the human world beyond this enclosed self, carries conviction and, incidentally, echoes Hegel's account of insanity as "a state in which the mind is shut up within itself, has sunk into itself, whose peculiarity...consists in its being no longer in *immediate contact* with actuality but in having positively separated itself from it."[38] This is from a passage in *The Philosophy of Mind* in which the reader will find a number of correspondences between Hegel's account of insanity and its cures (about which he is enlightened and compassionate) and the details of the Cairo asylum. For Hegel, the most effective cures for insanity involve bringing the sufferers out of the sealed world of their delusions so that "they are forced out of their diseased subjectivity and impelled towards the real world." An effective method, Hegel notes, is for someone to pretend "to enter into [the lunatic's] delusion and then suddenly doing something in which the patient catches a glimpse of liberation from his imagined complaint."[39] Peer, when confronted with the lunatics who implore help, does exactly the opposite: he maintains them in their delusions because he himself has no rational world into which to liberate them. Hegel posited this self-liberation as the task of every individual. Each human soul, Hegel declared, "on account of the infinite wealth of its content, may be described as the soul of a world, as the individually determined world-soul."[40] But to attain this mastery and comprehension of infinite spiritual wealth, we need to embark upon the very same conflict-filled journey that Peer has evaded. "What we have therefore to consider prior to the attainment of this goal, is the struggle for liberation which the soul has to wage against the immediacy of its substantial content in order to become completely master of itself and adequate to its Notion, namely, into that self-related, *simple* subjectivity which exists in the 'I'.[41] Attaining this elevation (which is only a phase of the soul's development) involves three stages: "the soul entangled in the dreaming away and dim presaging of its *concrete natural life*...the second stage [of] the standpoint of *insanity,* which means the soul divided against itself, on the one hand already master of itself, and on the other hand not yet master of itself.... Lastly in the third stage the soul becomes master of its natural individuality, of its bodily nature, reduces this to a subservient means..."[42]

This sequence, involving the mastery of the *dreaming, insane,* and *animal* (bodily) states, together with the goal of discovering in oneself, and comprehending, the infinite articulation of a "world-soul," seems to have direct bearing upon Peer's situation from youth to old age. *The Philosophy of Mind* (which is part 3 of *The Encyclopaedia of The Philosophical Sciences*, first published in 1830) would, I think, bear examining as a rich storehouse of ideas having relevance to Ibsen's conception of the human spirit within the world. Hegel describes the "subconscious" as a "night-like mine or pit in which is stored a world of infinitely many images and representations,"[43] and this calls to mind not only Peer and the troll world but also Ibsen's designation of himself, as poet, as a miner digging below with his hammer to reach the hidden ore. In Hegel's account of mind (*Geist*) we have, therefore, an infinitely rich inner world, or subconscious, and an infinitely rich outer world, the objective world, which is also the individual mind. Peer, as we noted earlier, has not dialectically overcome the conflicts of either the inner and lower or the outer and upper realms of spirit/mind and therefore has neither internal nor external "self." He is as confused a contradiction of animal and human as is the Egyptian Sphinx in Hegel's account. The inmates of the asylum resemble Peer in that they all have arrested their spiritual development at some earlier, "chrysalis" stage of evolution: primitive language (Huhu), historical nostalgia (the Fellah), and a world of mere paper intentions that never evolve into actions in the world.

The lunatic chaos of the asylum, therefore, would seem to be not a satire upon Hegel but an image of a world that has not undertaken the strenuous and painful labor of Reason enjoined by Hegel, so that it no longer is perceived to be the consummation of Absolute Reason which, Begriffenfeldt announces, "died last night." It might represent the *inherited* Hegelian system ("field of concepts") proliferating into pedantry, foreshadowing Lucky's manic learning in *Waiting for Godot*; and Peer's totally superficial relation to the world and the past (which is the exact opposite of Hegel's relation to reality) is an example of the very superficiality that Hegel so frequently attacked. For although the world is the embodiment of the Idea, of Absolute Reason, Hegel insists that the world can betray or inadequately realize the Idea which is substantiated only by painful struggle, both physical and intellectual. The "system," for Hegel, always has to be existentially affirmed.

Act 5 almost is a play in itself and is among the richest sequences in all Ibsen's writing, taking up the archetypal theme of the hero's homecoming and loading it with new and richly ironic meanings which search into the very heart of loss. The fragments of Peer's totally disintegrated consciousness appear as a bewildering procession of figures that are simultaneously inward and outward: they are aspects of Peer's subjectivity yet, at the same time, aspects of the objective world of spirit that Peer has failed to comprehend. Although the reader feels closer to Peer's existentialist despair than to the conventional piety of, for instance, the pentecostal choir, the act is an indictment of Peer's prodigal and misspent life, and, almost in the manner of the drowning man's swift recapitulation of that life, all its salient aspects reemerge in Peer's consciousness. The shipwreck is the real and somber repetition of the reindeer ride and plunge into the fjord; the Hegstad marriage feast turns into Ingrid's funeral with many of the same guests assembled; the story of Peer trapping the devil in a nut becomes that of the devil trapping a pig (Peer) under his cloak and producing the squeals of a porcine biography. Solveig appears immediately after, and Peer flees from her and finds himself in a burned-out wasteland that is the mordant contrast to the magnificent Ronde landscape of Peer's outlaw youth. Aase's voice mingles with that of the landscape, reproachfully recollecting her deathbed; the Troll King returns to the scene and the pietists reappear as the pentecostal churchgoers. Ibsen may have called *Peer Gynt* "a caprice," but he is as incapable of unstructured writing as Henry James is incapable of popular sensationalism. In the reappearance of these past patterns Peer is being reproached by the presence of the spiritual structures his life has attempted to deny.

The major metaphors with which Ibsen shapes the imaginative argument of this act are: shipwreck; death by drowning; funeral; wasteland and fire; debility; the terror of nonidentity; and, finally and poignantly, a tentatively adumbrated redemption. The rich transposition of archetypal models within the modern action, from both pre-Christian and post-Christian cultures, gives this sequence a texture anticipative of T. S. Eliot's *The Waste Land*, and the Morality Play figures of the Strange Passenger, the Troll King, the Button Molder, and the Lean One (the devil) extend the action of the play into the dimensions of metaphysical argument.

The shipwreck with which the act opens, proceeding to explore the total devastation on land, brings to mind Ibsen's words to Brandes a few years later: "There actually are moments when the entire history of the world reminds one of a sinking ship."[44] Such an apocalyptic vision of the world is encountered more than once in Ibsen's writings, so that it would not be too farfetched to see in this shipwreck, as in that which opens *The Tempest*, a metaphor for a whole world in confusion. The crew of the ship are no better than Peer; they callously refuse to rescue the survivors of a shipwreck, being involved only in their own well-being. Before his own shipwreck, Peer is visited by the Strange Passenger, an enigmatic figure variously interpreted as Death, the Devil, Kierkegaardian Angst, and even the poet, Ibsen, himself. The text warrants any one or all of these interpretations, which means only that Ibsen intends the figure to remain enigmatic. His reappearance at Peer's side in the sea deepens the enigma and effectively "darkens" the texture of the play. In a sense, all the figures Peer encounters in act 5 are aspects of himself: of his past and of his inward life; and much of their mysterious quality is due to the chaotic nature of Peer's subjectivity. Peer now is the inhabitant of a mental landscape where events and objects are as much psychical as physical. The Strange Passenger's appearance, which should instigate deep self-reflection by Peer, moves him only to evasion.

Reaching land, Peer first encounters the funeral of the peasant who struggled over a lifetime to maintain human existence in the inhospitable landscape. The priest's beautiful epitaph is Ibsen's tribute to the unglamorous and stubborn heroism of common humanity. But, beautiful as the passage is, it is, I believe, ambiguous. Peer's comment that the eulogy contained "nothing unpleasant to jar the mind" alerts us to the fact that the peasant's life established nothing in the world beyond the range of his own family's life.

In direct contrast to the crowd gathered with the priest to contemplate the "uplifting" example of the peasant's life is the next scene in which Peer sees another funeral crowd gathered to contemplate the dispersed and unedifying details of Peer's past. It is the first of a sequence of "wasteland" scenes, a "hillside with a dried-out river bed... a ruined mill. The ground is torn up; everything is desolate."[45] Ingrid, it seems, has died after a life of multiple and undistinguished infidelities, and Hegstad is in ruins. An auction is taking place at which all the objects for sale once belonged to Peer (from Aase's confiscated estate), and attached to these objects are legends relating to Peer. Peer enters the auction and offers to sell his own past life whose details are as dispersed and degraded as the auction objects. He offers the Ronde castle, Grane, the horse with which he drove Aase to Soria-Moria castle, "one dream of a silver-clasped book," from his memory of Solveig, his American empire, his prophet's beard, and the gray hair of a madman. He hears from the sheriff that Peer was an abominable fabricator, and from another that he was hanged somewhere abroad. The fable of the devil and the pig which Peer then tells, typically adapting another man's invention,[46] seems to rebuke the auction guests for their inability to recognize the reality of the life of Peer that they had just been relating; but it also is the reverse of his youthful Hegstad story of trapping the devil in a nut. In the new version the devil is in command, tormenting his victim.

After the auction, Peer enters a forest, on all fours, searching for food like an animal and proclaiming for himself the epitaph "emperor of all the other animals." He then descends lower and, in the famous scene, sees himself as an onion. In the auction scene he unfolded his life, for sale, in the sequence from youth (the Ronde castle) to his middle age in the asylum; now he sees layer after layer of his past identity unfolded in multiple roles lacking a center. Still in the animalistic posture, on all fours, he approaches what is actually the center he could not discover, Solveig's hut with its reindeer horns, signifying victory over the animal realm,[47] and he momentarily thinks he sees a mermaid "fish-shaped down from the navel"[48] —a recollection of the animalistic troll-woman. When Solveig appears, singing that the hut is waiting for Peer's visit at Pentecost, Peer rises, "hushed and deathly pale," from all fours to the human posture, for the first time fully recognizing, "Here is where my empire was!"[49] Aarseth suggests that, through a series of alarming encounters, Peer now will undergo a dark night of the soul and thereby transcend the animal identity in which he has been trapped to attain to his highest self, in Solveig "who is the image of the soul, without which he is lost."[50] Supporting the

idea that Peer now undergoes a new spiritual travail, which the
Strange Passenger attempted to instigate, is the fact that the subsequent episodes are all psychical, the scenes and figures of a spirit
world.

It is now *night*, and Peer finds himself on a moor with trees
burned by a forest fire. Unlike the degradation of the auction
scene, this wasteland implies a far more painful devastation.
"Charred tree trunks can be seen for miles around."[51] It is the
landscape of Peer's soul, and its elements directly reproach him
with the crying of children's voices. Whereas the charred scene
suggests purgatory, the children's voices suggest limbo, the realm
not of sinful but of unaccomplished things; and it is this non-
accomplishment with which Peer is reproached. Confronting this
limbo of evaded possibilities in the form of threadballs, leaves,
wind, and dew, Peer's "self" is further dispersed into the vegetable
and elemental levels of existence. Beneath these levels there can be
only a form of Ur-stuff, similar to the primeval slime to which
Julian, in his trance, sees material life reduced. In the next scene,
the Button Molder describes Peer's soul as precisely such a primeval
substance, as something that needs to be recycled for the reemer-
gence of new spiritual forms. Seeking to prove that he has created
out of his life an authentic identity, and so escape the recycling
ladle, Peer learns from the Troll King only that he has proved an
exemplary troll, living in complacent self-sufficiency. In his second
meeting with the Button Molder he is told that to be oneself is
to slay oneself, slaying false and inadequate selves in order to advance, as did Brand, to higher and truer identity. In terms of dialectics, the false or inadequate self can be slain only if it is explored
to the limits where it is forced to reveal its insufficiency and to
evolve to a more adequate identity.

By not developing his identity to this dialectical extreme, even
to the extreme of being a greatly negative force in the world, Peer
merits neither heaven nor hell, because he has not lived as if these
were realities shaping his life. In this, Peer is no worse than most
of his fellowmen, for the devil (the Lean One) reports that his
business has shamefully fallen off and that sins even worse than
Peer's, such as setting up idols in sermons, art, and literature, have
not qualified for damnation. Against the interpretations of Hem-

mer and Aarseth, who see a strongly Christian argument in the play, I would suggest that Peer and his age stand indicted for not having evolved to spiritual conceptions beyond, and higher than, those of traditional Christianity. The emphatic use of Christian imagery in very unconventional ways, as well as the vivid use of pagan images and themes, brings these old forms forcefully before us but as the terms of a spiritual condition to be superseded.

This, surely, is evident in the closing scenes. In the most moving speech in the whole play Peer, like a pagan, addresses an almost pantheistic hymn to the "beautiful sun and beautiful earth," as, also, the dying Julian will do. The lament is in terms of having failed to match the beauty of the earth, of neglecting to contribute to it; it is not the Christian's lament at having been ensnared by this beauty into foresaking the afterlife.

The pentecostal hymn of the churchgoers counterpoints Peer's speech in one of those pagan-Christian justapositions so frequent in Ibsen up to the close of *When We Dead Awaken.* The pentecostal hymn sets up a challenging vision: the tongues of God's kingdom struck the earth, and the earth, reborn, replied with the tongue of God's kingdom. In Peer's speech, the beauty and glory of the world are in the world itself; to the churchgoers the beauty is a miraculous visitation from God's heaven. Peer is not renewed by the hymn. On the contrary, he now reaches a pitch of total devastation and is ready to give in to the Button Molder. The Christian message of the hymn, therefore, is no revelation pointing Peer onto the right path; at most, it is the expression of one traditional, supreme orientation to one's self and the world from which Peer is conspicuously excluded.

Peer's salvation, if it lies anywhere, is with Solveig. That Solveig is, in a very special and unorthodox sense, Christian is undeniable, and it is obvious that Ibsen does invest her with attributes of the Virgin Mary interceding with the Father on behalf of the sinner. But Peer is not merely a sinner. In a sense he has been Solveig's salvation, also. Solveig is not given to hyperbole and when she tells Peer that he has made her whole life a beautiful song, we have to believe her. On the psychological level, we can see the force of Hemmer's argument that Peer lifted Solveig out of the world of the valley (incidentally removing her from the harsh life-denying pietism of her parents) and did awaken love in her.[52] Solveig has kept Peer "like a silver-clasped book" because he has value, and if we see Peer as only animalistic, rather than extend this term to include "pagan," it would be difficult to fathom this value. On the allegorical level, argued for convincingly by Aarseth:[53] even if we see Peer and Solveig as the lower and higher selves of the same identity, we must see this separation as harmful to Solveig as well as to Peer and the reintegration as just as necessary for the higher self. Peer, by taking on the guilty identity of the errant and wandering prodigal, has in many ways been the scapegoat, keeping Solveig free from sin—as he explicitly avows when he leaves Solveig in act 3 in order not to involve her in his degradation. But a virtue thus protected from the realities of the world is hardly a virtue at all—as any even indifferent Hegelian knows, and as any Ibsenite, schooled in the dramas from *Catiline* on, knows. Ibsen shares the Romantic impatience with Edenic innocence and the Romantic conviction of the necessity of the Fall.[54] If Peer, journeying through the dark night of the soul, finally attains to his highest (spiritual) identity in Solveig, in a pattern remarkably similar to that described by St. John of the Cross, as Aarseth argues,[55] we have to see that such a journey, which Solveig does not experience, is of spiritual value. In a very different way Brand reaches the height of the ice-church only after a tragic experience of the "lower" human world which the ice-church guardian, Gerd, has not undergone.

When Peer cries out his question to Solveig, as the day breaks:

> Where has Peer Gynt been since we parted...
> As first when he sprang from the mind of God?[56]

we are meant to consider this destiny, I think, as an aspiration for the future, like the third empire, and not as conformity to a traditional spiritual form. As Peer's "mother, *wife,* innocent woman" (the three phases of the eternal feminine that Peer has degraded), Solveig is more than the Virgin figure just as Peer is more than the beast, even though these identities are included in the Peer-Solveig union. Similarly, the "pure woman" that Julian seeks in *Emperor and Galilean* is more than an anticipation of medieval Mariolatry. There are, I think, a "cluster" of themes and images in this last

scene, as there are throughout *Peer Gynt*, from both pagan and
Christian traditions. The final breaking of the sun, for example, is
a pagan, a Christian, and a Romantic and Hegeliam emblem of the
divine spirit. In Hegel it is used constantly as the signal of a new
dawn of spirit, as in a superb passage in the Preface to *The Phenomenology of Spirit*.

The spirit has broken with what was hitherto the world of its existence and
imagination and is about to submerge all this in the past; it is at work giving
itself a new form. To be sure, the spirit is never at rest but always engaged in
ever progressing motion. But just as in the case of a child the first breath it
draws after long silent nourishment terminates the gradualness of the merely
quantitative progression — a qualitative leap — and now the child is born, so,
too, the spirit that educates itself matures slowly and quietly toward the new
form, dissolving one particle of the edifice of its previous world after the
other, while its tottering is suggested only by some symptoms here and there:
frivolity as well as the boredom that open up in the establishment, and the in-
determinate apprehension of something unknown, are harbingers of a forth-
coming change. This gradual crumbling which did not alter the physiognomy
of the whole is interrupted by the break of day that, like lightning, all at once
reveals the edifice of the new world.[57]

Hegel had in mind, in this passage, the new spirit following the
French Revolution and the Napoleonic reshaping of Europe, and
the dual image of childbirth and sunrise in this passage, used to
describe the sudden emergence of a new dawn of spirit after a long
process of the dissolving of old forms, has affinities with the last
scene of *Peer Gynt*. The *Pietà* image of Peer sleeping with his head
in Solveig's lap also brings to mind the icon of mother and new-
born child, the image of a tentative struggle forward, a new birth,
out of the ashes of the old world. If Peer, as the Prodigal Son, lost
himself in the world, that was partly because the world itself was
lost; devoid of any new sustaining spiritual principle, it became an
arena in which the human spirit *could* lose itself. Ibsen will repeat
this powerful image of the *pietà* later, in *Ghosts*, where the sun also
rises on mother and child after a whole cultural edifice has slowly
crumbled away, and in both instances, I think, the rising sun is the
symbol of possible spiritual rebirth from the ashes of the past.

Peer Gynt proved to be Ibsen's last verse-play, and his decision
to forsake verse-drama for the subtler theatrical poetry of realism

has been regretted by many. But Peer himself is a warning that the overtly poetic may be an evasion of authentic dialectic engagement with reality. Ibsen's poetry, from now on, will wrestle more earnestly than ever against the intractable particulars of everyday, fallen reality that resist the free and true emergence of spirit. Ibsen wants his poetry to work upon the world that he, as poet, inhabits with us, to search out its most secret places, and to reveal the archetypal and universal patterns, upon which everyday reality has turned its back, within the structure and texture of that reality.

Brand and *Peer Gynt* are great poetic parables, the parable proving, so far, to be the most effective form that modern verse-drama has adopted, as *Murder in the Cathedral* also demonstrates. But it is in the nature of the parable to be exemplary, somewhat distant, leaving the actual substance of our daily lives untouched, and both Ibsen and T. S. Eliot felt impelled to go beyond exemplary verse-parables into a drama of modern realism. Eliot's later method of concealing his verse beneath the skin of modern idiom, and Ibsen's method of structuring his great poetic arguments (what Hemmer calls his "poetic ideology")[58] beneath the images of everyday contemporary life, were similar attempts to bring poetry and reality closer together so that they might interact more consequentially. Such a form dramatizes our ordinary lives in all their ordinariness, but the spiritual epiphanies that might then occur would be all the more arresting for having engaged with the obstinate commonness of everyday existence. No more splendid a leave-taking from verse-drama can be imagined than this prodigious, prodigal *Peer Gynt*, which seems to contain so many earlier forms, from Gilgamesh and *The Odyssey* to *Faust*, and to presage so many forms to come.

THE MEDIOCRE ANGELS
OF *THE LEAGUE OF YOUTH*

In his Introduction to the Oxford translation of *The League of Youth* and *Emperor and Galilean*, J. W. McFarlane adroitly compares and contrasts the two works. "Common to both plays," he writes, "is then that they are both Germanic (yet how differently Germanic) and that they are both realistic (yet how differently realistic)."[1] Otherwise, he continues,

it would be hard to imagine two plays more unlike each other, or, indeed separately, more unlike Ibsen's other plays: the one parochial, locally allusive, comically Holbergian, stuffed with plots and schemes and double-dealing, people with caricatured figures of vanity and petty ambition and pomposity, and all rather desperately kept going by a creaking machinery of misplaced letters and contrived encounters; and the other epochal, distant, heroically proportioned, heavy with cosmic significance, sombrely mystical, chronicling the ineluctabilities of world-historical processes, and proclaiming an earnest if cloudy philosophy.[2]

I do not think the dramatic machinery of *The League of Youth* creaks as much as McFarlane implies. Today any dramatic plotting in the old style is likely to annoy modern audiences despite the fact that the original audience was meant to experience conscious pleasure at the deft deployment of conventional dramatic devices, just as those originally listening to sonata form were able to appreciate formal muscial conventions. But the contrast between the two plays is striking, as in MacFarlane's account. It is so striking, in fact, that one wonders if such a contrast were not intended by the poet; just as after completing *Brand* Ibsen was impelled to write its total opposite, *Peer Gynt*, so a similar process might have been at work in the composition of these two very dissimilar plays.

Ibsen's fondness for dialectical contraries encourages one to think that, after contemplating for so many years the huge subject matter of *Emperor and Galilean*, he was at some time intrigued by the idea of a total inversion of its themes. The two plays form a contrast of diametrically antithetical spiritual conditions requiring similarly antithetical form and subject matter. In *Emperor and Galilean* the energies are directed outward to vast imperial conquests, to the clash of empires, of world-historical forces, and to the gathering of mighty, invisible spiritual powers that will shape the life of people for centuries to come. In *The League of Youth* the energies are all turned inward, to a microcosmic human order incapable of expansion and governed by *de lokale forholde* (the local condition), a phrase that, McFarlane observes, is repeated thematically throughout the play—somewhat like a bubbling little *motif* in a Mozart *allegretto*.

Such a contrast in subject and in dramatic method might represent more, on Ibsen's part, than a virtuoso display of contrasting dramatic talents, though the display is impressive enough. It might represent more, too, than a desire to return to a salutary realistic and particularist form of artistry at a time when, engaged in the speculations of *Emperor and Galilean*, his writing all too easily could have lost its sharpness in the rarer ether of philosophico-historical abstraction. *The League of Youth* is as decisively a work for the *theater*, fully effective only in precise theatrical enactment, as *Emperor and Galilean* is a "mental drama" which would not gain from theatrical representation—except, perhaps, in terms of the cinema where it would prove highly effective. The implications of an intentional contrast between the two plays increase when we recollect that both plays were followed, immediately, by the twelve-play realistic cycle.

For *The League of Youth* has all the narrowly restricted topography of the plays of the realistic cycle without their active universal and archetypal content, whereas *Emperor and Galilean* has all the universal and archetypal content of the cycle without its sharp and accurate fidelity to the rhythms of the modern consciousness and its theatrical expression, for which the cycle is so notable. The gulf that we detect between the art and the subject matter of *The League of Youth* and *Emperor and Galilean* is bridged by the realistic cycle, in which the huge perspectives and shaping spiritual forces of the world-historical drama are infiltrated into the confined scene of *The League of Youth*. It is as if the two plays, separately, confronted Ibsen with his great dramatic problem and that, for the time being, he wished to set out this problem clearly before himself in its extreme form, placing on one side *de lokale forholde* and on the other *det tredje rike* (the third empire/kingdom). Each phrase is sounded as a *leitmotiv* in its respective play, and each is sounded to opposite effect.

That Ibsen felt the *lokale forholde* of Norway to be deadly to the development of a larger social, intellectual, and spiritual life—of the order dramatized by *Emperor and Galilean*—is evident in many of his pronouncements upon Norwegian cultural life. For instance, he wrote to Georg Brandes (in 1875, when he was in the unusually long period of artistic inactivity between the publication of *Emperor and Galilean* in 1873 and the completion of the first play of the realistic cycle, *Pillars of Society*, in 1877) deploring the parochialism of the Scandinavian countries:

Why do you and all of us whose standpoint is a European one feel so isolated at home? Because the state we belong to is not a complete, united organism, and because the people at home are parochial, not Scandinavian or nationalistic in their thinking, their feeling, and their general orientation. I set very little store by political organisations, but all the more by the welding together of our national ideas. You call your periodical *The Nineteenth Century*—but at the present moment isn't the physiognomy of this century quite different in Denmark, in Sweden, in Norway! And do you believe that the fraction of Europeanism each branch of the Scandinavian people has assimilated provides a sufficient foundation for everything you dream of building? Only entire nations can join in great intellectual movements. Advancing the front line of our conceptions of life and of the world is not a parochial matter. Compared with the other nations, we Scandinavians have not yet got beyond the point of view of the parish council. And have you ever heard of a parish council looking for and preparing the way for "the third kingdom?" [the third empire].[3]

In this letter the local conditions of the parish council are contrasted with the lofty imperatives of the third empire. This strongly suggests that Ibsen had his two immediately preceding plays in mind as he was preparing himself for the writing of the first play of the realistic cycle. (The confrontation reminds one somewhat of the later contrast between Shaw's determination to make his drama expressive of the larger intellectual currents of the world and the work of the Abbey Theatre playwrights determined to express the consciousness of Ireland.) Other pronouncements by Ibsen insist upon the spiritual parochialism of the world dramatized by *The League of Youth*. In that play, he tells Georg Brandes, "you will find everything ordinary and everyday, no strong passions, no profound moods, and above all no isolated thoughts."[4] To Peter Hansen, in 1870, he makes the famous comparison of the style of the play to "Knackwurst and Beer," adding that the point of view of his art has changed "because here I find myself in a society well-ordered to the point of boredom."[5] Since this society was that of Dresden, it is apparent that the spiritual parochialism depicted by the play was not confined to Scandinavia but represented a parochialism of the spirit discoverable in any society not activated by living universals. Nevertheless, it is to Scandinavia that Ibsen's thoughts turn in the next sentence: "What on earth will happen when I resettle at home! I shall have to find salvation in remoteness of subject. That is when I intend to begin *Emperor Julian*."[6] It is *Emperor and Galilean*, then, that will set the spirit free from the parochialism of *The League of Youth*.

In a world like that depicted in *The League of Youth*, all aspects of human life, from the immediately personal to the communal and public, are utterly without access to the spiritually sustaining, universal, and "archetypal" powers that alone can give meaning to life. Such a world exists in inadequate self-consciousness—that unexamined life which Socrates declared not to be worth living. *Det tredje rike* leads the consciousness through huge perspectives of the past to a spiritual crisis in the present that will be resolved only at some point in the distant future; the very sound of the phrase with its three broad monosyllables resembles a portentous summons to the lofty and infinite. *De lokale forholde,* on the other hand, conjures up the bustling petty spirit that it represents, quickly bringing the consciousness back to an awareness of the parochial present. The world of *The League of Youth* very much resembles the society of *Love's Comedy,* which has shut out the lure of great natural vistas, and Peer Gynt's conventional and nonvital valley community, which proffers Ingrid and the Hegstad farm as its great prize (Ingrid has become the much-sought-after Widow Rundholmen) and which is shut off from the vistas that supply Peer's spirit with an alternative world of possibilities. Stensgaard is a Peer who has helplessly got caught up in the coils of this petty society. More surprising to contemplate, Stensgaard also is a Julian born in a time and place bypassed by significant history.

The play depicts a mode of life denied knowledge of or access to the universal content of human life and consequently stifling in its mediocrity, the Chekovian condition of this most un-Chekovian of plays. Ibsen's analysis is performed with a great deal of skillful and zestful satiric thrust and humor, but the unbearable pettiness of such a condition continually is insisted upon by different characters in the play and the phrase *de lokale forholde* buzzes about the text like a gadfly. Only an awareness of the larger spiritual and historical forces that have gone into the shaping of our consciousness can restore a sense of meaning, perspective, and sanity to life, so that the passions and purposes of life can be directed to worthwhile ends and guided by essential and living principles. By the same token, such an awareness, alone, can prevent human talents and energies such as Stensgaard, however dubiously, possesses from atrophying totally or being squandered upon trivia.

The action of the play depicts an absurd storm in a teacup (and it is deliciously ironic that its premiere in Christiania should have occasioned another such storm) not unlike the social agitation of *Love's Comedy.* We see a society full of frantic and misdirected energies, wildly agitated within a tiny space, finally coming to rest in a complacent consciousness of its own mediocrity:

BRATTSBERG: ... truly, we have been groping and fumbling in darkness; but good angels were behind us.

LUNDESTAD: Oh, God help us, the angels were somewhat mediocre.
ASLAKSEN: Well, that comes of the local conditions, [*de lokale forholde*]
Mr. Lundestad.

(curtain falls.)[7]

If God is to help us (*Gud bedre oss*), he will have to send more alarming angels, or spiritual forces, as in the unnerving arrival from America of a Lona Hessel who, in *Pillars of Society,* will lift an equally mediocre and stifling community out of *de lokale forholde* to a glimpse, at least, of more universal and searching principles for living: "the spirit of truth and freedom."

For the realism of the cycle, it still is necessary to insist, is permeated by universals taking on potent particular forms. Beneath the immediately realistic surface we discover archetypal repetition and quotation (visual, verbal, and gestural), archetypal actions and characters, grave universal arguments opened up by the realistic fictions, where historical and spiritual forces deriving from the total past evolve into the life of the present and begin to shape the future. With the ending of *Pillars of Society* and its release of the dangerously dynamic spirit of truth and freedom, *de lokale forholde* are made to collide and dialectically engage with the forces of *det tredje rike.*

In *The League of Youth* the conditions of omnipresent and insurmountable pettiness create only a ludicrous parody of the universal and archetypal action that we detect in the play. It opens on the seventeenth of May, Norway's constitution day, on which the nation celebrates its independence (thus proclaiming the factional separatism Ibsen complained of), and then proceeds to enact the story of an aborted revolution which is a hilariously bathetic and miniscule parody of the satanic revolt in heaven. The play was at first subtitled "The Almighty and Co." Although this might be the dig at Bjørnson, who was in the habit of enlisting the Almighty to his cause, that interpreters have seen (and Bjørnson's association with God is a delicious example of the parochial concept of the cosmos held by his society) and although Ibsen deleted the subtitle just before the book was printed, we should be alerted to the playful parody the drama performs on its Christian archetype. Brattsberg is the obtuse God of his world, defended by his mediocre angels, whereas Stensgaard leads the younger rebel angels in revolt (in the name of the Lord), invading Brattsberg's realm until his ultimate disgrace and expulsion. Ibsen's satanic metaphors are frequent and playful in this fashion. We already have encountered them in *Kongs-emnerne* (The Pretenders) and in *Peer Gynt,* and they are going to resurface in the realistic cycle, but in *The League of Youth* the deeper levels of this archetypal rebellion are not explored. The potential of such metaphors, one might say, are aborted in the repressively narrow space of the play's limited sphere of action.

Stensgaard's idea of revolution, which does not get far beyond the idea that those in power should be out and those out of power should be in is, as Rolf Fjelde argues in another connection, "The traditional or conventional conception" of revolution:

Traditional revolution has been the prevailing form on countless occasions throughout the past, from the insurrections of 1848 back to earliest classic antiquity. The scenario for this conception pits a champion of the oppressed masses, or a party of the people, against the repressive forces of irrational authority vested in an individual tyrant or a small, self-perpetuating power elite. The traditional conception, holding the deprived majority to be right and the ruling minority to be wrong, adopts for its remedy the drastic expedient whereby Fortune's wheel, given a half turn, yields a full revolution: the outs are swept in, the ups are brought down—but beyond a redistribution of material goods, nothing further is won. The new establishment, in fact, immediately generates a new underground, plotting *its* program for the next half turn of the wheel.[8]

Ibsen's earliest depiction of such a conventional revolution, Fjelde notes, was his first play, *Catiline.* Its hero's dark and Byronic rebellion, with its satanic overtones, has its parodic resurrection in Stensgaard. The difference between this old form of revolution and the new (represented by Stockmann of *An Enemy of the People*) lies in *ideas:* in the generation of new *conceptions* of truth and freedom (as Ibsen insisted to Georg Brandes) rather than in particular freedoms.

Stensgaard's idea of revolution only too obviously is animated by no philosophic principle nor by any historical vision—as Lundestad, the sly conventional politician, quickly sees, realizing he can enlist Stensgaard in his ranks. But though Stensgaard is a consummate hypocrite and opportunist, he hardly is much worse than the society he so deviously works upon, for the pettiness of the local conditions that stifle and frustrate young energies also defend blatant injustices and false advantages. Instead of thoroughly knowing his petty society and thereby knowing his true strength and weakness within it, as does the doctor Fjeldbo—one of Ibsen's many sympathetic doctors—Stensgaard opposes to this society not the fundamental criticism and the indication of universal imperatives that might work to transform it but only a windy revolutionary rhetoric so unfocused that the arch-conservative Brattsberg is led to believe that Stensgaard's attack upon him is actually an attack upon one of his enemies.

Because Stensgaard never bothers to grasp his implication in the society he so rhetorically indicts, does not see that he "shares the guilt of the people to which he belongs," as Ibsen declared of himself, he is enmeshed quickly in contradictory actions in which he betrays allegiances, unscrupulously grasps at conflicting opportunities for self-advancement, and, finally, succeeds only in uniting all factions against him. This is a reductive travesty of Julian's nobly intentioned and profoundly searching actions. The comic desperation of Stensgaard's actions and the self-destructiveness of their results tell us that he is less an accomplished villain, for all his adroit hypocrisy, than he is a creature utterly bewildered and lost in the social confusion depicted by the play. In Halvdan Koht's illuminating phrase, he is a Peer Gynt of the political world. When he relates to Fjeldbo how, once, in a dream, he was visited by a vision of revolution, we believe he is telling the truth:

STENSGAARD: ...I once had a dream, or perhaps I saw it; but no, I dreamed it. But so vividly! I thought that the last judgment had come to the world. I could see the whole globe of the earth. There was no sun, only a stormy yellow light. Then came a gale, rising from the west and swept all things before it. First it swept the withered leaves and in the same way swept people...but they still kept on their feet. Their cloaks clung tightly to them so that they seemed to be sitting while in flight. At first they seemed to be like ordinary people that chased after their hats in the blast; but when they came nearer, they were emperors and kings and what they were chasing and which they always seemed on the point of reaching, but never did, were crowns and scepters. Oh, there were hundreds upon hundreds of all kinds and none knew what was happening. But many called out and asked, "Whence has it come, this terrible storm?" The answer came, "One Voice spoke, and the echo of that voice is the awakened storm."

FJELDBO: When did you dream this?

STENSGAARD: Oh, once—I don't remember. Many years ago.

FJELDBO: Probably there had been disturbances somewhere in Europe, and on top of that you had eaten heavily in the evening and read the newspapers afterward.

STENSGAARD: Exactly the same shiver, the same tremor down my spine, I felt this evening. Yes, I *will* achieve all that I desire. I will be the Voice...

FJELDBO: Now listen to me, my dear Stensgaard, you ought to stop and think about this. You will be "the Voice," you say? Good! But where will you be the Voice? Here, in the parish? Or, at best, in the country? And who will be the Echo that wakes the storm? People like merchant Monson or the local printer, Aslaksen, or that fat-assed genius, Bastian. Instead of the fleeing emperors and kings we'll see farmer Lundestad chasing after his parliamentary seat. What will come of all this? That which you saw at first in your dream, local parishioners in a gale.[9]

As in Ibsen's letter to Brandes, the great events in the world at large, in Europe, form a cruel contrast to the frantic little events in the parish, and even had Stensgaard been blessed with the integrity and imagination seriously to carry out a local "revolution," it could only have been another storm in a teacup. The little local agitation, in Stensgaard's dream, is blown up until it takes on the noble dimensions of world-historical events on the scale of *Emperor and Galilean:* kings, emperors, crowns, and scepters are whirled by the forces of historical change and of evolution impelled by superhuman forces represented by the Voice. The imagery recalls that of Shelley's *Ode to the West Wind* (the poem that Ibsen's friend, Brandes, hailed as the most revolutionary and prophetic of Romantic utterances)[10], and Stensgaard's account of his dream seems sincerely Romantic. But the rhetorical afflatus of this account, with its day of judgment, its storm gathering in the west and blotting out the sun, its multitudes of monarchs and emperors, its Voice in the whirlwind, already has lost sight of the local conditions and it is to the dispiriting pettiness of these conditions that Fjeldbo cynically returns him.

Stensgaard speaks as if he were caught in the drama of Julian, as if he were the possible vehicle of world-shaping forces, but meanwhile he has failed to understand either his own nature or that of the little society to which he is confined, so that, as Fjeldbo later will charge, he actually turns upon the representatives of what is best in that society. Brand and Falk similarly had been confined to crushingly restrictive little communities, but they had discovered in themselves the means toward authentic revolt which, though more modest in its imagery than Stensgaard's dream, was more courageous, and more consequential in its commitment. In the later realistic cycle the rebellious or awakening individuals will engage themselves with particular aims, particular aspects of reality, but through the depth of their engagement and its authenticity they will be participating in a universal spiritual emancipation. For beneath the modern surface lies layer after layer of the past with all its consequences upon the present; and within this vaster reality are more than the kings and emperors of Stensgaard's dream. All world history will be summoned to the agonizing séances in the drawing rooms of the later plays, so that to the awakened imagination, the present and its realities, far from being limited and restrictive and stifling the spirit, will reveal themselves to be the immensely vast arena for the spirit's self-fulfillment.

Although Fjeldbo pricks the balloon of Stensgaard's inflated dream imagery, this is done to call him back to a deeper awareness of social and political realities and not to an abandoning of radically critical activity. The call to Reason which Ibsen would seem to be making in *The League of Youth* is a call for a better knowledge of the realities with which the most ambitious criticism of life and the most ambitious poetry must learn to engage and, through engagement, transform.

Unsurprisingly, a revolutionary rhetoric as unreflective as Stensgaard's collapses at the first confrontation with reality. Content to be only the rhetorician of revolution, instead of its thinker or its committed activist, having no core of integrity, such as Thomas Stockmann possesses, from which to proceed to genuinely radical insight, and having no knowledge of the world that he professes to oppose, Stensgaard becomes hopelessly enmeshed in the complexities of this world as soon as it, in turn, engages with him. Fjeldbo's summary of Stensgaard's character describes the fundamental social and psychological confusions that account for his extraordinary actions:

Patchwork. I have known him since childhood. His father was a withered tramp, a lout, a—nothing; he ran a little huckster's shop and pawnbroker's business on the side—or, to be more accurate, his wife ran it. She was a sluttish, gross woman, the most unwomanly I ever knew. She had her husband declared incapable: she had absolutely no heart. And it was in this household that Stensgaard grew up. And then he went to grammar school. "He'll go to college," said the mother, "and there they'll make a good accountant of him." Squalor at home, high ideals at school, his mind, character, will and talents all going in different directions. What could it lead to but a completely split personality."[11]

Stensgaard's pitiably squalid origins were only too likely to create a character apt to confuse his "higher" ideals with baser self-interests. Ibsen's judgment on this type of unreflective ideological enthusiasm is very close to Hegel's notorious condemnation of J. F. Fries, the leader of a German league of youth, whose enthusiastic and rhetorical teutonism, which was to be combined with a rabid anti-Semitism, prefigured the ugliest development of German political life. Hegel's magisterial judgment on Fries is worth quoting at length because Stensgaard in many ways is a diminutive version of Fries:

A ringleader of these hosts of superficiality, of these self-styled 'philosophers', Herr Fries did not blush, on the occasion of a public festival which has become notorious, to express the following ideas in a speech on 'The state and the constitution': 'In the people ruled by a genuine communal spirit, life for the discharge of all public business would come from below, from the people itself; living associations, indissolubly united by the holy chain of friendship, would be dedicated to every single project of popular education and popular service', and so on. This is the quintessence of shallow thinking, to base philosophic science not on the development of thought and the concept but on immediate sense-perception and the play of fancy: to take the rich inward articulation of ethical life, i.e. the state, the architectonic of that life's circles of public life and their rights, uses the strict accuracy of measurement which holds together every pillar, arch and buttress and thereby produces the strength of the whole out of the harmony of the parts—to take this structure and confound the completed fabric in the broth of 'heart, friendship and inspiration'. According to a view of this kind, the world of ethics (Epicurus, holding a similar view, would have said the 'world in general') should be given over, as in fact it is not, to the subjective accident of opinion and caprice.[12]

A mentality like Stensgaard's, enthusiastic for high ideals—at least as invigorating catchwords that could lift his whole spirit out of the parental squalor—yet desperately craving self-advancement, is only too likely to devise a strategy, mostly unconscious because unpondered, in which the lofty idealism remains ineffectual rhetoric and so does not interfere with the baser machinations of self-interest. The relevant contrast is with Brand, who is from a similarly squalid home but who, instead of escaping from his misery to rhetorical and histrionic revolutionary attitudinizing, undertakes a profound examination of himself and his society and, in order to work out a mutual salvation, takes upon himself the most agonizing fidelity to his vocation. Stensgaard is too full of contradictions to be able to work out a smooth, machiavellian path to power, but his hypocrisy is impressively adroit. Lundestad is moved to admiration by Stensgaard's frequent display of this essential political gift—as when, hearing that Monsen's daughter is bankrupt, Stensgaard denies his love for her with the reflection that it was most unwomanly of her to be responsive to his proposal when her father was in financial trouble; and the funnier instance when, believing that Brattsberg's daughter will come into only a small inheritance, he renounces her, too, with the lofty declaration, "I will renounce the happiness of working in quiet modesty for the woman I love: I shall say to my people, 'Here I am—take me!'" To which Lundestad is moved to reply, "You truly possess great gifts, Mr. Stensgaard!"[13]

The character of Stensgaard is more richly comic if we see this hypocrisy as mostly *unconscious*, as the deft and habitual maneuvering of his mind whenever his self-interest is threatened. In a world whose complacent social order is unfairly loaded against the aspirations of persons of Stensgaard's origins, such persons are all the more likely not to question the propriety of highly advantageous situations: in Stensgaard's case, the patronage of men such as Monsen, the flattering attention of a Brattsberg, or the happy prospective combination of marital and financial felicity. Such unconscious ethical agility is a gift of a kind, and the astute politician

Lundestad predicts that even after his disgrace and expulsion, Stensgaard will return to sit "in the people's or the king's council — perhaps in both at once."[14] This is a tribute to Stensgaard's adroit opportunism, which will find a means of reconciling the irreconcilable, rather than a tribute to any tenacious political dedication, but it does acknowledge that his is an uncommon talent at work in the world. The character should be played, at the least, as a remarkable scoundrel whose maneuverings under pressure call to mind those of a recently disgraced American president.

The intellectual and cultural confusion that Stensgaard, at the center of the action, best exemplifies results from the drastic disruption of the traditional social order under the pressure of new economic, political, and ideological realities of which the too pragmatic characters are but dimly — if at all — aware. Even Fjeldbo, spiritually the most secure and certainly the most sympathetic character (as *raisonneur* he is a sort of sunny Dr. Rank), has no awareness of the wider dimensions of the social situation where, at the top, the son of the aristocratic Brattsberg has become ensnared in the capitalist schemes of Monsen and has been driven to the dishonor of forgery; where Aslaksen, in the past, was ruined along with Daniel Hejre; and where, at the bottom of society, emerging from the squalor, a Stensgaard is confusedly climbing to power. In an exchange between Aslaksen and Fjeldbo we see that social change no longer can be seen in the old (e.g., Shakespearean) way as divinely sanctioned justice or satanically inspired rebellion. Aslaksen's ruin has been attendant upon that of Daniel Hejre (who himself once rescued the now dominant Brattsberg from his financial troubles), and Aslaksen cannot see in the changes in the wheel of fortune any evidence of design in the affairs of men. He concludes the exchange with the reflection, "... it is strangely confusing! Daniel Hejre and Providence and Fate and Circumstances — and myself, also! I've often thought of sorting it all out and writing a book about it. But it is so damned complicated that..."[15]

It is not that Ibsen believes providence and fate are absent from the world; on the contrary, it is the attempt to identify these which so strenuously engages him in *Emperor and Galilean*. But the characters caught in the world of *The League of Youth* cannot *perceive* of Providence and fate as operating rationally and thereby giving meaning and dignity even to catastophe, for in the world of the play no convincing scheme of absolutes, no valid universal forces behind the mask of petty particulars, can be discerned. Whereas in the old order one could see providence in the fall of a sparrow, *now*, the crash of an entire family makes no sense. The contrast between this play and, say, *Rosmersholm* — which presents somewhat similar social conflicts but which, through the psychological and ideological commitment of the main characters, raises a far greater catastrophe to the spiritually sustaining level of universal significance — will allow us to see the drastic separation of particular from universal in *The League of Youth* which, for all its comic energy, depicts a spiritual hell.

The lack of *reflection,* of self-knowledge, is not confined to Stensgaard but is endemic to the whole society. The old order is represented by the obtuse Brattsberg and is wholly discredited intellectually although, as Fjeldbo observes, it is still the best that this mediocre society has got. The general disarray of values exemplified can be seen as a miniature and comedic version of the breakdown of postrevolutionary European society. The European social structure, now an anachronism, once had stretched back to the huge medieval synthesis (which succeeded the critical period dramatized in *Emperor and Galilean*) in which every aspect of human experience had its place in a God-given hierarchy of values. Losing this synthesis and unable to detect, or struggle toward, a new one, the society of *The League of Youth* lives in a world of meaningless ephemeral agitations, and thus the political confusion that the play depicts remains unremittingly petty, with no lesson learned in the end.

In *Brand* and *Peer Gynt* the *social* realm of the plays' actions (the realm to which the action of *The League of Youth* is confined) was curiously alien and negligible so that the only spheres in which the heroic spirit could expand were those of nature and of the spirit's long history; thus the heroes of both plays were singularly lonely. To be able to inhabit society in spiritual fullness one would have to, in Falk's phrase, "uplift the age of which one would be citizen." To do this, it would be necessary to infiltrate the repressive social patterns of the community with the universal imperatives on which it had turned its back, so that all human relations, of individual egos, of the sexes, of classes, and of conscious and unconscious forces within each individual and within the culture as a whole would be "awakened" by contact with the ever-present universal Spirit. This is the task I believe Ibsen set himself in the realistic cycle where, play by play, he opened up the contemporary life of his people to the spiritual forces that should be (and secretly *were*) operating upon them. Brandes records that at their meeting in Rome in 1872 when Ibsen was working on his world-historical drama *Emperor and Galilean*, he declared to Brandes:

Scandinavia lies outside the cultural mainstream. The unhappy consequence is that we never get anywhere until the rest of Europe has moved on.... It is as though one were to introduce astronomy into Madagascar and begin with the Ptolemaic system.[16]

In *Emperor and Galilean* Ibsen clarified for himself the nature of the spiritual crisis, as he saw it, in the life of Europe. He located the crisis to a period long before the medieval social-metaphysical synthesis, implying that humankind has been stumbling on the wrong path ever since, as he observed in a note to *Ghosts*. It is not important whether Ibsen is historically or philosophically "right" or "wrong" in his analysis (although a whole tradition of European letters from Chaucer to Nietzsche and beyond suggests that he has located a critical division in the life of Europe) nor whether his analysis is conducted with historical accuracy or philosophical rigor (in both cases it is not.) For a poet requires not so much a factually unimpugnable ideology as an imaginatively extensive ideology, one whereby his or her creativity can be led beyond the poet's most immediate preoccupations to the most profound, sublime, and universal, as well as to the most poignant and particular, vision of life.

The personal philosophy or world view that Ibsen claimed to have worked out in *Emperor and Galilean* seems to be, as Halvdan Koht suggests,[17] Hegel reconstituted through Kierkegaardian subjectivity. The huge Hegelian account of reality is now explored in terms of poignantly (existentially) personal human drama: the Hegelian "system," in Keats' phrase, "proved upon the pulses."

The League of Youth is the comedic account of a social order that refuses to undertake anything like a profound analysis of the forces that have gone into the shaping of its internal and external realities. The play is thereby doomed to mediocrity as Peer Gynt had been doomed to repetition. *Emperor and Galilean,* on the contrary, depicts a world in which such analysis was the obsessive preoccupation of every member of society, from the artisans whose theological disputes open the play, to the factions within the imperial court, and, finally, to the philosophers and mystics searching for some foundation of knowledge and some new direction of the spirit. The world of *Emperor and Galilean,* for all its tragic contradictions, *was* one in which the spirit was led outward and upward, through direct and agitated personal experience, to the highest and profoundest investigations into the mystery of existence.

THE THIRD EMPIRE
Emperor and Galilean

The most exalted action of Spirit would be the history of the world itself. We can conceive it possible that our poet might in this sense undertake to elaborate in what we might call the absolute Epos this universal achievement on the battlefield of the universal spirit whose hero would be the spirit of man, the humanus, who is drawn and exalted out of the confusions of consciousness into the clearer region of universal history. But in virtue of the very fact of its universality a subject matter of this kind would be unfitted for artistic treatment.

Hegel
Philosophy of Fine Art

In this passage Hegel had in mind a possible epic poem of vaster dimensions than Milton's *Paradise Lost,* for the entirety of Christian history would be only one of its "moments." This poetic enterprise, which Hegel sees both as the only adequate modern poem and as an impossible project, was bound to be a challenge and a lure to later ambitious poets. Imre Madách undertakes just such a universal poem in his drama *The Tragedy of Man,* and, unknown to Hegel, Goethe's own *Faust,* part 2, was to fulfill much of this requirement. In *Emperor and Galilean* and the realistic cycle that succeeds it, Ibsen undertakes a similar enterprise. Together the dramas enact universal history as the memory of the human race is recalled for a judgment day.

The tragic subject of *Emperor and Galilean* is not that of the fate of its hero, Julian, but that of the world-spirit itself. We watch the process of one world dying and the other struggling to be born. The universal tragedy, which gives to the whole work an elegiac quality, is the necessary death of a beautiful world order, the Hellenic, and the necessary triumph of a world order in many respects far less attractive, the Christian. The historical preoccupations that made up the arguments of *The Burial Mound* and *The Vikings at Helgeland* now are expanded to universal dimensions, and the early

224

portrait of Earl Skule in *The Pretenders* now is developed into the richly complex and articulate Julian.

To Edmund Gosse, Ibsen wrote his famous defense of the use of realistic prose as the appropriate medium for *Emperor and Galilean.*

The play is conceived in the most realistic style. The illusion I wished to produce was that of reality. I wished to produce the impression on the reader that what he was reading was something that actually had happened. If I had employed verse I would have counteracted my own intention and defeated my purpose ... We are no longer living in the days of Shakespeare ... Speaking generally the dialogue must conform to the degree of idealization [*den grad af idealitet*] which pervades the work as a whole. My new drama is no tragedy in the ancient sense. What I sought to depict were human beings, and therefore I would not let them talk "the language of the gods."[1]

These seemingly straightforward sentences are full of traps for the unwary interpreter. First, we note that the audience of the play is a *reader*, so that we are in a "mental theater," as in *Love's Comedy, Brand,* and *Peer Gynt,* where we translate the scenic notations on the page into the terms of an imagined real world, not a stage world. *Emperor and Galilean,* therefore, is attempting the same illusion of reality that the novel achieves, and Ibsen would seem to be requiring an authenticity of expression from the author and a sensitivity and vigilance from the reader which Flaubert and Henry James were to demand for the novel. (In the *theater,* in fact, the difference between verse and prose would be less evident than on the printed page, for the plausibility and dramatic urgency of the actor's speaking of his or her lines would take the audience's attention from the medium. As readers, however, we give a different order of attention to the verse of *Brand* and *Peer Gynt* than we do to the prose of *Emperor and Galilean.*)

More difficult to grasp is the stipulation that "the dialogue must conform to the degree of idealization [or ideality] which pervades the work as a whole." Ideality, in this connection, must mean aesthetic and poetic remoteness from everyday reality, the seeing of things in their most ideal and poetic terms. In *Emperor and Galilean* ideologies, beliefs, and ideals are championed and brought into conflict in the realm of every day experience. We are not presented with poetic symbols or abstractions of paganism and

Christianity, philosophy and faith, and so on, but with realistic situations in which ordinary human beings (living, it is true, in an extraordinary age) are agitated by ideas. Tragedy "in the ancient sense" was poetic and rhetorical; values and ideas were *affirmed* rather than rendered plausibly as actual experience. This left the values and ideas untested in terms of experience. The increasing tendency in nineteenth-century fictive writing (we can think of Flaubert, Tolstoy, Zola, James) was to establish its ideas and values only on the ground of a plausible facsimile of our actual experience and to distrust the affirmation of ideas and values that could not be thus rendered. Ibsen himself had begun with idealistic drama (inherited from Schiller), of which *Olaf Liliekrans* was the most extravagant example, but beginning with *Love's Comedy,* he insisted that the idealism he still retained be authenticated as livable experience. Not only does this bring the ideal realm "down" to the level of everyday life; it also lifts everyday life to the level of that ideality which can be so authenticated.

For the *reader,* verse would be an obstacle to the author's intention of attaining fidelity to the rhythms of everyday speech. This intention at first seems modest—a reduction of poetry's capacity to present images, metaphors, and symbols of universal realities such as Ibsen achieved so brilliantly in *Peer Gynt;* and we can understand the new method only if we see that, for Ibsen, the only valid universal values and ideas are those capable of being authentically enacted by recognizable humans in plausible modern situations. Everyday reality must be brought to engage with the ideal realm that it affirms "poetically" but actually evades, and the ideal realm must be tested to see if it is capable of human embodiment. But more than this is involved. Not only "values" but positive and negative spiritual and universal forces work upon life and must be engaged with if we are to function authentically, fully, and freely in life. These spiritual forces have their sources far back in time, before recorded history, and need to be acknowledged by us. Realism, far from turning its back on these forces, actually is resurrecting them, redeeming everyday life through them, by suffusing life in the numinous medium of universals and archetypes. This new, realistic aesthetic of authenticity is a more difficult artistic discipline than the discipline of the older rhetorical verse-drama.

The concern with authenticity, with fidelity to our actual experience of reality, is, in the best realists, not an unimaginative pragmatism but the manifestation of an integrity that was uneasy about the idealized "poetic" expression of a value that kept itself out of danger and unharmed by contact with actuality. The immense rigors the best realists set themselves testify to this aesthetic conscientiousness. Henry James noted Ibsen's beautiful obsession with unity of time, and we can discover an equal obsession with unity of place; both concerns posed tremendous difficulties. We, the audience, would gladly excuse the author from the rigors he sets himself, not objecting to changes of scene (especially if they took us to interesting *locales*) or to an easygoing deployment of time. Obviously, therefore, it is not from a desire to "fool" us with an illusory art that Ibsen sets himself such difficulties (for audiences are willing to be fooled by far less art); rather it is from a desire to establish his ideas authentically, to bring the ideas uncomfortably close so that the heightened dialectical action begins to reshape alarmingly yet significantly the image of reality to which we have assented. None of Ibsen's followers, not Strindberg, Chekov, Shaw, maintained this difficult discipline of a plausibly rendered image of reality that was urgently shaped into a dialectical, yet at the same time aesthetically perfect, structure. The tragic feeling of terror that we can experience from a performance of *Ghosts, Rosmersholm,* or *The Master Builder* derives from our perhaps unconscious sense that our reality is being disturbingly reshaped by the requirements of the play's argument.

Emperor and Galilean is the necessary completion of Ibsen's long preoccupation with the past before he integrates it into his image of the modern world, and it brings to its ultimate development the form of historical tragedy itself. The following conditions are necessary for an adequate historical tragedy:

(a) The hero must fail—in order to be tragic.

(b) His failure must establish an order—so that the action must be dialectical and rational.

(c) His opposition to the order esablished must itself have substantive, rational value.

(d) The drama, to be modern, must be both subjective and objective, that is, the larger ideological conflict must also be mirrored in the hero's personal and subjective reality.

It has been common in Ibsen studies to refer to *Emperor and Galilean* distantly and respectfully and then to hurry on to more congenial ground, in the apparent belief that its unarguably ideological subject matter, if taken too seriously, would interfere with the established idea of Ibsen as the pragmatist whose major concern is to depict real people in real trouble. Theodore Jorgenson, Paulus Svendsen, G. Wilson Knight, and Rolf Fjelde are among the relatively few who have shown how rewarding it is to take the play seriously and even to accept Ibsen's claim for it as his major single work. The first half of the play, *Julian's Apostasy*, strikes the present reader as the best thing that Ibsen has yet written once one is reconciled to its very special genre for its subject is not just a particular historical situation but is History itself. In fact, one of the best guides to the play would be Hegel's *The Philosophy of History*, particularly the Introduction, not because the play is a paraphrase of Hegel but because it obviously shares with the philosopher certain basic assumptions about the nature of history.

At an earlier stage in its genesis the entire drama was intended as a trilogy with three distinct phases: *Julian among the Philosophers*, *Caesar's Apostasy*, and *The Emperor Julian*—a movement from (a) inquiry to (b) apostasy to (c) power. Much of this triadic structure remains in the final version and I think would better have expressed its argument. In *Julian among the Philosophers* Ibsen creates a dramatic hero who ponders philosophic issues not in the conventional manner of Marlowe's Faust or Shakespeare's Hamlet, nor in the more original but less dramatic manner of Goethe's Faust, but in terms of a serious philosophical as well as personal quest, in the actual world, upon which he is willing to stake his life. Julian is a philosophic hero in a way unique to dramatic literature. The crises of the first three acts of the drama are crises of *thought*, an agon of the intellect in which the author and the audience are as implicated as the hero.

Julian does not just *exemplify* a historical condition analyzed from the advantage of hindsight by the playwright as in Schiller's *Wallenstein*—in other words, the hero is not smaller than the total condition of which he is the central consciousness. Nor is he the single mouthpiece of the author, delivering a wisdom beyond the comprehension of his fellow actors, as in Shaw's *Caesar and Cleopatra* — that is, he is not larger than the play's total action. The climax of Julian's intellectual and spiritual quest is the séance scene of act 3 in which the hero, as much as the reader, is confronted with the insoluble mysteries of free will and necessity and of choosing an individual vocation that would represent a significant spiritual contribution to the purposes of the world-will. Julian's failure to solve the problem, consciously, is as likely to be our failure, too, so that we share his predicament. We cannot see, as we can with Macbeth, where he obviously is making a "wrong" choice. When we later realize that Julian has taken a wrong path, we cannot see how he obviously should have discovered the right path. *Emperor and Galilean* ends on a note of bafflement as the Christian Macrina "corrects" her brother's confident account of Julian as the necessary rod of correction for the Christians:

Oh, brother, let us not seek to the bottom of this abyss... Erring human souls... if you were *forced* to err, allowance will be made on that great day when the mighty one shall come in a cloud to judge the living dead and the dead who live.[2]

If, in Rolf Fjelde's very suggestive phrase, Ibsen discovered "tragedy reborn from the spirit of history,"[3] *Emperor and Galilean* can be seen as most exhaustively developing that idea of tragedy. Hegel described history as the gradual development and embodiment of the concept or Idea, the completed realm of rationally apprehended reality, for which both "positive" and "negative" people and actions were necessary. He distinguished between individuals who, from the highest motives, "have resisted that which the advance of the spiritual idea makes necessary"[4] and those "whose crimes have been turned into the means—under the direction of a superior principle—of realising the purpose of that principle."[5] The former, though nobler as persons, possess only "a formal rectitude—deserted by the living spirit and by God."[6] Before Hegel, Andrew Marvell depicted such a contrast with the characters of Charles I and Cromwell in his *Horatian Ode* where the noble, fixed, and legitimate Charles must go down before the man of destiny, Cromwell. Earl Skule, of *The Pretenders*, stands in similarly poignant contrast to Haakon.

There is no complacent judgment upon Julian from historical hindsight, however, for Ibsen emphasizes, rather, the more disturbing theme of the inscrutability of the historical process by selecting a moment that invited the clear judgment of historical hindsight but creating, instead, the impression of overwhelming confusion and perplexity, a condition we share with the hero. Julian's degeneration and defeat is the consequence of his fine responsiveness to the subjective and objective aspects of this confusion, so that we experience the entire play from within the perplexities of its situation. True, by stubbornly insisting on imposing his own interpretations of events against all the "signs" Julian involves himself in disaster, but in this drama there is no Haakon, with an obviously superior principle to counterbalance the errant hero. We see no clearly preferable ideology before us which Julian should have embraced. Hellenism might have been a wrong choice for Julian, but it was not a wrong *cause,* and its values are envisaged as being retained in the future. The right choice would have entailed the timely recognition of the superior positive values of Christianity, and nowhere were these evident in Julian's empire until he had made his choice.

As Theodore Jorgenson noted, the two parts of *Emperor and Galilean* comprise dialectical antitheses.[7] In part 1 we watch the virtuous ascendant hero against the background of a Christianity in decadence and disarray; and in part 2 we see the hero in decline against a resurgent Christianity—a dialectical intention behind the play that makes Ibsen, in the second part, polemically unfair to his actually enlightened hero. This scheme also hurts the structure of the play for, in part 2, with the psychological center falling below our sympathy and frequently below our interest, we have nothing to focus upon. There is something of the same structural awkwardness in *Macbeth.* The demoniacally possessed Macbeth, struggling with this possession, fearfully giving way to it and driven to the heart of darkness, opposing an entire kingdom, is an enthralling center of our attention. But this attention is dissipated in the second part of the play when we move to the resurgent victims, Malcolm and Macduff, then back to Macbeth foiled by the equivocal powers of darkness and harried by his opponents, then back again to the victims and their gathering strength, then back to

Macbeth, and so on. One sees why this structure is necessary for the argument of the play, but it is unsatisfactory. The second part of Ibsen's play is even more hamstrung, for Macbeth's decline into despairing evil is histrionically less unfortunate than Julian's decline into pettiness and pedantry.

In the first part of *Emperor and Galilean* Julian is brought into conflict with both worldly and spiritual power, with emperor and galilean. Emperor Constantius personfies the tyrannously worldly power under which his subjects live and which can intimidate and direct to false ends the life of action. Constantius has reached into every aspect of Julian's worldly and spiritual existence; his family, his teachers, his vocation, the choice of his wife and even of his food—all are under the emperor's control But for all his totalitarian power Constantius is self-divided, fearful, and confused—almost the example of the tyrant as the most miserable of men in Plato's *The Republic.* Constantius therefore can stand for the objective world and its power over us, riddled with its own confusions.

To oppose the tyranny of worldly power—whether that of totalitarian Byzantium or the more hidden power of social tradition, culture, laws, mores, and public opinion (a theme of the modern realistic cycle)—the individual needs spiritual certainty and direction. Yet the spiritual world we inherit, of tradition, faith, and learning, is itself both bewildering and limiting, shutting us off from alternative spiritual possibilities. Searching his or her culture for a more adequate spiritual reality, the individual finds a culture divided by unresolved religious and ideological conflicts deriving from the life of the race; and to become liberated from confinement to a merely partial world view and even from the belief that the present cultural conflict is genuine and essential, the individual is forced to go behind historical causes and attempt to reach a more fundamental, primary source of the spirit's life. The wider and freer investigation of the total expression of our humanity has been the endeavor of artists and thinkers in Europe at least since the time of Blake.

The accidents of history, created by humanity's alienated and constrained consciousness, cannot claim to be the absolute values by which we should shape our lives. Constantine's possibly cynical decision to adopt Christianity as the totalitarian monotheism that could best prop up his imperial power (a monotheism which then set about excluding and exterminating all other persuasions of thought and faith) cannot be binding upon the modern mind that values truth and freedom, any more than can the edicts of the corrupt and politically motivated early church councils that formulated the creeds of the church according to political expediency.

The study of history, indispensable for an understanding of the present, is certain to call into doubt the absolute claims of present-day institutions and ideologies. Romantic thinkers who inherited the Enlightenment's indignation against these institutions and their histories searched for deeper spiritual processes, "behind" history, for the foundation of a new faith, looking to folk-legend, myth, primitive cults and rituals, as well as to the expressions of individual poets and thinkers.[8]

Superbly realized in *Emperor and Galilean* are the confusions of worldly life that infect the spirit and the spiritual confusions that infect the world. Ibsen brilliantly introduces the theme of his play through the character of Emperor Constantius, the Christian emperor whose conscience is tormented by the hideous crimes that maintenance of his worldly power requires, so that he constantly oscillates between cruel and murderous policy and galilean self-abasement. The figure of Constantius presents to Julian a spectacle of the human problem he attempts to overcome. His reaction against Christianity for infecting the will and inhibiting and distorting worldly heroism and beauty is justified by the spectacle of Constantius.

The historical moment the play explores is complex and subtle. It is the point in history where Christianity has achieved only uncertain political victory in the world and where the persecuted pagans are not decisively defeated. Within Christianity itself is an as yet unsublimated and powerful residue of paganism, so that the Christians of the play, for the most part, are infected by passions they deny but cannot control, giving way to ugly crimes. Julian, who *consciously* attempts to return to paganism, actually is infected with Christian conscientiousness, so that the revulsion with which he turns from the worldly corruption and spiritual dishonesty of Christianity is a response that not only a pagan but also a true Christian might share—and Julian's whole nature is predominantly Christian in its subjective, self-divided, and unhappy consciousness. He is Schiller's "sentimental" consciousness attempting a return to "naiveté." The marriage of Julian, the self-divided and other-worldly pagan, to Helena, the passionately sensuous and single-minded Christian, catches up the ironies inhering in the situation depicted by the play.

The ideological psychology of the characters is here subtler than anything Ibsen hitherto has created, and it will alert us, also, to the very same ideological dimensions in the portraiture of the later realistic cycle. Everywhere in *Emperor and Galilean,* with the exception of such simple characters as the Horatio-like pagan Sallust and the somewhat emasculated Christians Basil and Gregory, we find this theme of ideological division within individuals, reflecting the division within the empire itself. In these divisions, alternate aspects of human nature are not simply placed in opposition, with pagans on one side and Christians on the other, but are confusedly intertwined and mutually destructive within single individuals. Obviously Ibsen saw an affinity between the age of Julian and his own times and, in the character of his hero, was able to find an objective correlative to his own predicament as an artist. Much of the harshness, even unfairness, with which Ibsen judges his hero in part 2 probably derives from his determination to exorcise flaws from his own nature. The Hellenism that Julian futilely attempted to revive had a strong appeal for Ibsen, also, and in order to "burn this bridge" behind him, so that he could go forward with the *Zeitgeist,* Ibsen made Julian's revival of paganism more ridiculous and certainly more intolerant than history shows. Nevertheless, the main method of the play is analytic: the analysis of a certain condition of the world and of the human spirit within it, in which we are meant to observe the total condition rather than take sides with any of the contending forces.

The career of Julian parallels that of Macbeth, for the hero-villain seeks out and acts upon metaphysical counsel, seizes power, fails to establish it, falters in his reason, and, finally, dies in battle. But we cannot pronounce judgment upon Julian as we can upon Macbeth. Macbeth destroyed a positive "good"—Duncan's Scotland, with its divinely sanctioned social and spiritual order. Having destroyed ceremony, order, social distinction, and custom by an action, killing the king, that violates all these, Macbeth is confronted with a chaos of appearances that keep him in doomed and damned untruth. Julian, on the other hand, begins in a world of division and false appearances and attempts to transcend these by a strenuous and honorable quest for spiritual truth. His opponent and victim, Constantius, may claim divine sanction for his authority and Julian's rebellion against him does carry overtones of the satanic revolt that runs through so many of his plays (including the immediately preceding *The League of Youth*), but the victory of the Christian cause at the end of the play is not a victory for clarity, justice, and truth. In the long spiritual night that followed, Christianity was to "petrify" into a spiritual totalitarianism in which the vitality of paganism was to be stifled and subterranean until the Renaissance.

Like Skule before him, Julian exemplifies one of the tragic paradoxes of history described by Hegel, who noted:

Those who through moral steadfastness and noble sentiment have resisted the necessary progress of the spirit stand higher in moral value than those whose crimes have been turned by a higher purpose into means of carrying on the will behind this purpose. But in revolutions of this kind both parties stand within the same circle of disaster. It is therefore only a formal right, forsaken both by the living spirit and by God, which the defenders of ancient right and order (no matter how moral) maintain. The deeds of the great men who are the individuals of world history thus appear justified not only in their intrinsic, unconscious significance but also from the point of view of world history.[9]

The new philosophical ruler who, as Ibsen conceives Julian, wishes not only to represent but also to *further* the purposes of the world spirit no longer can rely on traditional sanctions of kingship. In the Hegelian, evolutionary scheme of historical reality, tradition—as Skule discovered—no longer is an adequate sanction; for tradition, however sacrosanct, can only give way before a new and higher spiritual principle to which the world is evolving by means of its world-historical individuals.

It is at this point that appear those momentous collisions between existing acknowledged duties, laws, and rights and those possibilities which are adverse to this system, violate it, and even destroy its foundation and existence.

Their tenor may nevertheless seem good, on the whole advantageous—yes even indispensable and necessary. These possibilities now become historical fact; they involve a universal of an order different from that upon which depends the permanence of a people or a state. This universal is an essential phase in the development of the creating Idea, of truth striving and urging toward itself. The historical men, world-historical individuals, are those who grasp just such a higher universal, make it their own purpose, and realize this purpose in accordance with the higher law of the spirit.[10]

In the contest between Haakon and Skule this Hegelian pattern was more clearly evident. In *Emperor and Galilean* it is more subtly and complexly presented because Julian's opponent is no single individual, like Haakon, but the spirit of Christianity itself, manifesting its power in a multitude of ways.

In what was to become the scenario for innumerable historical dramas, and a number of actual, momentous, historical events, Hegel outlined the course of a typical world-historical individual's career, that of Julius Caesar, in which Caesar was driven both by circumstances and by his own uncanny understanding of what the times required to bring about ends greater than he at first intended:

In accomplishing his originally negative purpose—the autocracy over Rome—he at the same time fulfilled the necessary historical destiny of Rome and the world. Thus he was motivated not only by his private interest, but acted instinctively to bring to pass that which the times required. It is the same with all historical individuals: their own particular purposes contain the substantial will of the world spirit. They must be called "heroes" insofar as they have derived their purpose and vocation not from the calm, regular course of things, sanctioned by the existing order, but from a secret source whose content is still hidden and has not yet broken through into existence. The source of their actions is the inner spirit, still hidden beneath the surface but already knocking against the outer world as against a shell, in order, finally, to burst forth and break it to pieces; for it is a kernal different from that which belongs to the shell.[11]

Haakon was one such hero, and, in his larger empire, Julian seeks to be just such a world-historical individual who, as in the example of a Moses, Alexander, or Jesus or, in modern times, a Napolean, Lenin, or Mao, can make his life's odyssey in thought and action a vital element of the growth of the world spirit. Julian desperately searches for direction from the inner spirit both of the world's process and of his own complex personality. But the paradoxical injustice of the world's process will deem that his deeper and more wide-ranging quest will be frustrated, though other individuals, of lesser stature morally and intellectually, will yet be in harmony with the world-will. Julian's recoil from the "lie" of the degenerate Christianity of his times, his search for deeper spiritual roots, and his fidelity to the ancient Hellenic order are noble and sympathetic errors deriving from far higher motives than, for example, Constantine's enforcement of Christian monotheism in his empire; but the world-will was on the side of Constantine and was against Julian.

The play is as much the tragedy and defeat of paganism as it is Julian's failure, defeat, and death. A once-great, moving, beautiful, variegated world order dies with Julian's death, and the confirmation of Christian totalitarianism is brought about. Ibsen does not use the death of paganism to indict Christianity, is not indignant on its behalf (as, for example, Gore Vidal seems to be in his *Julian*), for his fatalistic philosophy perceives the necessity of this death, a necessity which gives rise to that "tragedy reborn from the spirit of history" which Rolf Fjelde referred to. The elegiac quality of the play recalls Hölderlin's *Hyperion* or the vivid evocation of the spirit of Hellas in Hans Castorp's dream in Thomas Mann's *The Magic Mountain*, since the play derives from the same "area" of the European imagination. The sadness at the heart of *Emperor and Galilean* (which will be recollected in very different form in *Hedda Gabler*) is all the deeper for its unsentimental recognition that any attempt at a Hellenic revival can only turn into a ludicrous charade.

EMPEROR AND GALILEAN, PART 1

The play opens with emphatic contrasts of dark and light, symbolic details in Ibsen's art to which we should always pay attention. Behind the darkened gardens of the imperial palace, in the background, the court church is "blazing with light." In the imperial gardens are the "overturned statues" of the pagan gods and heroes, their beauty desecrated by the dirt, while in the blazing light, at the doors of the church, crowd "beggars, cripples and blind men." The images of strength and beauty have been overthrown and the central place now is taken over by weakness, debility, and misery to which the Church ministers. From the church comes the Easter anthem proclaiming the everlasting victory of Christianity unified in peace round the One Truth. The last word of the anthem is *helg*—holiness, sanctity—but even while the word is still sounding in our ears the stage quickly is given over to violent conflict and confusion, setting up another set of contraries to the darkness-light, beauty-ugliness, already presented: namely, the holiness and peaceful unity proclaimed by the Church as contrasted with the actual squalid conflicts within the Christian world.

The Easter hymn voices the Christian dream of the end of history and thus of significant life within the world. After the conquest of the earth by the Lamb, no further dialectical process is desired. But the scene presents us with so many unresolved conflicts that the Easter hymn takes on strongly ironic overtones; nor can we forget the appeal of the suppressed pagan world implied in the overturned statues.

The goldsmith, Potamon, enters, carrying a lantern and asking after the "emperor," and the word for "the emperor" (*keiseren*) is repeated four times in as many lines. In the dialogue and action that follow, in which the ascendant Christians first bully the pagans, then fall to squabbling among themselves, the terms "emperor" and "Christian" (or various sects of Christian) are juxtaposed, like contrasting motifs which later will be massively and symphonically developed.

The pagans are told to "wallow in the filth like your own gods." These words alert us to the fallen statues and perhaps also convey the Christian judgment on the myths and legends of paganism with their alien intimations of beauty, energy, and savagery. The ensuing scuffles among the alarmingly proliferating schismatic sects is broad ideological comedy, wittily, vividly, and dramatically driving home the spiritual confusions, both inner and outer, of this world, in obviously ironic contrast to the ecstatic theme of the Easter anthem.

The emphatically physical nature of this opening action, of scuffles, blows, and, later in the play, of spectacle and procession

culminating in full-scale battle and death would be difficult to enact plausibly in a theater but are indispensable to a reader's theater
where we need events vividly brought to our mind's eye and on a
suitably imposing scale. The realism of the later cycle will be of a
far more understated physical nature, which actors and actresses
could represent plausibly and which will draw our attention to the
inner, intellectual emphasis of the play underneath the physically
presented theatrical surface. In *Brand, Peer Gynt*, and *Emperor
and Galilean* Ibsen needs to supply strong visual details to make
the act of reading an imagined physical as well as mental event, for
there are neither actors nor a stage to supply this visual detail.
Ibsen understood that within the limits of modern realistic acting,
physical actions must be restricted to maintain credibility; nothing
is more dispiriting to the discriminating playgoer today than the
spectacle of actors attempting to approximate convincing sword
fights, savage blows, deaths by inches, and (a particular bane of
the present) convincing sexual activity. Only through highly sophisticated and nonrealistic theatrical conventions can violent
physical action be presented artistically and acceptably in the
theater. In the realistic cycle Ibsen never forgets that he is in stage-
space and that there is only so much that his realistic convention
permits him to present. But he compensates for this restriction of
the actor's gestures by displacing much of his poetry onto the
deeply and subtly rendered *scene* which often is given more violent
action than are the characters.

Such extreme subtlety of the actor's gestures would be out of
place in a mental theater like *Emperor and Galilean*, so that the
text concentrates instead on giving the greatest explicitness and
vividness to Ibsen's highly intellectual argument. This makes of
the play a curious literary phenomenon: a book to be read, where-
in the reader "sees" an action, without authorial commentary, as
in drama, and also meant to be experienced as actual life. It carries
to a further extreme the art of the realistic novel, for we have to
forget we are reading a book as we experience the rhythm of each
act to its climax and imaginary curtain, yet we also are meant to
forget this imaginary theater, also, and to imagine we are seeing
something that actually is happening. This represents the full
development of that "mental theater" sought by Byron, and the

reader's mind is called upon to perform complex acts of trans-position from printed page, through theatrical structure, to imag-ined reality. That it "works" I think any reader of Part 1 would agree; we experience the accelerated rhythm, urgency, and height-ened action of theater, yet we enjoy the reader's privilege of entering into a fuller and more convincing rendition of reality than theater could supply while having the opportunity to ponder the nature of our experience. If we compare Ibsen's play to Gore Vidal's *Julian*, an extremely accomplished novel and in many ways more easily enjoyable reading, we can see how the dramatic form of *Emperor and Galilean* gives its argument far more urgency and its reality far more immediacy. Whereas Vidal's novel is a relaxed, urbane reflection upon the historical events, Ibsen's play forces us to become urgently and inescapably implicated in these events—a far more unsettling experience and a far more difficult achieve-ment. For to bring off an *acted* scene (as against a narrated one), to enter into a part, making it sustain itself without any relaxation of attention, without the opportunity, as in the novel, to direct the reader's attention elsewhere and to supply commentary or indicate the unspoken—all of which let the novelist "off the hook"—demands from the writer the highest level of mimetic and imaginative activity, and requires a more strenuous act of atten-tion by the reader.

The physically violent opening of the play, with its intrinsic contradictions, its ideological conflicts agitating even the common-est ranks of society, alerts the vigilant reader to watch for the development and expansion of these conflicts in the later action. The satiric scene ends with the words, "the emperor!" and with the repetition of the Easter hymn, thus returning full circle to the opening juxtaposition of Christian and emperor. Therefore, we are not surprised, when this Christian emperor and his court come into view "in stately procession," to see the same symptoms of di-vision and unease that we have observed in society. The emperor, a physically distinguished young man, is spiritually tormented. His eyes are "gloomy and suspicious," and his whole deportment betrays weakness and unease. The "stately" procession contains, also, the pale and delicate empress and the prince Julian who is "awkward and impetuous in his manner."[12] Only Helena and Memnon, the slave, seem at all at ease. This imperial group, therefore, making its way to the church, visually establishes victory neither for emperor nor galilean, as the ensuing dialogue, on the steps of the church, indicates. The emperor is manipulated by his slave, and he betrays pathological symptoms of suspicion and fear, at one point scream-ing aloud in terror. Suspicious of everyone around him, he also is inwardly tormented by guilt: both the fear and the guilt deriving from his inability to reconcile the claims of being both a Christian and the emperor.

To gain power and to maintain it, Constantius has had to com-mit enormous crimes against others, including large-scale murder—Julian's family being one of the principal groups of victims— and these crimes torment his Christian conscience which, after bouts of self-abasement, is ready for even worse crimes. His Christianity making him a weak emperor, his imperial ambitions making him a guilty Christian, Constantius is the very symbol of the spiritual condition that Julian will have to overcome.

As Constantius moves toward the church, a cripple, hoping to be cured, touches the hem of his imperial garment and a blind man prays to the emperor to restore his sight—mordant travesties of the New Testament miracles. The confusion of emperor and galilean values and powers is total, and Julian recoils in disgust from the scene.

When his young friend Agathon unexpectedly appears, Julian's character emerges as one perplexed and struggling to free itself of the spiritual inauthenticities of the empire. Within Julian the confusions of the time are most acutely developed—as in all of Ibsen's dramatic writing from the beginning, the condition of the consciousness of the central character or characters is a microcosm of the confusion within a whole culture—and it is this fine respon-siveness to the spiritual condition of his age that will bring about his tragedy. His imagination is deeply divided between love of the heroic and classical world with its active and intellectual heroes, and his deep Christian yearning for an authentic faith that will give him clear spiritual direction.

He recalls his boyhood when he read Homer's account of "hero meeting hero in battle...and the gods above inciting them," and the time when he led Agathon from the "darkness of paganism into light everlasting."[13] This is an ironic image in a dialogue held at night, in the confused world of Byzantium, where Julian is standing in the darkness of the imperial garden with its overturned pagan gods while behind is the light of a church into which a visibly corrupt Christian community has just entered. His boyhood was a time, Julian recalls, when songs of praise were in the air like a ladder between heaven and earth; the images of both the song and the ladder are to be repeated later in the play. The boyhood encounter between Hellenic culture and Christian faith had an ideal character which has since become obscured, confused, and trivialized in the corrupt world of Byzantium. Julian now lives in an atmosphere of court intrigue, of enmity between Christians and pagans and between Christians and Christians. Philosophers, such as Libanius, now are feared and hated by the Christians, and the advance of new knowledge and the growth of the spirit are termed heresy and are abandoned for the crassest conflicting dogmas and superstitions.

The tormented and degraded world revealed in Julian's conversation with Agathon suddenly is contrasted with a totally different spiritual world, as the philosopher Libanius and his disciples cross the stage to leave the corrupt air of Constantinople. This procession, "with ivy leaves in their hair," led by the tall, handsome philosopher carrying papers and parchments and conversing with his laughing, noisily happy young followers, is a vision of a poignantly attractive, Western spiritual tradition that is an alternative to totalitarian dogmatism, but, in the course of the play, it will reveal itself to be spiritually bankrupt. At this stage of the drama, however, we are meant to respond to the attractive human possibility represented by the group: their laughter and easy friendship make the strongest possible contrast with the atmosphere of the Christian world of mutual suspicions, hostility, blows, heresy hunting, and dogmatic polemic, where laughter has not sounded except derisively.

This happy, noisy group awakens one memory from the western imagination—the Athens of Socrates—just as the Easter hymn at the opening of the play looks back to the Jerusalem of Christ. And just as we detected a contradiction within the Christian evocation of its highest vision—the peace that has come to the earth following the death and resurrection of the Lamb—so we detect a contradiction within this Athenian image of the free philosopher and his group of disinterested disciples who extend the life of the spirit in friendly and honest intellectual contest. Libanius at first seems a latter-day Socrates victimized by society while equably adjuring his "happy friend" Gregory to guard knowledge as a treasure more precious than gold. A scene direction tells us that Libanius recognizes Julian, but the philosopher proceeds, politically, as if he did not know him. This undercuts Libanius's Athenian identity since such duplicity, for practical and political ends, is alien to the Socratic tradition of open and honest discourse. Ibsen departs from the historical records to give this defect to Libanius, so that it is obvious he wishes to demonstrate how the once-vital spirit of Greek philosophy has passed away.

Libanius and Hellenic culture seem to offer Julian the possibility of freely creative intellectual combat where "the fight and fighters are bathed in light and joy . . . keen edged swords of wit clash in the combat; the serene gods sit smiling in the air"[14]—the image suggesting that these intellectual combats are the spiritual sublimation of the earlier Homeric battles that Julian recalled from his boyhood. Hellenic culture seemed to have been able to effect this sublimation, which would be necessary if Julian is to be the "Achilles of the spirit" prophesied by his mother's dream. Julian's formula is a further elaboration of Blanka's exhortation, in *The Burial Mound*: to sublimate Viking warriorship into a *spiritual* fight, "on silver seas of thought."

The night-world of Constantinople shrinks from such knowledge; its light is only the artificial light of the church, not the great free light of Helios, the sun, to whom Julian will dedicate himself. Before he exits, Libanius sums up the challenge of the Hellenic ideal in which happiness and spiritual progress go hand in hand. In the Hellenic world, Libanius claims, "life is an endless festival, among statues and temple songs, with foaming goblets full, and roses in the hair. Bridges span the dizzy void from spirit to spirit, away to the farthest stars in space."[15] In this "vast and sunny realm" eternal bliss is a pantheistic "reunion with the primal source,"[16] instead of the Christian longing for personal immortality. Libanius, of course, is giving a highly "edited" account of Hellenic culture, an account calculated to impress the learned young prince with whose circumstances the philosopher has taken pains to acquaint himself; but despite the duplicitous intention of the speech, the genuine appeal of Hellenism, with its celebration of physical and spiritual life, emerges.

Libanius and his group, going out into the darkness and across the sea "to Athens," leave the stage emptied of their ideal, rendering the scene perceptibly impoverished. The play now jarringly returns to the harsher themes of Christian intolerance and murderous hatred of the intellect. Agathon declares Julian's attraction to Libanius to be "the work of the devil," and he then gleefully recounts a particularly savage attack by Christians upon pagans, during which the Christians pillaged the pagan's possessions and "many houses were set on fire; many pagans perished in the flames; we killed still more as they fled. Oh, it was a great day for the glory of God!"[17] After this dubious exercise for the faith (a capsulated history of the Church in the world), Agathon, hysterical and exhausted, retired, and in a feverish sleep received a vision which he interprets as a call to Julian to "wrestle with the lions."

We now come upon one of the most "awkward" aspects of the play for the modern reader: Ibsen's serious use of visionary experience, dream, prophecy, and miracle. Many of these details could be accounted for as subjective delusion, as with Agathon's feverish dream, or as cleverly manipulated charlatanism, which is the way Gore Vidal views Maximus's séances, but it is obvious that Ibsen intends the important spiritual experiences in the play to be taken seriously. He too obviously does *not* view Maximus as a charlatan, in striking contrast to the commonly held modern view from Gibbon to the present day. We have to accept the even more awkward fact that we, as readers, are meant to take the spiritual experiences as true and serious. Ibsen's point may be that, at a time when the spiritual traditions of western culture still were vital, people did, as many accounts insist, see visions, hear voices, and make prophecies and that the extent to which this now is alien to us measures the extent of our spiritual loss.

The "mental stage" of *Emperor and Galilean* is inhabited by greater and more indiscreetly direct spiritual identities than we are used to encountering in the naked prose of realism, and it is probable that Ibsen chose the realistic method not so much to make his subject matter more *plausible* but to make it more alarming and unsettling. Edmund Gosse's regret that the play was not in verse may reflect his sense of Ibsen's tactlessness. For whereas in verse one literally can accept anything (from articulate dead stars, in *Manfred*, to the declarations of love between planets, in *Prometheus Unbound*), in prose the invasion of everyday reality by spiritual forces is alarmingly incongruous and to bring it off requires the utmost authenticity of expression and of commitment by the author.

For the remainder of act 1 we are treated to a searching analysis of the psychology of a degenerate Christianity. Agathon's fanaticism conceals from itself its own contradictions and self-interests (which include sanctified theft and murder); Hecebolius's more comic hypocrisy (anticipating Pastor Manders) is able, triumphantly, to prove virtuous intention through manifest double-dealing (by lying to Julian about the pagans he proves, by this sin, his selfless devotion to Julian's interests); and Constantius is able once again to act unjustly and cruelly in the world now that his soul has been purified in church. These are all shrewdly depicted traits of the compromised Christian spirit in its dealings with the world.

Julian's half-brother, Gallus, lacking Julian's fearful and distrustful alertness while possessing a physical beauty and headstrong courage that make him an Achilles of the flesh, is, for all his Christian orthodoxy and cruelty, an innocent pagan warrior (a Fortinbras to Julian's Hamlet) who can only be destroyed in the world of Byzantine intrigue and spiritual confusion; on the other hand, Julian's complex contradictions and doubts better equip him for survival. By the end of act 1 all the major themes of the play have been brilliantly stated. The Christian-Hellenic antinomies are complexly juxtaposed both in their ideas and their debased actual realities, and the implications for the human spirit of their mutual opposition and inner contradictions are clearly and vividly brought out. The philosophic and historical condition is forcefully rendered as a human predicament into which, if we are fully attuned to our cultural situation, we enter with concerned interest. G. Wilson Knight observes how, in this play, "rival sounds and groups clash to fine effect,"[18] and the series of images Ibsen gives us to reflect upon carry as much of the philosophical meaning of the play as do the speeches. It is a drama in which our intellect, and with it our historical and cultural consciousness, is keenly aroused and remade into poignant experience. The play creates a fine *conceptual* poetry, reminding us of Shaw's dictum that, after Wagner, drama's significant development could lie only in a theater of *ideas*, for Wagner had done all that could be done with the drama of expression, of feelings. Darkness and light, falling stars, the pagans crossing the stage momentarily to recollect, and to betray, our dream of Hellenism before disappearing into the night, the sharp discords of physical and mental conflict, the two imperial processions, the first, entering the church, divided, tortured and terrified, the second, exiting from the church, ruthless, dangerous, dispensing offices and destinies—all gradually build up a powerful conceptual design inviting us to meditate upon its shape and movement.

Act 2 presents the contrasts between a degenerate Hellenism and the living spirit, between "books" and "life." In act 1 we were presented with the flawed Christian world of Constantinople across which, momentarily, Libanius and his companions disdainfully moved as if descended from another and higher realm of spirit. Across the corrupt pagan world of act 2 the simplistic Christians Basil and Gregory move with equal disdain. Act 1 took place at night streaked by falling stars, animated by brilliant centers of artificial light, such as the church front and the imperial processions. Act 2 opens on a vivid memory of the classical world: an open square or agora surrounded by colonnades and statuary—the idealized "golden" Athens of innumerable European paintings. Ibsen wishes to present this poignant idealization, rather than a true picture of the classical world, so that the reality of actions and speeches played out against this setting will be all the more discomfiting, for we are to share Julian's deep disillusion with the dream of Hellenism. Against the colonnades are groups of students sitting or strolling about (as in Raphael's *School of Athens*), the whole scene bathed in the glow of a setting sun. Although the setting sun casts a warm glow over the scene, it also indicates the passing of a phase, adding an elegiac tone to this recollection of Athens, which is very different from the fierce antithesis of light and dark of act 1.

The square, the fountain, the colonnades, the statues, and the students all suggest the region of the intellect and of the arts—of Reason—where the spirit is refreshed and exercised. Ibsen wishes to awaken our nostalgia for this Athens and to remind us of the spiritual values it still possesses for us, so that the disillusioned judgment against it that we are induced to make will be all the more painful. Julian's journey from Constantinople to Athens to Ephesus is a spiritual quest in which we, as readers, are meant also to take part. In Constaninople we see a faith fiercely set against the world and therefore unable to deal with it; in Athens we see the finest expression of belief in this world and of human fulfillment within it, but spiritual direction is lacking; in Ephesus Julian and Maximus search for a new source of faith that will advance the spirit yet reconcile it with the world.

Athens is a way of life that could give beauty to Alcibiades and Socrates, to the poets and philosophers, to the *polis* as itself a supreme work of art, and if we are to go beyond Athens we cannot join in the priggish revulsion from this beauty in decline which Basil and Gregory express. Nor is Ibsen's celebration of Athenian freedom and joy-of-life academic and sterile. He explicitly honors instincts and actions that are still irrationally and fearfully tabooed by the modern world:

JULIAN (*after a short pause*): Tell me, Basilios, why was pagan sin so beautiful?

BASILIOS: You are wrong, friend; beautiful poems have been sung and tales told of this pagan sin. But it was not beautiful.

JULIAN: Oh, what are you saying. Wasn't Alcibiades beautiful when, burning with wine, like a young god, he burst through the streets of Athens at night? Wasn't he beautiful in his boldness when he made fun of Hermes and banged on people's doors, when he called to their wives and daughters while the women inside shuddered in breathless, gasping silence, longing for nothing more than to...

BASILIOS: Oh, I implore you, listen to me...

JULIAN: And wasn't Socrates beautiful in the symposium? And Plato and all the joyful, riotous companions. And yet they did those things that the swinish Christians out there would deny on oath were they accused of them. And then think of Oedipus, Medea, Leda.

BASILIOS: Fiction, fiction; you are confusing truth and fiction.

JULIAN: Are not the poetic imagination and the will subject to the same creative laws? And only look at *our* holy writings, both the old and the new. Was sin beautiful in Sodom and Gomorrah? Didn't Jehovah's fire punish what Socrates did not turn away from? Oh, as I live this life of riotous pleasure I wonder if truth *should* be the enemy of beauty.[19]

The nineteenth-century hesitations of this passage do not conceal the remarkable endorsement of all aspects of the Hellenic spirit. Not just the selected and emasculated "virtues" of classicism honored in the academic textbooks but the whole celebration of the instinctual as well as the spiritual life is embraced, including that homosexuality so embarrassing to the fainter-hearted Hellenists of the post-Christian world. The tone of this passage, which reflects the hindsight of Ibsen's nineteenth century that was emerging from the long Christian repression of the body and the mind, brings to mind Nietzsche's indignation against the Christian slander of the instincts, and we will encounter it again, in Ibsen's writing, when Osvald Alving angrily defends his Parisian friends against the slanders of the equally "swinish" respectable Norwegian tourists in Paris.

Christians, we notice do not refrain from pagan sins—they only deny they have committed them. Unable to banish the instincts from the world, they at least make them shameful and unmentionable. It was the Church's genius to condemn as sinful ineradicable instincts and then to offer its penitents conditional absolution; but it is a spiritual condition exemplifying what Ibsen was to call "the lie" and against which those who would be free (a not too numerous band, as Dostoievsky's Grand Inquisitor observed) must rebel.

Julian's entry upon this Athenian scene, with roses in his hair and surrounded by young disciples praising his wisdom, has all the elements of desperate make-believe and of wish-fulfillment. Like many an educated man, Julian has dreamed of returning to one of the more notable phases of cultural history and of playing a star role—here, that of Socrates in Athens. Futilely trying to bring this dream to palpable reality, Julian discloses its lifelessness to us. All such attempts to return to the past must fail, for history has tougher and more painful purposes than this. Athens may be an ever-living reality for the human spirit but only, in the Hegelian paradox, after it has first *died*, in all its inessential aspects, so that its essential aspects can be taken up and "sublimated" within succeeding spiritual forms. Part of the essential reality of Athens is its *death*; and truly to possess the Hellenic heritage, we must also possess that poignant, necessary death. This is what Julian is brought to do in this act which opens with his acting the role of pagan sage. He stages a mock trial of his Christian friend Gregory, taunting him with the question, asked of Christ, of what is due to Caesar and what is due to God. To answer the question by relegating the actual, objective world to Caesar and the spiritual, subjective world to God is to be willing to be passive before worldly wrong and to confirm the nonsacred nature of the world. If one allows that the realm of God extends into this world and if the emperor should encroach upon it, then courageous choice is necessary between the emperor and God, a choice Gregory evades, deliciously, by protesting, "I'll not answer. It is disrespectful ... both to God and the Emperor."[20] To claim that one's "faith" alone belongs to God is to make of one's faith a totally private, nonsubversive entity. In *Peer Gynt* the Troll King gladly allowed Peer to keep his Christian faith so long as Peer agreed to conform to all demands relating to his dress and behavior. The answer, "Render unto Caesar that which is Caesar's and unto God that which is God," therefore, is an unhelpful and evasive formula, merely a rephrasing of the question, not an answer to it. This theme is central to the argument of the play, so that the mock trial is more than just a dramatic diversion.

The intellectual rout of the Christians is immediately followed by the exposure of the pagan philosopher Libanius, who is hungry to sell his wisdom to the highest bidder, like the worst of the Sophists denounced by Socrates. Libanius resembles the world of learning in the modern age, too: he is eloquent, urbane, impressive, dignified, conscious of recognizing and preserving "values," yet, in confrontation with the realities of economics and power, as self-deceiving and sycophantic as the Church. Julian, who perceives this in Libanius and suffers from the knowledge, betrays in himself qualities of pedantry and academic vanity, slight enough in the first half of the play but disastrously taking over his character in part 2.

Letters arrive from Antioch detailing crimes of lust and murder in the Christian community so that, as in our impression of Constantinople, we see how the antinomies of paganism and Christianity are inflaming each other to madness. Just as Agathon's fervid account of ecstatically robbing and murdering pagans betrayed a frighteningly unconscious mixture of self-interested ferocity and bigoted spirituality, of gainful murder for higher ends typical of Christian history, so the squalid crimes in Antioch, with their aftermath of hysterical public denunciations and confessions, show the same lethal collision of antithetical cultural and psychic forces within individuals and within the empire. Although Julian shares these confusions, he stands above his age by being aware of them and by struggling to overcome them.

The catalog of the fleshly crimes of the Christians is contrasted with Julian's account of the beauty of "pagan sin" in a culture in which Socrates could equably accept what St. Paul abominated. But this beauty is a thing of the past, and Julian's attempt to revive it, later, will lead to ridiculous charades of Dionysiac revels. Athens itself is a spiritual museum, prolonging the pagan ideal after it has been abandoned by history. The Christians, on the other hand, for all the violent contradictions of their natures, in fact because of these contradictions, reveal that they are the vehicles of the new forward thrust of history.

Julian's very confusions deprive him of the ability to confidently embrace a partial role or partial vision in the manner of his simpler-minded opponents. Just as his lack of faith and his ambivalence, in Constantinople, were a more adequate response to the conditions of Christian culture than was Agathon's fanatic faith, so his falseness of tone and gesture and his lapses into pedantry, in Athens, more truly reflect the contradictions into which the Hellenist and Humanist tradition has sunk than does Libanius's urbanity and easy solemnity.

Both the center of faith, Constantinople, and the center of learning, Athens, insist that the truth is to be found in books, but books clearly are not vitalizing the spirit of the age. The intellectual realm of Athens is even more barren than that of Constantinople, for it has severed its "wisdom" from the realities of practical and political power. With the established spiritual, intellectual, and political forces of the empire clearly revealing their inadequacy and corruption, Julian is impelled to explore beneath them on his quest for truth and toward the comprehension of the purposes of the world-will itself. In this primary realm, behind that of the world of appearances, "spirit talks to spirit"—a dialogue Julian terms "the goal of all wisdom." It is the mystic philosopher, Maximus, who seems to be moving toward this goal and so Julian abandons Athens, the seat of Reason, to journey to Ephesus and the mystery.

Act 3, set in Ephesus, presents the greatest obstacles to the modern reader. *Emperor and Galilean* is written in prose because, Ibsen claims, he wishes to give the reader "the illusion . . . of reality," that what is happening in the play really is taking place. Yet in this act we are to attend a séance, presided over by a highly solemn magician, in which spirits from the human past and its legends are summoned to prophesy ambiguously to Julian on the course of the world's future. We are to move beyond the familiar categories of space and time to confront the generative world-will itself, begetting new realities like the realm of Demogorgon in Shelley's *Prometheus Unbound*. We are shocked to see the supernatural inadequately clothed in prose—and understandably so, for unless the dramatic action is heightened to near ritual, it cannot acceptably convey areas of reality that transcend the terms of everyday experience.

The realistic prose presentation of the séance tells us that Ibsen believes in the supernatural forces he is presenting and that he wants us to feel them as vividly *actual* in the mental theater that we create when reading his play. He prevents us from dismissing the supernatural aspects of the scene as merely Julian's overwrought subjectivity or Maximus's charlatanism by having Julian uncannily predict the arrival of his two guests, Basil and Gregory, so that when they arrive he has already prepared a meal for them. It would have been much easier on the author and on us had Ibsen left the issue of the reality of the supernatural experiences in doubt or had he explained them, as does Gore Vidal, by depicting Maximus as a fraud. Ibsen makes no such concessions to our common sense but presents the spiritualist episodes of the séance and other supernatural episodes as direct realities which we have to accept. Reading the séance scene, entering into its spirit, we do, I think, find it convincing; and it is here that the *dramatic* method of the book, with its ability to present us with immediate and highly wrought actions, with a heightened experience of the events, is so effective. Flaubert chose the method of the mental theater for his presentation of the supernatural in *The Temptation of St. Anthony*, no doubt for the same reason as Ibsen: to convey the experience of the supernatural with maximum force.[21]

Maximus the mystic was a disciple of the philosopher Iamblichus, who had reduced the mystical and supernatural elements of Neoplatonic philosophy to magic, an indication of the extent to which Hellenic thought had been corrupted. There can be no doubt that Maximus was a charlatan, though perhaps convinced of his powers, and that Libanius's disrelish for him was justified. Far from being a new direction of spirit leading away from Hellenic decadence, this mysticism and magic was a symptom of decadence: of the corruption of Hellenic rationalism by Asiatic mysticism. Many of the Mithraic traditions to which Maximus adhered went into the development of Christianity, for the Church looted the spiritual as well as the material riches of the faiths it exterminated. At most, one might say that the extraordinary spiritual fervor, including mysticism and magic, of the time of Julian was the symptom of an age seeking by many means to identify its true spirit and that the supernatural was a legitimate experiment. Ibsen apparently endorses this endeavor, and we have to recognize the fact and its consequences for our idea of the author. We will not understand his later "realism" if we conveniently ignore the quite serious and emphatic belief in the spiritual elements that are the foundations of his realism.

Julian tells Basil and Gregory that he once received a great revelation while in a trance. The trance is vividly and impressively described. After prayer and fasting Julian felt himself "transported far away . . . far into space and beyond time . . .

around me was bright shimmering sunlight, and I was standing alone on a ship with slackened sails in the glassy sparkling Greek sea. Islands towered up, like airy banks of cloud at anchor, far off, and the ship lay heavy, as though it slept, on that wine-blue surface—

But see! The surface grew more and more transparent, lighter, thinner; at last it was no longer there and my ship hung over an empty terrifying abyss.

No foliage, no sun, down there, only the dead, slimy black seabed in all its ghastly nakedness.

But high above, in the infinite arch of the sky, which before had seemed to me empty—there was life; there the invisible took on form; and silence became sound. Then I grasped the great redeeming realization... That which is, is not, and that which is not, is.[22]

The three stages of this entranced revelation are: the Greek seascape (the world at its most beautiful and ethereal) taken out of definite time and place; the disappearance of *this* layer of beautiful reality and the appearance of the abyss with its dark and slimy bed over which Julian's ship floats suspended without support; and, finally, the etheric realm of the sky where the invisible takes shape and silence becomes sound.

This trance state is a release from confinement to a particular time and place, to an awareness of dimensions of reality outside time and space. At one extreme is the matrix of all life forms, the dark and slimy seabed whose formless matter is the opposite extreme of the matterless form of the etheric heights. Within an individual psyche one could see these extremes as those of idlike instincts and energies before they have taken on definition, and the highest level of conscious life, that of the absolute spirit. We have encountered these vertical spiritual extremes in *Olaf Liliekrans*, *Love's Comedy*, *Brand*, and *Peer Gynt*, and they are taken to their farthest limits in Julian's vision. Outside the realm of the individual psyche, the extremes might resemble those of the Aristotelian chain of being from formless matter to matterless form. The gnomic pronouncement "That which is, is not, and that which is not, is" is thoroughly in the tradition of western philosophy from the pre-Socratics to Schopenhauer, in which we find the distinction between being and appearance, particulars and universals, phenomena and forms, the eternally present spirit versus the process of becoming, or the world as will and as representation. In this tradition the true reality (that which is not, is) is that of universals, forms, archetypes—the absolute unperishing but not existing for the five senses, giving form to sensuous experience which, being in a state of constant flux (that which is, is not), has no reality. Julian's revelation, therefore, is an existential grasping of a traditional philosophic idea.

Julian's awareness of this spaceless and timeless reality behind the appearances of existence lifts him above the schismatic controversies of the Byzantine world and above the disenchanting intellectual aridities of Athens. He feels in contact with the creative principle of reality from which any new, vital spiritual revolution must emerge, both "objectively" and "subjectively."

He has experienced this reality not as unreflective ecstasy channeled through orthodox and dogmatic formulas, as in Byzantium, nor as speculative propositions of the academic mind, as in Athens, but as "proved upon the pulses" of personal exploration and spiritual receptivity. Christianity could offer Julian only a fanatic and overweening faith in individual, personal immortality — a belief that affronts any educated idea of the cosmos; Libanius, on the other hand, offered only a soulless pantheism where the individual's immortality is merely a reunion with the earth that nourished him or her, as the rotting leaf is reunited with the soil. But Julian is aware of a cosmic and spiritual power, a creative principle, behind the world of appearances and behind the categories of the intellect — not unlike the creative evolutionary speculations of Shaw's *Back to Methuselah.* The individual becomes immortal by comprehending this reality, so that immortality would not be the endless continuation of individuality nor the endless recycling of earthly life but awareness of the point at which, here on earth, the individual raises himself or herself to eternal significance; it would be one of the "moments" or aspects of the purposeful life of spirit. Julian makes it clear that Maximum's concept of immortality, which he endorses, does not hinge upon an afterlife:

JULIAN (to Basil): What you, like any slave, hope for, is precisely what the great mystery aims at providing for all initiates *here,* in this earthly life of ours. What Maximum and his disciples seek is our restoratior, . . . our lost likeness to the deity.[23]

This restoration was the goal of Brand who saw the spirit of his age as resembling the fragments of a broken statue that needed to be restored to wholeness as the pure young Adam. In each successive generation, Julian continues, the "pure Adam" has been reborn, as Moses, Alexander, Christ, but in all these forms he lacked "the pure woman," who alone can unite with the hero to create a new race of beauty, harmony—a spiritual step forward for the human race analogous to evolutionary advance in biology. The aspiration seems uncomfortably unrealistic (nowhere is it specified what a "pure" woman *is*); but if, as Ibsen and so many other nineteenth-century thinkers concluded, we have come to the end of a whole line of human and cultural development, humanity would need to evolve a new identity for itself. If we were to universalize the awkward concept of the "pure woman," seeing in it more than a mere idiosyncrasy of Julian's imagination, we might say that, previously, human history has undergone its major spiritual evolution through the active male principle represented by such archetypes as Adam, Moses, Alexander, and Jesus, and that true spiritual wholeness would require spiritual androgyny. In the plays that follow the active interplay of equal male and female consciousnesses and their problematic union will be a major theme.

The séance in which Julian and Maximum commune with the world-will demonstrates the difficulty Ibsen faced in presenting a "positive" view of human history and destiny. By means of a ritual in which the senses and the forces of the unconscious are activated, even to synaesthesia, the spirit is released from its separate individuality while dancing girls sing of losing oneself in Dionysiac ecstasy. As much as he can, Ibsen tries to get the reader to experience the excited, trancelike state of Julian. Sounds, sights, movements, light and darkness arouse and bewilder so that the voice from the flame emerges with maximum effect, lifting the conundrums of free will and necessity into the realm of gripping drama. (In fact, one somewhat uneasily realizes what superb cinema it is.) Julian's confrontation with the spirits, reminiscent of Macbeth's second visit to the equally prophetic and equally equivocal witches, is the climax of his search within himself and within the world he inhabits, for spiritual direction, and by presenting this climax in the form of a séance at which voices from the world-will speak directly to Julian, Ibsen gives his hero's philosophical quest the strongest *dramatic* expression. It would have been easy to present his hero, Hamletlike, soliloquizing on the insoluble problems of fate and free will, recalling the spiritual archetypes who preceded him in world history. But a soliloquy is an implausibly audible subjective dialogue with the self, and in *Emperor and Galilean* Ibsen seeks to emphasize that his play is a drama of the objective world, also, not reducible to Julian's subjectivity.

The séance, therefore, for all its great risks, is the most reasonable as well as the most effective solution to the problem of presenting the vital connection between subjective and objective spiritual realities. The voices that speak to Julian are equivocal, as oracles traditionally are, putting upon the inquirer both the freedom and the obligation of interpreting, and the first voice that answers Julian carries an ominous echo. Julian is told to "establish the empire," and the reader who knows his Herodotus remembers how, on another occasion, Darius was promised by the Delphic oracle that if he crossed a river to battle he would destroy a mighty empire—a prophecy he fulfilled by destroying his own. This ambiguity (which empire?) is characteristic of the ambiguity of the whole séance, not because the world-will is a tease but because predictions must be ambiguous. The oracle or the mystic can predict results to be brought about by human agency but cannot predict exactly or predict the means by which the ends will be brought about, for this either would give the fated inquirer the foreknowledge whereby he or she could forestall the predicted event (an impossible paradox), or it would remove individual freedom of action, the freedom by which the fated events are to be brought about. The necessity that governs the world, to this way of thinking, reveals itself *after* the event, as in *Oedipus Tyrannos,* and the prediction is shown to have been fulfilled in a way unguessed at by the forewarned victim. (In T. S. Eliot's *The Cocktail Party* Sir Henry Harcourt-Reilly "sees" Celia Coplestone's face "after" her future death, but he does not know how her death will come about.)

If Julian is to establish the empire, only after his death is it revealed which empire, this being, it appears, that of the Christians. But the ambiguity goes deeper. Julian, as the scourge of the Christians, rejuvenates their flagging faith; yet this rejuvenated Christianity is itself merely a transitional phase or stage to a higher empire of spirit which is waiting for the fullness of time. Thus Julian does contribute to the establishment of the third empire, the goal envisaged by Maximus.

Julian is "free" to commit error, although, of course, this free-

dom is illusory. In Hegel's paradox the only true freedom is syn-
onymous with necessity, for it will be the freedom to will and to
do that which *has* to be done. Until one's subjective will thus is
the expression of the objective world-will, and vice versa, as it was
for Haakon in *The Pretenders*, the will can act only arbitrarily, not
freely; just as in a science, such as mathematics, freedom comes
from the comprehension of its necessary laws, not from the arbitrary flouting of them. Antigone is free when she sees she has no
choice but to defy Creon and to die. Ismene, mediating ineffectu-
ally between Antigone and Creon, is trapped, her predicament not
of her own choosing, while Creon blundering between contradictory choices to the end is, for all his power against his victim,
totally unfree. Ibsen confessed that with *Emperor and Galilean* he
had become a "fatalist," and in the Sophoclean world of this play,
as in Hegelian philosophy, all action, whether opposition or support (opposition being as necessary as support) fulfills the Idea.
The great nay-sayers, the opposers and negative forces of human
history (whom Ibsen, with somewhat parochial Christian bias, sees
as Cain, Judas, and, by implication, Julian), are figures who willed
what they had to will, their negative actions being essential to the
purpose of the world-will which, like Hegel's "cunning of Reason,"
has lured them into painful action. The freedom of these great
negators lay in the realization, the fulfillment, of their essential
identities which thus became significant processes in the world—a
lesson the Lean One and the Button Molder vainly try to impart to
Peer Gynt. Thus "the way of freedom" is "the way of necessity":
of comprehending the laws and processes of the world, even if unconsciously, and acting in accord with those processes. One commentator observes that for Hegel "necessity is the matrix of freedom," or, as Hegel would say, the truth of necessity, therefore, is
freedom.[24]

The philosophic hero is faced with the problem of being able to
read correctly both the riddle of the self—the subjective spirit—
and the riddle of the world—the objective spirit; and we saw how,
on encountering the emblems of these as the Boyg and the Sphinx,
Peer Gynt failed miserably even in seeing that the riddles exist. By
thoroughly entering into the dilemma of Julian instead of display-
ing it, from a distance, as an example of tragic error, Ibsen brings
the form of historical drama as far as it can go. That is, he brings

it to the point at which the author himself enters the labyrinth of evolving historical processes until he, as author, no less than the hero he is creating, is brought up, finally, to the central mystery: the problem of truth and freedom within the complex movement of historical destinies.[25]

A particular problem that Ibsen set himself is that Julian's tragedy exists on two levels: the level of Julian as philosopher with the errors to which he tragically is led—the tragedy of his intellect; and the tragedy of Julian the man and his human suffering. What would be tragic for the man would not necessarily be tragic for the philosopher. The integration of hero with philosopher, thinker with man, is humanly desirable but, as a dramatic identity, the unity is extremely difficult to bring off. Ibsen does bring it off, making Julian's tragedy as much that of his intellect as of his individual character, but the result is drama of a very esoteric kind.[26]

The *adequate* hero of a modern drama must be an intellectual, for he must act adequately, that is, make a serious attempt at understanding the nature of reality. Yet reality, to the modern thinker, is a formidably problematic thing to fathom, so that the hero, in order to both think and act adequately, would need to be a combination of Hegel and Napoleon at once.[27] If he is to be a tragic hero, his tragedy must be as much a tragedy of thought as of feeling, involving his intellect as well as his body. His thought, too, must be the most adequate conceivable, and if he is to arrive at a tragic dilemma, such as Julian's, it cannot be one that patently is unnecessary or arbitrary. *Julian among the Philosophers* seems to seek an integration of artwork, religious quest, and philosophic inquiry that Ibsen later formulated as the future direction of the spirit:

I believe that poetry, philosophy and religion will fuse together to form a new category and a new power in life, of which, however, we who are now alive are incapable of forming any clear impression.[28]

The dramatic crisis of *Julian among the Philosophers* is the moment when, through the art of *drama* and by means of a Dionysian ritual, Julian's *philosophic* quest is brought to a central *spiritual mystery*.[29] The confusions, both subjective and objective, that face the complex mind (such as Julian's) inevitably create a world in which "the signs conflict"—as Maximus warns Julian. Ambiguous

events in the outer world of politics and power seem to corre-
spond to the equally ambiguous messages from the spirit world and
to the forces within Julian's own character with its conflicting aspirations. The séance leaves in doubt whether Julian or Maximus is
the third great negator who will be the instrument of the advance
of spirit.

From the dangerous and duplicitous outside world of the empire
arrive messengers, interrupting the séance and its interior quest,
announcing the murder of Gallus and proclaiming Julian the new
Caesar. Seeing in this striking coincidence the response by the outside world to the promptings of the spirit at the séance, Julian,
despite Maximus's misgivings, embraces the world of earthly power
and glory. Three empires and three possibilities for the spirit are
presented to the reader in an ascending order of significance: the
world empire of power, intrigue, and military conquest offered by
Constantius through his messengers; the theological empire of
spirit, with its factious and intriguing bishops, which Basil, the
Christian, urges Julian to embrace; and the future integration of
these two within a "third empire" whose time is not yet come.
Julian's fateful acceptance of the objective and earthly empire is
the consequence of his return to paganism, and it will impel him
against the second, self-divided empire of the Christian world,
forcing it into unity.

Act 3 ends with an intertwining of two values, power and knowledge, body and mind. Julian Caesar believes he can realize Plato's
dream of the philosopher-ruler, like Marcus Aurelius, at a time
when the realities of his world have left this dream behind:

Caesar, after his elevation, will remain what he was...the poor philosopher
who received all by the Emperor's grace.[30]

The three acts of *Julian among the Philosophers* are the culmination of a development of Englightenment and Romantic drama
from Lessing on, a development to which Byron and Shelley,
Schiller, Goethe, and Kleist all contributed. The ambition of this
drama was to be philosophical, to recover for dramatic art the conceptual boldness and freedom it possessed under the Greek dramatic poets. Because there was no theater in Europe able to sustain
so formidably intellectual a drama, Ibsen was forced to create a
reader's theater, but in these three acts and the two that follow,

Ibsen renders his great argument in terms of brilliant actions and visual metaphors. Although less "engaging," by far, than *Peer Gynt,* the play is far more "engaged" in its wrestling with the imponderables of its argument; and it makes for more vivid and more exciting drama than does *Brand.* Ibsen's decision to present the play's lofty, idealist philosophy through the medium of prose realism was a courageous act, and one can see how, once he had taken this step, there could be no turning back to the more indulgent and easygoing convention of verse-drama. The commitment to plausibility of presentation puts the poet's idealism on trial.

Acts 4 and 5, which complete part 1 of *Emperor and Galilean,* make up a unity by themselves and originally were fused under the title *Julian's Apostasy.* At the same time they bring the dramatic action full circle to the opening of the play, for act 5 ends with the images of the church in a blaze of artificial light against the darkness and with a singing choir, with which the play opened. In these two acts Julian and Maximus are shown anxiously awaiting the "signs" from the outer world of imperial power and from the inner world of spirit. The emphasis of Julian's quest, however, shifts decisively from spiritual and "inner" to temporal and "outer" concerns. The world of the emperor Constantius reaches directly and murderously into Julian's life, taking Gallus, then Helena, and finally threatening the life of Julian himself. The change of quest drives Julian farther from the spiritual empire he had hoped to found and into the tortuous confusions of Constantius's empire.

Act 4 opens on this theme of confusion. Helena anxiously waits for news of the great battle in which Julian is engaged, but the rumors conflict so that when Julian enters in consternation Helena assumes that the battle has been lost. Julian's explanation that he has suffered far worse than defeat—a resounding victory—and his account of the way in which the totalitarian rule of Constantius controls and regulates every aspect of Julian's life underscore the complexity of the world of intrigue against which Julian must engage. As Caesar he is far less free than he was as a student in Athens.

An example of Consantius's power over Julian's life is there before us: Helena, chosen by the emperor as Julian's wife. Helena is a brilliant, almost Dostoevskyan, portrait by Ibsen. Her fervid Christianity only too patently is an unsuccessful sublimation of intense eroticism which, because it does not acknowledge itself, becomes sick, evil, openly expressing itself only in the delirium of her death agonies. The totalitarian control over individuals, the efficiency of the surveillance and espionage, depicted by the play, with the spectacle of opposing ideologies engaged in social and international conflict for control of thought as well as of political power, seem frighteningly closer to twentieth- than to nineteenth-century conditions.

The entry of Decentius, the sinister ambiguity of which Julian immediately detects, derives its dramatic power from the reality of the dangers in the world that Ibsen so imaginatively has created. Excellently rendered is the language of lethal deception on both sides. Helena's solicitous questions about Constantius's health stem from her desire for his death, as Decentius, by his urbanely ambiguous replies, shows he is aware. Julian uses this language better than Helena as a means of trapping the false courtiers with whom he is surrounded, of conveying his hostility toward Constantius, and of enlisting the army on his side while still speaking the language of loyalty until Decentius, himself highly adept at this sort of discourse, is completely outwitted and helplessly has to witness Julian's adroitly managed revolt. Ibsen enters into this murderous and duplicitous language with fine mimetic skill. The deadliness of the reality beneath the political language, which Julian clearly perceives, is made manifest when Helena is murdered by eating poisoned fruit from the emperor—a gift Julian himself presumably was to share.

As is true of all the details in this play, Helena's death-agonies, in which the perversity of her Christianized eroticism is revealed, disclose further layers of the emperor-galilean conflict. It is the death of Helena with the revelation of her infidelities that most likely changes decisively the course of Julian's quest; for his earlier quest, in which he would have been the leader of a new spiritual empire while his brother, Gallus, would have controlled the material empire, required, for its fulfillment, the love of "a pure woman," a role he incongruously saw Helena as fulfilling. In act 5 Helena will be sanctified as the pure woman by the wily priests who need a miracle to impress their wavering congregation. No irony in the play is greater than the contrast between Helena's actual deathbed confession and her afterlife sanctification. Throughout the play the name of Basilios's sister, Macrina, is sounded significantly, and it is Macrina who will speak the last words of the play over Julian's body. Macrina, it seems, is the "pure woman" who might have been Julian's spiritual partner, in poignantly ironic contrast to the sordid actuality of his marriage with Helena.

Act 4 closes with a superbly rendered scene, full of conflict, complexity, ambiguity, and irony, scored for contrasting individual and *ensemble* voices. In the scene Julian adroitly isolates his enemies, wins his army to his cause, and then cleverly feigns reluctance as he accepts the imperial role. The brilliant handling of such dynamically clashing forces, in which the dramatic writing is fully adequate to the highly sophisticated and cynical political realities of the Byzantine empire, fully justifies Ibsen's own high estimate of his play; for it represents his imaginative emancipation to the wider realm of world-historical drama. The complex objective world he failed to create in *Catiline* now is rendered with impressively convincing substantiality.

Act 5 is built around a vertical symbolic structure whose extremes stretch from the voice high in the dome of the brilliantly lit church proclaiming the sanctification of Helena, down to the voices of Maximus and Julian, deep in the lowest crypt of the catacombs searching for a sign and calling upon Helios in the depths and darkness. Ibsen's customary vertical symbolism is here used with greater significance than ever. At the brilliantly lit summit of the church's dome is "the lie," whereas down in the darkness and the depths of the tomb lies the truth.

The *scene* of the action—the stage space into which these sounds from the heights and the depths penetrate—is itself strikingly vertical. We face the cavernous arched interior of the catacombs, with steps reaching from its vault to the floor and further steps lead from this floor to passages below. A separate "winding passage" also leads upward, out into the agitated world above.

Above this scene the empire searches for directives on the problems of power and faith, and the confusion is paralleled in the lower and inner world where Julian and Maximus search for a "sign" that also will unlock the riddles of power and faith. The Church, through its priests and choir, proclaims a miracle performed by the corpse of Helena—a clear "sign" to the wavering faithful. The army, feeling itself betrayed, clamors for Julian's life. Oribases and Eutherius waver between the equally doubtful causes of Constantius and Julian. Sallust urges Julian to act decisively in the political-military world, but Julian and Maximus search for certitude in the darkness. The entire scene, from the contrived miraculous voice high in the dome of the church to its mirror-reversal in the voices of Maximus and Julian in the lowest depths, seems to represent the material and worldly embodiment of Julian's vision, recounted to his friends in act 3, of being suspended between an abyss like a black and slimy seabed at one extreme and the ethereal, endless firmament at the other, for at the end of this act, as Julian is about to emerge from the depths, Maximus will exclaim, "Ah, these slimy things about my feet!" The earlier vision seems the prototype or Platonic idea that the world perhaps continually embodies, in age after age. Below, in the darkness, is the matrix of the new order that Julian seeks to further and to serve; above, is the world as it, too, is taking shape under the pressure of the world-will. It is a brilliant and audacious scenic metaphor, superbly scored for clashing sounds and images. It would make stunning "epic" cinema.

Julian's dry account of Helena's sanctification is peppered with biting, satiric references to her sexual incontinence. "An angel came down each night to her room and called to her."[31] The account of the fraudulent miracles that are drawing crowds of believers to the church vividly exposes "the lie" within the world, against which the later realistic cycle also will engage. Against this fraudulently manipulated, politically corrupt, and frantically agitated world, imprisoned within its noisy confusions, Maximus and Julian's searching in the depths (like the Miner's digging, in Ibsen's famous poem) for some answer to the mystery of the riddles of spiritual regeneration obviously is the nobler endeavor. Julian's poignancy as a tragic world-historical hero is that he has to search desperately for the answer because he himself is not the answer. With all his great gifts he will be abandoned by the world-will because he is not one of the elect, one of "die Kinder des Hauses."

Events in the world of ideas and in the world of arms and politics again parallel each other. Maximus mentions how Julian's old "army" of Christian believers now, in the realm of thought, is put to flight, and soon Julian will put the Christian emperor's army in full flight. Sallust, the pagan soldier, becomes Julian's military adviser, just as Maximus, the pagan mystic, becomes his spiritual adviser. Julian's antipathy to Christianity grows with his increasing revolt against the emperor's power and his revulsion against the spiritual life of the Church. "All human emotions have been forbidden since that day the seer of Galilee began to rule the world."[32] he exclaims, anticipating the complaints of Nietzsche, Swinburne, and others. (His description of the Christians as "hollow-eyed, pale-cheeked, flat-chested" brings to mind, also, Stephen Daedelus's recoil from the priesthood, in James Joyce's *Portrait of the Artist as a Young Man,* when he observes a procession of similarly unprepossessing Catholic novices walk by.)

Maximus implores Julian to *surmount* the Galilean, but Julian, recoiling in disgust from the fraudulent "miracles" performed by the sanctified Helena's corpse, rejects Christ altogether and retreats to paganism as to a source of spiritual authenticity. This understandable, even commendable error will frustrate and bring into confusion Julian's entire reign. The fateful decision is made with a fine crescendo of sights and sounds. The church choir praises the holy Helena; the army clamors for Julian's life; Oribases and Eutherius plead for peace; Sallust calls on Julian to take command of the increasingly tumultous army; Maximus calls down to Julian to choose freedom; and Julian himself, calling upon Helios in the darkness, emerges blood-spattered from the sacrifice and ascends to the door, opening it onto the brilliantly lit church and its singing choir. As Julian proclaims, "Mine is the kingdom," the pagan, Sallust, adds, "and the power and the glory," while the choir counterpoints with the same words from the paternoster concluding with "for ever and ever, Amen." Part 1 of *Emperor and Galilean,* therefore, ends with a powerful recapitulation of its main themes of temporal and spiritual values. The old conundrum that Christ failed to answer, of what is God's and what is the emperor's, with which Julian had embarrassed his Christian friends in Athens, is restated in terms of overwhelming dramatic action. We see how superbly the "argument" of *Emperor and Galilean* is organized in a form of poetic/philosophic counterpoint.

In the true world-historical Caesar of the future, presumably, the dichotomy between what is God's and what is the emperor's would be overcome, for the emperor's will would be the expression of God's (the Absolute's) will. G. Wilson Knight notes how the ideal of the play looks forward to Nietzsche's prophetic formulation of "a Roman Caesar with the soul of Christ" in *The Will to Power*.[33]

Ibsen more than once proclaimed *Emperor and Galilean* to be his greatest work, and for part 1 this claim is plausible. It marshals its clashing forces in a brilliant *montage* of sights and sounds with a dramatic *immediacy* unlike anything else in Ibsen. This immediacy looks forward to cinematic methods and, if one could overcome the average audience's terror at the presence of serious thought in dramatic art, the play also might prove effective in the theater. I have suggested that the play belongs to the special dramatic genre of reader's theater and that we should be responsive to the nature of the artistry suitable to this form of theater, but G. Wilson Knight argues convincingly for the stageworthiness of the play:

Emperor and Galilean may seem unwieldy, but it is stageworthy. Unlike *Brand* and *Peer Gynt* it is conceived dramatically, even theatrically. From now on rival sounds and groups clash to fine effect, and under a spectacular production the result could be triumphant. Cutting would, certainly, be necessary; the theme lacks appeal of a normal kind; all depends on our interest in the one grand opposition. That granted, Julian and his plight are humanly drawn, and so are the rest. Excitement is maintained; new events, new life, seethe and crash, all history is before us, turning on the one axial problem.[34]

EMPEROR AND GALILEAN, PART 2

Various reasons have been given for the very noticeable drop in dramatic power of part 2 of *Emperor and Galilean*. It is said that Ibsen finally lost interest in the play with which he had been wrestling so long, and the fact that he did not submit this second part of the drama to the process of creative revision and condensation that is typical of his artistry at its best bears out this supposition. Theodore Jorgenson's observation that the dramatic initiative now shifts from the hero to the amorphous world he is opposing also would explain the slackness of much of the dramatic action, for although Julian's enemies can be said now to possess the dramatic initiative, they cannot be said to have any commanding dramatic presence.

The division of part 2 into five acts does not seem justified; the original plan of a three-act drama seems more suitable. All the more frustrating to the reader is the fact that a gripping three-act drama (having undergone the Ibsen process of condensation) seems called for by the story. Act 1 would have shown Julian attempting to introduce benign and tolerant rule over his empire against fierce opposition; act 2 would have revealed Julian betrayed by historical circumstances into establishing repressive rule; act 3 would have presented his disgusted departure from Antioch to found a new kingdom, and his death in battle against the Persians. The opportunity of seeing a better play in his material than Ibsen has been able to write is of a rarity that is breathtaking; but we can return to earth by reflecting that this, after all, does seem to have been Ibsen's earlier plan, too. Perhaps the desire to balance a "part 1" of his drama with an equal-sized "part 2" led Ibsen to produce so unwieldy and shapeless a play.

Compared with the superb part 1, much of the second half of the play seems strangely uninspired writing. We find little of the metaphorically constructed and contrasting scenes and images, of concepts rendered into the vital dramatic metaphors of light and darkness, height and depth, inner and outer, that make the action of part 1 so compelling. Whole stretches of dialogue in the second part are unaccompanied by vivid action (recalling a similar slackness in act 4 of *Peer Gynt*), so that Julian's pedantic garrulity often renders his stage-presence tedious. Many of the most striking occurrences are rendered as messenger reports of "offstage" miraculous events to which no intelligent modern can be expected to give credence. William Archer's devastating criticism of this second part of the drama, though too severe, contains a great deal of truth. With a pragmatist's distaste for abstractions, Archer ascribes to Ibsen's concept of a world-will the faults of the play;[35] but, we reflect, the world-will also was operative in the superb part 1. It is not the philosophical concept, therefore, but its aesthetically inadequate treatment, that vitiates the dramatic art of the second part.

More to the point is Archer's case against Ibsen's travesty of the historical records. Julian, one of the most tolerant and benign of rulers, against whom the Christians' chief complaint was that he denied them, by his tolerance, the bliss of martyrdom, is made by Ibsen into a frantic Macbethlike tyrant and, far more fatal to his dramatic character, into a ludicrous pedant and credulous dupe of the most crassly obvious court flatterers. It is almost impossible to maintain interest in, or feel sympathy for, a character who establishes so little that is admirable and so much that is criminally obtuse. Ibsen commits the error of making Julian's faults those of a stupid man; this is unwarranted either by the historical records or by Ibsen's own account of Julian in part 1. It is almost as if, in part 1, we see the Christians from Julian's viewpoint, then, in part 2, we see Julian only through the distorted lens of the most fanatic Christian viewpoint. If this is, indeed, Ibsen's procedure (and it would be an interesting artistic intention), it does not seem to be carried out with sufficient consistency.

Archer observes that Julian is made to commit crimes more abhorrent than those of which even the most fanatic and libelous Christians accused him.[36] At the same time, the hero's efforts are thwarted by the most astounding supernatural portents, as if the world-will were a melodramatist (to which Julian obtusely pays no attention); for this reason Archer's uncomfortable comparison with the Victorian melodrama *The Sign of the Cross* (a forerunner of the Hollywood biblical epic) is unhappily apt. Gibbon's drily ironic recounting of cosmic miracles and marvels (the laws of nature suspended by God on behalf of the Christian community, though observed by no reputable historians) should have terminated for ever the serious use of such events in literature; yet Ibsen uses them with a lavishness that suggests the Enlightenment never occurred.

Despite these, admittedly severe, qualifications, it is still possible to admire much in part 2, at least in terms of its dramatic argument. Perhaps just because Ibsen shared the German Romantic nostalgia for Hellas and all it stands for, finding in it a powerfully seductive lure against the necessary and painful maturing of the spirit, he was led to depict Julian's attempt to turn back the clock as a ludicrous charade. The immensity of the theme of the play, and the universal poignancy of the extinction of a beautiful world order, lie behind the dramatic action. The search for a vitalizing faith that, while reconciling us joyfully to the world, will not be crassly materialistic but will creatively engage all the spiritual and physical faculties in terms of a regenerated human community looks as much to the condition of the modern world as it looks back to the Romantic endeavor.

Ibsen paints on the broadest historical canvas (that of a whole empire hesitating fatefully before its momentous decision to evolve into the new Christian world order) because he sees that the configuration the human community as a whole will take on emerges only from a multitude of conflicting wills and passions, not from the neat historical decisions made by man "between breakfast and supper" and "within the antechamber of a prince," as in earlier historical drama. The old, shapely, "Schillerian" historical drama (*Don Carlos; Mary Stuart*) in which the dialectical interplay of a few, highly articulate individuals stood for momentous turning points in the history of the race was rendered invalid by the new ideas of history inaugurated by Hegel. In part 2 of *Emperor and Galilean* this condition of historical determism seems particularly in evidence, so that the play becomes less the drama of Julian than that of his empire.

The final death-struggles of a once vital and beautiful world order, despite Julian's efforts to keep it alive, bring to mind Hegel's account of the death of cultures:

Existence has become, so to speak, external, sensuous; it is not absorbed any more in its purpose. Thus individuals die, thus peoples die a natural death. Although the latter continue in existence, it is an uninterested, lifeless existence; its institutions are without necessity just because the necessity has been satisfied — all political life is triviality and boredom. If a truly general interest is desired, then the spirit of the people would have to come to the point of wanting something new — but whence this something new? It would be a higher, more universal idea of itself, transcending its present principle; but this, precisely, would manifest the presence of a wider principle, a new spirit.

Such a new principle does indeed come into the spirit of a people which has arrived at its completion and actualization. It not merely dies a natural death, for it is no merely single individual, but has spiritual, universal life. Its natural death appears rather as the killing of itself by itself. The reason for this difference from the single, natural individual is that the national spirit exists as a genus, and consequently carries its own negation within itself, the very universality of its existence. A people can die a violent death only when it has become naturally dead in itself . . . [37]

Because the living spirit has left the forms that Julian wishes to revive, he is forced into pedantry, ludicrous mimicry, and poignantly empty rituals more ridiculous than the most fanatic excesses of his Christian opponents. The cruelties Ibsen makes him inflict upon the Christians are more to demonstrate the vitality of the Christian spirit under persecution (compared with that of the persecuted pagans) than, I think, to indict Julian, for Ibsen clearly maintains sympathy with Julian. The contrast is between two world orders, one dying, the other struggling to be born, and the perceptive reader was to read in the confusions of the Byzantine history a "model" of the *kulturkampf* of Ibsen's own times in which the old Christian order was undergoing the same process.

Ibsen's determination to demonstrate the death of paganism in spite of the seductive influence of its abidingly subversive beauty makes him direct against Julian and his pagan followers a satirical technique that frequently is too broad. The technique at times is almost Brechtian, as when Julian and Libanius stage a rhetorical reconciliation before a sycophantic audience of applauding courtiers. The scene cruelly demonstrates the hollowness of their intellectual friendship, in sad contrast to Julian's youthful dream of intellectual heroes returning arm in arm from honest and open conflict. The too broad satirical thrust makes it difficult for us to "see" Julian three-dimensionally and so maintain the interest in him as a living human being which will be necessary for the pathos of his deepest moments.

In part 2 the drama shifts from the intense personal exploration of the hero that we saw in part 1 to the contrast and clash of rival rituals, processions, and, finally, armies. Nothing is sadder than the spectacle of Julian conducting pedantic ceremonies before the uncomprehending and jeering crowds of Antioch, or the contrast between his invocation to the "beautiful earth, home of light and life, home of joy, home of happiness and beauty, — what you once were, you shall be again!" [38] and the hymn of the life-renouncing Christians,

Blissful to suffer, blissful to die,
Blissful after life's woes to arise![39]

And the contrast (which recalls Peer's invocation to the earth
counterpointed by the Pentecostal choir in *Peer Gynt,* act 5, scene
10) is not only to Julian's disadvantage. Julian cannot revive the
life of Hellenism, but its beauty and appeal are acknowledged. The
living spirit may be with Christian fanaticism and life-renunciation,
but the repellant aspects of this creed are noted, and if Julian degenerates into a tyrant this is partly because his intolerant opponents drag him down to their level.

The miracles by which Julian's attempts to restore paganism
are reproached makes one feel that the spirit of history itself is
inferior in intellect to Julian. It is as if a Romantic hero were to
find himself defeated by the God of the medieval mystery cycles.
Similarly, the determination at every opportunity to demonstrate
that the pagans are spiritually bankrupt means that Ibsen, untypically, is not "seeing" them objectively and adequately. Libanius,
in actuality a courageous champion of the oppressed, is depicted
by Ibsen as a mercenary opportunist, and Gregory, similarly in
defiance of history, is shown as a heroic opposer of the emperor.
Not only is Ibsen libeling his characters; far worse, the historical
characters are dramatically more interesting than the caricatures
of Ibsen's demonstration. The realistic method which so superbly
rendered the complex characters of part 1 now is giving way to a
one-dimensionalism that defeats the realistic aesthetic Ibsen
created.

The ludicrous nature of Julian's attempts to revive pagan rituals,
accompanied by the unflagging pedantry of his commentaries on
them, suggest that Ibsen's target is primarily the academic Hellenism of his own time and that Ibsen was concerned to acknowledge
to himself that however moving and alluring this academically
revived Hellenism might be it is not the dynamic new direction for
the spirit required by his age. A more dynamic Hellenism or neo-
paganism, curiously, was to emerge while Ibsen was completing
Emperor and Galilean, for Nietzsche's *The Birth of Tragedy*
appeared in 1872 to outrage classical philologists, to proclaim
the rebirth of Dionysos from the spirit of Richard Wagner's

music, and to begin a philosophical transformation of German culture.

If Julian's cause is to be defeated by the resurgent Christianity his apostasy roused, Ibsen makes it clear that this Christianity is as unacceptable (as a *total* spiritual form) as the old paganism. Maximus does not reappear in the drama until act 3, after Julian has run his course of disillusion, when he tells the emperor:

Friend, if illusion is necessary to you, go back to the Galileans. They will receive you with open arms.[40]

Just as striking is Julian's encounter with Basil and Macrina in act 4 during which Macrina detects a power in Julian fatal to Christianity. "In him is a greater one. Don't you see, Basil . . . in him the Lord God will strike us until we die." And she concludes, "Alas, Basil, here or there, all is finished."[41] Maximus insists that decisive, world-historical figures appear in ever more adequate embodiments of the total human spirit:

There is *one* who always returns at certain intervals in the life of the race. He is like a rider breaking in a wild horse in the arena. Again and again it throws him. Soon he is in the saddle again, each time more secure and expert; but down he had to go in all his incarnations up to this day. Down he had to go as the god-created man in Eden's grove; down he had to go as the founder of the world empire; down he must go as the prince of the empire of God. Who knows how often he has walked among us, recognized by no-one. How know you, Julian, that you were not in him you persecute.[42]

Julian, however, obsessed with his mission of *defeating* the Galilean instead of surmounting him, does not learn from Maximus. Although Macrina sees that, for the Christians, "the sun is setting over our home; hope is sinking and the light of the world! Oh . . . that we should live to see the night,"[43] Julian still has to be taught this lesson about the pagan faith he is vainly attempting to restore to life. He now turns desperately to omens and sooth-sayers, this futile search for external "signs" signifying the loss of his inner faith and direction. The omens show nothing, whereas dreams and visions bring Julian to the edge of madness. In these scenes the power of the dramatic writing increases considerably as Julian actually sees the spirit of the Galilean he has spent so many years opposing. Now engaged in a campaign against the Persians, he burns his fleet, antagonizes his Christian soldiers, and, finally, rushes recklessly into battle where he is killed by his old Christian friend Agathon who has been driven mad by persecution and torture. As he dies, unrepentant, Julian calls to mind again the beauty of the pagan world and of the "beautiful earth . . . beautiful life on earth." Opening his eyes for the last time, he exclaims, "Oh, sun, sun, why didst thou deceive me,"[44] and Maximus, bending over him, speaks his obituary:

Led astray like Cain. Led astray like Judas . . . Your God is a wasteful god, Galileans! He is lavish with souls. Were you, Julian, not the chosen one, this time either, you sacrifice on the alter of necessity. What is the value of living? Everything is sport and mockery. To will is to *have* to will.

Oh, my beloved . . . all signs deceived me, all omens spoke with two tongues, so that I saw in you the mediator between the two empires.

The third empire will come! The human spirit shall reclaim its birthright, and then shall burnt offerings be made for you and your two guests in the symposium.[45]

While Basilos complacently appropriates Julian's defeat and death to the Christian cause, Macrina, taking in the import of Maximus's words, sees no such clear purpose behind Julian's defeat and death:

Oh brother, let us not seek to fathom this abyss. (*She bends over the body and covers the face*) Erring soul of man — if you *had* to err, it will be accounted to your good on that great day when the mightly one comes in a cloud to judge the living dead and the dead who live![46]

The living dead and the dead who live; the spirit world that seeks to repossess the world by inhabiting the souls of the heroic consciousnessess that yearn for universal significance, as did Julian — these are the perennial themes of Ibsen's imagination. Julian, seeking to revive the beautiful world of Hellenism, to embody its meaning in himself and to see the old banished powers walk again on the earth, was impelled into universally significant conflict from which, alone, the human spirit can grow and attain its full potential. For all the falling off in artistic effort of the second part of the play, *Emperor and Galilean* is the mightiest and most complex version, so far, of Ibsen's dramatic dialectic. It is indispensable to our understanding of the realistic cycle that immediately succeeds it.

EPILOGUE
Toward the Realistic Cycle

In *Emperor and Galilean* Ibsen employed historical realism within the context of a mental drama, inventing a literary form that combined the detailed realism of the historical novel with the urgent immediacy of the drama. In this play he "named the forces," as it were, that he saw operating upon human life. These forces, which consisted of a host of archetypal and mythic figures from man's spiritual evolution, ranged themselves into two distinct value systems: one, pagan and Hellenic, celebrating the beautiful life of human fulfillment upon earth, the other, proclaiming galilean self-denial for a truth above and beyond that of the earth. The two systems required but resisted synthesis, and the failure of this synthesis set up a historical conflict that continued from Julian's Byzantium to the life of Ibsen's own age.

During the long artistic odyssey that led from *Catiline* and the early critical writings to the conclusion of *Emperor and Galilean*, the poet was all the time increasing the conceptual content of his art and devising the most adequate artistic expression of that content. This odyssey prepared Ibsen for the greatest of his artistic undertakings: the creation of a cycle of plays whose modern scenes, characters, actions, dialogues, and urgent modern issues rediscover, by resurrecting, the spiritual forces explored by Ibsen's

earlier writing. It might be as well, at this point, to remind ourselves of the nature of the art of the realistic cycle.

In Hegelian philosophy, reality (including, of course, all that we
call "life") is the result of the Concept leaving its realm of abstractions and taking on material existence as the phenomena of a cosmos and its history. To understand reality fully, therefore, is to
discover the idea, or concept, it embodies. Such knowledge is a
self-discovery, for to comprehend reality fully is to be the Absolute
Spirit comprehending itself. One of the highest forms of Absolute
Spirit's self-comprehension is Art; and drama, for Hegel, is the
highest form of Art. Dramatic art, if it is philosophically "awakened," can mediate between the Concept, which lacks concrete
manifestation, and our actual world, in which the presence of the
Concept can be obscured both by the multitude of confusing particulars *and* by the way in which everday alienated reality in great
part negates its Concept—a theme repeated in the text of Hegel's
aesthetic writings.

By seeing an Ibsen play as a dramatized Concept, an "idea," we
should avoid reducing it to an abstract argument, for this would
deny its imaginative reflection on *life*; nor should we reduce it
merely to the plausible simulation of "real life," for this would
deny the play's struggle to reveal the idea within life that Ibsen
perceives. At present there is evidence of a very welcome recognition by Ibsen interpreters that his plays contain a mythopoeic
content, so that even so blasé and modern a product as *Hedda
Gabler* organizes many of its crucial details to reenact a mythic
pattern.[1] This is a significant advance in interpretive sophistication from the naive belief that the dramatic structures were the
expressions of real people in real trouble. But interpretation also
must seek to give a rational account of the purpose of this mythic
content in Ibsen's modern plays; otherwise the account of the
plays will remain reductive even if in different terms. Within the
total concept of each play one might see a mythic *substratum* or
matrix whose form or movement decides the configurations of the
later structures that make up the dramatic concept: historical,
literary, ideological, philosophical, and so on. All these structures
constitute the deeper content of contemporary life whose details
the play, at *first* glance, merely is copying. Many of the details are

"there" in an Ibsen play not simply or even primarily because they best explain or express a particular character or social issue but because only by inserting such details can Ibsen cunningly infiltrate the full content of his dramatic concept into the play and most cogently and adequately present his full dramatic "argument."

The dramatic argument must be presented in terms of compelling human experience subject to the accelerated rhythm of theatrical timing, and the dramatist must "pace" the audience's attention with carefully timed crises of perception which intensify the human drama while increasing our aesthetic awareness of its underlying import. The characters who create, suffer from, and clarify the argument must possess a histrionic quality unusual in everyday life, but they must also continuously sustain our faith in the dramatized fiction. It is a difficult tightrope for the artist to walk, getting from one moment of illuminating intensity to another while carrying sufficiently convincing realistic detail; for the dramatist cannot impede the movement of the play with the minute explanatory detail of the novelist's method. If the argument is universal, the strictly realistic aspect of the dramatized fiction is certain to reveal some awkward gaps, some sleight of hand, and some inconsistencies—if subject to the kind of scrutiny for which the play was not designed. We should not, for example, reflect too long upon the improbable situation upon which *Oedipus the King* depends: that Oedipus and Jocasta, in the course of their long married life together, should not have brought up the subject of their extraordinary pasts; and we can as easily discover equally great improbabilities in the tragedies of Shakespeare. Lesser playwrights would have taken better care of such matters; Sophocles and Shakespeare have other things to attend to. So does Ibsen who, nevertheless, in his modern realistic plays asks for fewer concessions from us than most. It is our awareness of the larger and more complex purposes of the dramatist's art that prevents our bringing to that art the criteria of a Thomas Rymer on Shakespeare or, more recently, a Ronald Gray on Ibsen[2]—the philistine criteria of a common sense that refuses to make any concessions to the difficulties of the *major* dramatist.

Ibsen's realistic drama achieves its expressive power through the creation of a perceptible theatrical tension deriving from our consciousness of the moment-by-moment fatefulness of each tiniest gesture and detail that occur onstage. We become acutely aware of the way in which time and space are being stretched to an almost unbearable tautness, so that each word, each movement, each nuance occurs with maximum effect. We noted, in our account of *Lady Inger of Østraat*, that this new theatrical "notation" increased the acuity of our experience of the play, raising that experience to enthralled attention, and thus created a compelling alternative to the powerful Wagnerian music-drama. Only after he had fully explored his dramatic world in the great "mental dramas" did Ibsen proceed to perfect this theatrical ritual. In the plays of the realistic cycle the audience's attention is elevated to almost hallucinatory awareness as it links itself to the carefully sustained rhythm of the play. This dramatic rhythm is found in, for example, *Ghosts, Rosmersholm, Hedda Gabler,* and *When We Dead Awaken;* in these plays the most urgent tension is sustained and nothing extraneous, nothing that is mere decorative detail, is allowed to intrude to disturb the taut structure. It is an art similar to chamber music or modern functional architecture. These dramatic structures are solipsist, closed systems that can be elucidated adequately only from their own internal details.

In the manner of the Romantic drama from which it derived, Ibsen's earlier drama, from *Catiline* to *Peer Gynt*, embodied its Concept in a form poetically distanced from our experience of the actual world and so left unanswered the question whether the idea *could* be embodied by actual life—whether, in fact, it was only a poetic and theatrical idea. Ibsen turned to realism, beginning with *Emperor and Galilean*, because he wished to prove that his universal and ideal argument could be authenticated as livable experience and because he wished to prove that everyday life does contain the universals that had always made up his larger dramatic argument. Just as the Absolute Idea or Spirit does not rest until it becomes the rich phenomena of the world, so the phenomena of the world, even if unconsciously, are struggling to reveal the presence of the Absolute Spirit. The details of any of Ibsen's realistic modern plays are not struggling to be mere simulations of everyday reality; they are struggling to reveal the universal elements of the spirit within life, drawing upon archetypal characters and actions that better embody these universal elements, and upon a dialectical method that subverts unawakened reality's claim to be an adequate expression of the spirit. For this claim of one-dimensional reality actually results in the repression of our full spiritual potential, our right to call on all the powers that can aid our self-determination to truth and freedom. The revival of the most outlandish cults, myths, gods, beliefs might be instrumental in this attempt to recover and express our full humanity. A *totalitarian* system stunts the development of our full potential when it refuses to permit us to call upon these powers. The realistic cycle is, in many ways, a vast séance where hosts of the excluded powers reexpress themselves through modern actors.

This theme goes back to the origins of Romanticism, when poets and thinkers saw humankind as inhabiting an alienated reality that had created structures of repression and untruth while preventing the expression of much that was our rightful potential: the ideal of our total humanity which the spirit should struggle to "realize." This repression was not external, merely; man himself was subjectively alienated from his full identity, even feared that identity, and needed to be awakened to develop his full potential, his birthright. A dual liberation was needed: the liberation of the objective world of repressive institutions and conventions, and the liberation of the self into an awareness of its neglected possibilities (the clear argument of *Love's Comedy* and *Brand*).

False cultures and false consciousness were negations of truth and freedom, what Ibsen, in *Emperor and Galilean*, calls "the Lie" and what Brand calls "a feast of liars celebrating lies." To overcome the Lie, we need to "negate the negation," a process that rarely is voluntary or welcome, for it requires shaking us to the very depths of our spirit. For Hegel, a full awakening requires the critical reexperience of the entirety of objective and subjective reality.

In the realistic cycle it is *this* world, and not an ideal poetic world, that Ibsen reconciles with its neglected universals. Whereas Ibsen, therefore, might have agreed to Georg Büchner's disparagement of Schiller and "those so-called Idealist poets" for not creating real flesh-and-blood characters, he would not have been driven to the despairing pragmatist fragmentation of Büchner's dramaturgy; for Ibsen, like James Joyce after him, was to find within the fallen world of nonidealist reality the presence of universals again, within the very structures of that modern reality which seemed to have turned its back upon them. In the long history of the world these universals have taken on certain archetypal identities and actions and, as it were, wait for their opportunity to live again in the world. We can see this as a form of spiritual "vampirism" in which the living dead need to enter modern characters so that their archetypal dramas can be reenacted, and in which living human beings need to be invaded by these presences to attain universal, that is, eternal significance. It probably is no accident that the cultural period that gave this theme its loftiest philosophical expression also produced Bram Stoker's *Dracula*. A play like *Ghosts* — or *Rosmersholm* — contains both the abstract philosophic quest and a quite healthy basis of lurid melodrama, just as *Hamlet* fuses Renaissance speculative thinking with the most lurid revenge melodrama.

Watching a modern Ibsen play, we should see the way in which the fragmented particulars of everyday life are, as in a metaphysical kaleidoscope, being rearranged into their truer configurations, reenacting many of the themes of the plays from *Catiline* to *Emperor and Galilean* within nineteenth-century Norwegian drawing rooms and thus better revealing the universal elements of modern reality. Behind the modern action we will find the reenactment of a ghostly, more ancient, and universal drama, as, in *Ghosts*, the spirits of Greek drama return through the details of the modern story. The ghosts that return are not always welcome and often are painful to us, but they must be acknowledged and reexperienced because they more adequately represent aspects of our total spiritual identity than do the unillumined particulars of everyday life. The raising of the ancient specters is an indication that the modern protagonists are beginning to live essentially and not arbitrarily. Their painful liberation into truth and freedom brings them to the rhythms of tragedy — for tragedy is the privilege of those who live essentially.

Redeeming modern reality by suffusing its details with the forces of the universal spirit, recharging modern life and making it glow with archetypal presences and forces, is the great theme of an

Ibsen play. This argument is sufficiently thrilling for us to concede to the author of the modern plays the inevitable minor implausibilities created by the needs of the dialectical argument and of the fateful return of the past. Dramatists occupied with smaller matters easily escape the difficulties with which Ibsen's great art wrestles. For the purpose of Ibsen's art is, as far as is possible, to bring the nineteenth-century Norwegian audience to the experience of the full content of the human spirit, both the "good" upon which that audience had turned its back for a smaller inheritance and the "evil" which it complacently had considered alien to it. If the poet, in Ibsen's words, must engage in a lifelong struggle against the trolls within the mind and heart, this self-education and self-mastery could become that of the poet's people, too—the theme, we discovered, of *Brand*.

The later realistic cycle opens with the play *The Pillars of Society*, in which the human community is totally unawakened, professing principles it betrays, denying itself possibilities it fears or condemns, and living in a false consciousness of moral self-sufficiency. Evil is what other communities do at the other end of sea routes or railway lines, and it is considered utterly foreign. The reality of this society is a mass of unacknowledged contradictions and conflicts needing dialectic development into fuller spiritual self-knowledge, into a fuller exploration of a vaster and more complex spiritual terrain of both good and evil, in order to fulfill the Apollinian injunction, "Know thyself." When the leading citizen of this community, Karsten Bernick, is brought to an awareness of the false consciousness in which he and his society exist, and of the depth of evil which, though hitherto projected complacently onto other communities, must now be acknowledged as part of his own identity, he begins the spiritual growth that may release this community from its tomb (a growth which will require eleven more plays for completion). Bernick's frantic crimes, therefore, are to be welcomed as the process of the spirit coming to know itself, painfully, by acknowledging as its own what once had seemed totally alien. "This thing of darkness I acknowledge mine," Bernick might say, echoing Prospero's acknowledgment of Caliban. This taking possession of a problematic and even dangerous new spiritual terrain parallels Bernick's action of secretly getting his community to open "a new branch line" onto the problematic terrain of other communities and their influences. In the dialectic movement of the play, which Ibsen already had established in *The Feast at Solhoug* with Margit's painful journey to knowledge of evil (a fortunate fall, or *felix culpa*, that Ibsen obviously endorses), the complacent consciousness of virtue turns out to be evil whereas experience of evil is good because it teaches painful self-knowledge and instigates fateful dialectical evolution. So, paradoxically, by being impelled to contemplate committing the greatest crimes, including mass murder, Bernick, like Margit, is a hero of spiritual growth. It is for this reason, I think, that Ibsen lets him off so lightly; for the dramatist is interested not in the vulgar business of satisfying his sense of morality by punishing what he considers evil and rewarding what he considers good but in the more distinguished business of depicting the process of painful self-knowledge toward which, at the close of the play, Bernick tentatively is moving.

In the plays that follow *The Pillars of Society*, this process of discovering seemingly alien spiritual identities and acknowledging them as one's own is continued, in greater depth. The much desired and delightful doll house becomes the intolerable prison to the once dolllike Nora who discovers in herself the possible qualities of a tragic heroine. The Puritan Mrs. Alving recognizes and acknowledges the joy-of-life she had earlier tried to suppress and extirpate; whereas the good doctor and friend of society, Stockmann, discovers, much to his surprise, that he is its enemy, no longer fighting its physical evils and delighting in healthy growing bodies, but fighting its spiritual evils and delighting in the prospect of creating healthy growing young minds. By reluctantly laying claim to seemingly alien terrain, where, under dialectic pressure, things turn into their opposites, reality is opened up to the excluded forces, both good and evil, that, in spite of the havoc they wreak upon decorous modern reality, are the instruments of spiritual liberation. Hilde Wangle urges Solness not to fear to call upon "those enchanting little devils, both the fair and the dark," for his creative liberation requires them both. Not only is nothing in humanity alien to me (this could be the motto of *Emperor and Galilean*); everything humanity is capable of is part of my universal human identity, and the intellectual laziness or timidity that cannot acknowledge this inheritance cannot overcome it and so is helpless before it and, because of this helplessness, is capable of committing the greatest evil—generally in the name of the seven deadly virtues.

The acknowledgment of our total human identity, including its unwelcome aspects, had been the purpose of the plays from *Catiline* on, and Ibsen's heroes and heroines are those who are impelled to embark upon such dangerous spiritual voyages. In the present volume we have traced the astonishingly rich development of this theme from the drama of Catiline to that of Julian, encountering on the way one figure, Peer Gynt (and his shadow, Stensgaard), who evaded the journey to self-knowledge. On the journey the most varied spiritual forms were encountered and the depths and heights of the soul were explored. Ibsen, in Norway, may well have felt he was liberated into a larger imaginative world by his artistic comprehension of even the darkest aspects of the spirit; that this form of liberation is absolutely fundamental to his imagination can be gauged from the fact that he makes it the theme of his matriculation essay in 1848:

Of all the branches of thought the investigation of our own nature is among those in which the sharpest observation and impartiality are necessary if one is to arrive at that which is the goal of every inquiry, namely the truth. Self-knowledge demands the most careful study of ourselves, our inclinations and actions, and only by the results of such an analysis is it really possible for a human being to reach a clear and truthful understanding of what he really is.... Even if a man, by acquiring this self-knowledge, gets to know his worst characteristics, and thereby finds himself required to humble himself in his own eyes, such humiliation can in no way impair his self-respect, since it provides evidence of a strong will and an honest quest for what should be man's goal in life—the development of his spiritual gifts and a care for his temporal well-being.[3]

In the first version of *Catiline* the hero finally achieved the insight that authentic life is an endless battle between antithetical forces within the human spirit, and all of Ibsen's subsequent writing has been the expansion and enrichment of the terms of this "mental fight." In Ibsen's earliest and clumsiest plays one can see taking shape, in embryo, what will become the rich and multidimensional forms and terms of his later art. The purpose of this art is always our spiritual liberation, and in each of the modern plays of the realistic cycle this liberation is attempted through raising the forces of the past and "naming the powers" that operate upon our lives so that we better can take control of our full spiritual inheritance. Because this collective, universal inheritance is the birthright of each of us, the poet who seeks to serve it is led to develop a fierce individualism; for continually, in his or her world, the poet will find institutions and powers, temporal and spiritual, that try to deny us access to parts of this full inheritance. For Hegel, true individuality is the synthesis of the particular with the universal and not the cultivation of eccentricity or isolation, and Ibsen, it seems, shares this concept. Ibsen's most memorable and free characters have the quality of becoming "possessed" by universal forces and by the "demons" of the human spirit, "both fair and dark," which need to be acknowledged, served, and mastered.

This pattern of being responsive to both the light and the dark aspects of our psyches was established as early as *Catiline* and in the plays we have studied in this volume it gradually takes on richer and richer content until it culminates in the world-historical perspectives of *Emperor and Galilean*, the drama that brings to a close, as Rolf Fjelde observes,[4] the first half of Ibsen's poetic career. In the second half there emerged an utterly different form of poetic drama—the cycle of twelve realistic plays. Yet for all the radical change in dramatic method, and however great the enrichment of his art by the more ambitious program of the realistic cycle, one is aware of not only a firm continuity but even a form of dialectical evolution in Ibsen's career, from the first play to the last.

Provocatively, it is the modern and realistic plays that are the more "primitive" in the sense of returning the theater to its ritual purposes. Rolf Fjelde notes how Ibsen's visual symbolism seems to recover a conviction of the primitive mind. He quotes Theodore Gaster's comment on the "extended self. The primitive believes that the self, or identity, of a person is not limited to his physical being, but embraces also everything associated with it and everything that can evoke his presence in another person's mind."[5] Fjelde observes that Ibsen seemed to possess some "intuitive grasp ... of this notion of the extended self, of the individual as a field of force entering into and appropriating certain personally expressive objects to fulfill its ends [which] appears to be the principle underlying much of the use of the symbols in the plays."[6] We have seen how this method of displacing psychic energy onto objects appeared first in *The Burial Mound*. In that work the argument of the play and the spiritual lives of the characters are "charged," as it were, by contact with the symbol, taking on a deeper, more elemental, but also a higher and more universal meaning.

In the modern, realistic plays, this psychic extensiveness and fatefulness of symbolic objects is both greatly increased and greatly subtilized; indeed, the greater restrictedness and confinement of the realistic scene, in which the characters are locked into one *milieu* and its inescapable history, makes all the more overpowering the operation of the spirit through these symbolic objects. The world of the dramatic performance, no longer historically or exotically remote from us, being instead the very form and substance of our age, becomes a psychic ritual of the modern bourgeois mind. Within this ritual our ghosts and demons are resurrected and better understood and our collective consciousness more adequately apprehended. Ibsen, as a poet of the modern "wasteland" theme, saw the spiritual crisis—of loss of spiritual identity—of which his culture was unaware. He sought to "awaken" this collective consciousness through dramatic rituals of spiritual liberation, raising the bright and dark specters of the past that still lay within us, reactivating their repressed, excluded, or unacknowledged power, and thus clarifying them for us. And by this ritual, he perhaps tried to prepare us for the more difficult and dangerous job of individual liberation in the world outside the theater.

NOTES

NOTES

PREFACE

1. Rolf Fjelde, "The Dimensions of Ibsen's Dramatic World," in *Contemporary Approaches to Ibsen*, vol. II, Proceedings of the Second International Ibsen Seminar, Cambridge, August 1970, ed. Daniel Haakonsen (Oslo: Universitetsforlaget, 1971).

2. *Ibid.*

3. Asbjorn Aarseth introduced this term into Ibsen studies and encountered some resistance from Ibsen scholars. But the term is useful in indicating the range and depth of investigation proper to the interpretation of literary texts. It is used by the great critic Walter Benjamin as well as by the philosophers and writers of the Hegelian Frankfurt school.

4. Jørgen Haugen, "The Riddle of the Sphinx," *Scandinavian Review*, 4 (1968), p. 39. The sphinx's riddle, as it emerges from this article, is a minute and dismal affair.

5. *Ibid.*

6. Ronald Gray, *Ibsen: A Dissenting View* (New York: Cambridge University Press, 1977).

THE CRITICAL WRITINGS

1. Samuel Beckett, *Endgame* (New York: Grove Press, 1958), p. 57.

2. *The Oxford Ibsen*, ed. James W. McFarlane, (London: Oxford University Press, 1960), I.588-89.

3. G. W. F. Hegel, *Aesthetics*, trans. T. M. Knox (Oxford: Clarendon Press, 1975), II.1068-69.

4. *Oxford Ibsen* I.589.

5. *Aesthetics* II.1111.

6. *Oxford Ibsen* I.590.

7. Isaiah Berlin, *Vico and Herder* (New York: Viking Press, 1976), pp. 179-83.

8. Albert Goldman and Evert Sprinchorn, *Wagner on Music and Drama* (New York:: Dutton, 1964), p. 91.

9. *Oxford Ibsen* I.591-92.

10. *Ibid.,* 599-600.

11. The relevant passages in Hegel seem to be in *Aesthetics* II.1124-28.

12. My translation. Cf. *Oxford Ibsen* I.599-600.

13. *Oxford Ibsen* I.600.

14. *Aesthetics* II.1159.

15. M. H. Abrams, *Natural Supernaturalism* (New York: Norton, 1971), pp. 192-93.

16. *Oxford Ibsen* I.600-603.

17. *Ibid.,* 601.

18. *Ibid.,* 602.

19. *Ibid.,* 608-10.

20. *Aesthetics* II.1046-47.

21. *Oxford Ibsen* I.609.

22. *Ibid.*

23. *Oxford Ibsen* I.672-84.

24. *Ibid.,* 672.

25. *Ibid.*

26. *Aesthetics* II.1048-50.

27. *Oxford Ibsen,* I.672.

28. *Ibsen: Letters and Speeches,* ed. Evert Sprinchorn (New York: Hill & Wang, 1964), p. 208.

29. *Ibid.,* p. 214.

30. *Aesthetics* II. 1174-78.

31. *Ibid.,* 1064-65.

32. *Oxford Ibsen* I.673.

33. *Aesthetics* II.1049-50.

34. *Ibid.,* 1153.

35. *Oxford Ibsen* I.674.

36. *Ibid.*

37. *Ibid.*

38. *Aesthetics* II.1161 (and *passim*).

39. *Oxford Ibsen* I.674.

40. *Ibid.,* 675.

41. *Ibid.*

42. *Oxford Ibsen* I.676.

43. *Ibid.,* 676-77.

44. *Ibid.,* 678.

45. *Ibid.,* 680.

46. *Ibid.*

47. *Oxford Ibsen* I.683.

48. *Ibid.,* IV.241.

THE SUBJECTIVITY OF *CATILINE* / THE OBJECTIVITY OF *THE BURIAL MOUND*

1. James Hurt, *Catiline's Dream* (Urbana: University of Illinois Press, 1972).

2. In the series *Main Currents of Nineteenth Century Literature*, vol. VI *(passim)* New York: Boni & Liveright, 1924).
3. G. W. F. Hegel, *Aesthetics*, trans. T. H. Knox (Oxford: Clarendon Press, 1975), II.1224.
4. *The Oxford Ibsen*, ed. James W. McFarlane (London: Oxford University Press, 1960), I.676.
5. James Hurt, in *Catiline's Dream*, sees in the plot of the play and in the dream that Catiline experiences, a psychic myth which, in all its essentials, will be repeated throughout Ibsen's dramatic career. Hurt's study is fascinating and ingenious and of obvious importance, but as a key to Ibsen's creative identity and to his entire artistic production — which it purports to be — it is, like so much psychoanalytic interpretation, reductive. The perennial psychic myth that Ibsen's work reveals, according to Hurt, is classically schizoid. The hero begins in a polluted and stifling "primary home" — usually a lowland, valley, or fjord. He might recollect a joyful, innocent period, which constitutes a memory of loss. He leaves this polluted home to reach a higher point of detachment and perspective usually represented as "On the Heights" (as in Ibsen's poem of that name), from which he enjoys an overarching view of reality. He rejects his home and adopts a "project of the will," a goal to which he devotes himself. At this point there occurs the "first child death," and a "fascinating" woman and a "gentle" woman make their appearance. The fascinating woman tempts the hero to some fatal action, usually to follow her to the mountainpeaks. But the hero resists her temptation and returns to the valley where he establishes a secondary home and unites with the gentle woman, with whom he works on a "project of the will." The relationship deteriorates, embittering them both and often ending in the death of the gentle woman. "At this point the project of the will collapses, a second child death occurs, and the hero ascends to the peaks to die an ecstatic death, often in the company of the fascinating woman" (p. 8). This account, which I have paraphrased from Hurt, is, as Hurt admits, a composite myth, taken from the details of many plays and never present altogether in any single play. This fact calls into doubt much of Hurt's procedure which tends to see radically dissimilar plays as essentially struggling to reveal this single myth.

The psychoanalytic account of this mythic pattern which Hurt finds in Ibsen's entire work is compelling and perhaps indicates a fundamental part of the poet's imagination. If, as Hurt, quoting R. D. Laing, asserts, we are all to a degree schizoid and thus responsive to this schizoid myth, the plays will have universal interest. Hurt interprets the myth as an expression of the schizophrenic division between Love and Will, using the somewhat simplistic scheme of Rollo May. Love is feared because it renders vulnerable, and even threatens to devour, the emerging ego, whereas Will, which consciousness adopts as a defense against this threatening aspect of Love, necessitates isolation and danger and a rigidity that eventually leads to the defeat and collapse of the project of the will. This account has much in common with the more Freudian account of Charles Lyons's *Henrik Ibsen: The Divided Consciousness* (Carbondale, Ill.: Southern Illinois University Press, 1972), and one can also see in Hurt's account of the schizoid myth strong resemblances to the Jungian thesis of Erich Neumann's *The Origins and History of Consciousness* (with a Foreword by C. G. Jung, trans. R. F. C. Hull [New York: Pantheon, 1964]).

Undoubtedly the entirety of human expression could be made to reveal such fundamental strategies of the consciousness, from the Gilgamesh epic to the latest fiction of today. The psychoanalytic hypothesis, just like the Christian or Marxian hypotheses, is a mental structure that can be used persuasively to interpret all human reality, and each, if given a great and varied body of writing to interpret, such as Ibsen's lifework, to doubt could construct an equally compelling pattern. Such detection of a pattern can be in-structive, but if the hypothesis actually *replaces* the artwork, so that all other details such as conscious aesthetic and idealogical choices are mere distractions, the procedure becomes the reverse of illuminating.

Mythopoeic and archetypal interpretation based upon psychoanalytic theory is parti-cularly vulnerable. Psychoanalytic evidence is at once imaginatively compelling and scientifically dubious, and what is established at one time as a classic expression of schi-zoid behavior, for instance, is later challenged as being fallacious. The literary critic, who must remain an amateur in this field, finds the psychoanalytic terms exciting and com-pelling and when, as in e.g. Rollo May's and Neumann's work, the terms appear to cover the entirety of human expression with the minimum of conceptual difficulty, they seem ideal tools for analysis. But the scientific controls we are then able to exert over our activity as amateur psychoanalytic literary critics are feeble, if they exist at all.

Obviously psychoanalytic evidence can be relevant to our interpretation of a formal artwork, whether by Ibsen, Bach, Mozart, or de Kooning; but it is relevant only after we have assured ourselves of that highly conscious, intentional, controlled *aesthetic* activity which, after all, is what makes our subject an artist and not a psychoanalytic case study. When we have grasped much of the artist's intention, it often will turn out that what we had taken for unconscious or subconscious expressions (welling up from the individ-ual or the collective mind) are in fact highly conscious thematic choices deriving from a common stock of ideas, images, and "arguments" within the artist's cultural inheri-tance. Because critics' use of various schools of psychoanalytic theory has had such an effect upon modern interpretation of fictional literature (it has done far less damage in the other arts), it is worth attempting to see in what way the "classic schizoid pattern" of Hurt's composite myth is capable of other explanation.

All the ingredients of Hurt's myth are typical metaphors of Romantic literature in fiction, poetry, aesthetic theory, and philosophy, making up the terms of discourse of Romanticism. The "polluted primary home" from which the hero feels alienated and from which he might recall an earlier, blissful condition before this fall derives from the many versions of the lost golden age, including the influential lost paradise of the Christian adaptation of this myth. The myth was taken up and modified with consider-able frequency by European writers from Rousseau, Kant, and Herder, to Schiller, Fichte, Hegel, and many others. Schiller, in his *The Aesthetic Education of Mankind,* describes modern man awakening, looking about him, and discovering himself in a pro-foundly alienating (i.e. polluted) reality, in which he cannot recognize what he discerns as his true self and which denies the functioning of his best and freest nature. By the recollection or contemplation of a natural (naive) condition, like childhood, and by the historical recollection of seemingly unalienated cultures (especially the Hellenic), a more joyous and wholesome condition, one of unity and wholeness between man and nature (including his own natural impulses which are tragically at odds with the mores of modern society), can be glimpsed. This lost wholeness and unity is something for which the modern alienated consciousness must strive, not by returning to primitive innocence (as with Aurelia's lure to Catiline) but by energetically striving to overcome alienation (a project of the will) and so attaining to the lost unity but at a "higher" level.

The modern, alienated, fragmented consciousness poignantly aware of its severance from nature is termed by Schiller, in his most famous essay, *sentimentalisch,* and it is contrasted with the *naiv* consciousness which, like that of the child or the animal, is happily unaware of any such separation between nature and the human world. Schiller, developing the potent argument of Rousseau, inaugurates the modern concept of "alienation," and his dichotomy of naive and sentimental will beget a long procession of similar dualisms in modern thought and fiction, Nietzsche's Dionysos *(naiv)* and Apollo *(sentimentalisch)* and Jung's extrovert and introvert being notable variations. The sentimental or self-reflective mind, Schiller movingly relates, feels self-divided, remote from life, alienated, and labors to overcome this condition. In Romantic writing this frequently entails the hero's ascent to mountain heights. Hurt analyzes the "mythic" action in Ibsen's poem *On the Heights* where the narrator leaves his home, meets a strange hunter who takes possession of his will, and later sees his mother's home ablaze in the distance. He is induced by the hunter to stifle his agony and instead aesthetically to enjoy the pictorial "effect" of the blaze. A year passes with the narrator still on the heights; now he is able detachedly to observe his fiancée in the distance riding to her wedding. He concludes that only on the heights are freedom and God to be found, whereas in the valley men grope in servitude. This action of "putting into perspective" and thus detaching oneself from the close and stifling context of one's life with others is a common action of the Romantic hero in poetry and fiction (Childe Harold was the famous prototype), and the only distinct aspect of this story is the emphatic "aesthetic" nature of the detachment. This was not unique in Romantic literature, becoming, in fact, a major literary movement of the later nineteenth century.

The classic instance of the poem in which the narrator leaves his surroundings, muses on his home, responds to the anarchic wildness of nature, and reaches a "height" from which to attain to philosophic perspective is Schiller's *The Walk (Der Spaziergang)* which in its action is similar to, though less startling than, Ibsen's poem. Ibsen's metaphoric landscape with its many levels of human consciousness is seen frequently in Romantic writings; one need only call to mind the use of the landscape in Wordsworth, Byron, Schelley, Goethe, Schiller, Richard Wagner, and the Nietzsche of *Thus Spake Zarathustra.*

Child death as a metaphor for the loss of the state of innocent consciousness is another Romantic commonplace, found in Blake and Wordsworth, in Dickens and Henry James, as well as in much popular fiction. The emblem of the duel between the gentle woman and the fascinating woman is perhaps the most pervasive of all the Romantic details that Hurt interprets as private schizoid myth. It long precedes Romanticism in the earliest representations of beneficent and terrible goddesses and in the myth of Lilith and Eve. In Homer's *Odyssey* it occurs twice in the contrasts between Nausicaa and Circe and between Penelope and Calypso. To remind the reader of only the most familiar examples, there is Cordelia and her sisters, Racine's Phèdre and Aricie, the women of Coleridge's Christabel, of Schiller's *Don Carlos* and *Mary Stuart,* of Wagner's *Lohengrin, Tannhäuser,* and *Parsifal* (where Kundry combines both aspects), and, the most explicit version, Hawthorne's *The Marble Faun* in which the blonde and gentle Hilde lives in a tower surrounded by white doves, whereas the dark and fascinating Miriam is associated with the underworld. In opera, with its *penchant* for the most blatant contrasts, there are versions of this theme: Bellini's *Norma* (early parodied by Ibsen), Bizet's *Carmen,* Verdi's *Aida,* and Puccini's *Turandot.* So pervasive is the theme, especially in Romantic and post-Romantic literature, that it would be more surprising were it absent from Ibsen's drama.

In Hurt's psychoanalytic myth, the hero attempts to sustain himself on the heights by a project of the will, but in his divided allegiance between the two kinds of women he hardens into fanaticism. The death of one of the women signals the collapse of his strategy of the will, whereas the reappearance of the other "marks the return of the suppressed side of his nature, and the second child-death marks a second ego-crisis" (p. 35).

By an ascent to the peak, however, there takes place "a triumphant rebirth of the self" and a "killing of the self in self transcendence and in the brilliant clarity of the dawn being reborn, whole and undivided," bringing to an end "the restless quest that dominates the lives of Ibsen's protagonists" (p. 35). This interpretation of the pattern in terms of schizoid experience fits not only the work of Ibsen but also that of many Romantic writers and thinkers and, perhaps, a great part of the literature and legends of humankind, so that as a tool for understanding Ibsen's particular intentions and his uniqueness as an artist, it has its limitations.

Death transcendence on the peaks, for instance, is another Romantic commonplace. In fact, once Romanticism had established its metaphoric natural scenography—which it did early on—all forms of spiritual transcendence, of which death transcendence was the ultimate manifestation, would be associated with heights, just as regression, or a sinking back into the unconscious, would be associated with depths. It might, of course, be possible to detect in Romantic literature a schizophrenia affecting a whole culture, or even a schizophrenia endemic to man that was first fully explored by Romanticism, but if we grant this we also must admit that the terms "schizoid" or "schizophrenia" in their clinical sense are not very helpful and that a less reductive terminology, capable of embracing a wider spectrum of cultural phenomena, would be preferable.

Romantic archetypal and mythopoeic imagery was a literary "public domain" upon which the young Ibsen was free to draw. It was part of a general discourse into whose ongoing arguments a young poet would be drawn—for there would have been no alternative intellectual/metaphoric structures (apart from, say, rigorous Christian orthodoxy) available at that time. Granted that Ibsen's creativity, like that of all artists, drew upon unconscious sources within his mind; but much of the development of that creativity, even where it expressed the poet's subjectivity, was inevitably "programmed" by the terms of the Romantic themes and images. In the same way, a modern writer, employing Marxian or Freudian themes, or conventional Christian themes, would be obeying laws of development within these disciplines as much as expressing unconscious impulses. The completed artistic identity, in terms of successfully objectified artworks, would be a synthesis of these two "systems," the personal and the public.

If we keep this in mind, while responding to the highly suggestive pattern that Hurt usefully discovers, we will not reduce Ibsen's plays, which are objective works of art, to private and subjective stratagems, mostly unconscious, concealed beneath ultimately irrelevant aesthetic externals. Rather, we will be aware of the gradual evolution of Ibsen's creativity from a springboard of subjective compulsions to the controlled aesthetic transformation of a whole world of objective reality in which the artist's adoption of archetypal themes and images, actions and characters, speaking powerfully to subjective and subconscious areas within ourselves, is part of a fully rational aesthetic program. The tendency of much modern interpretation to reduce artistic phenomena to psychological phenomena—and even to indications of psychic *disorder*—actually is a refusal to allow the function of art, which is to create an aesthetic *order* of objective significance. Thereby one protects oneself from the challenging and potentially subversive consequences of art; one denies the dialectical intention of art to effect change upon the viewer and, instead, one decides to effect change upon the artwork: to "reinterpret" it in other than aesthetic terms. This even makes the interpreter, who is more aware than the artist of the "true" psychological strategies performed by the work, the artist's superior.

6. The creation of an undefined stage space where the actor's facility of moving in and out of sight begets the opportunity for the most implausible concealments and revelations, and where the characters act in defiance of psychological probability and of

common sense, is a typical fault of Romantic drama—taken to extremes of skillful inanity in Victor Hugo's *Hernani*. The relaxation of artistic discipline which the Romantics introduced into dramatic form permitted the most resonant verbal and physical histrionics unchecked by any compelling theatrical discipline. Ibsen's great achievement is that he gradually will recover for modern theater an authentic, subtle, difficult discipline of theatrical conventions—the notation of modern realism—in which the extravagent Romantic histrionics are refined into equally ambitious but incomparably more convincing psychological and aesthetic experience.

7. This female duality, as Ibsen's first biographer Henrik Jaeger pointed out, continues throughout the plays.

8. Neumann, *The Origins and History of Consciousness.*

9. Percy Bysshe Shelley, *Poetical Works* (London: Macmillan, 1907), pp. 451-52.

10. My translation.

11. My translation.

12. If Ibsen's youthful intention had been to create a drama about an objective situation and if this goal was later frustrated by his inability to control his own subjective and "schizoid" condition, one cannot see why Ibsen would, with such *conscious* effort, draw our attention to the play's subjective nature. Exactly the opposite seems to be true: that Ibsen is consciously creating a highly literary drama of Romantic subjectivity for which the historical and external details act as a convenient dress. One can say that most "dream sequences" in literature are highly conscious devices employed by the authors to signal the realm of the subconscious or the occult and that we should not read them as uncontrolled, unmediated expressions of the poet's subjective life. Genuinely unconscious expression in art, if it were possible, would not, one imagines, be able to distinguish between dream and reality but, instead would merely create dreamlike reality, as with the "art" of the mentally disturbed.

13. Halvdan Koht, *Life of Ibsen,* trans. Einar Haugen and A. E. Santaniello (New York: Blom, 1971), p. 44.

14. The play has much in common, in fact, with the often quite atrocious "archetypal" art and fiction admired by Jungians and created under the influence of Jungian theory. Archetypal interpretation, however, can have considerable merit in discovering underlying thematic patterns and structures in a poetic work, an underlying unit beneath the mass of particulars. The method is used, I think successfully, in Asbjarn Aarseth's study of *Peer Gynt (Dyret i Mennesket* [Oslo: Universitetsforlaget, 1975]).

15. My translation.

16. *Caspar David Friedrich,* Tate Gallery Catalogue, 1972, p. 81.

17. Otto Lous Mohr, *Ibsen som Maler* (Oslo: Gyldendal, 1953), see e.g. p. 49.

18. *Oxford Ibsen* I. 151.

19. Heinrich Heine, *Selected Works,* trans. and ed. Helen M. Mustard (New York: Vintage Books, Random House, 1973), pp. 417-18.

20. My translation.

21. My translation.

22. By my computation, Blanka would have been just five years old when she converted the fierce old Viking Audun to the new faith. Even for a religion in which miracle is commonplace, this seems extravagent.

23. My translation.

24. *Oxford Ibsen* I. 151.

25. My translation.

26. *Oxford Ibsen* I. 13.

THE RECOVERY OF THE PAST:
ST. JOHN'S NIGHT TO *THE VIKINGS AT HELGELAND*

1. *The Oxford Ibsen,* ed. James W. McFarlane, (London: Oxford University Press, 1960), I. 591-92.

2. One of the overriding concerns of European Romanticism was the desire to discover true and original sources of national consciousness, its purest springs, and by these to escape from the alienated social reality and alienated consciousness created by history. The Rousseauist disparagement of modern, developed culture, the Wordsworthian belief in the need of the modern urban mind to recover its affinity with the natural world, and Schiller's famous contrast of the naive and the sentimental (alienated) consciousness also brought forth among the less reflective an enthusiasm for the simplest and most artless products of the folk spirit since these belonged to a time and condition before the onset of the painful fragmentation of society into hostile classes and ideologies, and before the individual mind was aware of painful self-division. Thus the often admirable program of cultural nationalism in many countries manifested itself in forms that were ripe for parody.

3. *Oxford Ibsen* I. 231.

4. G. W. F. Hegel, *Aesthetics,* trans. T. M. Knox (Oxford: Clarendon Press, 1975), II. 1206.

5. *Ibid.* 1207.

6. *Ibid.*

7. *Ibid.*

8. *Ibid.*

9. *Ibid.,* 1225-26 and 1231.

10. *Oxford Ibsen* I. 372.

11. *Ibid.*

12. *Oxford Ibsen* I. 374.

13. G. W. F. Hegel, *The Philosophy of Fine Art,* 4 vols., trans. F. P. B. Osmaston (London: Bell & Sons, 1920), IV. 113.

14. *Aesthetics* II. 1153.

15. Raymond Williams, *"Hamlet* and *The Feast at Solhoug,"* in *Drama in Performance* (London: Penguin, 1954), pp. 75-84.

16. My translation.

17. *Oxford Ibsen* I. 672.

18. *Ibid.,* 676.

19. *Ibid.,* 230.

20. *Oxford Ibsen* II. 64.

THE ACHIEVED ART: *LOVE'S COMEDY* AND *THE PRETENDERS*

1. Bjorn Hemmer, *Brand; Kongsemnerne; Peer Gynt* (Oslo: Universitetsforlaget, 1972), pp. 9-21.

2. G. Wilson Knight, *Henrik Ibsen* (New York: Grove Press, 1962).

3. By taking highly audacious liberties with historical fact in order to reveal the higher truth behind the facts, Friedrich Schiller recreated historical circumstances as a poetic drama of semi-mythic conflicts and dialectic not greatly dissimilar to those found in Greek literature. The result, however, as Richard Wagner saw, was a dramatic form (and a theatrical ritual) that was not timelessly mythic, for it purported to reveal and illuminate specific historical processes, yet was not truly historical because its extreme

freedom with the facts, which could always be altered or discarded if they contradicted or confused the "idea" behind them reduced these facts to the status of fictions without mythic sanctions. Schiller's dramatic arguments are enlightenment pseudo-myths vulnerable, as myths are not, to refutation. If historical figures are translated into semi-mythic figures, much of their *historical* identity is irrelevant and even hostile to the mythic purpose. By offering insights into historical processes, these semi-mythic works are claiming scientific/philosophic value which is open to historical dispute. Schiller had the genius to get away with his method, but one can see how it could quickly degenerate into offering an interpretation of history with no other discipline than one's own imaginative response to a few select historical accounts.

4. For this reason it is inappropriate to explicate plays like *Love's Comedy, Brand, Peer Gynt,* or the plays of the realistic cycle by speculating on the author's personal life until one is satisfied as to the nature of the play's internal and coherent principles of structure. These principles might imply a "world view" derived from or influenced by some external source, for example, as I have suggested, the Romantic heritage and Hegelian aesthetics, and, as Bjorn Hemmer has suggested, the structure of traditional Christianity; but the text of the work itself is the ultimate means of verification of our interpretations. A religious or philosophic system, an aesthetic theory or discipline will be valid as tools for interpretation if they illuminate more aspects of the poetic structure than hitherto, and invalid if they require one to ignore aspects of that structure. Asbjorn Aarseth has formulated the principle for such an interpretive (or hermeneutic) discipline. "[The] task of the interpreter is to arrive at a hypothesis concerning the fundamental structural properties of the chosen text, a hypothesis which appears to be inferior to none in its capacity to account for the complexity as well as the interrelations of the parts making up the finished text." (*Dyret i Mennesket* [Oslo: Universitetsforlaget, 1975], pp. 275-76 [author's English précis].)

5. Knight, *Henrik Ibsen,* p. 15.

6. My translation.

7. George Bernard Shaw, *The Quintessance of Ibsenism* (New York: Hill & Wang, 1957), p. 186.

8. By this means the play usefully exorcises the Romantic idea of "eternal love" from serious modern literature. Romeo and Juliet, settled in respectable marriage, would quickly lose their great appeal; and there is a tragicomic aspect, of which Shakespeare is deeply aware, in Antony and Cleopatra's repeated attempts to affirm an ideal and all-consuming love in the context of a world that actually has to be lived in, and despite the fact that they frequently are disenchanted with each other. The most ardent artist in the cause of Romantic love, Richard Wagner, also expressed its tragic impossibility in the actual world, in *Tristan and Isolde.*

9. This is pointed out by Bjorn Hemmer in his study *Brand; Kongsemnerne; Peer Gynt,* p. 16. Hemmer's major theme is that the "Ibsen-hero" of the dramas in the period 1862-67 is expected to realize God's plan for him, which is to overcome the "fall" of alienated reality and its spiritual life, to return to Edenic wholeness and innocence, and to be rewarded, in spite of great isolation and suffering, with a divine, as against an earthly crown. Falk and Brand are examples of such positive heroes, and the antithesis to such a hero would be a negative figure, like Bishop Nicholas in *The Pretenders,* who is directly linked to Satan and the diabolic hold upon the world. Earl Skule and Peer Gynt are errant heroes, who evade the destiny God has chosen for them, who mistakenly seek an earthly crown (as does Julian in *Emperor and Galilean*), and who are dragged down into error and degradation, only at the last moment undergoing a genuine penitence and self-humbling and receiving a redemptive illumination.

Much of Hemmer's thesis is in line with my own. I would question whether the hero (or the poet, Ibsen) wishes to return to Edenic innocence; this is contrary to almost universal Romantic lore which acknowledges the necessity for the Fall and which insists that a return to innocence (the overcoming of alienation) must be attained at a *higher* level than that of Eden. Edenic innocence, like Aurelia's lure to antiheroic love, is not the "wholeness" Brand wishes to restore, for wholeness requires the knowledge of good and evil. See M. H. Abrams, *Natural Supernaturalism* (New York: Norton, 1971), especially the chapter "The Circuitous Journey: Through Alienation to Reintegration," pp. 199-252. Although I agree with Hemmer that a major source of this heroic action of self-realization is traditional Christianity (more Old Testament than New, as Hemmer concedes), the pre-Christian (Hellenic) and post-Christian (Romantic) versions of this quest myth are as predominant.

10. My translation.

11. In a fine critical introduction to this play (in volume II of the *Oxford Ibsen*, 1962), J. W. McFarlane notes that the Haakon-Skule contrast is similar to Schiller's distinction between the "naiv" and the "sentimentalisch" types of creative imagination. Schiller was led to this distinction after considering the difference between Goethe's Bjørnsonlike naturalness and confidence and his own more alienated, selfreflective character. One could, in fact, create long parallel columns of such character contrasts out of the major literature of the modern world from the time of Schiller to that of Thomas Mann. Schiller's great essay *On Naive and Sentimental Poetry*, "The greatest of all German essays," according to Thomas Mann, portrayed the wistful, envious stare of the alienated spirit at the natural gracefulness of the "naive" spirit and its relation to its world. The legacy of this confrontation would include the following:

Naive	Schiller	*Sentimental*
Dionysos	Nietzsche	Apollo
Extrovert	Jung	Introvert
Mary	Mary Stuart	Elizabeth
Tasso	Torquato Tasso	Montecatino
Prince Frederick	*Prince of Homburg*	Elector Frederick
Harriet Smith	*Emma*	Emma Woodhouse
Peer Gynt		Brand
Ulfheim	*When We Dead Awaken*	Rubek
Billy Budd	*Billy Bud*	Captain Vere
Shen Te	*Good Person of Setzuan*	Shui Ta
Estragon	*Waiting for Godot*	Vladimir

This game could be played indefinitely. The prevalence of this theme (what Jane Austen designated Sense and Sensibility) in the writing of the Romantic period and after indicates a major division in our cultural life which reaches its extreme in the distance between popular and avant-garde art.

12. Hemmer, *Brand; Kongsemnerne; Peer Gynt.*

13. Georg Brandes, *Main Currents of Nineteenth Century Literature* (London: Boni & Liveright, 1924), IV. 125.

14. Mircea Eliade, *Cosmos and History: The Myth of the Eternal Return* (New York: Harper & Row, 1951), see pp. 3-51, "Archetypes and Repetition."

15. John C. Pearce, "Hegelian Ideas in Three Tragedies by Ibsen," *Scandinavian Studies*, 34, no. 4 (1962), pp. 245-57.

16. *Ibid.*, p. 245.

17. Albert Goldman and Evert Sprinchorn, eds., *Wagner on Music and Drama* (New York: Dutton, 1964), pp. 144-45.

18. *The Oxford Ibsen,* ed. J. W. McFarlane (London: Oxford University Press, 1962), II.22.

19. My translation.

BRAND: THE TRAGEDY OF VOCATION

1. This is one of the many examples in the drama where the scenic conventions are pictorial rather than theatrical, suited to a mental theater rather than to an actual stage.

2. Freidrich Schiller, *Willian Tell,* trans. Gilbert J. Jordon (New York: Bobbs-Merrill, 1964), p. 62.

3. *Ibid.,* p. 89.

4. Gerard Manley Hopkins, *Poems and Prose,* ed. W. H. Gardner (Baltimore: Penguin, [1954, c. 1963]), p. 61.

5. Although it is heresy, I confess I find this true of Shakespearean drama which is always profounder reading, or hearing, than it is viewing. Henry James, when simultaneously reviewing *Richard III* and *Little Eyolf,* complained that the "acted Shakespeare no longer is to be borne" and declared his preference for Ibsen's play for the purposes of theatrical production.

6. Rolf Fjelde, "The Dimensions of Ibsen's Dramatic World," *Contemporary Approaches to Ibsen,* vol. II, Proceedings of the Second International Ibsen Seminar, Cambridge, August 1970, ed. Daniel Haakonsen (Oslo: Universitetsforlaget, 1971), pp. 161-80.

7. My translation.

8. "Triple alliance" brings to mind the "holy alliance" of the three great reactionary powers of Europe: Prussia, Austria, and Russia, who fought to undo the entire work of the French Revolution. The weapons of this holy alliance were similar to those denounced by Brand: (1) intellectual reaction and frivolity; (2) crass materialism in which the bourgeois culture turned its back upon the old idealist imperatives; and (3) fanaticism and mysticism that set themselves resolutely against the establishment of freedom and justice. These great forces of reaction in the world at large are also present in each individual, resisting the spiritual liberation that Brand calls for. If I am correct in hearing an echo, in Ibsen's *tripelallians,* of the reactionary forces that sought to maintain unfreedom in Europe (and Ibsen's letters show that he was highly responsive to political events in Europe — *Brand* itself has been interpreted as an angry reaction to the Dano-Prussian War), this would suggest that the poet believed the inward spiritual struggle of each of us is of as great a consequence as the great and fierce struggles for freedom in the political/ideological arenas of the world. His "mental drama" would then be a contribution to the creation of another powerful, inward arena in which the cause of spiritual freedom could be served.

9. *Love's Comedy,* act 3. My translation.

10. Søren Kierkegaard, *Either/Or,* trans. David F. Swenson and Lillian Marvin Swenson, with revisions and a foreword by Howard A. Johnson (New York: Doubleday, 1959), II.355.

11. This idea appears as parody in *Peer Gynt.* Peer envisages founding a new city, Peeropolis, in the south but, as Asbjorn Aarseth notes, entirely in the *animalistic* terms of stud breeding — in contrast to the *spiritual* terms of Brand and Agnes's vision. In

Emperor and Galilean Julian also takes up this idea, of founding Heliopolis whose blend of the physical and spiritual would integrate the galilean-emperor opposition of Brand and Peer.

12. Act 2. My translation.

13. Act 2. My translation.

14. Act 2. My translation.

15. Precisely at the time when modern reality was becoming that of urban and industrial society, with all its attendant problems, many of the keenest poetic imaginations among the Romantics and Victorians turned their backs on this reality, creating alternative worlds of "nature" and "imagination." Even the novelists, who took upon themselves the closer exploration of the spirit within the alienated world, did not examine in depth the economic and political issues analyzed by the economists and by Hegel and Marx — at least not until Emile Zola. Balzac's great novels are brilliant descriptions of modern society but they are not deep *analyses;* the ruminations of a George Eliot in a novel like *Middlemarch* do not really grasp the drastic transformation of technological, economic, political, social, and ethical realities that is occurring.

16. Taking responsibility for the entire history of the race was a *hubris* to which many Romantic artists and thinkers were prone, particularly William Blake, Hegel, Ibsen, Richard Wagner, and James Joyce. In this coming to terms with the total past, both personal and universal redemption was at stake; the Romantic thinker was somewhat of a Captain Ahab in pursuit of the white whale even at the risk of jeopardizing the safety of the world. The fervor with which the actions of recollecting and recreating the spiritual past were undertaken is startling to the modern reader.

17. J. P. Sartre, "Existentialism and Human Emotion," *Literary and Philosophical Essays,* trans. from the French by Annette Michelson (London: Rider, 1955).

18. By choosing his *vocation,* Brand ensures that his personal salvation is bound up with that of the world existentially; one attains authentic identity only through an individually affirmed relation to the world. In a world of fatalistically accepted identities like the Hellenic, or of a God-sanctioned and conventional hierarchy of identities, both good and evil, like the Christian, such a poignant need to choose and sustain identity would not have made sense. Nor does it make sense in, e.g., the Marxian world, for identity here is not a matter of individual choice but of alien class relationships, whose abolition would end alienation and reconcile the individual to his or her role in a "pastoral" order of justice. Ibsen's drama is truly existentialist, in Sartre's terms, because the authentic identity of his heroes has to be chosen, questioned, and maintained, minute by minute. Henry James shrewdly remarked that Ibsen's characters do not *play* with life because they are too busy learning to live. If they *do* play, as is true of Peer Gynt and the Ekdals, they live in a limbo of inauthenticity and nonidentity. In the Christian world view one may be judged by whether or not one attains one's full Christian value within as assigned identity; the Prologue to Chaucer's *The Canterbury Tales* and Calderon's *The Great Theater of the World* give us the image of orthodox hierarchies of identity from monarch (or knight) to peasant and reveal the discrepancy between the individual and his or her role. Shakespeare's monarchs, nobles, liegeman, and peasants similarly may transgress against their given roles (Macbeth being the most vivid example), but they do not, by an act of Will, individually discover, choose, and existentially affirm them. Richard II is "determined to be a villian," as he explicitly tells us, but, as he equally explicitly explains, this is because Nature already has shaped him for the part. Most pertinent of all is the figure of Hamlet whose famous vacillations over his conventional roles of Christian prince and of pagan revenger derive from condi-

tions of cultural dissolution which for Brand, by contrast, are the very means for the assertion of his identity and vocation.

19. This is the dilemma built into the vocation of priest in the Protestant tradition, which holds up individual authenticity and certitude against the compromises permitted by the older, more catholic institutionalized religion. The secularization of this idea of authenticity into the areas of philosophy, art, politics, and ethics (and Ibsen insisted that Brand's drama was not that of priest, only) ensures for humanity a great deal of spiritual discomfort.

20. M. H. Abrams, *Natural Supernaturalism* (New York: Norton, 1971), pp. 143-95.

21. Johann Gottfried von Herder, *Reflections on the Philosophy of the History of Mankind* (Chicago: University of Chicago Press, 1968), p. 6.

22. George Gordon Noel Byron, *Poetical Works* (London: Oxford University Press, 1970), p. 11.

23. *Ibid.*, p. 390.

24. The prototype of the reflective hero, Hamlet, so often invoked by Romantic writers, is not a spiritual hero in this sense. Hamlet is a modern (Renaissance-Elizabethan), reflective sensibility called upon to be the hero of a primitive revenge drama, and his vacillations between acceptance of and resistance to this destiny do not question its validity. Hamlet questions his own worthiness, laments that the kingdom of Denmark has lost its old heroic value, and doubts that he is the suitable mender of these disjointed times. He sees modernity (corrupt machiavellianism) as the curse upon the kingdom, the disease that needs lancing. But he is himself corrupted and is superseded, apparently with Shakespeare's approval, by the simplistic figure of Fortinbras whose armored figure appearing at the end of the play, by "echoing" the armored figure of the old king's ghost at the beginning, brings the kingdom back full circle to its condition of health. Where Hamlet does act resolutely, as in the killing of Polonius, the trapping of Rosenkrantz and Guilderstern, the decision not to kill Caludius at prayer but only when he can ensure his damnation, and when he abets in the carnage of the last scene, he is acting *below* his highest reflective level; but when he reflects at this level he is incapable of action. Samuel Johnson — in many respects the best commentator on Shakespeare because his rationalism did not permit the intellectual and aesthetic abasement before the bard that has been seen in later commentators — was not disposed to see contradictions, incongruities, weak devices, and poor plotting as evidence of virtues too deep for rational understanding. His summary of the virtues and faults of *Hamlet* is performed with a telling succinctness that must have seemed brutal to Romantic enthusiasts. He notes that Hamlet's feigned madness allows the prince to do nothing "that he might not have done with the reputation of sanity," and, in line with our argument, sees Hamlet as "rather an instrument than an agent." (*Johnson Prose and Poetry*, selected by Mona Wilson [London: Rupert Hart Davis, 1963], p. 618.) After the Romantic revolution, tragic heroism becomes inseparable from intellectual heroism and (as in Brecht's *Galileo*, for example), tragic villainy is inseparable from intellectual villainy.

25. Restoration tragedy, for example, is to the modern taste an arena of impossibly false histrionics, whereas Restoration comedy, for all its exotic nature, still can be appreciated on much the same terms as it was originally. When Lessing promulgated reform in modern drama, he seized upon post-Racinian neoclassical tragedy as an example of all that was absurdly false and overblown in current dramatic practice. His own *Emilie Galotti*, a tragedy of the middle class, is, to our taste, almost as false in its histrionics as Voltaire's tragedies already were to Lessing. Neoclassical comedy, however, and

Lessing's comic and mixed-genre plays, *Minna von Barnhelm* and *Nathan der Weise*, are still capable of pleasing and moving us.

THE PARABLE OF *PEER GYNT*

1. This account of *Peer Gynt* owes much to Rolf Fjelde's Foreword to his fine translation of the play (New York: New American Library, Signet Classic, 1964) which is to be reissued by The University of Minnesota Press in 1980.

2. Asbjorn Aarseth, *Dyret i Mennesket* (Oslo: Universitetsforlaget, 1975).

3. The question of Peer's moral character has created a debate as contentious as that on Hamlet's indecisiveness. Some critics see Peer as damned, others as saved by means of his poetic imagination. Solveig is concerned with saving the sinner in some accounts and is attracted to the poet in others. The debate cannot be resolved because, as with *Brand*, the drama is ambivalent — it transcends conventional moral categories.

4. The list of comic liars and boasters is far too long to give here. Both tragedy and comedy are built upon the perception of *disparity* between appearance and reality, between what is and what should be. Tragedy seeks to overcome the contradiction at all costs; comedy exploits the contradiction, delights in it, and survives it.

5. M. H. Abrams, *Natural Supernaturalism* (New York: Norton, 1971), p. 165.

6. *Ibid.*, p. 172.

7. Theodore Jorgenson, *Henrik Ibsen: A Study in Art and Personality* (Northfield, Minn.: St. Olaf College Press, 1945), pp. 218-54.

8. I do not know if Ibsen was acquainted with *Jedermann* or with medieval Morality drama, but he would have known of the use of allegorical figures in medieval literature and art.

9. Bernard E. Dukore, *Dramatic Theory and Criticism* (New York: Holt, Rinehart & Winston, 1974), p. 581.

10. George Steiner, *After Babel* (London: Oxford University Press, 1975), p. 227. It is not Ibsen, however, who endorses the "life-lie" but the highly compromised Relling.

11. Aarseth, *Dyret i Mennesket*, pp. 74-75 and 85-86.

12. The battle between the Lapiths and centaurs, signifying the mind's victory over the body, was related to the battle between the Greeks and the Amazons which, in Greek thought, represented the victory of masculine rationality over the feminine passions. Both battles appear on the temple friezes.

13. Aarseth, *Dyret i Mennesket*, p. 91.

14. *Ibid.*, p. 85.

15. Critics of Peer sternly note that all his stories are only embellishments of the fictions or exploits of others; but by this severe rule we would have to condemn most fictive writing from the Greeks to the present. What would this rule make of Shakespeare, for example? And the disapproving critic or interpreter is even more of a parasite on the work of others.

16. My translation.

17. Ibsen too often has been saddled with the repressive attitudes of his culture toward the erotic when, in fact, he is constantly undermining the life-denying attitudes that he is presenting.

18. Joyce, a lifelong admirer of Ibsen, might well have seen the link between the Circe's island descent into animality and the troll sequence.

19. Quoted by Walter Kaufman in *Hegel: Reinterpretation, Texts, and Commentary* (New York: Doubleday, 1965), p. 391.

20. In an article by Jules Zentner, referred to by Aaarseth. See *Dyret i Mennesket*, pp. 208-9.

21. Not of pre-Romantic European vocabulary except for rare instances such as Henry Vaughan. The discovery of the sublimity and beauty of mountain scenery and its use as a symbol of spiritual elevation was a Romantic revival of pagan (Hellenic) ideas. Christian artists and thinkers before the Romantic movement saw in mountainous landscape the horrendous evidence of the natural cataclysms that accompanied the Fall. Even so urbane a writer as Samuel Pepys records that the sight of the Cumberland scenery, which Wordsworth was to celebrate a century later, filled him with such dismay that he pulled down the blinds of the coach in which he was traveling! It came as a surprise to me, when touring Greece, to discover that the "classical" Greeks chose as sites for their holy buildings natural scenes that would have entranced Romantic writers and artists. Delphi, which the Greeks considered the most beautiful place in the world (it might well be), is set in the most enthralling "Romantic" landscape. As Nietzsche remarked in *The Birth of Tragedy*, the Greeks still elude and baffle us.

22. Lionel Trilling devoted an entire book, the fine *Sincerity and Authenticity* (Cambridge, Mass.: Harvard University Press, 1972), to a study of the ramifications of the "disintegrated consciousness" as analyzed by Hegel in *The Phenomenology of Mind*.

23. In an important study of the play, "Peer Gynt, Naturalism and the Dissolving Self" *The Drama Review* (Winter 1968), pp. 28-43, Rolf Fjelde offers a very intriguing account of the place of this drama in the European tradition of art and thought, in fact seeing it as exemplifying a turning point in the development of artistic and philosophical perceptions of reality.

24. *Ibid.*, p. 37.

25. Aaarseth, *Dyret i Mennesket*, pp. 179-83.

26. This is pointed out by Aarseth who notes that the idea is taken from horse-breeding in which the sturdy dale horse is crossed with the swift Arabian horse.

27. Ibsen hardly can be satirizing Hegel's immensely difficult, deeply thought-through philosophy of history with Peer's totally superficial survey of the past.

28. Henrik Ibsen, *Peer Gynt*, trans. Rolf Fjelde, p. 165.

29. Aarseth, *Dyret i Mennesket*, pp. 127-41.

30. G. W. F. Hegel, *Aesthetics*, trans. T. M. Knox (Oxford: Clarendon Press, 1975), I.360.

31. *Ibid.*, 358.

32. It is here that, I hope not discourteously, I have to disagree with Aarseth, whose study of *Peer Gynt* I greatly admire. Aarseth, insisting that every reference to the animal in the play is negative, sees the phoenixlike birds also as negative animalistic aspects; but birds *always* function, in Ibsen, as symbols of spiritual qualities. In pagan and Christian iconography they represent the soul or the spirit. Even the hawk of *Brand* is spiritual — "the spirit of compromise." In *The Wild Duck* the bird is symbolic of the fallen *spirit*.

33. *Aesthetics* I.361.

34. *Ibid.*

35. This, in fact, is a constant theme in Hegel, who is acutely conscious of the difficulty of the whole human enterprise. In the Preface to *The Phenomenology*, Hegel warns: "Those who invoke feeling as their internal oracle are finished with anyone who does not agree: they have to own that they have nothing further to say to anyone who does not find and feel the same in his heart — in other words, they trample underfoot the roots of humanity. For it is the nature of humanity to struggle for agreement with others, and humanity exists only in the accomplished community of consciousness.

The anti-human, the animalic, consists in remaining at the level of feeling and being able to communicate only at the level of feeling." (Kaufman, *Hegel*, p. 454.)

36. Fjelde's translation of *Peer Gynt*, act 4, scene 13, p. 168.

37. *Ibid.*

38. *Hegel's Philosophy of Mind* (Oxford: Clarendon Press, 1971), p. 131.

39. *Ibid.*, p. 138.

40. *Ibid.*, p. 90.

41. *Ibid.*, p. 91.

42. *Ibid.*, pp. 91-92.

43. *Ibid.*, p. 204.

44. *Ibsen: Letters and Speeches*, ed. Evert Sprinchorn (New York: Hill & Wang, 1964), p. 114.

45. Fjelde's translation of *Peer Gynt*, p. 201.

46. Phaedrus, *Fabulae*, V, 5, "Scurra et Rusticus."

47. This is pointed out by Asbjorn Aarseth, who, mistakenly I think, disputes Rolf Fjelde's claim that Peer descends farther into the vegetative and elemental levels of nonidentity. If the imagery that describes Peer is predominantly animalistic, as Aarseth demonstrates, this is to a great extent because the animal state, being closest to the human, is the one Peer most easily can adopt and because it is the most *dramatic* of the lower identities. The inertia of the condition of the vegetable and mineral states would make them difficult to employ vividly; only in rare instances could the hero dramatically descend to the condition of Peer in the onion and threadball scene (as Osvald, in *Ghosts*, finally descends to a level beneath that of the animal). It is only as *animal* that man can be *actively* below himself, as with the example of the predominant animal imagery in *King Lear*. *Peer Gynt* employs, I think, a spiritual/material hierarchy which might be set out as: Absolute/God; demigod (Hero); man; animal; vegetable; mineral; "primary stuff" (Button Molder's material).

48. Fjelde's translation of *Peer Gynt*, p. 209.

49. *Ibid.*

50. Aarseth, *Dyret i Mennesket*, pp. 283-84. Aarseth joins Hemmer in seeing the play as developing an emphatically Christian argument. I would suggest that the Christian structure in the play is only part of the total ideological structure which already looks forward to the pagan (pre-Christian), Christian, and post-Christian argument of *Emperor and Galilean*.

51. Fjelde's translation of *Peer Gynt*, p. 210.

52. Bjorn Hemmer, *Brand; Kongsemnerne; Peer Gynt* (Oslo: Universitetsforlaget, 1972), pp. 163-64.

53. Aarseth, *Dyret i Mennesket*, pp. 195-222.

54. Just two years after completing *Peer Gynt*, Ibsen wrote to Georg Brandes, "Raphael's art has never really moved me. His people belong to a period before the fall of man." (Sprinchorn, *Letters and Speeches*, p. 86). The concept of the *Felix culpa*, or fortunate fall, continually appears in Christian arguments, and Milton's great *Paradise Lost* is its epic expression. Romantic writers, however, developed the idea beyond its Christian confines to denote a cultural and psychological alienation of the modern sensibility, the overcoming of which would elevate human existence beyond its previous peaks of paradisical innocence or Hellenic humanism.

55. Aarseth, *Dyret i Mennesket*, pp. 213-15.

56. Fjelde's translation of *Peer Gynt*, act 5, scene 10, p. 239.

57. Kaufman, *Hegel*, p. 380.

58. Hemmer, *Brand; Kongsemnerne; Peer Gynt*, pp. 9-21.

THE MEDIOCRE ANGELS OF *THE LEAGUE OF YOUTH*

1. *The Oxford Ibsen*, ed. J. W. McFarlane and Graham Orton (London: Oxford University Press, 1963), IV.3.
2. *Ibid.*
3. *Ibsen: Letters and Speeches*, ed. Evert Sprinchorn (New York: Hill & Wang, 1964), p. 155.
4. *The Oxford Ibsen* IV.552.
5. *Ibid.*
6. *Ibid.*
7. My translation.
8. *Ibsen: Four Major Plays*, ed. and trans. Rolf Fjelde (New York: New American Library, Signet Classics, 1970), vol. II, pp. xvi-xvii.
9. My translation.
10. Brande's judgment appeared in his volume *Naturalism in England* (1875) as vol. IV of *Main Currents of Nineteenth Century Literature* — six years after the appearance of *The League of Youth*. Brandes, however, probably was repeating what was a common verdict on Shelley's by now famous poem.
11. My translation.
12. G. W. F. Hegel, *Philosophy of Right*, trans. T. M. Knox (Oxford: Oxford University Press, 1952), p. 16.
13. My translation.
14. My translation.
15. My translation.
16. Michael Meyer, *Ibsen: A Biography* (New York: Doubleday, 1971), p. 362.
17. Halvdan Koht, *Life of Ibsen*, trans. Einar Haugen and A. E. Santaniello (New York: Blom, 1971), pp. 276-88.

THE THIRD EMPIRE: *EMPEROR AND GALILEAN*

1. *Ibsen: Letters and Speeches*, ed. Evert Sprinchorn (New York: Hill & Wang, 1964), pp. 144-45.
2. *The Oxford Ibsen*, ed. James W. McFarlane and Graham Orton (London: Oxford University Press, 1963), IV.459.
3. Henrik Ibsen, *Four Major Plays*, trans. Rolf Fjelde (New York: New American Library, Signet Classsics, 1965), vol. I. p. xxxi.
4. G. W. F. Hegel, *The Philosophy of History*, trans. J. Sibree (New York: Dover, 1965), p. 61.
5. *Ibid.*
6. *Ibid.*
7. Theodore Jorgenson, *Henrik Ibsen: A Study in Art and Personality* (Northfield, Minn.: St. Olaf College Press, 1945), p. 275.
8. Whereas Enlightenment thinkers attempted to account for major cultural changes by looking to archetypal "sages" and Great Individuals like Zoroastra (Mozart's Sarastro), Moses, or Solon, Romantic thinkers searched for spiritual origins *behind* the stage of isolating individuation — in the products of an anonymous "folk," in myth and tribal legend and ritual. The origins go back to the dimmest distances in time, as in the postulated "original oneness" of human consciousness in Nietzsche's *The Birth of Tragedy* or as in the folk-myths of Wagner's sources, the myriad spiritual currents of the race traced in Grimm's *Teutonic Mythology*, and in Hegel's search for a "starting point" for his

great odyssey of consciousness in *The Phenomenology of Spirit*. I think it would be possible to see a continuation of this Romantic endeavor in the psychological theories of Freud and Jung. *Emperor and Galilean* belongs to this tradition.

9. Hegel, *Philosophy of History*, p. 67.

10. *Ibid.*, p. 39.

11. *Ibid.*, pp. 39-40.

12. *Oxford Ibsen* IV.203.

13. *Ibid.*, 208.

14. *Ibid.*, 217.

15. *Ibid.*, 219.

16. *Ibid.*

17. *Oxford Ibsen* IV.220.

18. G. Wilson Knight, *Henrik Ibsen* (New York: Grove Press, 1962), p. 38.

19. My translation.

20. *Oxford Ibsen* IV.232.

21. Dismaying though the séance sequence may be to modern readers, they should reflect that it agrees with the recorded history of the human race until modern times. For the greater part of his history man has claimed to live in a numinous world and has recorded his experience of the supernatural. The Ephesus sequences establish in the play another order of reality, one in whose existence Ibsen seems to have believed, which lies behind and beyond the immediate present and for which he must, in this drama, devise the appropriate form of expression.

22. My translation.

23. *Oxford Ibsen* IV.253.

24. See Hegel, *Philosophy of History*, pp. 37-39.

25. *Ibid.*, pp. 82-83.

26. Ibsen, in fact, illustrates the dilemma of the modern writer. European drama until the time of Schiller reflected conventional systems of concepts of reality which it shared with its audience. Modern drama, beginning with Schiller's employment of Kantian philosophy, broke loose from conventional explanations of reality to learn from radical technical philosophy so esoteric that literature based on its premises was not likely to appeal to the public at large. The artist therefore has to choose between creating an art adequate to his or her philosophically radical understanding of reality and establishing an art of popular appeal. Such a situation has evolved into the extreme esotericism of modern art, and the drastic division of the public into popular and conventional taste on the one hand, and the taste of the cognoscenti on the other. Ibsen's plays, designed for the large theaters of Europe, now are most likely to be performed in the little theaters of minority taste.

27. This, more than any other single reason, strikes me as the cause of the demise of tragic drama in the modern world. Ibsen's solution, in the realistic cycle, was to create a whole world of universal tragic causes and consequences of which the principal actors were only dimly aware, for they could not mentally grasp the entire realm of meanings that alone made sense of their sufferings and sacrifice. They act more wisely than they think and so become tragically exemplary *for us* rather than for themselves. Julian, on the other hand, mentally grasps the universal drama in which he becomes the tragic sacrifice.

28. From a speech given at a banquet in Stockholm on September 24, 1887. *Ibsen: Letters and Speeches*, ed. Evert Sprinchorn (New York: Hill & Wang, 1964), p. 267.

29. The complexity of Julian's quest, and of his own mind that conceives this quest,

takes him far beyond the usual interests of the average theatergoer or the average reader. A more simpleminded hero would be a reversion to a relative primitivism. Creeds may set before us exemplary heroes and heroines whose simpler natures reflect laudable aspects of their respective faiths, but these will not carry the weight of sufficient mental complexity, of an adequate response to the totality of our reality, to interest the most thoughtful outside the closed circle of the creed. The modern *intellectual* hero must, to be tragic, run the risk of total *intellectual* devastation.

30. *Oxford Ibsen* IV.269.

31. *Ibid.,* 301.

32. *Ibid.,* 309.

33. Knight, *Ibsen,* p. 46.

34. *Ibid.,* p. 38.

35. *The Collected Works of Henrik Ibsen,* ed. William Archer (New York: Scribner's, 1920), vol. V, pp. xxvii-xxxv.

36. *Ibid.,* pp. xxv-xxvi.

37. G. W. F. Hegel, *Reason in History,* trans. Robert S. Hartman, The Library of Liberal Arts (Indianapolis, Ind.: Bobbs-Merrill, 1953), pp. 90-91.

38. Part 2, act 2. My translation.

39. Part 2, act 2. My translation.

40. Part 2, act 3. My translation.

41. Part 2, act 4. My translation.

42. Part 2, act 4. My translation.

43. Part 2, act 4. My translation.

44. Part 2, act 5. My translation.

45. Part 2, act 5. My translation.

46. Part 2, act 5. My translation.

EPILOGUE

1. "Mythic Patterns in *Hedda Gabler:* The Mask Behind the Face," paper read by Elinor Fuchs at the Ibsen Sesquicentennial Symposium, Pratt Institute, New York, May 12, 1978.

2. Ronald Gray, *Ibsen: A Dissenting View* (New York: Cambridge University Press, 1977).

3. Michael Meyer, *Ibsen: A Biography* (New York: Doubleday, 1971), p. 36.

4. *Ibsen: Four Major Plays,* ed. and trans. Rolf Fjelde (New York: New American Library, Signet Classics, 1965), vol. I, Foreword, p. ix.

5. *Ibid.,* p. xviii.

6. *Ibid.*

SELECTED BIBLIOGRAPHY

SELECTED BIBLIOGRAPHY

The scholarly and critical literature on Ibsen is a multilingual, voluminous, and irreversible industry. As with the academic writing on all major authors, this industry has created something of a great Tesmanian reef upon which the eager student can be stranded without reaching the rich and lofty poetic mainland. If the purpose of a bibliography is to help the reader arrive at the best ideas about the subject, it must inevitably be selective. More complete bibliographies can be found in M. S. Barranger, "Ibsen Bibliography, 1957-1967," *Scandinavian Studies*, 41, No. 3 (August 1969), 243-58; Hjalmar, Petterson, *Henrik Ibsen, 1828-1928* (Oslo: Cammermeyer, 1928); Ingrid Tedford, *Ibsen Bibliography, 1928-1957* (Oslo: Oslo University Press, 1961); Mariann Tiblin, Lise-Lone Marker, Harald S. Naess, et al., *"Ibsen Bibliography: Norwegian Literature; Theatre and Drama."* *Scandinavian Studies*, annual supplements.

The standard Norwegian text is the Centennial edition, *Samlede Verker* [Hundreårsutgaven], ed. Francis Bull, Halvdan Koht, Didrik Arup Seip, 21 vols. (Oslo: Gyldendal, 1928-58). A more convenient but less complete Norwegian text is *Samlede Verker,* ed. Didrik Arup Seip, 3 vols. (Oslo: Gyldendal, 1960). This edition omits *Kjaempehøien (The Burial Mound), Sankthansnatten (St. John's Night),* and *Olaf Liliekrans.* The reader without a knowledge of Norwegian now is handsomely served by the new "Oxford" Ibsen translations: Henrik Ibsen, *The Oxford Ibsen,* trans. and ed. James W. McFarlane et al., 8 vols. (New York: Oxford University Press/London:

307

Oxford University Press, 1960-77). These translations of the plays contain the most complete collections in English of Ibsen's notes, earlier drafts, and the dramatist's comments on his works. By studying the evolution of a play from first notes and sketches to the final version, the reader is provided with a rare opportunity of following the creative process of a major writer. American readers probably will prefer the translations of Rolf Fjelde, *Four Major Plays*, 2 vols. (New York: New American Library, Signet Classics, 1965, 1970). Highly recommended, also, is *Peer Gynt*, trans. Rolf Fjelde (New York: New American Library, Signet Classics, 1964). This Signet edition is at present out of print but will be reissued in 1980 by the University of Minnesota Press. These Signet editions are particularly valuable for their fine "Forewords" which rank among the best contemporary Ibsen criticism. Rolf Fjelde recently completed translations of all twelve plays of the realistic cycle, *Ibsen: The Complete Major Prose Plays*, trans. Rolf Fjelde (New York: Farrar Strauss & Giroux, New American Library, 1978).

All students of Ibsen will confess their gratitude to William Archer who, with Edmund Gosse, pioneered Ibsen's conquest of the English-speaking world. Although the Introductions to his translations reflect an Anglo-Saxon pragmatism at odds with Ibsen's continental idealism, they are filled with insights into details of the plays. See *The Collected Works of Henrik Ibsen*, ed. William Archer, 12 vols. (London: Heinemann, 1906-12). The "Penguin" translations of Una Ellis-Fermor and Peter Watts employ a more sophisticated critical approach in the Introductions but still remain within a predominantly social, ethical, and psychological area of interest, as if Ibsen were a dramatic John Stuart Mill with strong anticipations of Freud. (Penguin volumes translated by Una Ellis Fermor [London: Penguin Books, 1950, 1958]; and by Peter Watts [London: Penguin Books, 1964, 1965, 1966].)

The best biography is Halvdan Koht's *Life of Ibsen*, trans. Einar Haugen and A. E. Santaniello (New York: Blom, 1971). Koht admirably seeks to relate the life that Ibsen lived to the imaginative life of the poet's spirit. Michael Meyer's *Ibsen: A Biography* (New York: Doubleday, 1971) is concerned with the minuter details of the artist's personal life and the manner in which he was perceived by his contemporaries.

It is the theme of my argument that Ibsen consciously made himself the heir to the intellectual/spiritual heritage of civilization and that the archetypal conflicts and characters from this rich past reappear in his dramatic structures — including the plays of the realistic cycle. "You ought to make a thorough study of the history of civilization, of literature and art," Ibsen wrote to a young aspiring writer, John Paulsen — and these words, and those that immediately follow, should be addressed to the student of Ibsen also. "An extensive knowledge of history is indispensable to a modern author, for without it he is incapable of judging his age, his contemporaries and their motives and actions except in the most incomplete and superficial manner." *(Ibsen: Letters and Speeches,* ed. Evert Sprinchorn [New York: Hill & Wang, 1964], p. 181.) Paulsen, it seems did not take the advice for he later angered Ibsen by writing a novel in which Mr. and Mrs. Ibsen all too evidently were the models for the fictive persona, reminding one of those Ibsen interpreters who, not seeing the larger archetypes and metaphors in the plays, prefer to read them as runes of the dramatist's private life.

For accounts of Ibsen's artistry, the reader should consult William Archer, *Playmaking* (New York: Dover Publications, 1960), which is an excellent discussion of the technical aspects of the well-made play; also, Archer's *The Old Drama and the New* (London: Heinemann, 1923), which reveals the limitations of Archer's idea of the theater. By his philistinic attitude toward the older poetic drama and his ludicrously modest idea of what constitutes dramatic greatness (the book hails Arthur Wing Pinero as Ibsen's great successor), Archer prompted much of the reaction against Ibsen by such adherents of poetic drama as T. S. Eliot. Jennette Lee, *The Ibsen Secret: A Key to the Prose Dramas of Henrik Ibsen* (New York: Putnam's, 1907), drew attention to the similarities between Ibsen's symbolism and the *leitmotif* method of Richard Wagner. Her examination of the symbolism of the later plays long anticipates, and may have influenced, the similar work on Shakespeare's imagery instigated by Caroline Spurgeon. Francis Fergusson's *The Idea of a Theater* (Garden City, New York: Doubleday, 1953) offers a challenging assessment of Ibsen. P. F. D. Tennant's *Ibsen's Dramatic Technique* (Cambridge: University Press, 1948) contains a valuable account of Ibsen's theatrical apprenticeship and of the stage facilities at Ibsen's disposal. J. D. Northam's *Ibsen's Dramatic Method* (London: Faber, 1952) examines Ibsen's scene directions and interprets the plays from a psychological perspective. Maurice Valency's *The Flower and the Castle* (New York: Macmillan, 1963) traces the larger themes within the plays, as does G. Wilson Knight's *Henrik Ibsen* (Edinburgh: Oliver & Boyd, 1962) which manages, in its few packed pages, to encompass more of Ibsen's poetic imagination than volumes of previous commentary.

Eric Bentley is one of those authors that I realize, with each rereading, I have been unconsciously plagiarizing for years, and on more than Ibsen matters. He has proved a wise, witty, and persuasive champion of Ibsen in many of his writings. *The Playwright as Thinker* (New York: Reynal & Hitchcock, 1946); *The Modern Theatre* (New Haven, Conn.: Yale University Press, 1948); and *In Search of Theater* (New York: Vintage, 1954), contain many of his best discussions of Ibsen. Henry James's *The Scenic Art* (New York: Hill & Wang, 1948), a collection of articles on the nineteenth-century theater in Paris and London, records James's at first reluctant fascination with Ibsen that modulates into almost unqualified admiration. George Bernard Shaw's *The Quintessence of Ibsenism: Now Completed to the Death of Ibsen* (London: Constable, 1913) is, for all its quirkiness, one of the few studies to get the intellectual measure of Ibsen. Passages on Ibsen and Ibsen themes recur throughout Shaw's writings on music and drama, in which Richard Wagner and Henrik Ibsen tower above all others, the first as the great tone-poet of feeling, the second as the chief architect of the new literature of the intellect. These superbly nonacademic observations can be found in George Bernard Shaw, *The Perfect Wagnerite* (London: Constable, 1923/London: Dover, 1967); *Our Theatre in the Nineties* (London: Constable, 1931); *Music in London, 1890-94*, 3 vols. (London: Constable, 1932). (A selection from Shaw's musical criticisms can be found in *The Great Composers: Reviews and Bombardments by Bernard Shaw*, ed. Louis Crompton [Berkeley and Los Angeles: University of California Press, 1978]). The reader also should note the many references to Ibsen in the Prefaces to the plays. Shaw's great value, which he shares with many of his contemporaries, is in maintaining the discourse on Ibsen at the high level of the history of European civilization which Shaw, together with Ibsen, is conscious of inheriting and being responsible toward. Shaw may sometimes be eccentric or wrong about Ibsen, but he never reduces the dramatist to one of the subjects offered by a Scandinavian or Drama department!

W. B. Yeats's deeply ambivalent, often hostile, and always provocative judgments on Ibsen are expressed in *Plays and Controversies* (London: Macmillan, 1923). Yeats's desire to create a new poetic drama made him see Ibsen's intellectual success in England as a threat to be attacked. His fellow countryman James Joyce pronounced his youthful, ardent admiration for Ibsen, which he was to retain throughout his lifetime, in the essay on *When We Dead Awaken*, "Ibsen's New Drama," *Fortnightly Review*, n.s. 67 (1 April 1900), pp. 575-90.

Hugo von Hoffmansthal's *Die Menschen in Ibsen's Drama* (1891) has been translated and excerpted by Carla Hvistendahl and James McFarlane and appears in McFarlane's *Henrik Ibsen: A Critical Anthology* (London: Penguin, 1970), pp. 132-41. An equally appreciative excerpt from Rainer Maria Rilke's *Aufzeichnungen des Malte Laurids Brigge (The Notebooks of Malte Laurids Brigge)* (Leipzig: Im Insel, 1910/trans. John Linton, London: Woolf, 1930) is also included in the McFarlane anthology, pp. 214-5. There is a fine chapter on Ibsen in Benedetto Croce's *European Letters in the Nineteenth Century*, trans. Douglas Ainslie (London: Chapman, 1924), pp. 326-43.

Extensive accounts of Ibsen's earliest plays are rare enough in Norwegian and almost nonexistent in English. *Catiline* has received most attention by scholars probing this embryo for omens of Ibsen's later development. James Hurt, in *Catiline's Dream* (Urbana: University of Illinois Press, 1972), sees the play as establishing the prototypical psychic myth found in all Ibsen's subsequent writing. At the opposite extreme is John C. Pearce's "Hegelian Ideas in Three Tragedies by Ibsen: *Catilina, Kongsemnerne, Kejser og Galilaeer*," *Scandinavian Studies*, 34 (1962), pp. 72-77.

For accounts of *The Burial Mound (Kjaempehøien)*, readers are referred to M. B. Ruud, "Ibsen's *Kjaempehøien*," *Scandinavian Studies and Notes*, 5 (1918-19), pp. 309-37, and A. M. Sturtevant, *"Kjaempehøien* and Its Relation to Ibsen's Romantic Works," *Journal of English and Germanic Philology*, 12 (1913), pp. 407-24. Sturtevant, continuing to discuss plays omitted from William Archer's edition of the Collected Works (already cited), includes articles on *St. John's Night* ("Ibsen's *Sankthansnatten*," *Journal of English and Germanic Philology*, 14 [1915], pp. 357-74) and on *Olaf Liliekrans* (*"Olaf Liliekrans* and Ibsen's Literary Development," *Scandinavian Studies and Notes*, 5 [1918-19], pp. 110-32.

Lady Inger of Østraat has received little attention from English-speaking critics, so that the best accounts of the play are to be found in the Introductions to Archer's and McFarlane's translations. *The Feast at Solhoug* was made the subject of unfavorable comparison with older poetic drama in Raymond Williams's *Drama in Performance* (London: Penguin, 1954), "*Hamlet* and *The Feast at Solhoug*," pp. 75-84.

For discussions of the series from *Love's Comedy* to *Emperor and Galilean*, the reader is recommended to consult two anthologies of Ibsen criticism: James McFarlane's *Henrik Ibsen: A Critical Anthology*, previously cited, and Rolf Fjelde, ed., *Ibsen: A Collection of Critical Essays* (Englewood Cliffs, N.J.: Prentice-Hall, 1965). G. Wilson Knight includes fine accounts of these plays in his *Henrik Ibsen*, cited earlier, p. 309, which contains perhaps the best account of *Emperor and Galilean*. Philip H. Wicksteed's *Four lectures on Henrik Ibsen Dealing chiefly with His Metrical Works* (London, 1892) is still instructive. W. H. Auden's brilliant contrast of *Brand* and *Peer Gynt* can be found in McFarlane's *Critical Anthology*, pp. 331-45. A more traditional approach, but one which contains fine studies of *Brand*, *Peer Gynt*, and *Emperor and Galilean*, is Theodore Jorgenson's *Henrik Ibsen: A Study in Art and Personality* (Northfield, Minn.: St. Olaf College Press, 1945). Asbjorn Aarseth's *Dyret i Mennesket (The Beast in Man)* (Oslo: Universitetsforlaget, 1975) has proved to be one of the most interesting and original studies of *Peer Gynt* in some time. Bjorn Hemmer's *Brand; Kongsemnerne; Peer Gynt* (Oslo: Universitetsforlaget, 1972) discusses what Hemmer terms Ibsen's "poetic ideology" from a thoughtful, if somewhat restrictedly Christian, point of view.

For the Romantic argument of Ibsen's plays, E. M. Forster's "Ibsen the Romantic" in *Abinger Harvest* (London: Arnold, 1936), pp. 81-86, is a good starting point. Otto Lous Mohr's *Henrik Ibsen som maler (Henrik Ibsen as a Painter)* (Oslo: Gyldendal, 1953) reveals Ibsen's indebtedness to and affinities with Romantic landscape painters, and the reader should search out the paintings of the "Dresden" school of Caspar David Friedrich and his Norwegian colleague J. C. Dahl. The symbology of Friedrich's meticulously realistic landscapes could tell us much about Ibsen's realism with its use of natural scenes, changes of weather and of light and dark, and its stage props. To appreciate the intellectual range and depth of Ibsen's imagination, a comprehensive study of Romantic art and thought is a necessary beginning. Such writers as Rousseau, Lessing, Herder, Kant, Schiller, Goethe, Hegel, Kleist, Buechner, Heine, Hebbel, Richard Wagner, and Nietzsche are indispensable because they created the intellectual world that Ibsen shared and because their ongoing discourse, or argument, was taken up by him. The English Romantics, from Blake to Carlyle, reveal striking correspondences with German thought (there are surprising similarities between Blake and Hegel) and, in such instances as Coleridge and Carlyle, gratefully record their debt to the German thinkers. Ibsen's friend Georg Brandes superbly mapped out the intellectual landscape of Europe following the collapse of the French revolution in his *Main Currents of Nineteenth Century Literature,* 6 vols. (London: Heinemann, 1924). Brandes is concerned with depicting the extravagancies, follies, and evasions of the reactionary forces of the European spirit and their struggle against the forces of critical reason, a conflict which recently has been forcefully described by Herbert Marcuse, *Reason and Revolution* (New York Humanities Press, 1954). For the student of literature, the best account of Romantic art and thought is M. H. Abrams's *Natural Supernaturalism: Tradition and Revolution in Romantic Literature* (New York: Norton, 1973). Abrams's demonstration of the close interdependence of imaginative literature and technical philosophy, especially the philosophy of Hegel, in the Romantic period supports much of the argument of my book. Lionel Trilling's elegant and stimulating *Sincerity and Authenticity* (Cambridge: Harvard University Press, 1972), similarly stresses the centrality of Hegel's *The Phenomenology of Spirit* to postrevolutionary European culture.

Many will feel that Hegel is the unwelcome dark shadow that has simultaneously emerged with the light case on Ibsen by my approach. The Hegel of notorious legend, the apologist for German militarism, the theoretical instigator of both fascist and communist totalitarianism, is now seen as a bogeyman. Hegel, who insisted that the philosopher should refrain from "edifying," has been charged with advocating the processes that he is conscientiously and objectively describing and analyzing — just as Darwin was accused by the thoughtless of advocating the processes of natural selection. The present Hegel revival has exposed the absurdity of the method and conclusions of Karl R. Popper's *The Open Society and Its Enemies* (New York: Princeton, 1950). For this *political* aspect of Hegel's thought, the reader is referred to the entertainingly acrimonious debate in *Hegel's Political Philosophy*, ed. Walter Kaufmann (New York: Atherton Press, 1970). Schlomo Avineri's *Hegel's Theory of the Modern State* (London: Cambridge University Press, 1972) should finally dispel all doubts about Hegel's decency as a thinker. The reader who wishes to study Hegel in order to understand the intellectual world that Ibsen inherited and adapted (often in non-Hegelian ways) will be pleased to learn that an "Oxford" Hegel is appearing to accompany the "Oxford" Ibsen. So we can now follow the sometimes parallel and sometimes divergent flights of the owl of Minerva and the northern falcon. The most approachable of Hegel's writings are the lectures on history and on aesthetics, the first available as G. W. F. Hegel, *The Philosophy of History,* trans. J. Sibree (New York: Dover, 1956), and the second in the edition G. W. F. Hegel, *Aesthetics,* trans. T. M. Knox, 2 vols. (Oxford: Clarendon Press, 1975). For the influence of Hegel on the plays of the realistic cycle, see Brian Johnston, *The Ibsen Cycle* (Boston: Twayne Publishers/G. K. Hall, 1975). Those who wish to tackle Hegel's most brilliant but most difficult work should read G. W. F. Hegel, *The Phenomenology of Spirit,* trans. A. V. Miller (Oxford: Clarendon Press, 1977). To recommend further reading of Hegel on logic, nature, mind, the state, the history of philosophy, and the philosophy of religion would be to dismay the Ibsenite. What, for the poet in a cultural backwater of Europe, might have proved to be the most enthralling intellectual liberation available is, for the modern, a most daunting investigation of the history of ideas. Hegel's world view, nonetheless, is compelling, and Ibsen is an imaginative writer of sufficient stature to merit the effort.

The best guides to Hegel are Alexandre Kojève, *Introduction to the Reading of Hegel* (New York: Basic Books, 1969); J. N. Findlay, *Hegel: A Reexamination* (London: Macmillan, 1958/New York: Collier Books, 1962), Walter Kaufmann, *Hegel: A Re-interpretation: Texts and Commentary* (New York: Doubleday, 1965); and J. Loewenberg, *Hegel's Phenomenology: Dialogues of the Life of Mind* (La Salle, Illinois: Open Court Publishing, 1965).

Whereas the structure of Ibsen's world view, and his sense of truth and freedom as emerging only from dialectical conflict, are distinctly Hegelian, Ibsen seems *temperamentally* closer to Kierkegaard and Nietzsche, those wayward heirs of Hegel. There is no point in blandly recommending to the reader the collected works of both thinkers, for parallels with Ibsen's thought occur in innumerable places in the writings of the two philosophers. For a beginning, the reader could do worse than consult two excellent anthologies of Nietzsche's writings: *The Portable Nietzsche,* selected and trans. Walter Kaufmann (New York: Viking Press, 1954), and *The Philosophy of Nietzsche,* ed. Geoffrey Clive (New York: New American Library [A Mentor Book], 1965). Kierkegaard's most influential work is *Either/Or,* trans. Walter Lowrie, 2 vols. (New York: Doubleday, 1959). Both Ibsen and Nietzsche shared an antipathy to John Stuart Mill and to the whole British pragmatic culture which they felt permitted itself just so much ethical questioning as would be consonant with self-interest. Mr. Cotton of *Peer Gynt* is a portrait of the type, and Ibsen's *animus* is similar to the many Nietzschean animadversions on the British. There are some cruel words about Ibsen among the fragments of Nietzsche's writings that were gathered under the title *The Will to Power,* trans. Walter Kaufmann and R. J. Hollingdale (New York: Vintage Books, 1968), but, as the editor, Kaufmann, comments, Nietzsche seems not to have read Ibsen. Kaufmann also notes the resemblances between Ibsen and Nietzsche (pp. 52-54). Halvdan Koht records Ibsen's favorable remarks on Nietzsche in his *Life of Ibsen,* p. 436.

For the larger background of the history of ideas leading up to Ibsen's day, a few sources might prove useful. The battle between paganism and Christianity, a major theme of Ibsen's plays and one that attained climactic significance in *Emperor and Galilean,* has been brilliantly treated in a number of studies. Jean Seznec's *The Survival of the Pagan Gods: The Mythological Tradition and Its Place in Renaissance Humanism and Art,* trans. Barbara F. Sessions (New York: Pantheon Books, 1953) should be followed by Peter Gay's *The Enlightenment: An Interpretation. The Rise of Modern Paganism* (New York: Knopf, 1966). Gilbert Highet's *The Classical Tradition* (New York: Oxford University Press, 1953), places the subversive classicism and paganism of the nineteenth century within the context of the history of Europe. This theme appears prominently in Heinrich Heine's essays "The Romantic School" and "Concerning the Religion and Philosophy in Germany," both of which provide lively accounts, by one of Hegel's most brilliant pupils, of the Romantic *Zeitgeist.* They can be found in Heinrich Heine, *Selected Works,* trans. and ed. Helen M. Mustard (New York: Vintage Books, 1973). Less amiable by far, but at least as important for brassily proclaiming the great *kulturkampf,* are Richard Wagner's pronouncements on the state of nineteenth-century life and art, mercifully pruned and brought together in one volume in *Wagner on Music and Drama,* selected and arranged, with an Introduction, by Albert Goldman and Evert Sprinchorn (New York: Dutton, 1964). Oscar Walzel's *German Romanticism,* trans. Alma Elise Lussky (New York: Putnam's 1932), is a very useful account of many aspects of the Romantic background. Much of the mythological content of northern paganism — which, contradicting Hegel's unsympathetic judgment on northern mythology, was to be almost as subversive of Christianity as the paganism of the south — was uncovered by the great German scholar Jacob Grimm. Grimm's magnificent *Deutsche Mythologie* (2nd ed., 1844) is available in English: Jacob Grimm, *Teutonic Mythology*, trans. James Steven Stallybrass, 4 vols. (London: Bell, 1883-88/New York: Dover, 1966). Ibsen's Swedish contemporary, Viktor Rydberg, a doughty anti-Christian, also wrote a fascinating *Teutonic Mythology*, trans. Rasmus B. Anderson (London and New York: Norroena Society, 1907).

The general political background is well described in Benedetto Croce's *History of Europe in the Nineteenth Century*, trans. Henry Furst (New York: Harcourt, Brace & World, 1933). Except for this general reading, which may lead to more adequate conceptions of Ibsen's stature as an artist, no guide can be given but the reader's own curiosity, interest, and intelligence. Nothing less than all of human expression, at least from Homer and Hesiod, the Greek dramatists and philosophers, the Bible and the "history of civilization, of literature, and of art," up to the most signigicant work of the present, will suffice for us to adequately recognize Ibsen's place among his great equals. I am sure this is what he would have desired of us.

INDEX

INDEX